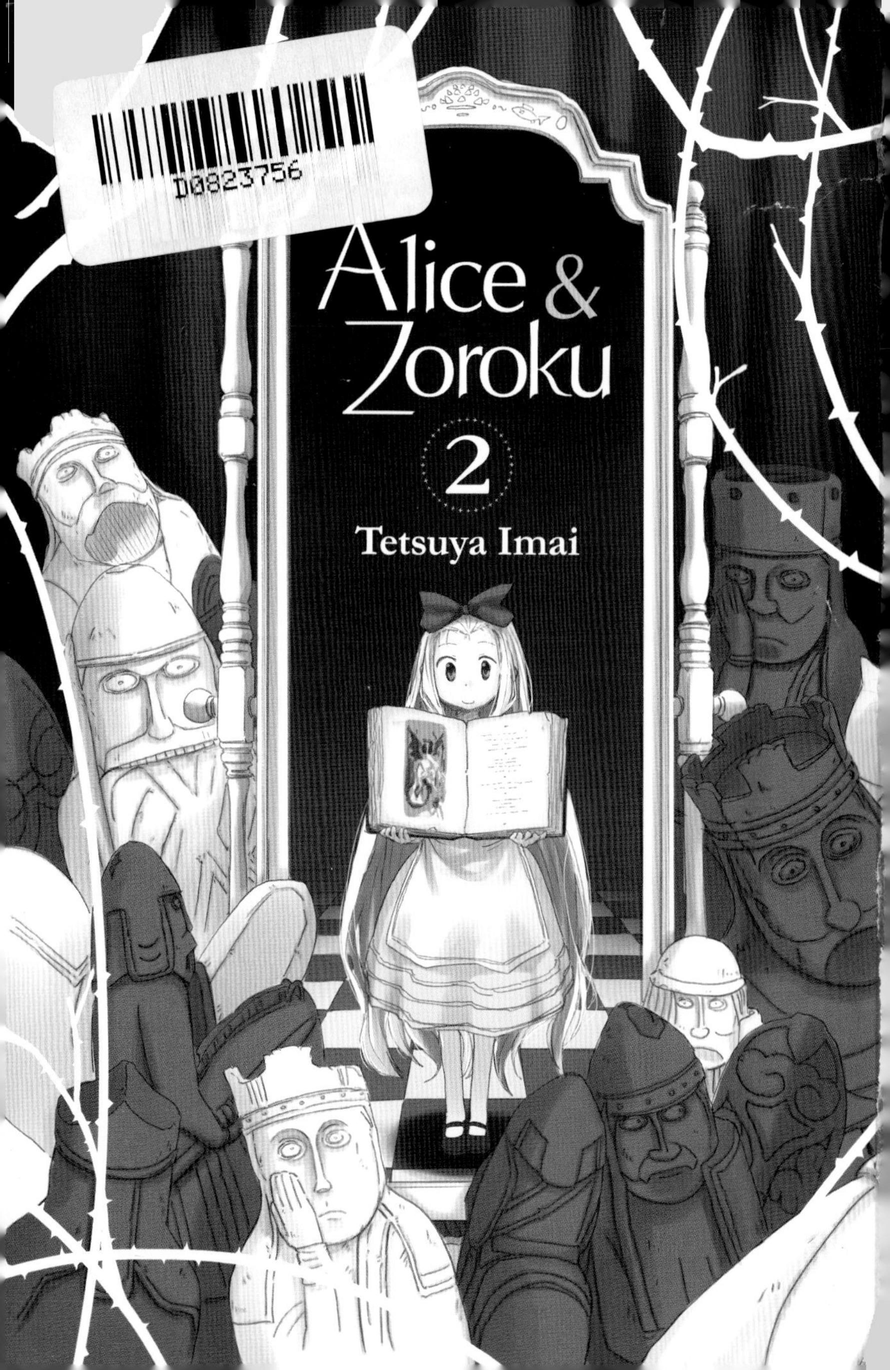
Alice & Zoroku
2
Tetsuya Imai

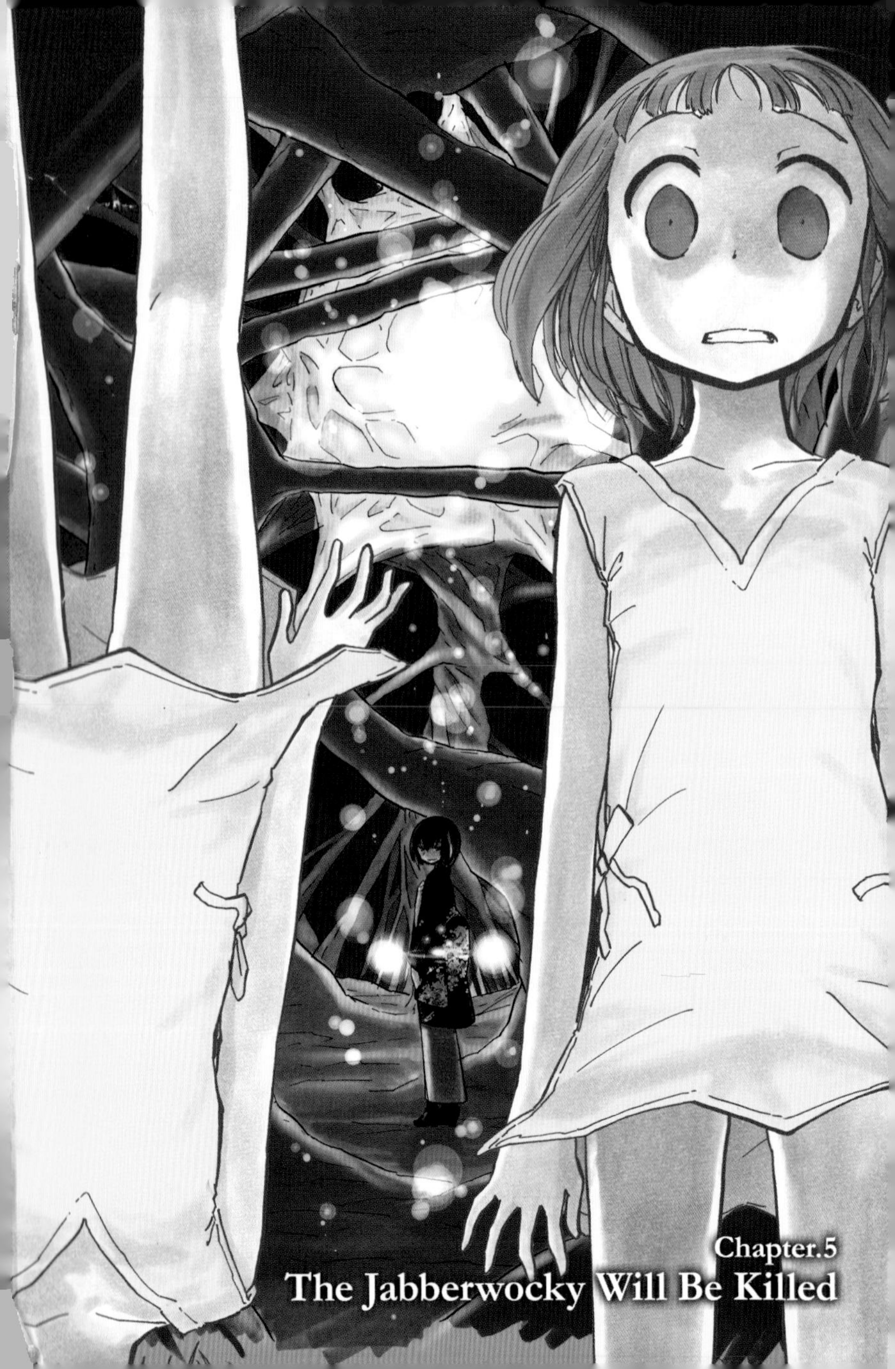
Chapter.5
The Jabberwocky Will Be Killed

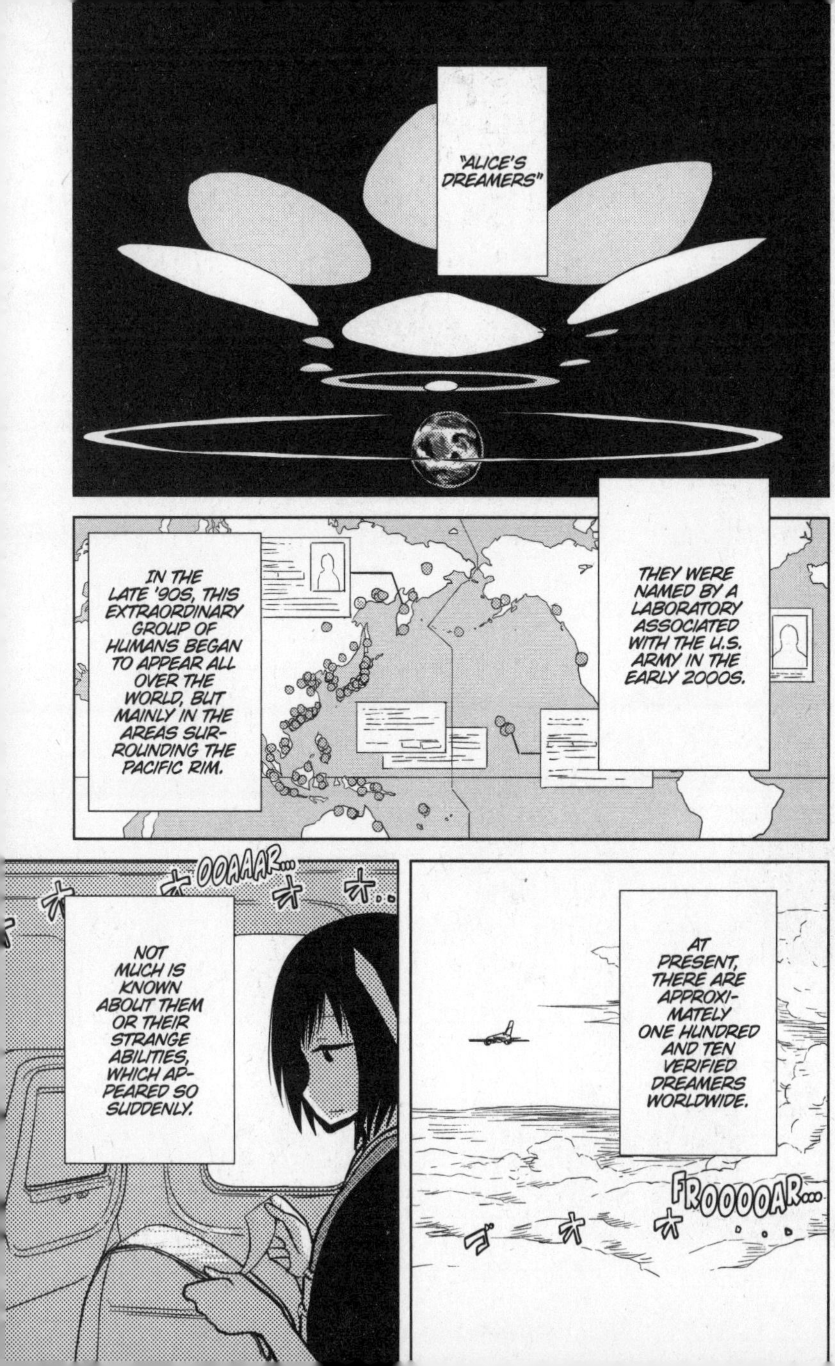
"ALICE'S DREAMERS"
THEY WERE NAMED BY A LABORATORY ASSOCIATED WITH THE U.S. ARMY IN THE EARLY 2000S.
IN THE LATE '90S, THIS EXTRAORDINARY GROUP OF HUMANS BEGAN TO APPEAR ALL OVER THE WORLD, BUT MAINLY IN THE AREAS SUR-ROUNDING THE PACIFIC RIM.
AT PRESENT, THERE ARE APPROXI-MATELY ONE HUNDRED AND TEN VERIFIED DREAMERS WORLDWIDE.
ゴオオ
FROOOOAR...
OOAAAR...
NOT MUCH IS KNOWN ABOUT THEM OR THEIR STRANGE ABILITIES, WHICH AP-PEARED SO SUDDENLY.

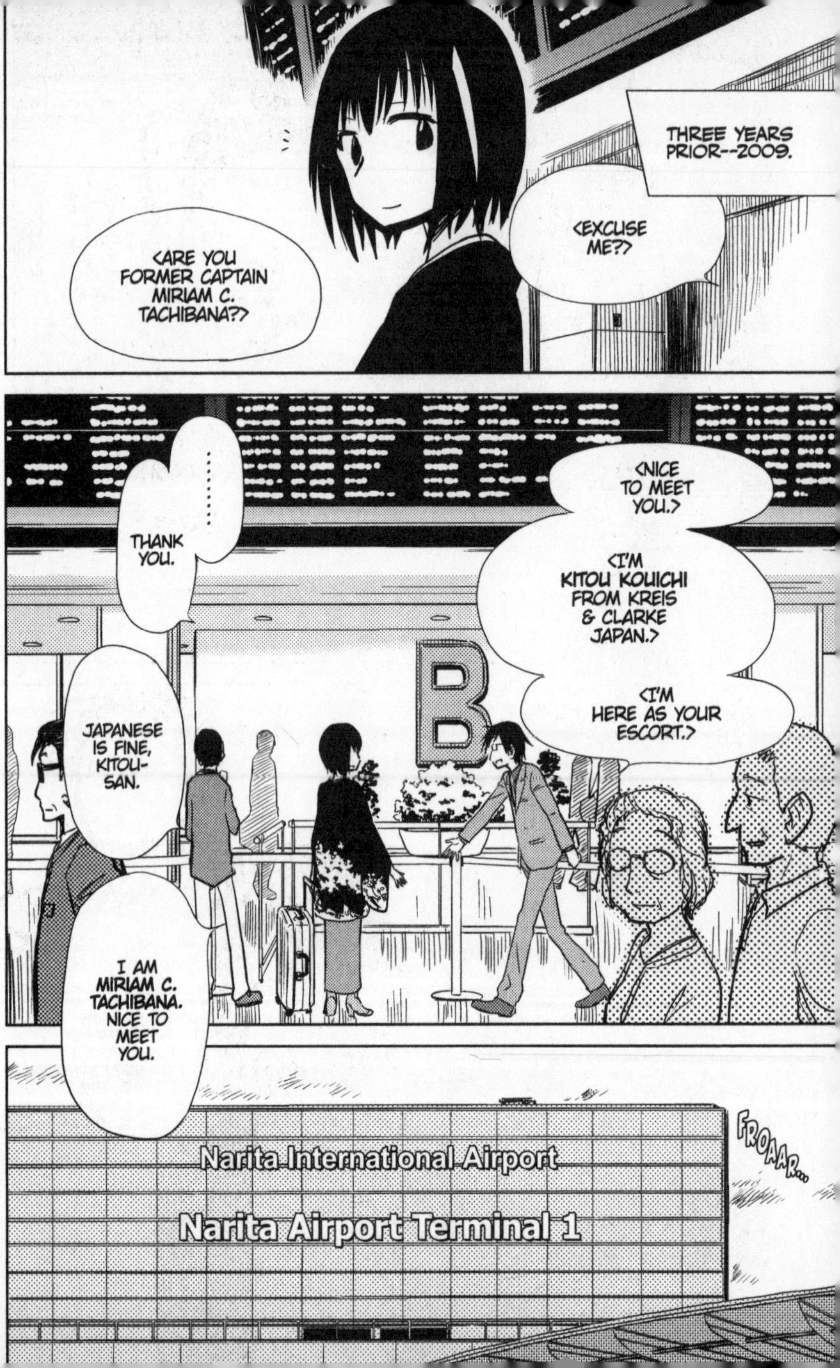
THREE YEARS PRIOR--2009.
<EXCUSE ME?>
<ARE YOU FORMER CAPTAIN MIRIAM C. TACHIBANA?>
<NICE TO MEET YOU.>
<I'M KITOU KOUICHI FROM KREIS & CLARKE JAPAN.>
<I'M HERE AS YOUR ESCORT.>
...... THANK YOU.
JAPANESE IS FINE, KITOU-SAN.
I AM MIRIAM C. TACHIBANA. NICE TO MEET YOU.
FROAAAR...
Narita International Airport
Narita Airport Terminal 1

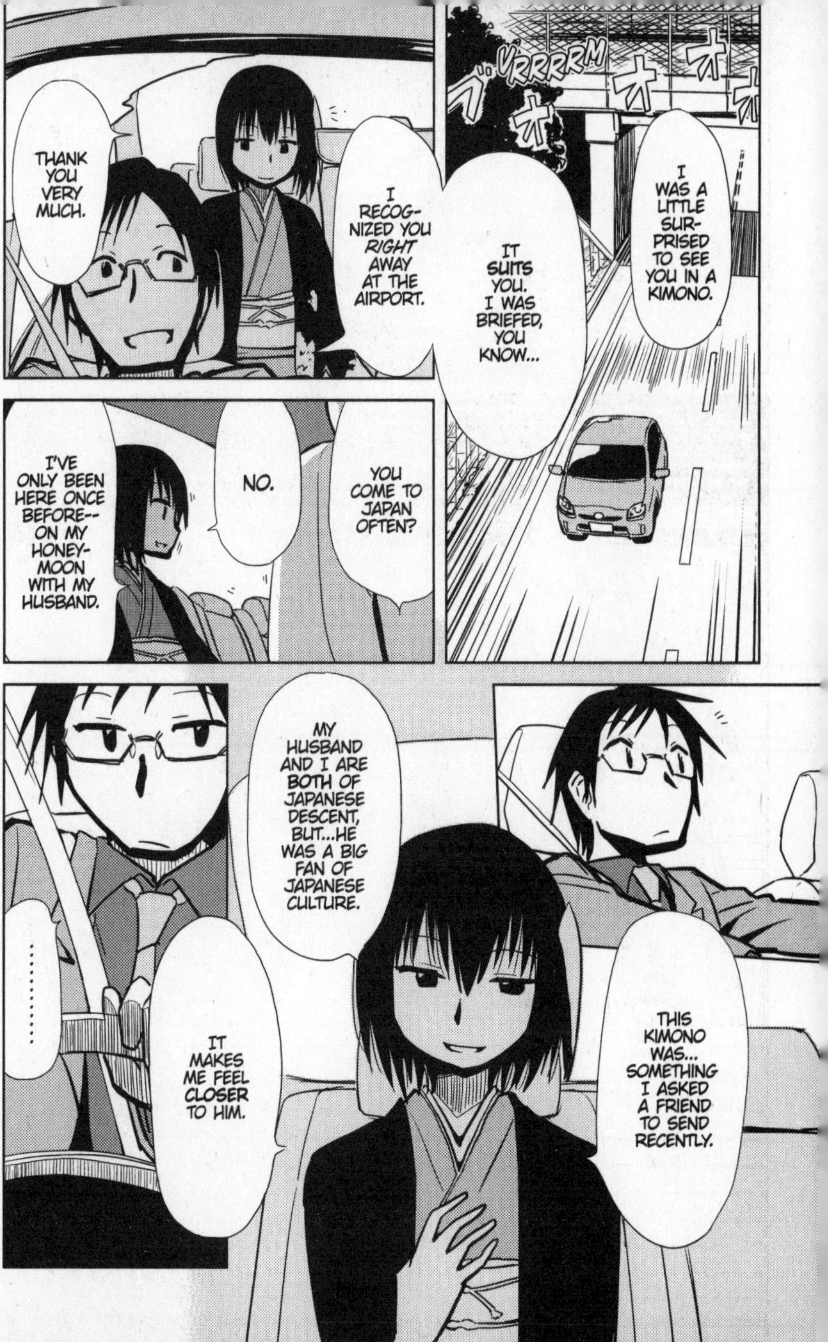
VRRRRM
I WAS A LITTLE SURPRISED TO SEE YOU IN A KIMONO.
IT SUITS YOU. I WAS BRIEFED, YOU KNOW...
I RECOGNIZED YOU *RIGHT* AWAY AT THE AIRPORT.
THANK YOU VERY MUCH.
YOU COME TO JAPAN OFTEN?
NO.
I'VE ONLY BEEN HERE ONCE BEFORE--ON MY HONEYMOON WITH MY HUSBAND.
THIS KIMONO WAS... SOMETHING I ASKED A FRIEND TO SEND RECENTLY.
MY HUSBAND AND I ARE BOTH OF JAPANESE DESCENT, BUT...HE WAS A BIG FAN OF JAPANESE CULTURE.
IT MAKES ME FEEL CLOSER TO HIM.
.........

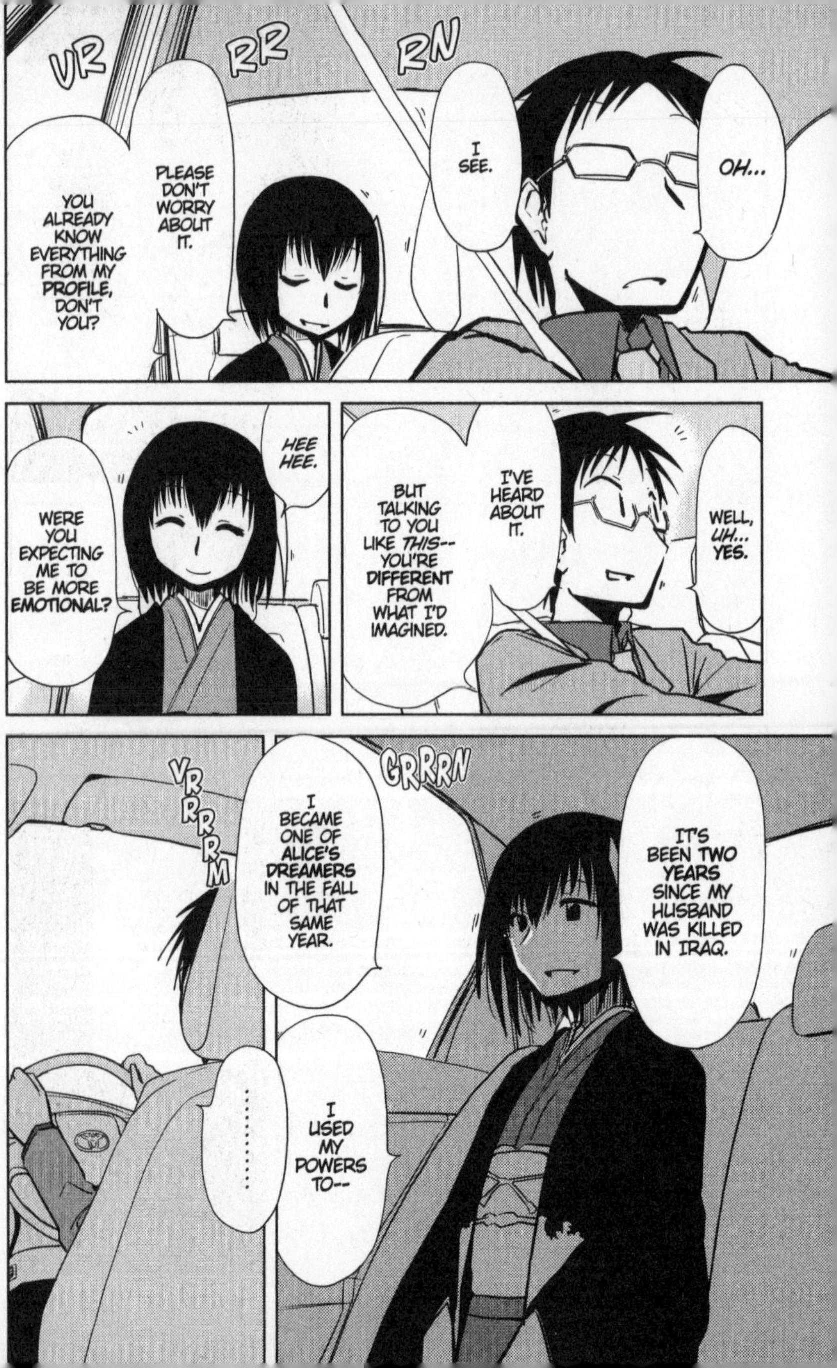
VR RR RN
OH...
I SEE.
PLEASE DON'T WORRY ABOUT IT.
YOU ALREADY KNOW EVERYTHING FROM MY PROFILE, DON'T YOU?
WELL, UH... YES.
I'VE HEARD ABOUT IT.
BUT TALKING TO YOU LIKE *THIS*-- YOU'RE DIFFERENT FROM WHAT I'D IMAGINED.
HEE HEE.
WERE YOU EXPECTING ME TO BE MORE EMOTIONAL?
GRRRN
IT'S BEEN TWO YEARS SINCE MY HUSBAND WAS KILLED IN IRAQ.
I BECAME ONE OF ALICE'S DREAMERS IN THE FALL OF THAT SAME YEAR.
VRRRRM
I USED MY POWERS TO--
......

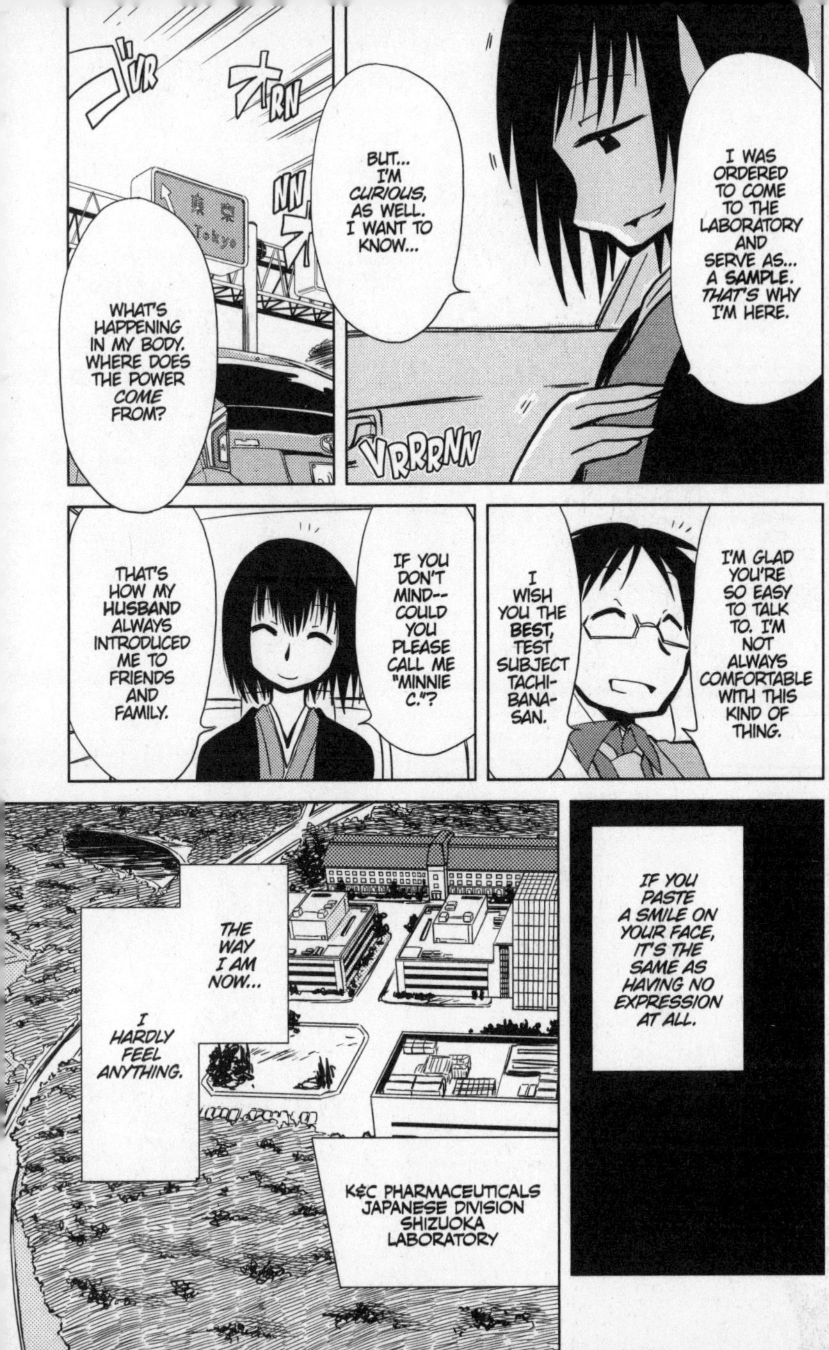
I WAS ORDERED TO COME TO THE LABORATORY AND SERVE AS... A SAMPLE. *THAT'S* WHY I'M HERE.
BUT... I'M *CURIOUS*, AS WELL. I WANT TO KNOW...
VRRRNN
VR
RN
NN
東京
Tokyo
WHAT'S HAPPENING IN MY BODY. WHERE DOES THE POWER *COME* FROM?
I'M GLAD YOU'RE SO EASY TO TALK TO. I'M NOT ALWAYS COMFORTABLE WITH THIS KIND OF THING.
I WISH YOU THE BEST, TEST SUBJECT TACHIBANA-SAN.
IF YOU DON'T MIND-- COULD YOU PLEASE CALL ME "MINNIE C."?
THAT'S HOW MY HUSBAND ALWAYS INTRODUCED ME TO FRIENDS AND FAMILY.
*IF YOU PASTE A SMILE ON YOUR FACE, IT'S THE SAME AS HAVING NO EXPRESSION AT ALL.*
*THE WAY I AM NOW...*
*I HARDLY FEEL ANYTHING.*
K&C PHARMACEUTICALS JAPANESE DIVISION SHIZUOKA LABORATORY

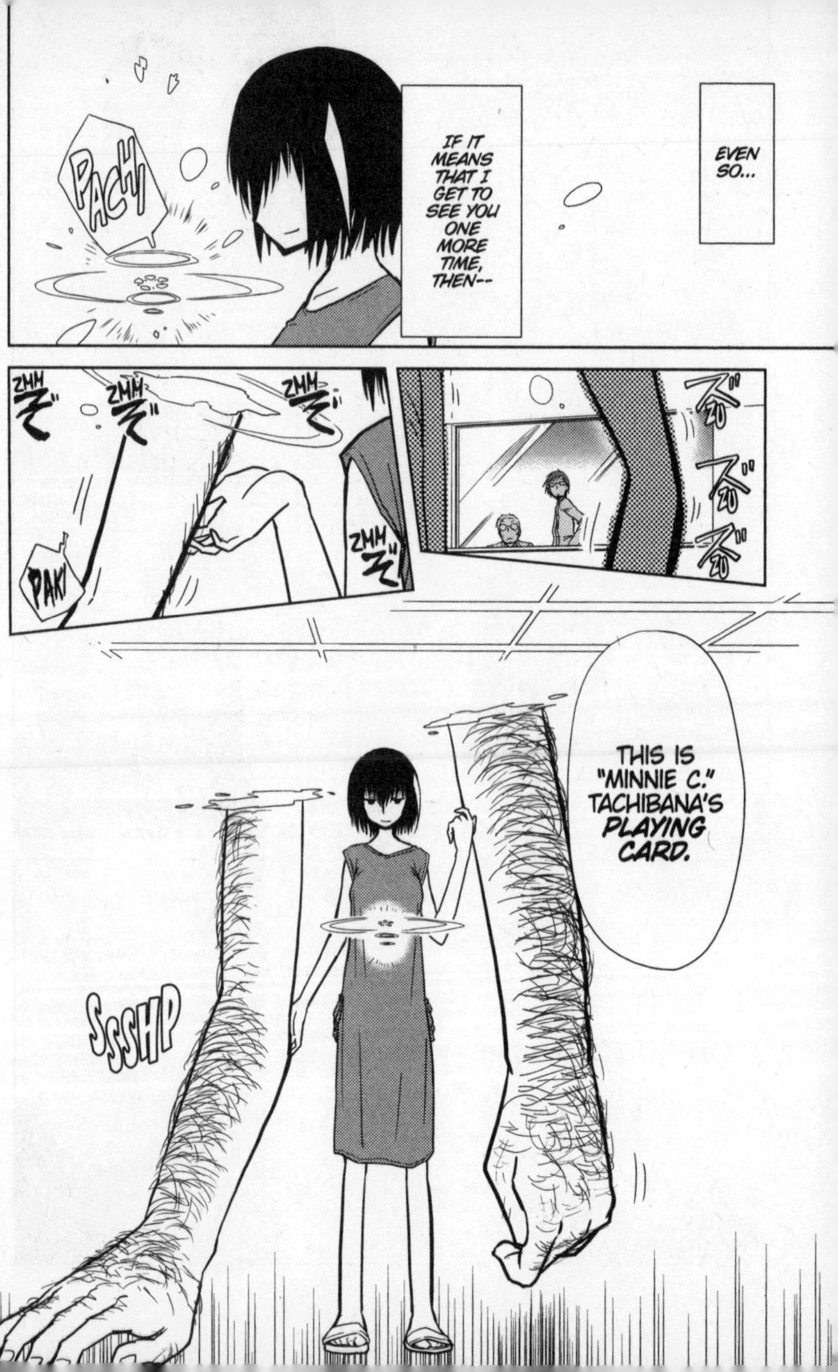
EVEN SO...
IF IT MEANS THAT I GET TO SEE YOU ONE MORE TIME, THEN--
PACHI
ZU ZU ZU
ZMM
ZMM
ZMM
ZMM
PAKI
THIS IS "MINNIE C." TACHIBANA'S PLAYING CARD.
SSSHP

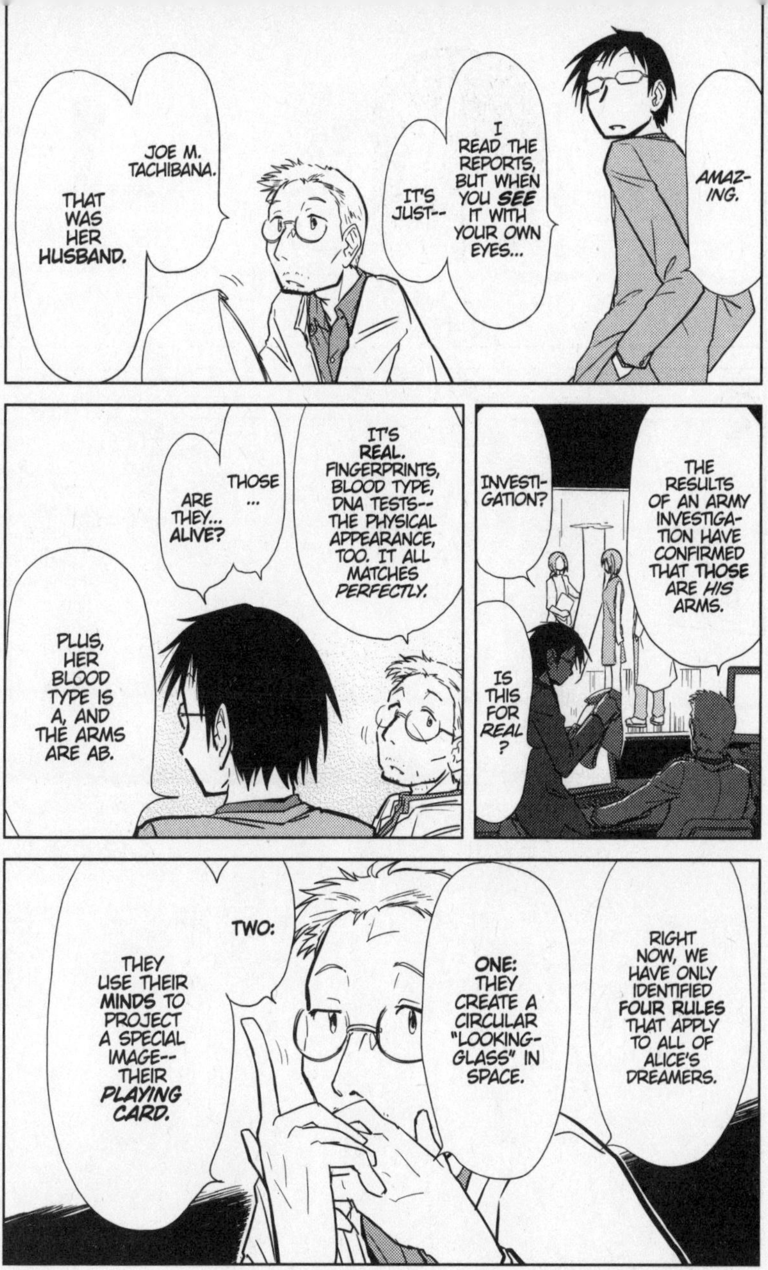
AMAZING.
I READ THE REPORTS, BUT WHEN YOU *SEE* IT WITH YOUR OWN EYES...
IT'S JUST--
JOE M. TACHIBANA.
THAT WAS HER HUSBAND.
THE RESULTS OF AN ARMY INVESTIGATION HAVE CONFIRMED THAT THOSE ARE *HIS* ARMS.
INVESTIGATION?
IS THIS FOR *REAL*?
IT'S REAL. FINGERPRINTS, BLOOD TYPE, DNA TESTS-- THE PHYSICAL APPEARANCE, TOO. IT ALL MATCHES *PERFECTLY.*
THOSE...
ARE THEY... ALIVE?
PLUS, HER BLOOD TYPE IS A, AND THE ARMS ARE AB.
RIGHT NOW, WE HAVE ONLY IDENTIFIED FOUR RULES THAT APPLY TO ALL OF ALICE'S DREAMERS.
ONE: THEY CREATE A CIRCULAR "LOOKING-GLASS" IN SPACE.
TWO:
THEY USE THEIR MINDS TO PROJECT A SPECIAL IMAGE-- THEIR *PLAYING CARD.*

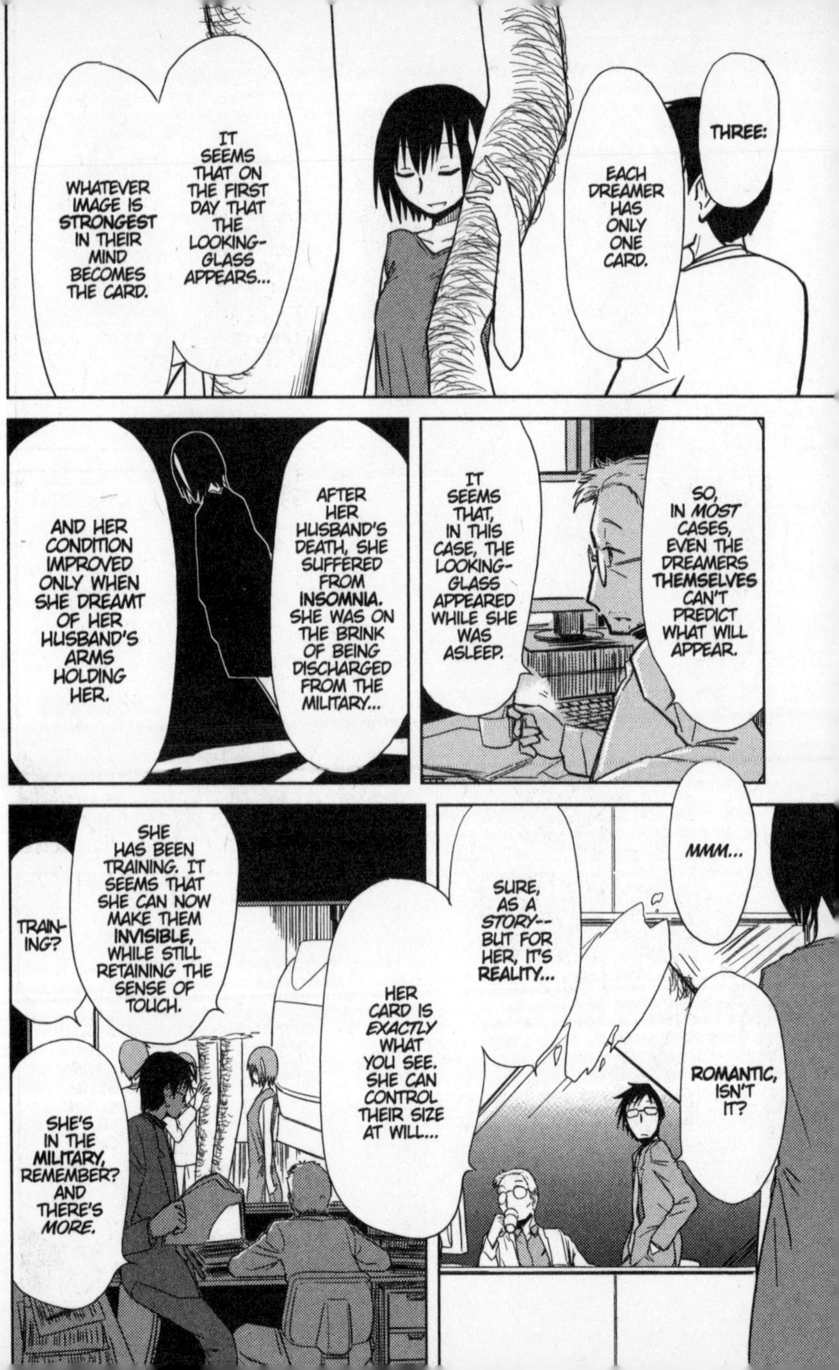
THREE:
EACH DREAMER HAS ONLY ONE CARD.
IT SEEMS THAT ON THE FIRST DAY THAT THE LOOKING-GLASS APPEARS...
WHATEVER IMAGE IS STRONGEST IN THEIR MIND BECOMES THE CARD.
SO, IN *MOST* CASES, EVEN THE DREAMERS THEMSELVES CAN'T PREDICT WHAT WILL APPEAR.
IT SEEMS THAT, IN THIS CASE, THE LOOKING-GLASS APPEARED WHILE SHE WAS ASLEEP.
AFTER HER HUSBAND'S DEATH, SHE SUFFERED FROM INSOMNIA. SHE WAS ON THE BRINK OF BEING DISCHARGED FROM THE MILITARY...
AND HER CONDITION IMPROVED ONLY WHEN SHE DREAMT OF HER HUSBAND'S ARMS HOLDING HER.
*MMM...*
SURE, AS A *STORY*-- BUT FOR HER, IT'S REALITY...
ROMANTIC, ISN'T IT?
HER CARD IS *EXACTLY* WHAT YOU SEE. SHE CAN CONTROL THEIR SIZE AT WILL...
SHE HAS BEEN TRAINING. IT SEEMS THAT SHE CAN NOW MAKE THEM INVISIBLE, WHILE STILL RETAINING THE SENSE OF TOUCH.
TRAINING?
SHE'S IN THE *MILITARY*, REMEMBER? AND THERE'S *MORE*.

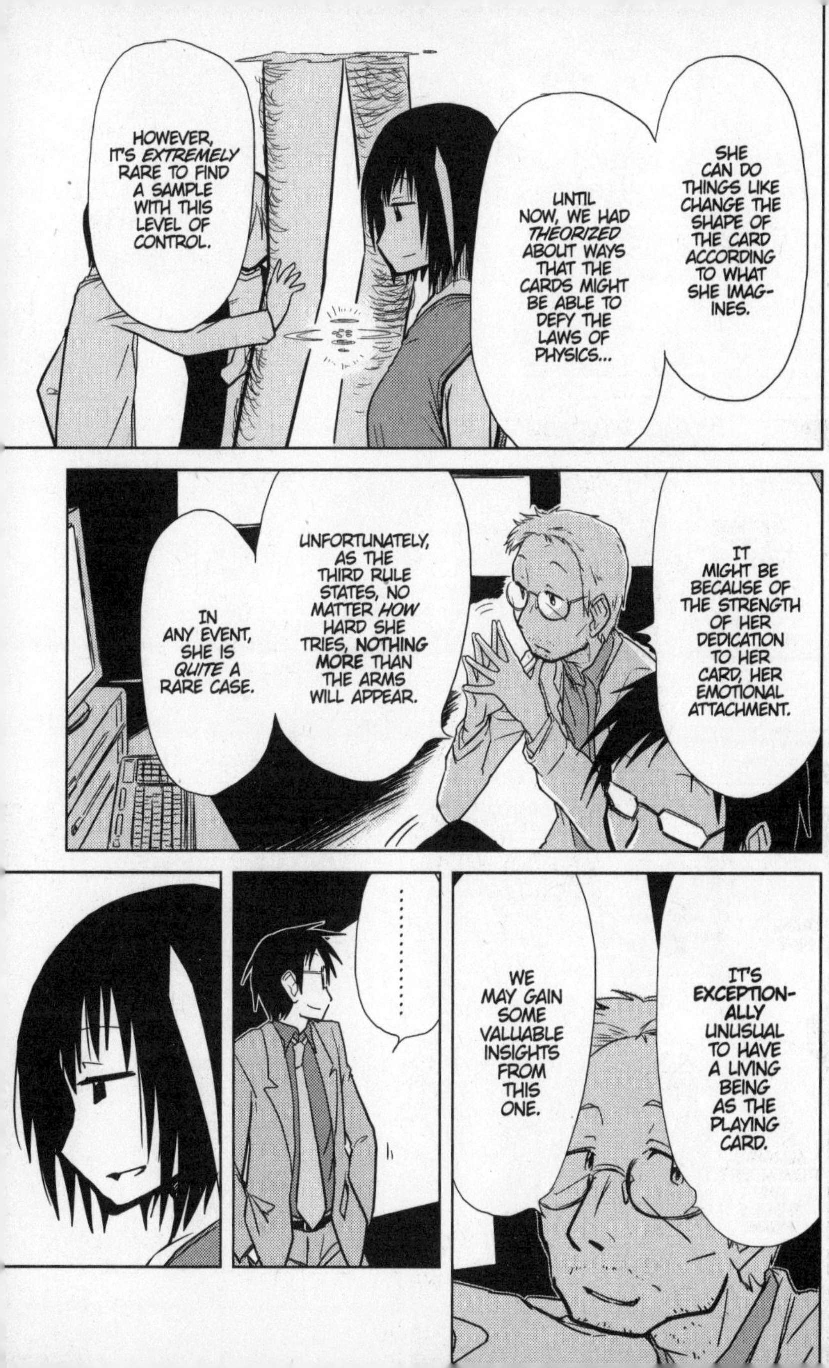
SHE CAN DO THINGS LIKE CHANGE THE SHAPE OF THE CARD ACCORDING TO WHAT SHE IMAGINES.
UNTIL NOW, WE HAD *THEORIZED* ABOUT WAYS THAT THE CARDS MIGHT BE ABLE TO DEFY THE LAWS OF PHYSICS...
HOWEVER, IT'S *EXTREMELY* RARE TO FIND A SAMPLE WITH THIS LEVEL OF CONTROL.
IT MIGHT BE BECAUSE OF THE STRENGTH OF HER DEDICATION TO HER CARD, HER EMOTIONAL ATTACHMENT.
UNFORTUNATELY, AS THE THIRD RULE STATES, NO MATTER *HOW* HARD SHE TRIES, NOTHING MORE THAN THE ARMS WILL APPEAR.
IN ANY EVENT, SHE IS *QUITE* A RARE CASE.
IT'S EXCEPTIONALLY UNUSUAL TO HAVE A LIVING BEING AS THE PLAYING CARD.
WE MAY GAIN SOME VALUABLE INSIGHTS FROM THIS ONE.
......

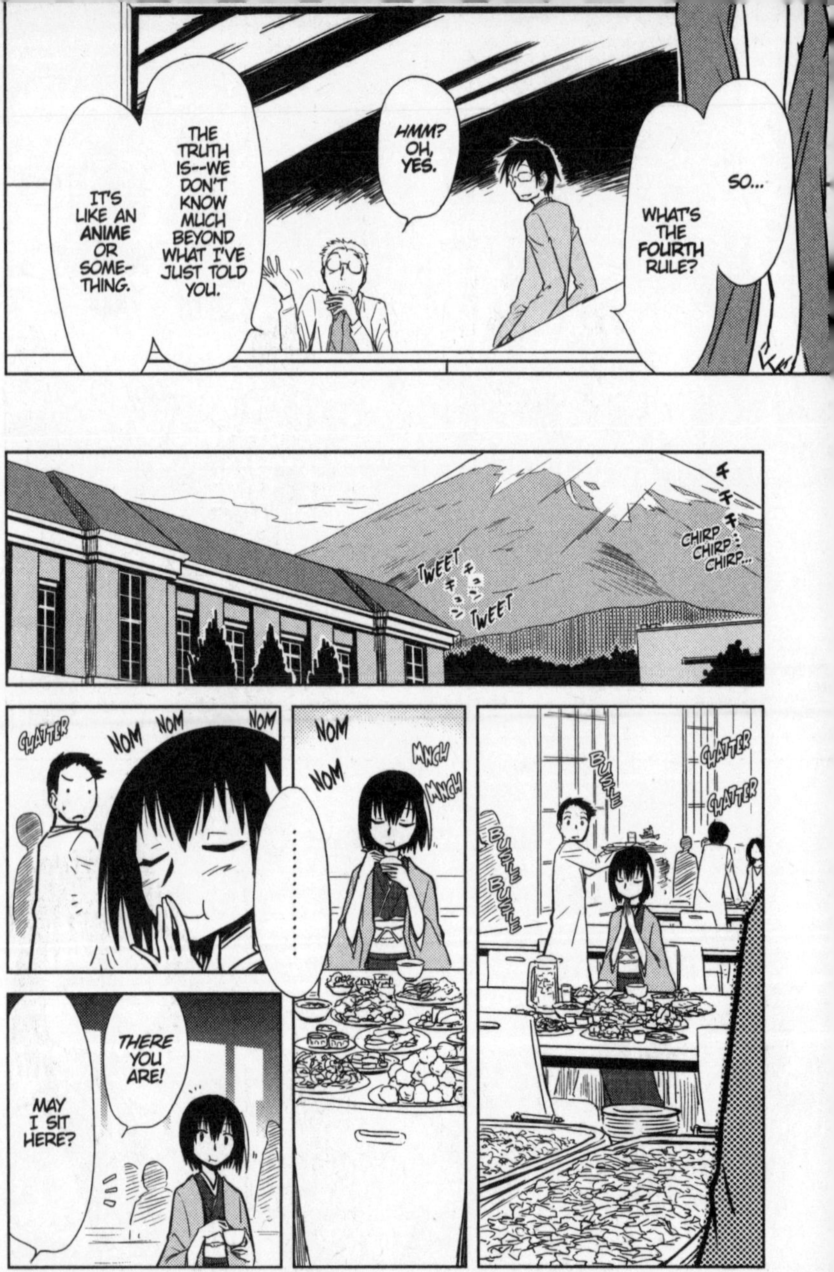
SO...
WHAT'S THE FOURTH RULE?
HMM? OH, YES.
THE TRUTH IS--WE DON'T KNOW MUCH BEYOND WHAT I'VE JUST TOLD YOU.
IT'S LIKE AN ANIME OR SOME-THING.
チチチ
CHIRP CHIRP CHIRP...
TWEET
チュンチュン
TWEET
CHATTER
CHATTER
BUSTLE
BUSTLE BUSTLE
MNCH
MNCH
NOM
NOM
......
NOM
NOM
NOM
CHATTER
THERE YOU ARE!
MAY I SIT HERE?

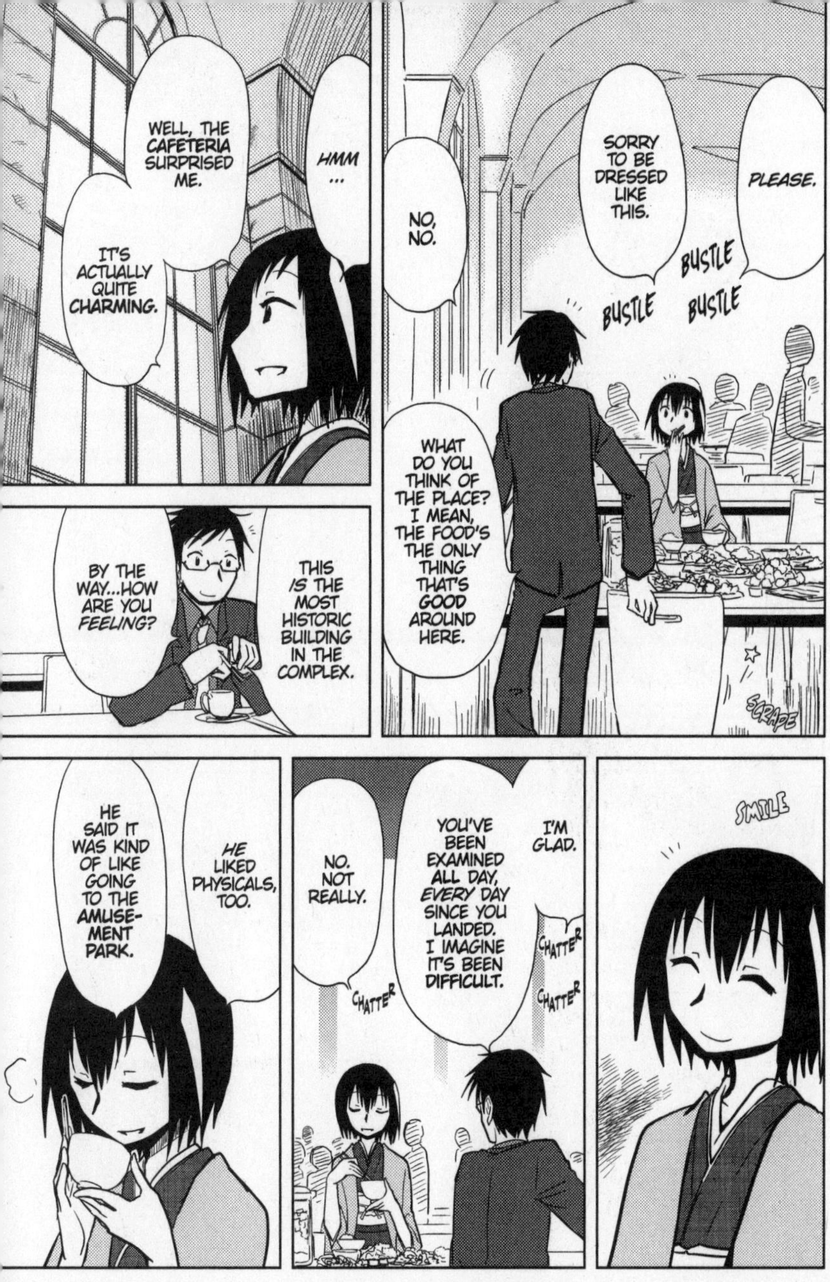
PLEASE.
SORRY TO BE DRESSED LIKE THIS.
BUSTLE
BUSTLE
BUSTLE
NO, NO.
WHAT DO YOU THINK OF THE PLACE? I MEAN, THE FOOD'S THE ONLY THING THAT'S GOOD AROUND HERE.
SCRAPE
HMM ...
WELL, THE CAFETERIA SURPRISED ME.
IT'S ACTUALLY QUITE CHARMING.
THIS *IS* THE MOST HISTORIC BUILDING IN THE COMPLEX.
BY THE WAY...HOW ARE YOU *FEELING*?
SMILE
I'M GLAD.
YOU'VE BEEN EXAMINED ALL DAY, *EVERY* DAY SINCE YOU LANDED. I IMAGINE IT'S BEEN DIFFICULT.
CHATTER
CHATTER
NO. NOT REALLY.
CHATTER
*HE* LIKED PHYSICALS, TOO.
HE SAID IT WAS KIND OF LIKE GOING TO THE AMUSEMENT-MENT PARK.

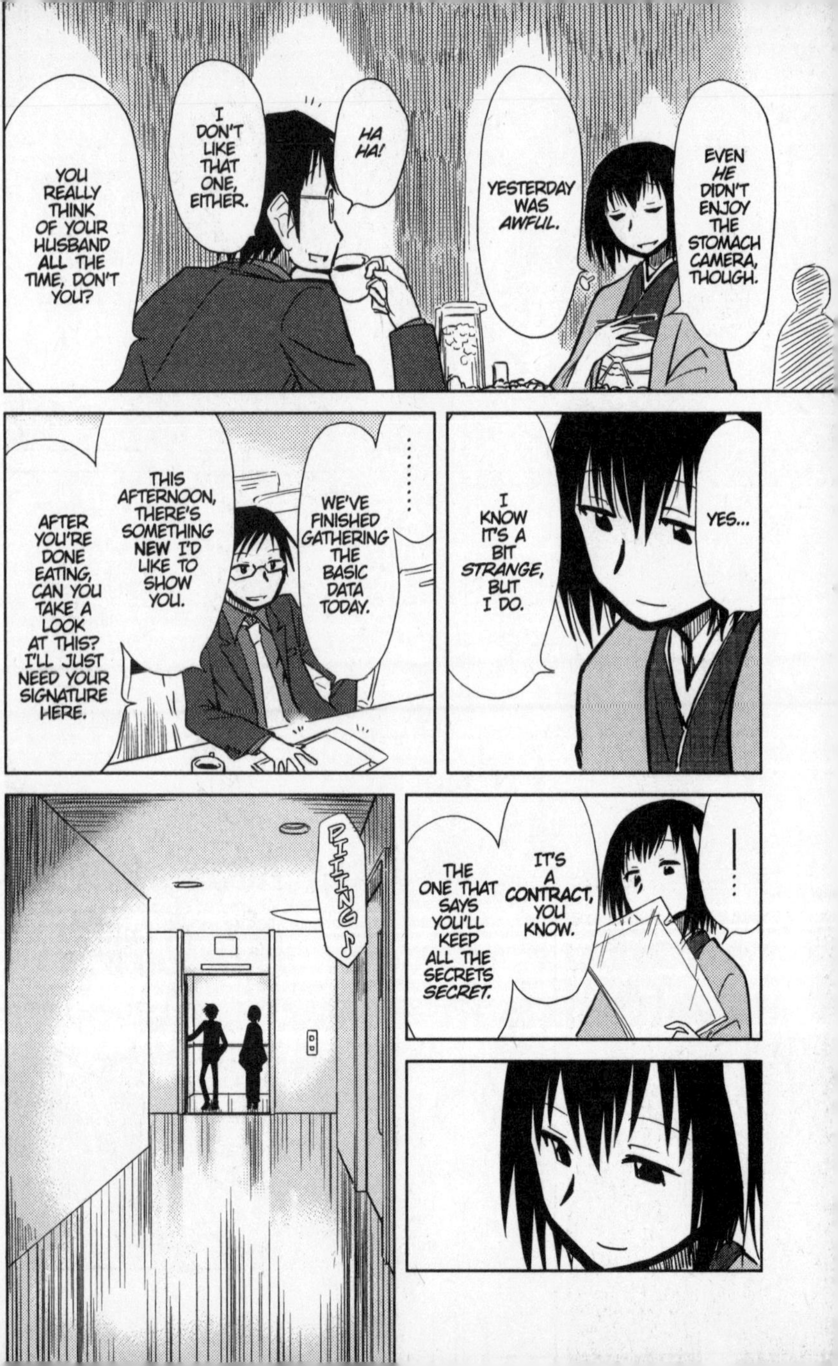
EVEN *HE* DIDN'T ENJOY THE STOMACH CAMERA, THOUGH.
YESTERDAY WAS *AWFUL.*
*HA HA!*
I DON'T LIKE THAT ONE, EITHER.
YOU REALLY THINK OF YOUR HUSBAND ALL THE TIME, DON'T YOU?
YES...
I KNOW IT'S A BIT *STRANGE,* BUT I DO.
......
WE'VE FINISHED GATHERING THE BASIC DATA TODAY.
THIS AFTERNOON, THERE'S SOMETHING NEW I'D LIKE TO SHOW YOU.
AFTER YOU'RE DONE EATING, CAN YOU TAKE A LOOK AT THIS? I'LL JUST NEED YOUR SIGNATURE HERE.
—...
IT'S A CONTRACT, YOU KNOW.
THE ONE THAT SAYS YOU'LL KEEP ALL THE SECRETS *SECRET.*
PIIING♪

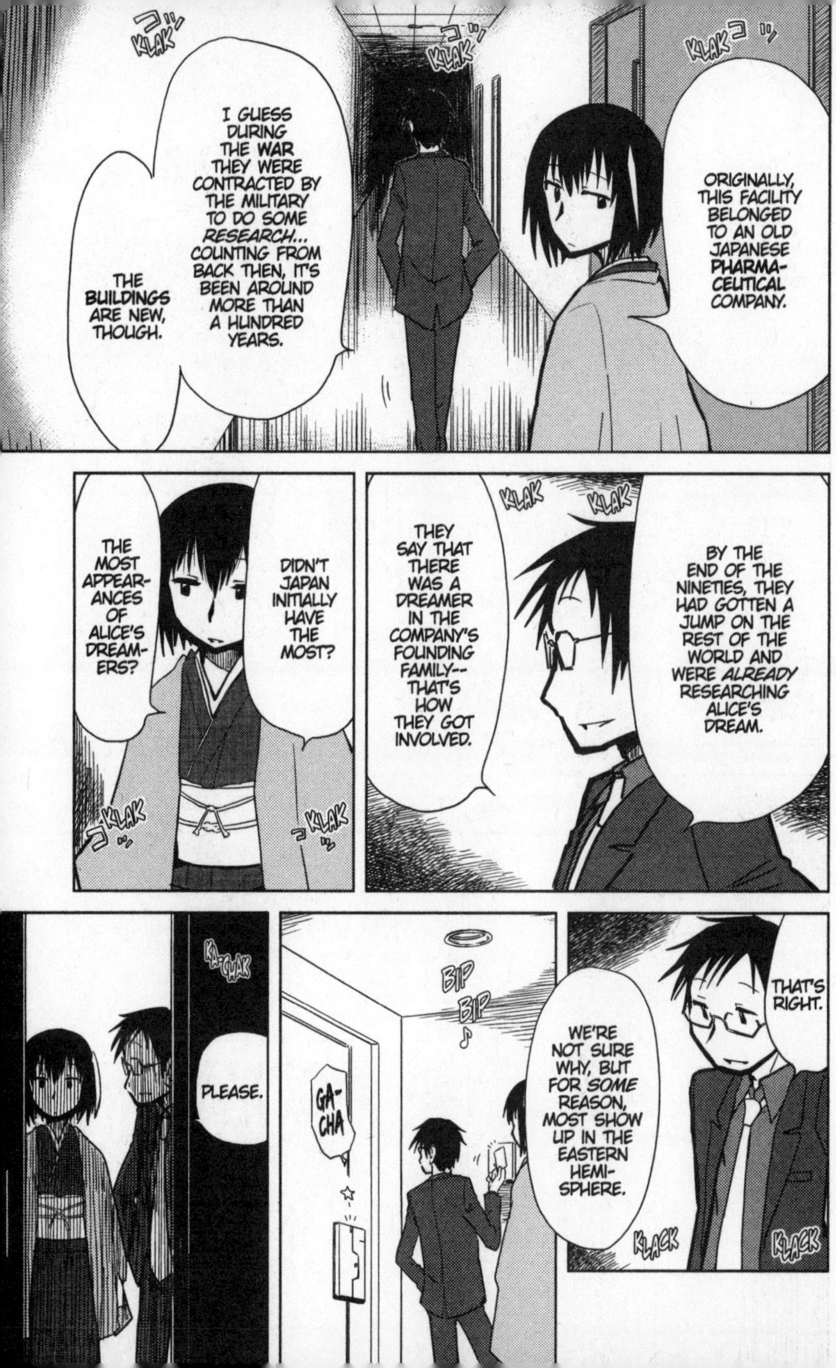
KLAK
KLAK
KLAK
ORIGINALLY, THIS FACILITY BELONGED TO AN OLD JAPANESE PHARMA-CEUTICAL COMPANY.
I GUESS DURING THE WAR THEY WERE CONTRACTED BY THE MILITARY TO DO SOME *RESEARCH*... COUNTING FROM BACK THEN, IT'S BEEN AROUND MORE THAN A HUNDRED YEARS.
THE BUILDINGS ARE NEW, THOUGH.
KLAK
KLAK
BY THE END OF THE NINETIES, THEY HAD GOTTEN A JUMP ON THE REST OF THE WORLD AND WERE *ALREADY* RESEARCHING ALICE'S DREAM.
THEY SAY THAT THERE WAS A DREAMER IN THE COMPANY'S FOUNDING FAMILY-- THAT'S HOW THEY GOT INVOLVED.
DIDN'T JAPAN INITIALLY HAVE THE MOST?
THE MOST APPEARANCES OF ALICE'S DREAMERS?
KLAK
KLAK
THAT'S RIGHT.
WE'RE NOT SURE WHY, BUT FOR *SOME* REASON, MOST SHOW UP IN THE EASTERN HEMI-SPHERE.
KLACK
KLACK
BIP
BIP
GA-CHA
KA-CHAK
PLEASE.

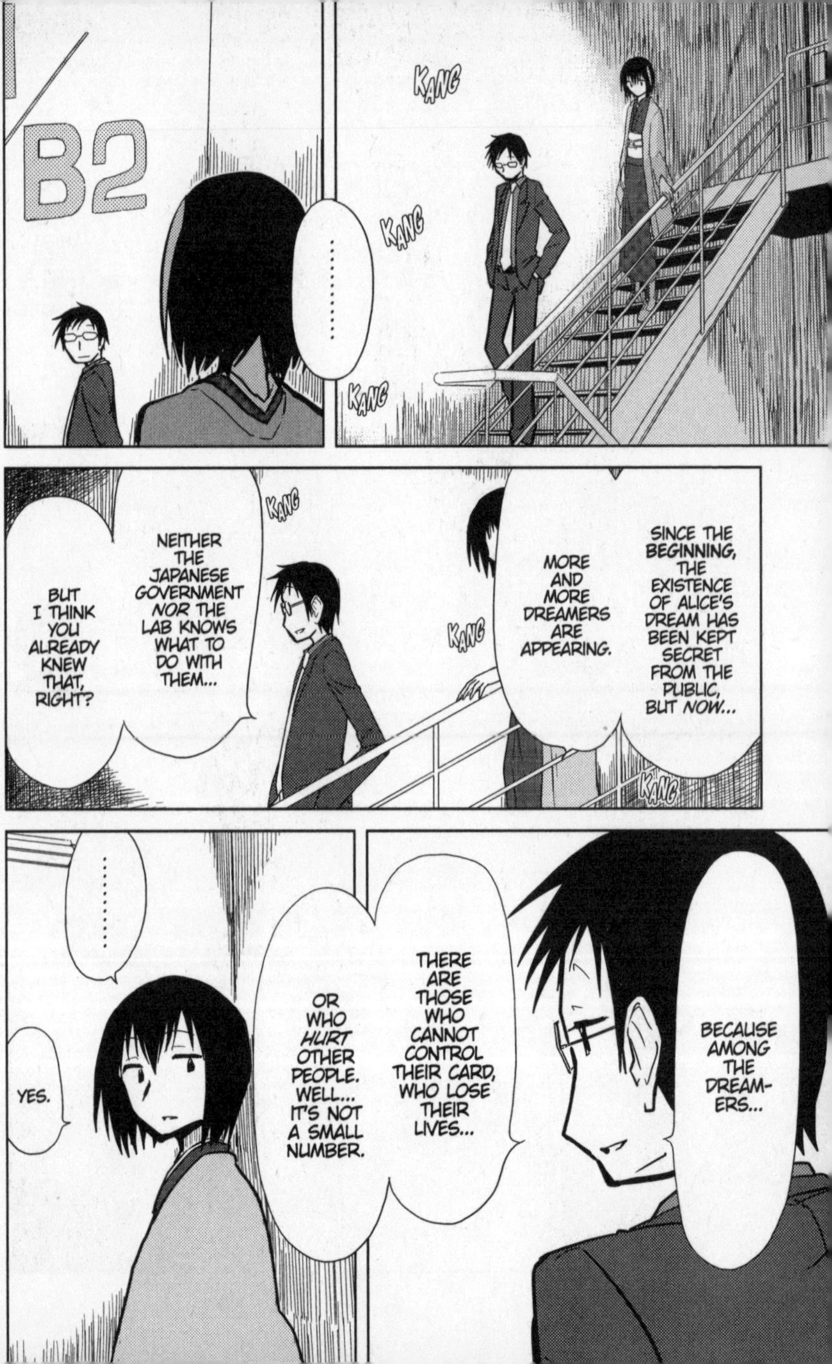
KANG
KANG
KANG
B2
......
SINCE THE BEGINNING, THE EXISTENCE OF ALICE'S DREAM HAS BEEN KEPT SECRET FROM THE PUBLIC, BUT *NOW*...
MORE AND MORE DREAMERS ARE APPEARING.
KANG
KANG
NEITHER THE JAPANESE GOVERNMENT *NOR* THE LAB KNOWS WHAT TO DO WITH THEM...
BUT I THINK YOU ALREADY KNEW THAT, RIGHT?
KANG
BECAUSE AMONG THE DREAM-ERS...
THERE ARE THOSE WHO CANNOT CONTROL THEIR CARD, WHO LOSE THEIR LIVES...
OR WHO *HURT* OTHER PEOPLE. WELL... IT'S NOT A SMALL NUMBER.
......
YES.

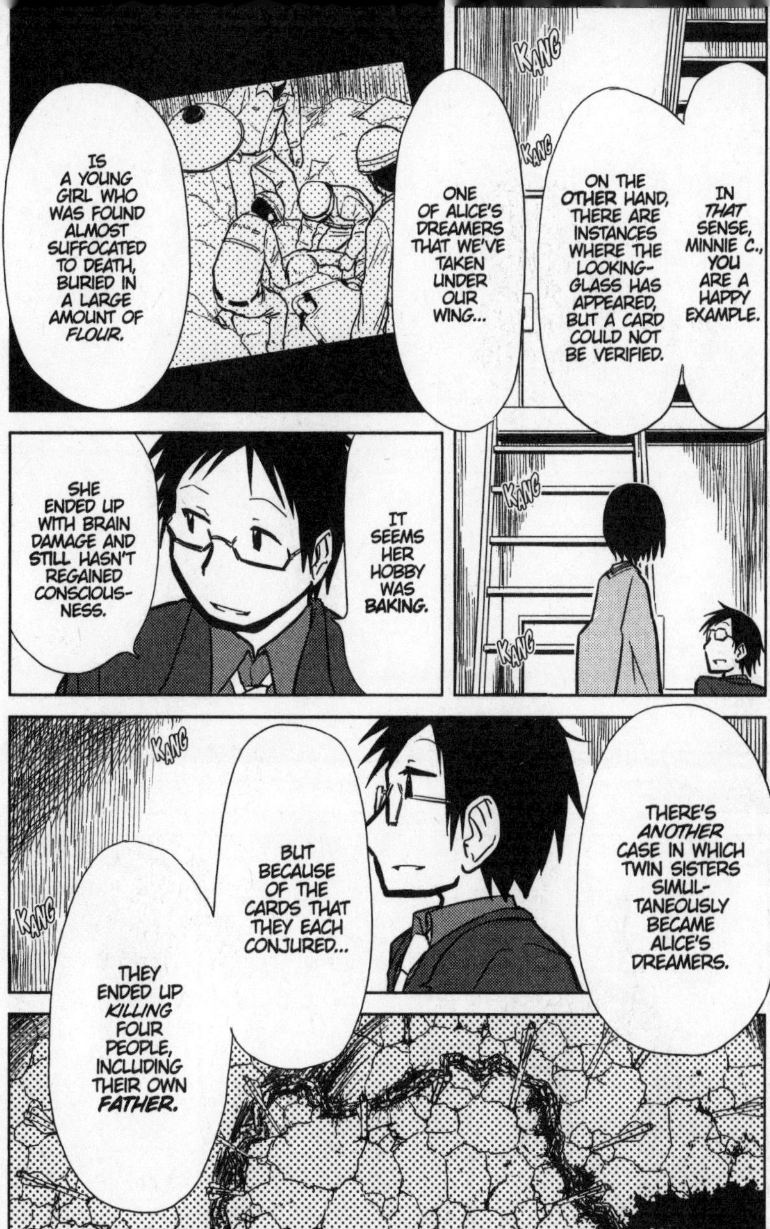
KANG
KANG
IN THAT SENSE, MINNIE C., YOU ARE A HAPPY EXAMPLE.
ON THE OTHER HAND, THERE ARE INSTANCES WHERE THE LOOKING-GLASS HAS APPEARED, BUT A CARD COULD NOT BE VERIFIED.
ONE OF ALICE'S DREAMERS THAT WE'VE TAKEN UNDER OUR WING...
IS A YOUNG GIRL WHO WAS FOUND ALMOST SUFFOCATED TO DEATH, BURIED IN A LARGE AMOUNT OF *FLOUR.*
KANG
KANG
IT SEEMS HER HOBBY WAS BAKING.
SHE ENDED UP WITH BRAIN DAMAGE AND STILL HASN'T REGAINED CONSCIOUS-NESS.
KANG
THERE'S *ANOTHER* CASE IN WHICH TWIN SISTERS SIMUL-TANEOUSLY BECAME ALICE'S DREAMERS.
BUT BECAUSE OF THE CARDS THAT THEY EACH CONJURED...
KANG
THEY ENDED UP *KILLING* FOUR PEOPLE, INCLUDING THEIR OWN *FATHER.*

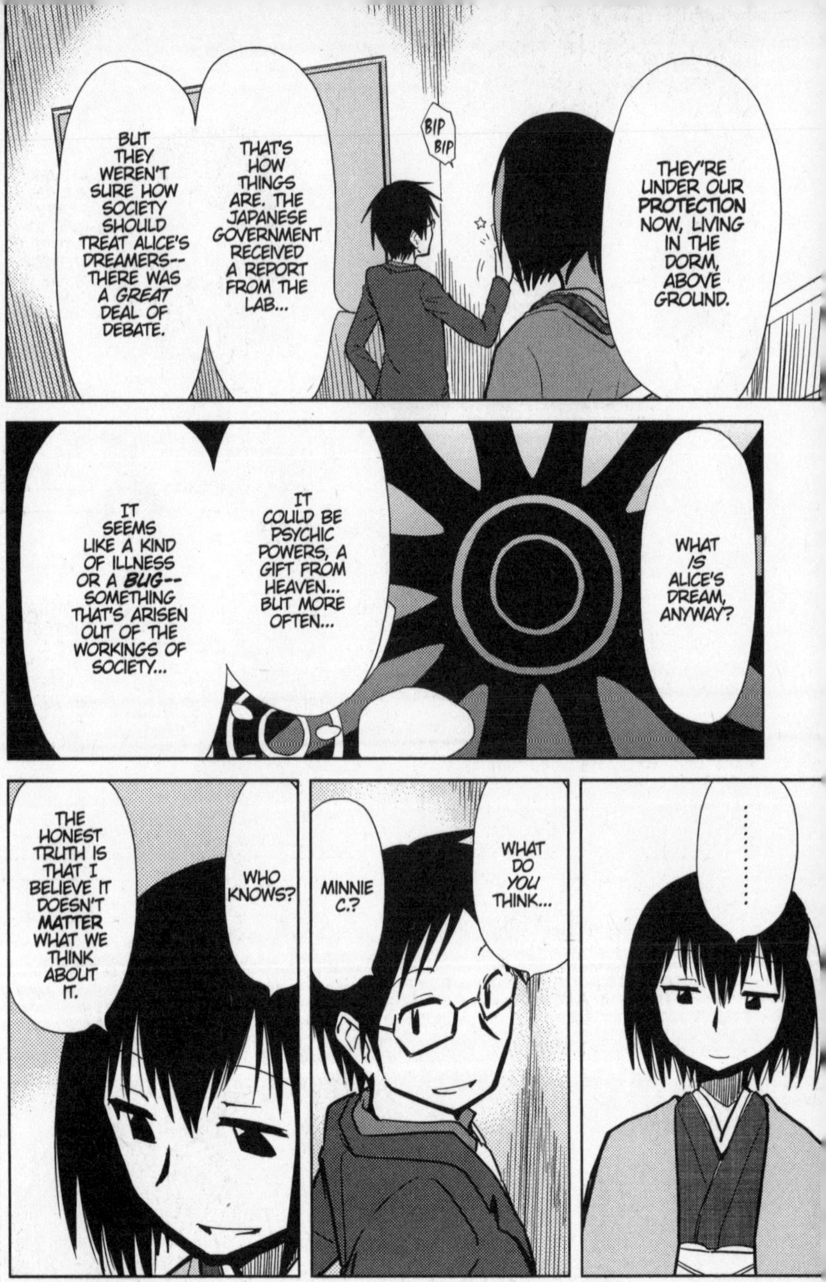
THEY'RE UNDER OUR PROTECTION NOW, LIVING IN THE DORM, ABOVE GROUND.
BIP BIP
THAT'S HOW THINGS ARE. THE JAPANESE GOVERNMENT RECEIVED A REPORT FROM THE LAB...
BUT THEY WEREN'T SURE HOW SOCIETY SHOULD TREAT ALICE'S DREAMERS-- THERE WAS A *GREAT* DEAL OF DEBATE.
WHAT *IS* ALICE'S DREAM, ANYWAY?
IT COULD BE PSYCHIC POWERS, A GIFT FROM HEAVEN... BUT MORE OFTEN...
IT SEEMS LIKE A KIND OF ILLNESS OR A ***BUG***-- SOMETHING THAT'S ARISEN OUT OF THE WORKINGS OF SOCIETY...
........
WHAT DO *YOU* THINK...
MINNIE C.?
WHO KNOWS?
THE HONEST TRUTH IS THAT I BELIEVE IT DOESN'T MATTER WHAT WE THINK ABOUT IT.

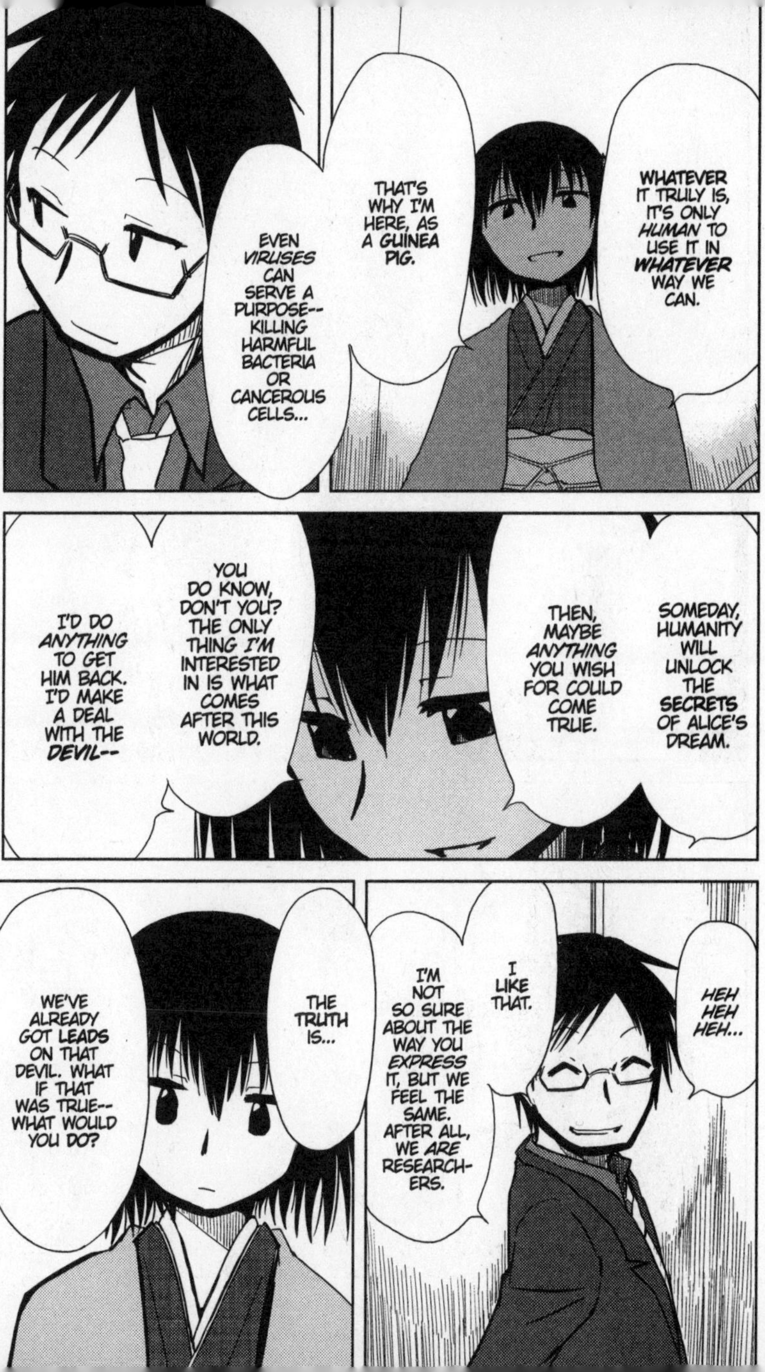
WHATEVER IT TRULY IS, IT'S ONLY *HUMAN* TO USE IT IN ***WHATEVER*** WAY WE CAN.
THAT'S WHY I'M HERE, AS A GUINEA PIG.
EVEN *VIRUSES* CAN SERVE A PURPOSE-- KILLING HARMFUL BACTERIA OR CANCEROUS CELLS...
SOMEDAY, HUMANITY WILL UNLOCK THE SECRETS OF ALICE'S DREAM.
THEN, MAYBE *ANYTHING* YOU WISH FOR COULD COME TRUE.
YOU DO KNOW, DON'T YOU? THE ONLY THING *I'M* INTERESTED IN IS WHAT COMES AFTER THIS WORLD.
I'D DO *ANYTHING* TO GET HIM BACK. I'D MAKE A DEAL WITH THE ***DEVIL***--
*HEH HEH HEH...*
I LIKE THAT.
I'M NOT SO SURE ABOUT THE WAY YOU *EXPRESS* IT, BUT WE FEEL THE SAME. AFTER ALL, WE *ARE* RESEARCHERS.
THE TRUTH IS...
WE'VE ALREADY GOT LEADS ON THAT DEVIL. WHAT IF THAT WAS TRUE-- WHAT WOULD YOU DO?

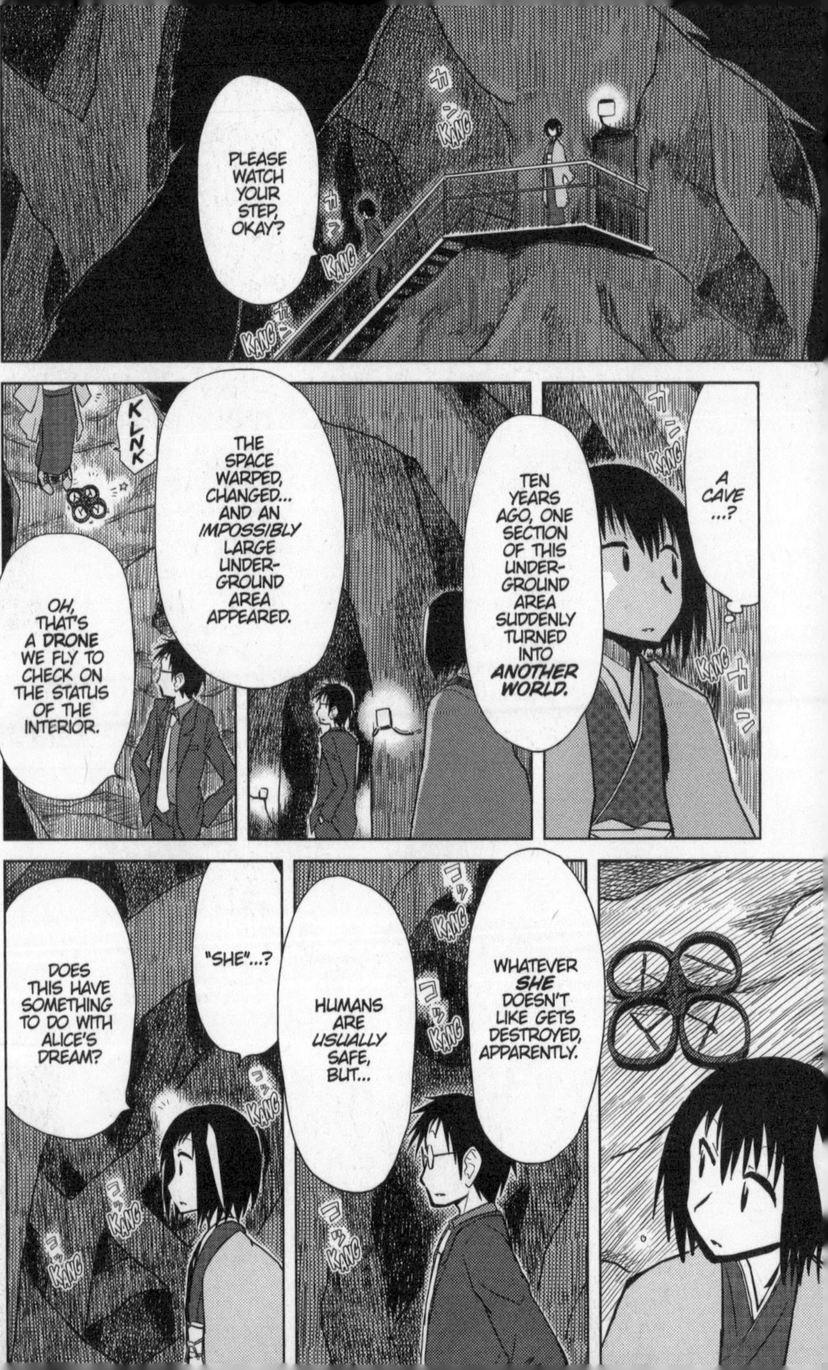
KANG
PLEASE WATCH YOUR STEP, OKAY?
KANG
KANG
KANG
A CAVE ...?
TEN YEARS AGO, ONE SECTION OF THIS UNDERGROUND AREA SUDDENLY TURNED INTO *ANOTHER WORLD.*
KANG
THE SPACE WARPED, CHANGED... AND AN *IMPOSSIBLY* LARGE UNDERGROUND AREA APPEARED.
KLNK
OH, THAT'S A DRONE WE FLY TO CHECK ON THE STATUS OF THE INTERIOR.
WHATEVER *SHE* DOESN'T LIKE GETS DESTROYED, APPARENTLY.
KANG
KANG
HUMANS ARE *USUALLY* SAFE, BUT...
KANG
"SHE"...?
DOES THIS HAVE SOMETHING TO DO WITH ALICE'S DREAM?
KANG
KANG
KANG

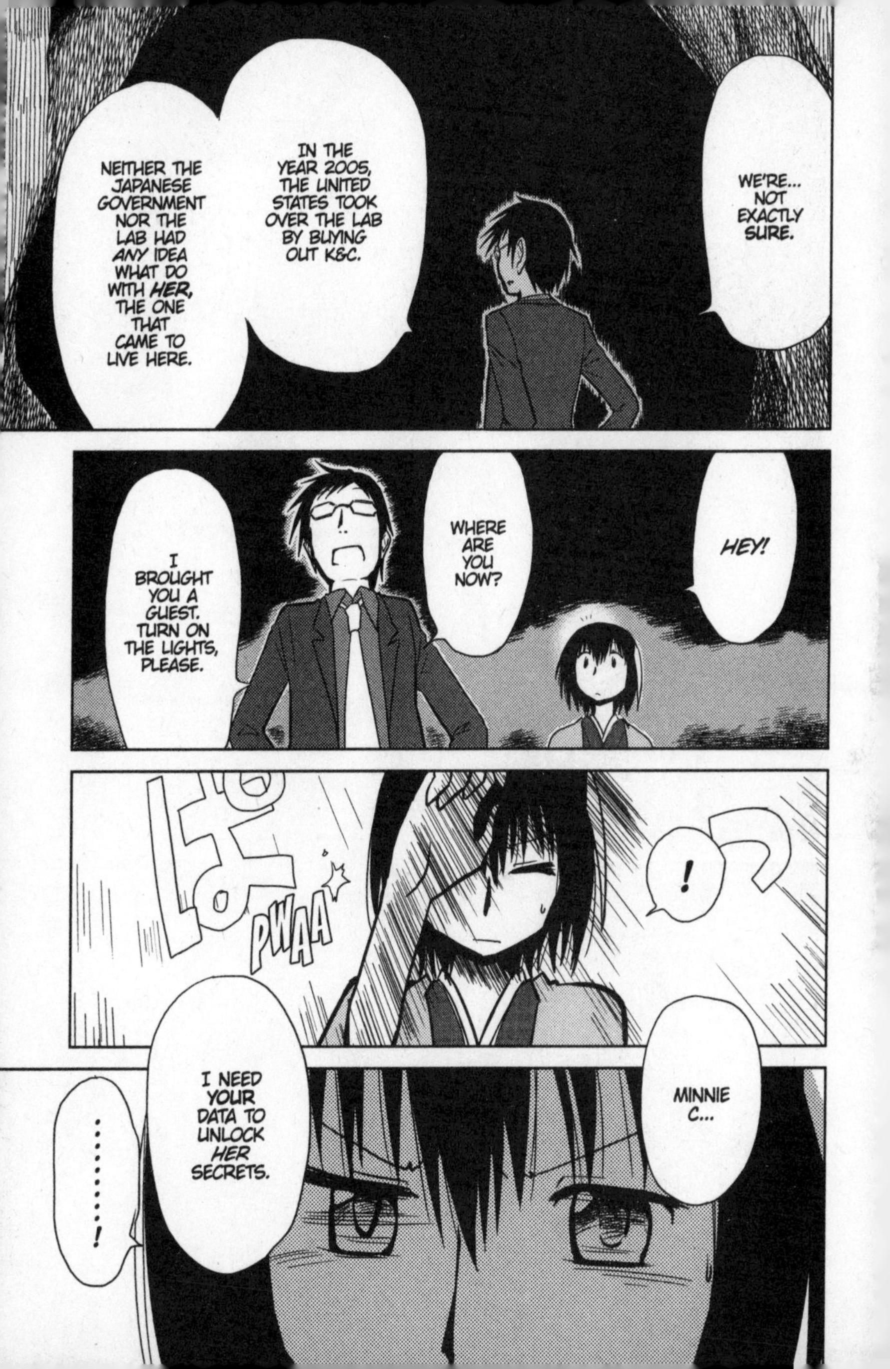
WE'RE... NOT EXACTLY SURE.
IN THE YEAR 2005, THE UNITED STATES TOOK OVER THE LAB BY BUYING OUT K&C.
NEITHER THE JAPANESE GOVERNMENT NOR THE LAB HAD *ANY* IDEA WHAT DO WITH *HER*, THE ONE THAT CAME TO LIVE HERE.
*HEY!*
WHERE ARE YOU NOW?
I BROUGHT YOU A GUEST. TURN ON THE LIGHTS, PLEASE.
!
PWAA
MINNIE C...
I NEED YOUR DATA TO UNLOCK *HER* SECRETS.
.........!

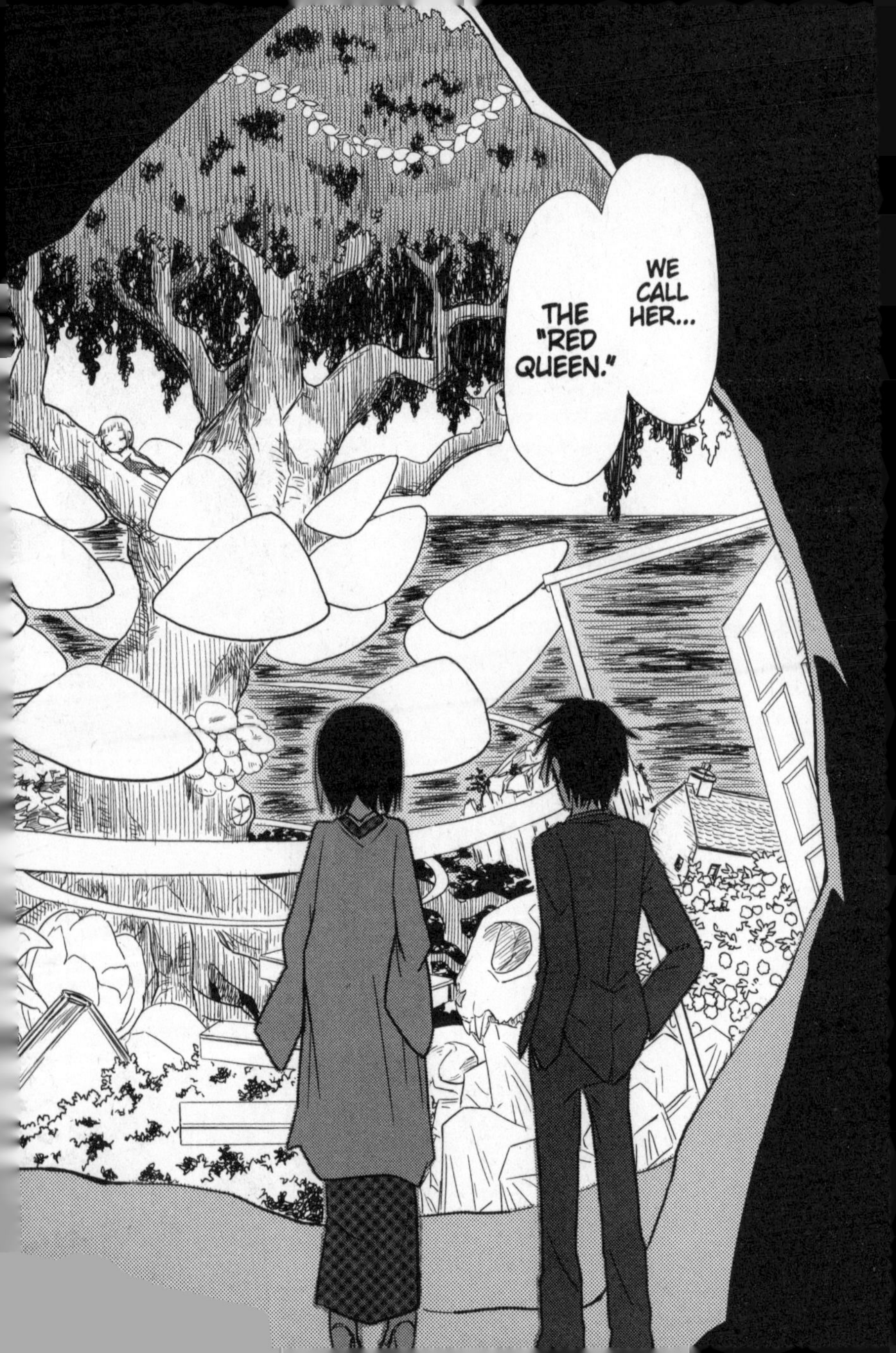
WE CALL HER... THE "RED QUEEN."

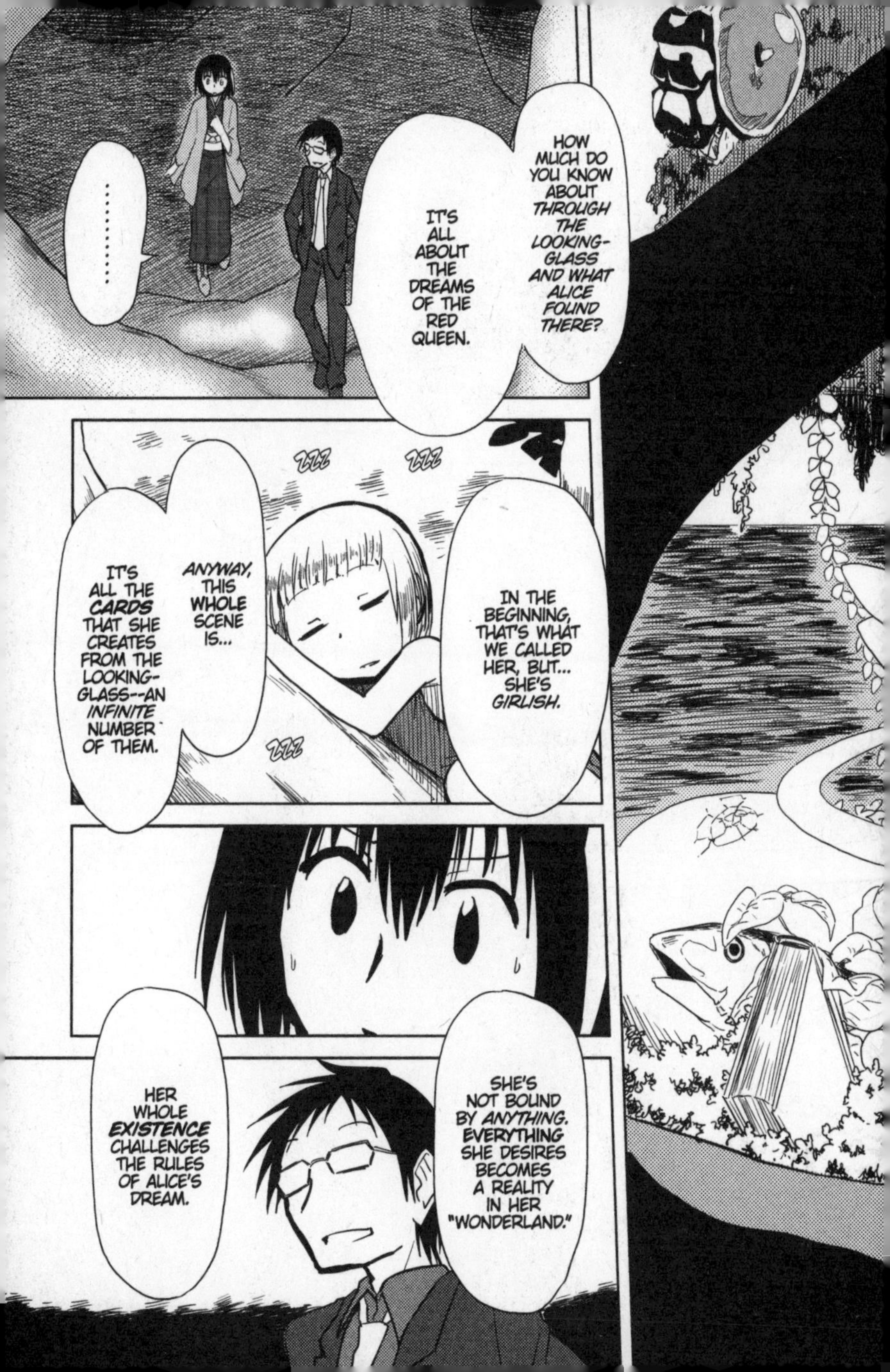
HOW MUCH DO YOU KNOW ABOUT *THROUGH THE LOOKING-GLASS AND WHAT ALICE FOUND THERE?*
IT'S ALL ABOUT THE DREAMS OF THE RED QUEEN.
......
ZZZ
ZZZ
IN THE BEGINNING, THAT'S WHAT WE CALLED HER, BUT... SHE'S *GIRLISH.*
*ANYWAY,* THIS WHOLE SCENE IS...
IT'S ALL THE ***CARDS*** THAT SHE CREATES FROM THE LOOKING-GLASS--AN *INFINITE* NUMBER OF THEM.
ZZZ
SHE'S NOT BOUND BY *ANYTHING.* **EVERYTHING** SHE DESIRES BECOMES A REALITY IN HER "WONDERLAND."
HER WHOLE ***EXISTENCE*** CHALLENGES THE RULES OF ALICE'S DREAM.

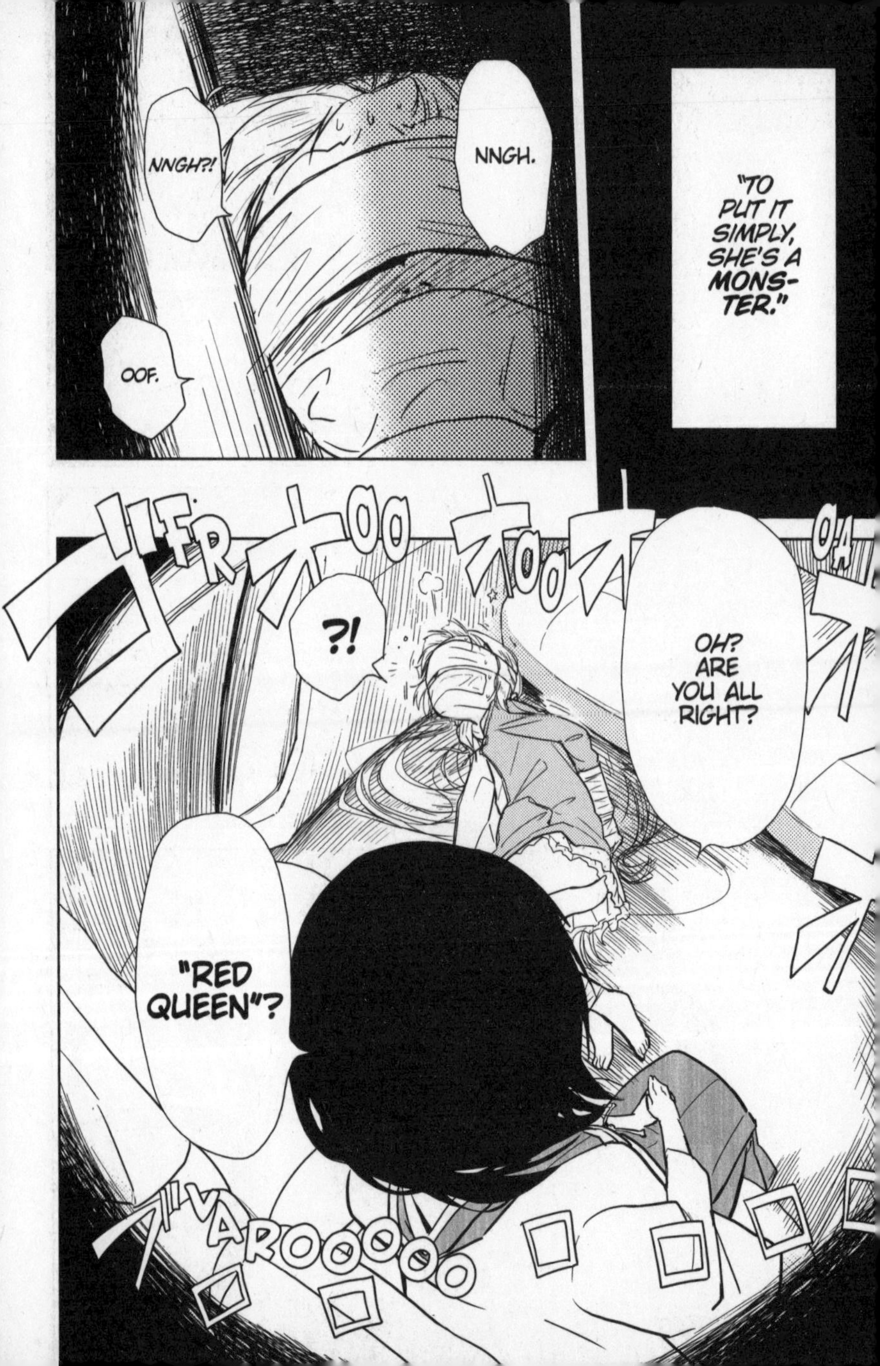
"TO PUT IT SIMPLY, SHE'S A MONSTER."
NNGH.
NNGH?!
OOF.
OH? ARE YOU ALL RIGHT?
?!
"RED QUEEN"?
VAROOOOOO

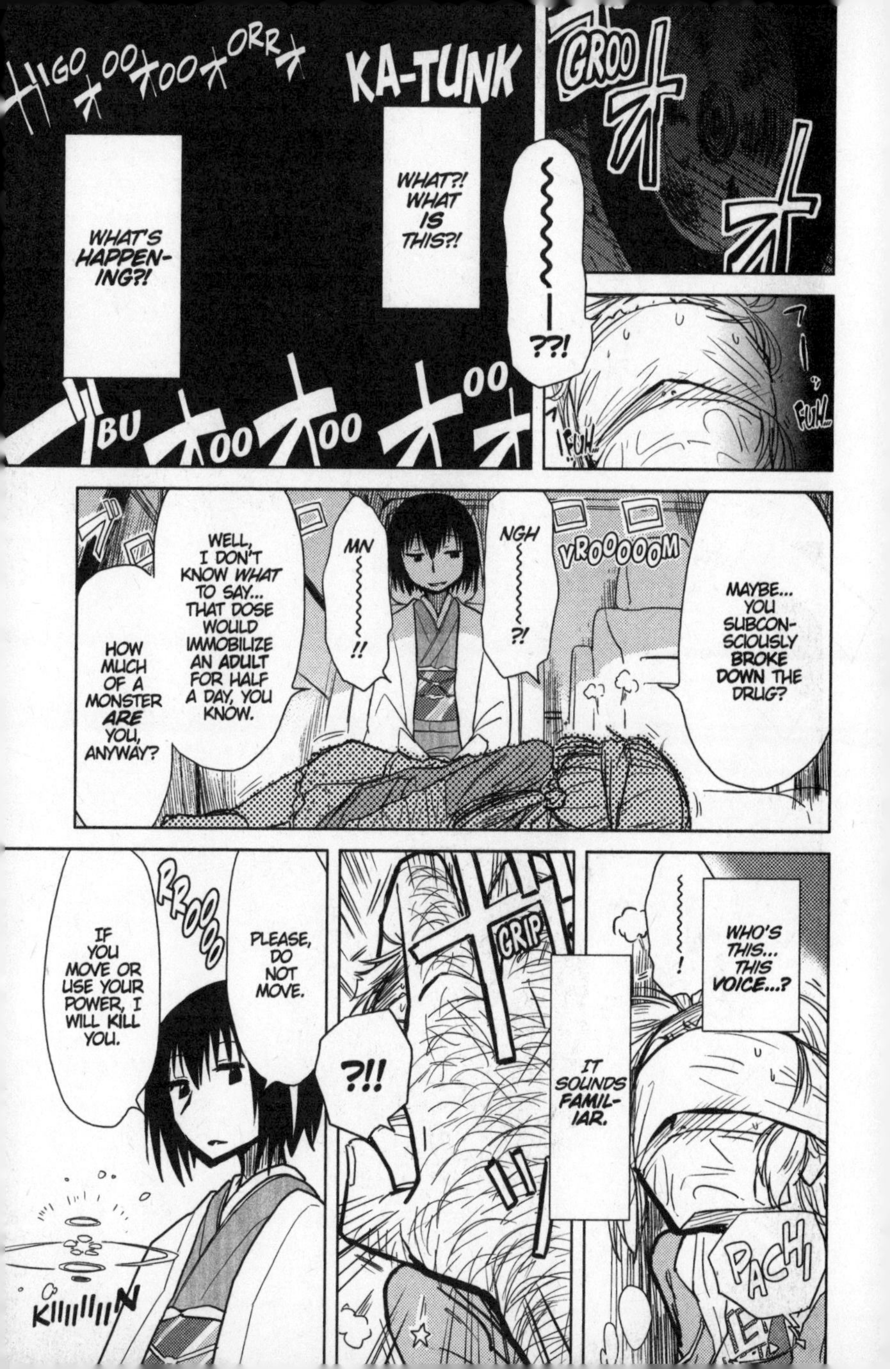
GROO
~~~~~~~~
??!
FUH...
FUH...
KA-TUNK
WHAT?! WHAT IS THIS?!
HIGO OO OO ORR
WHAT'S HAPPEN-ING?!
BU OO OO OO
MAYBE... YOU SUBCON-SCIOUSLY BROKE DOWN THE DRUG?
VROOOOOM
NGH ~~~~~~ ?!
MN ~~~~~~ !!
WELL, I DON'T KNOW *WHAT* TO SAY... THAT DOSE WOULD IMMOBILIZE AN ADULT FOR HALF A DAY, YOU KNOW.
HOW MUCH OF A MONSTER *ARE* YOU, ANYWAY?
WHO'S THIS... THIS *VOICE*...?
~~~~~~ !
PACHI
GRIP
IT SOUNDS FAMIL-IAR.
?!!
PLEASE, DO NOT MOVE.
RROOOO
IF YOU MOVE OR USE YOUR POWER, I WILL KILL YOU.
KIIIIIIIN

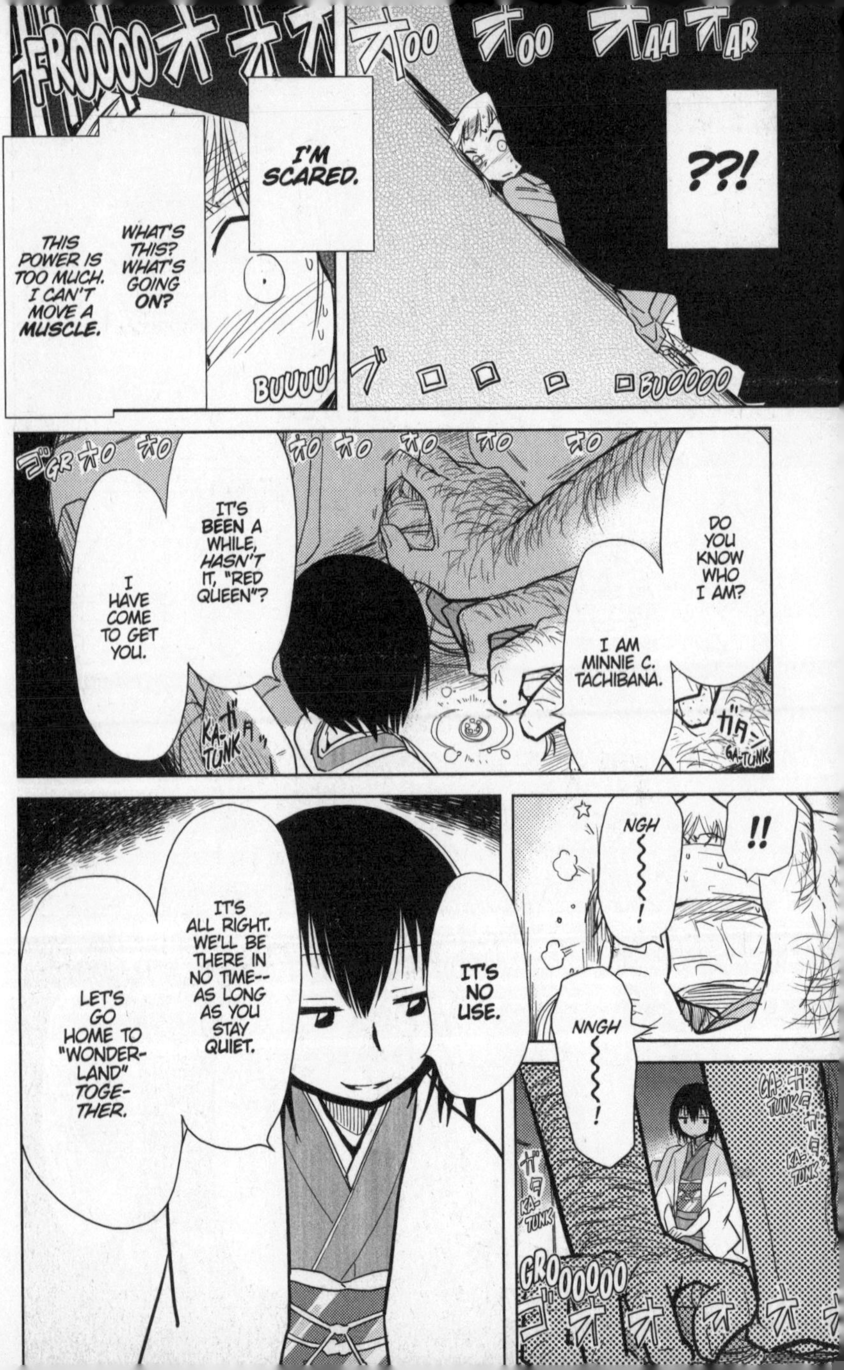
FROOOOOOOOOAAAR
??!
I'M SCARED.
BUUUUBUOOOO
WHAT'S THIS? WHAT'S GOING ON?
THIS POWER IS TOO MUCH. I CAN'T MOVE A MUSCLE.
GR
DO YOU KNOW WHO I AM?
I AM MINNIE C. TACHIBANA.
GA-TUNK
IT'S BEEN A WHILE, HASN'T IT, "RED QUEEN"?
I HAVE COME TO GET YOU.
KA-TUNK
!!
NGH~!
NNGH~!
GA-TUNK
KA-TUNK
KA-TUNK
GROOOOOO
IT'S NO USE.
IT'S ALL RIGHT. WE'LL BE THERE IN NO TIME--AS LONG AS YOU STAY QUIET.
LET'S GO HOME TO "WONDERLAND" TOGETHER.

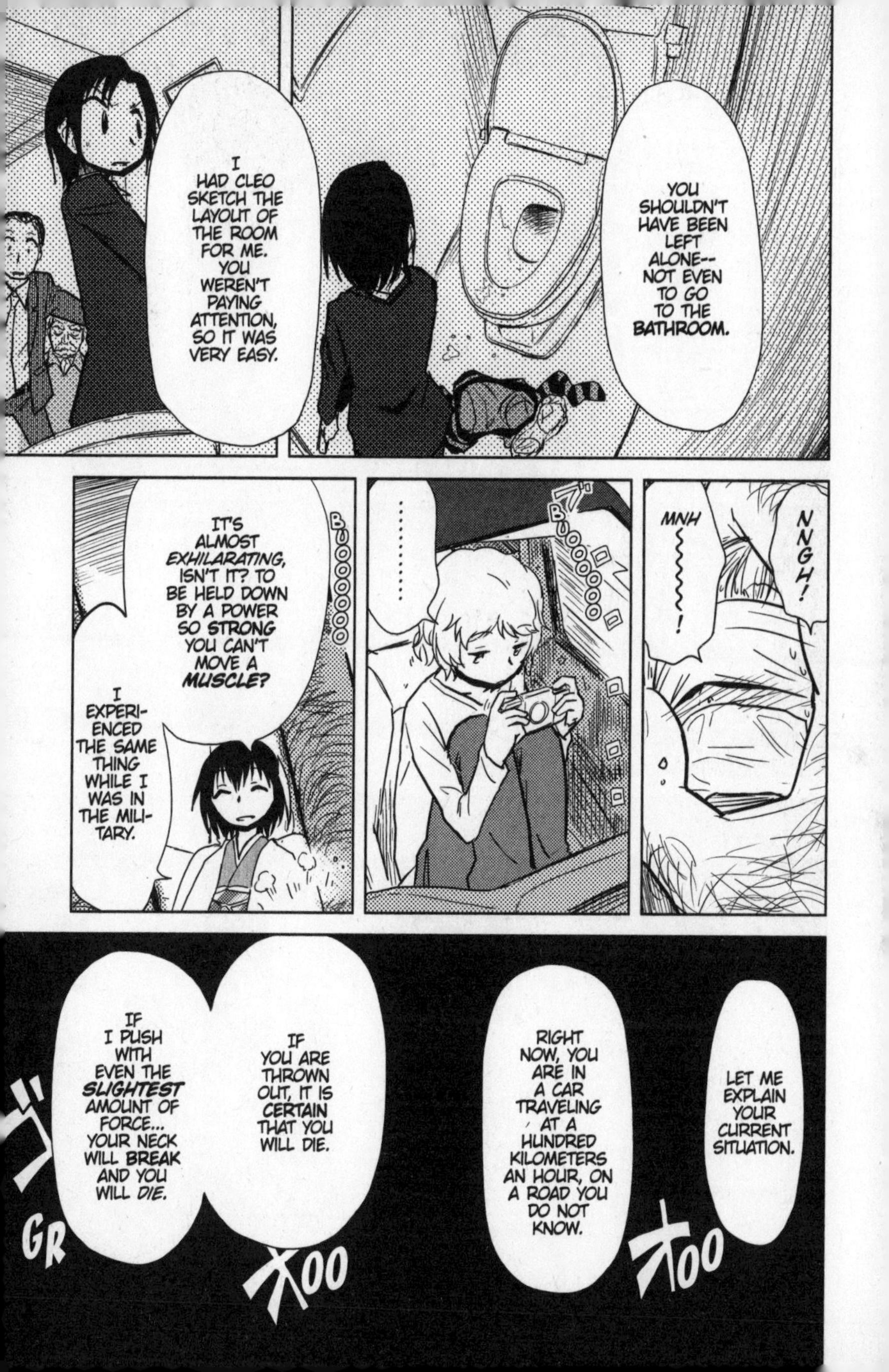
YOU SHOULDN'T HAVE BEEN LEFT ALONE-- NOT EVEN TO GO TO THE BATHROOM.
I HAD CLEO SKETCH THE LAYOUT OF THE ROOM FOR ME. YOU WEREN'T PAYING ATTENTION, SO IT WAS VERY EASY.
NNGH!
MNH~~~!
BUOOOOOOO
......
BUOOOOOO
IT'S ALMOST EXHILARATING, ISN'T IT? TO BE HELD DOWN BY A POWER SO STRONG YOU CAN'T MOVE A MUSCLE?
I EXPERIENCED THE SAME THING WHILE I WAS IN THE MILITARY.
LET ME EXPLAIN YOUR CURRENT SITUATION.
RIGHT NOW, YOU ARE IN A CAR TRAVELING AT A HUNDRED KILOMETERS AN HOUR, ON A ROAD YOU DO NOT KNOW.
OO
IF YOU ARE THROWN OUT, IT IS CERTAIN THAT YOU WILL DIE.
IF I PUSH WITH EVEN THE SLIGHTEST AMOUNT OF FORCE... YOUR NECK WILL BREAK AND YOU WILL DIE.
OO
GR

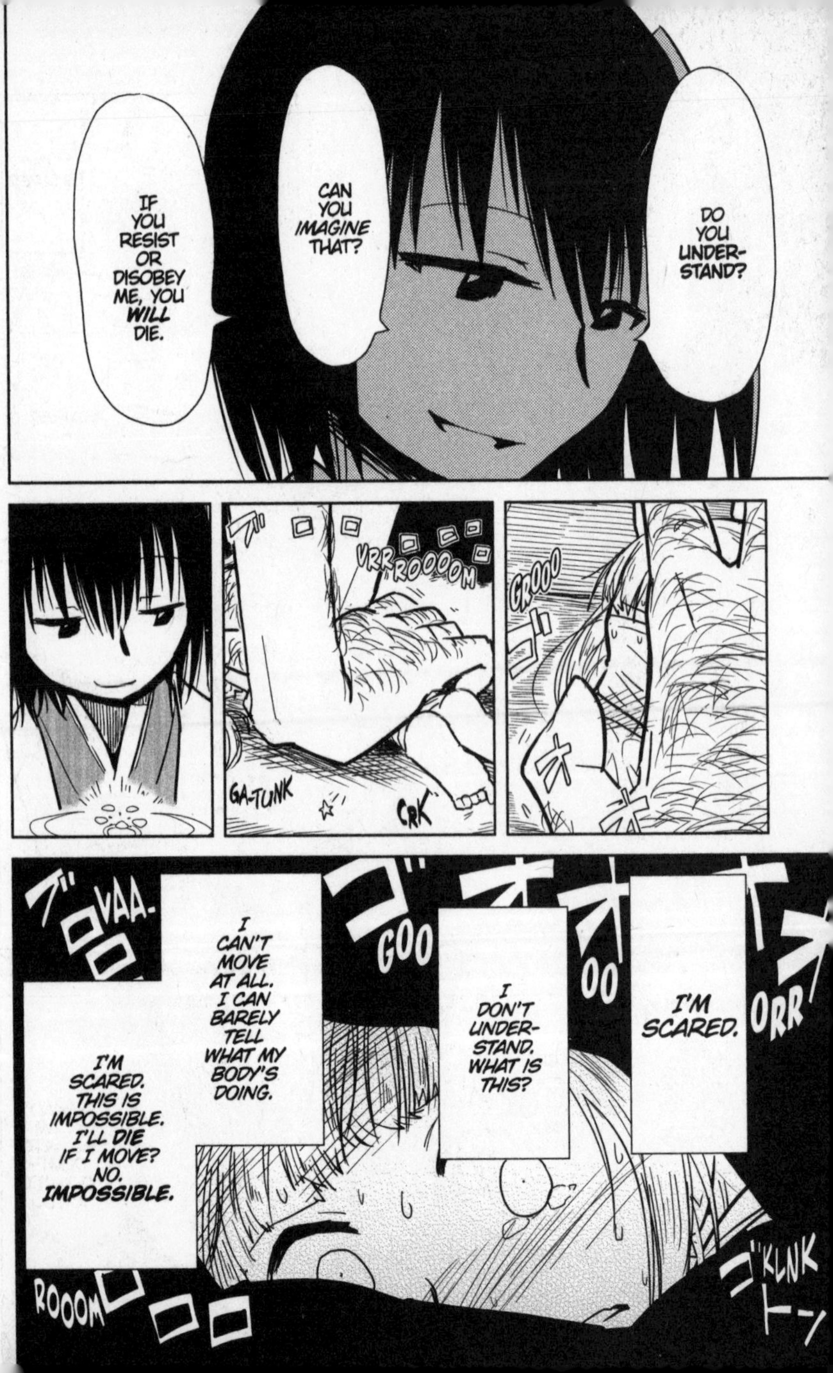
DO YOU UNDER-STAND?
CAN YOU IMAGINE THAT?
IF YOU RESIST OR DISOBEY ME, YOU WILL DIE.
GROOO
VRRROOOOOM
GA-TUNK
CRK
I'M SCARED.
ORR
I DON'T UNDER-STAND. WHAT IS THIS?
OO
GOO
I CAN'T MOVE AT ALL. I CAN BARELY TELL WHAT MY BODY'S DOING.
VAA-
I'M SCARED. THIS IS IMPOSSIBLE. I'LL DIE IF I MOVE? NO. IMPOSSIBLE.
ROOOM
KLNK

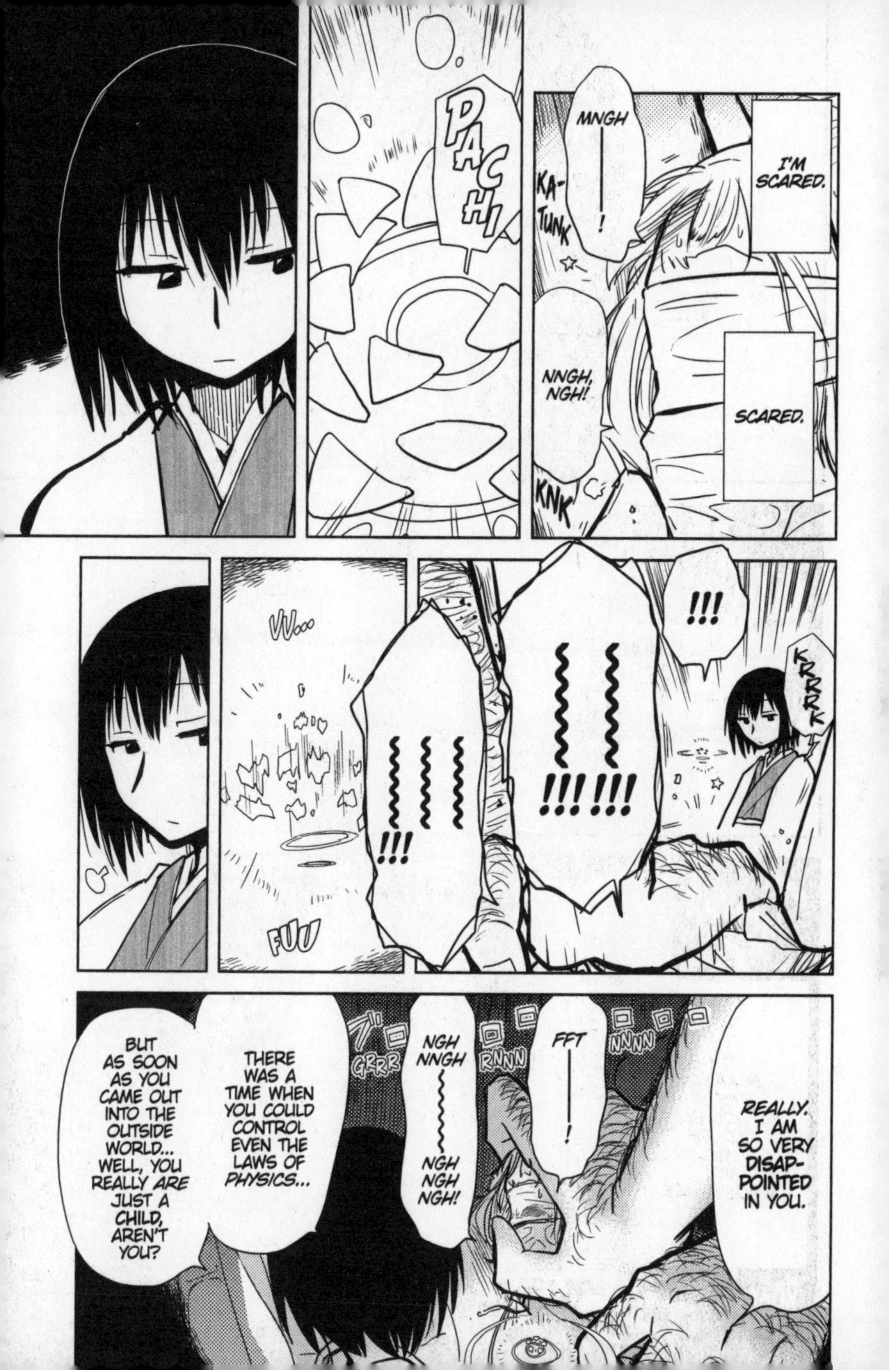
I'M SCARED.
SCARED.
MNGH—!
KA-TUNK
NNGH, NGH!
KNK
PACHI
!!!
KRRRK
~~~!!!!!!
~~~!!!
VV...
FUU
REALLY. I AM SO VERY DISAP-POINTED IN YOU.
FFT—!
NNNN
RNNN
NGH NNGH~ NGH NGH NGH!
GRRR
THERE WAS A TIME WHEN YOU COULD CONTROL EVEN THE LAWS OF *PHYSICS*...
BUT AS SOON AS YOU CAME OUT INTO THE OUTSIDE WORLD... WELL, YOU REALLY *ARE* JUST A CHILD, AREN'T YOU?

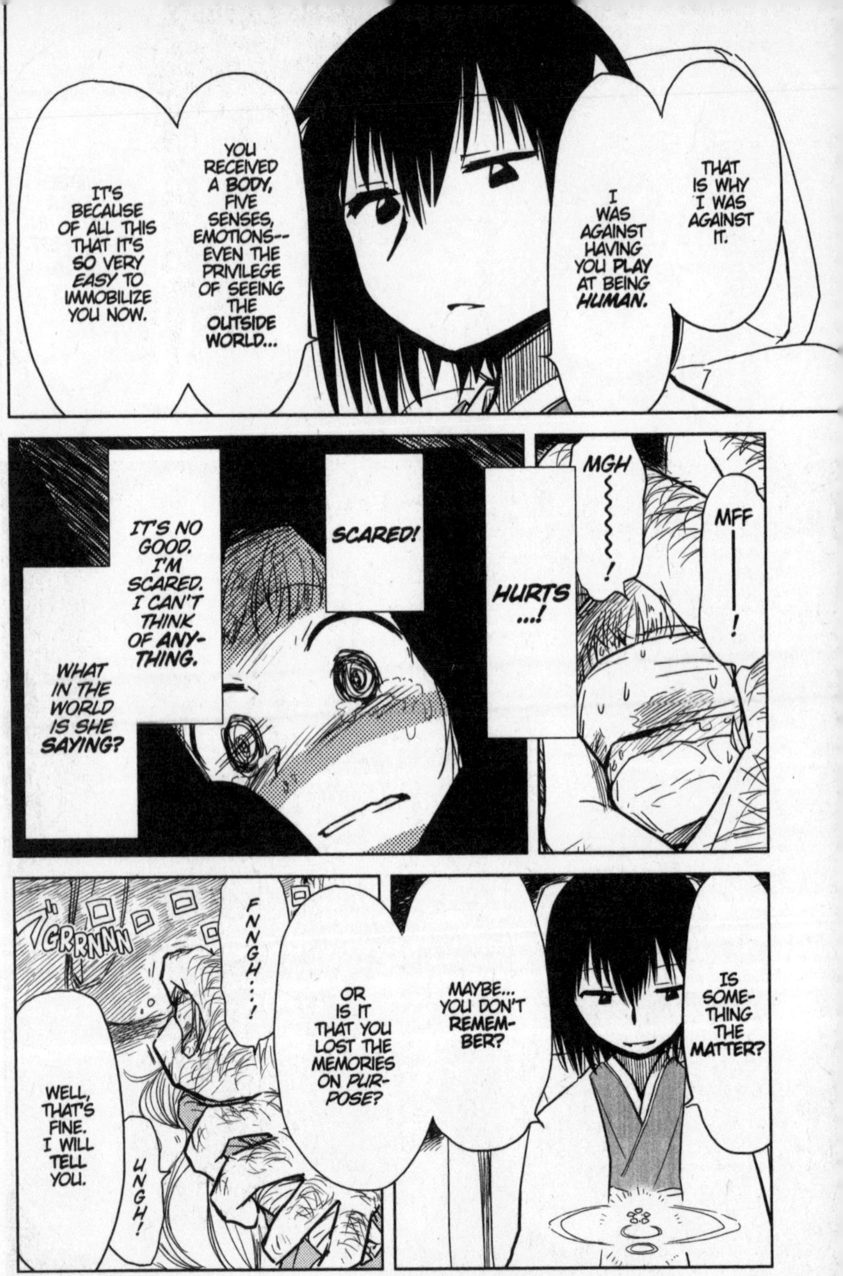
THAT IS WHY I WAS AGAINST IT.
I WAS AGAINST HAVING YOU PLAY AT BEING *HUMAN.*
YOU RECEIVED A BODY, FIVE SENSES, EMOTIONS-- EVEN THE PRIVILEGE OF SEEING THE OUTSIDE WORLD...
IT'S BECAUSE OF ALL THIS THAT IT'S SO VERY *EASY* TO IMMOBILIZE YOU NOW.
MFF—!
MGH~~~!
HURTS...!
SCARED!
IT'S NO GOOD. I'M SCARED. I CAN'T THINK OF **ANY-THING.**
WHAT IN THE WORLD IS SHE **SAYING?**
IS SOME-THING THE MATTER?
MAYBE... YOU DON'T REMEM-BER?
OR IS IT THAT YOU LOST THE MEMORIES ON *PUR-POSE?*
FNNGH...!
GRRNNN
WELL, THAT'S FINE. I WILL TELL YOU.
UNGH!

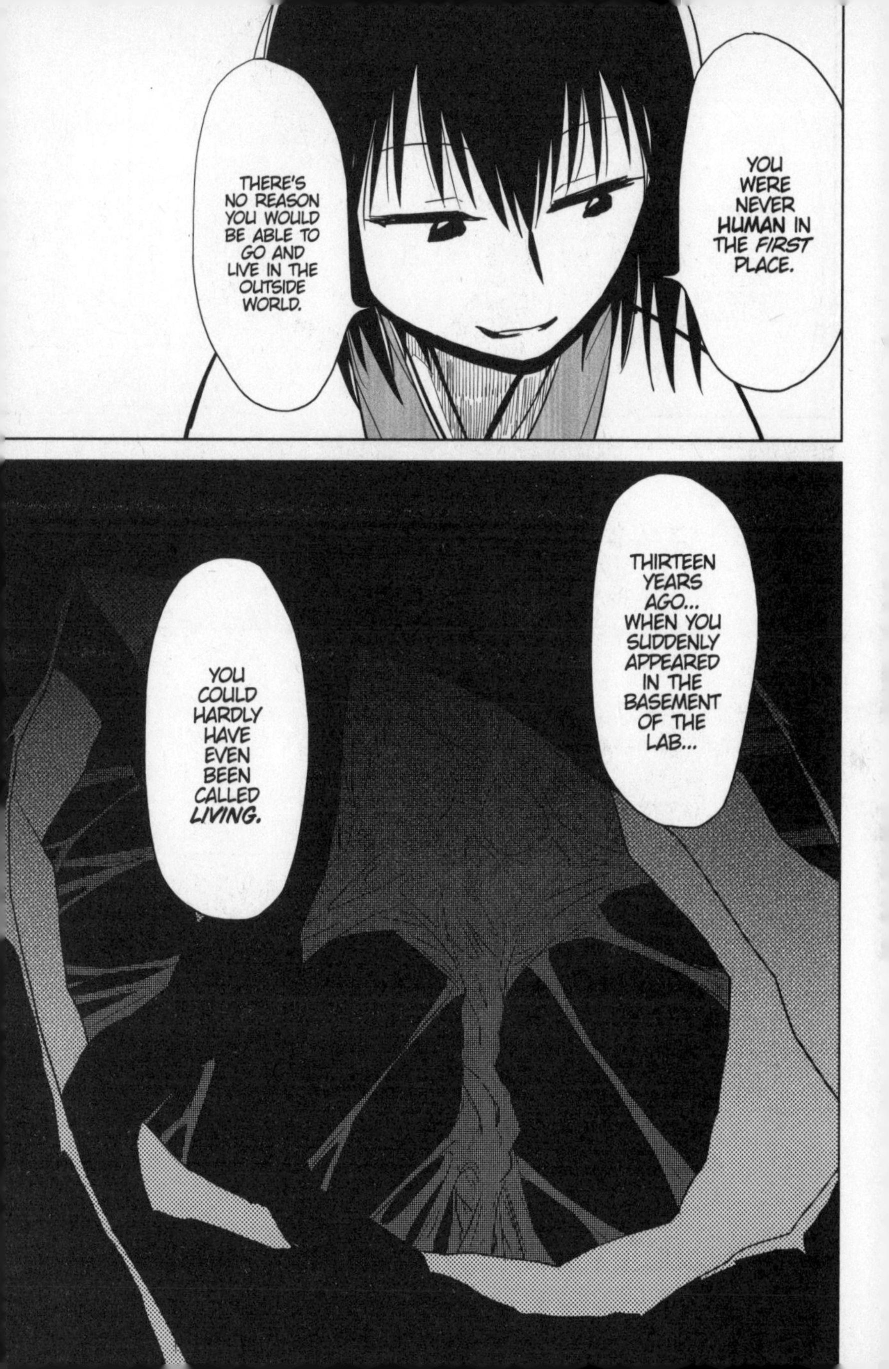
YOU WERE NEVER HUMAN IN THE *FIRST* PLACE.
THERE'S NO REASON YOU WOULD BE ABLE TO GO AND LIVE IN THE OUTSIDE WORLD.
THIRTEEN YEARS AGO... WHEN YOU SUDDENLY APPEARED IN THE BASEMENT OF THE LAB...
YOU COULD HARDLY HAVE EVEN BEEN CALLED ***LIVING.***

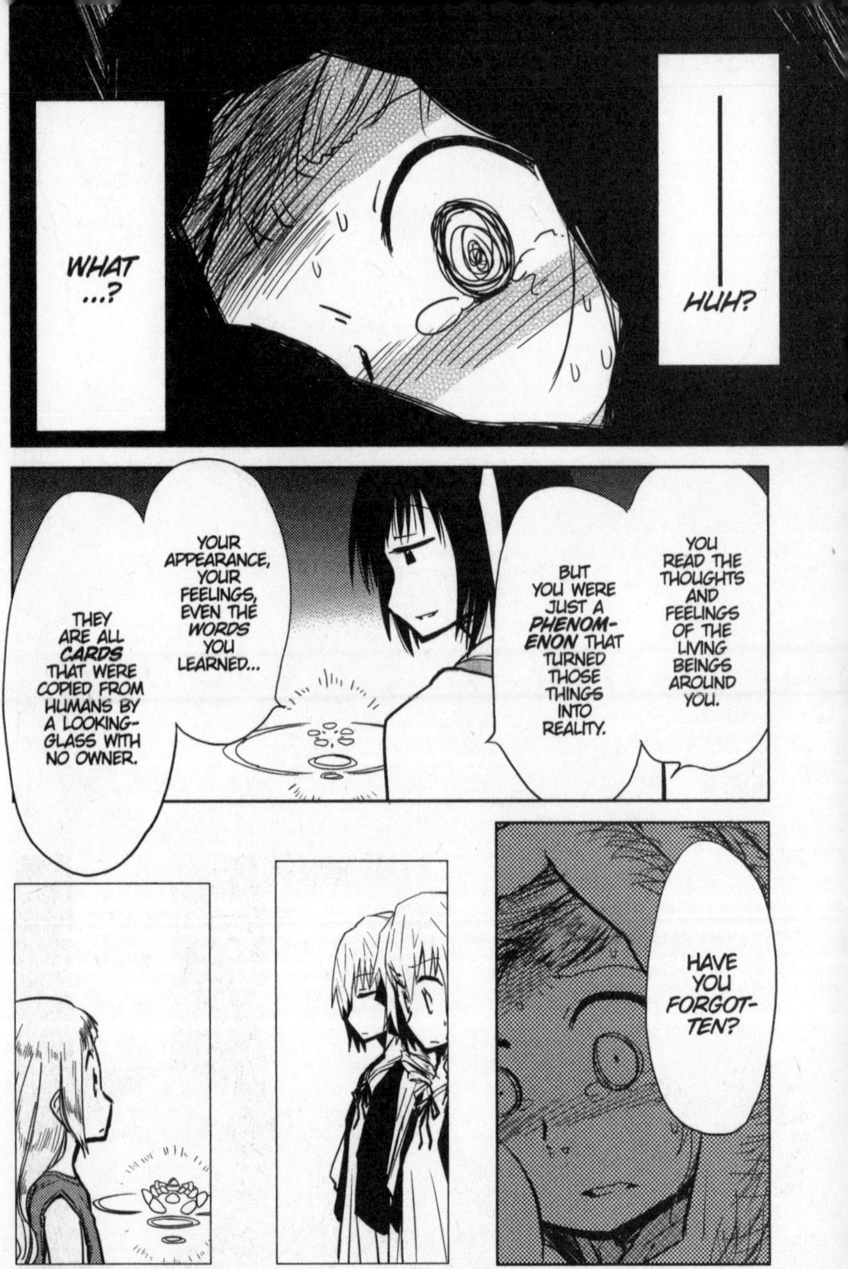
HUH?
WHAT...?
YOU READ THE THOUGHTS AND FEELINGS OF THE LIVING BEINGS AROUND YOU.
BUT YOU WERE JUST A PHENOMENON THAT TURNED THOSE THINGS INTO REALITY.
YOUR APPEARANCE, YOUR FEELINGS, EVEN THE WORDS YOU LEARNED...
THEY ARE ALL CARDS THAT WERE COPIED FROM HUMANS BY A LOOKING-GLASS WITH NO OWNER.
HAVE YOU FORGOTTEN?

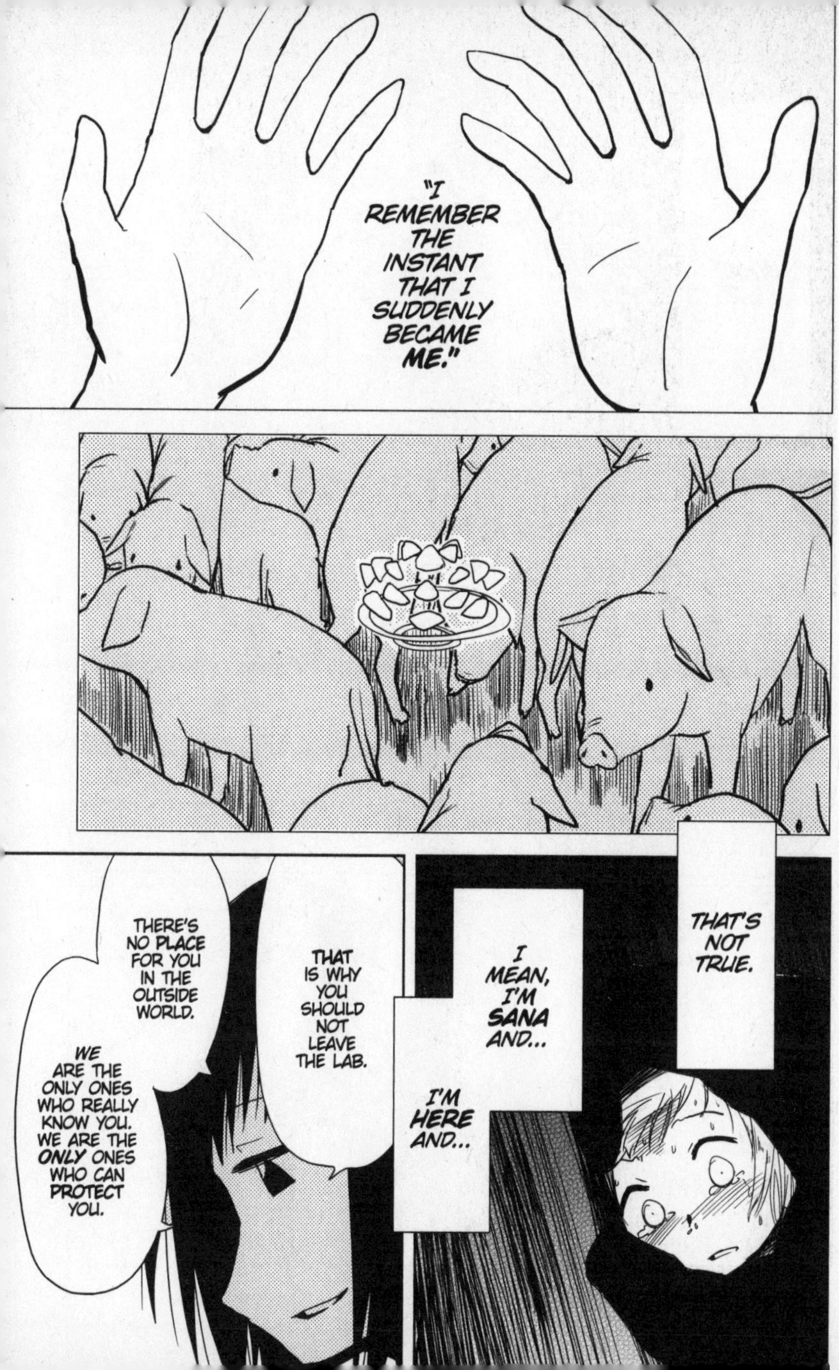
"I REMEMBER THE INSTANT THAT I SUDDENLY BECAME **ME**."
THAT'S NOT TRUE.
I MEAN, I'M **SANA** AND...
I'M **HERE** AND...
THAT IS WHY YOU SHOULD NOT LEAVE THE LAB.
THERE'S NO **PLACE** FOR YOU IN THE OUTSIDE WORLD.
WE ARE THE ONLY ONES WHO REALLY KNOW YOU. WE ARE THE ***ONLY*** ONES WHO CAN **PROTECT** YOU.

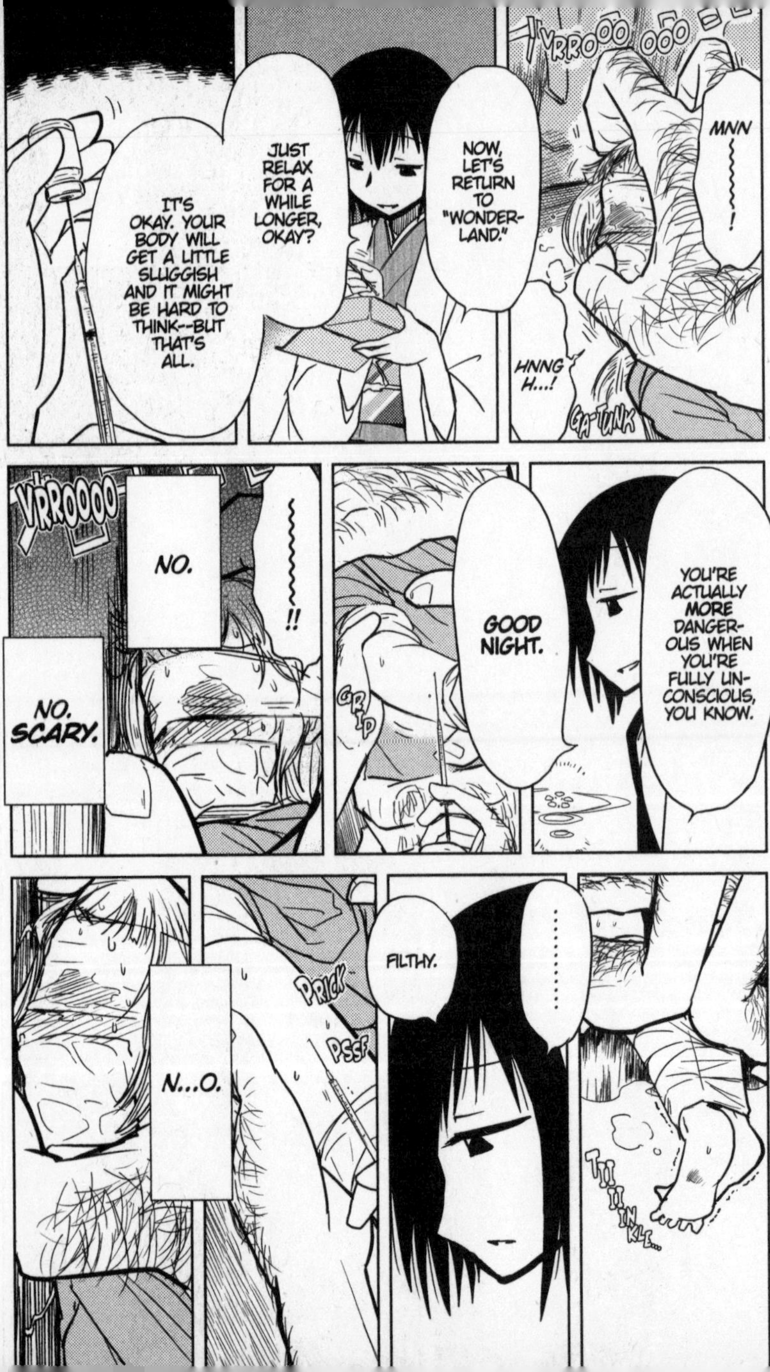
VRROOO OOO
MNN~~~~~!
HNNG H...!
GA-TUNK
NOW, LET'S RETURN TO "WONDER-LAND."
JUST RELAX FOR A WHILE LONGER, OKAY?
IT'S OKAY. YOUR BODY WILL GET A LITTLE SLUGGISH AND IT MIGHT BE HARD TO THINK--BUT THAT'S ALL.
YOU'RE ACTUALLY MORE DANGER-OUS WHEN YOU'RE FULLY UN-CONSCIOUS, YOU KNOW.
GOOD NIGHT.
GRIP
VRROOOO
~~~~~~!!
NO.
NO. SCARY.
TIIIINKLE...
......
FILTHY.
PRICK
PSSF
N...O.
~~~~~~

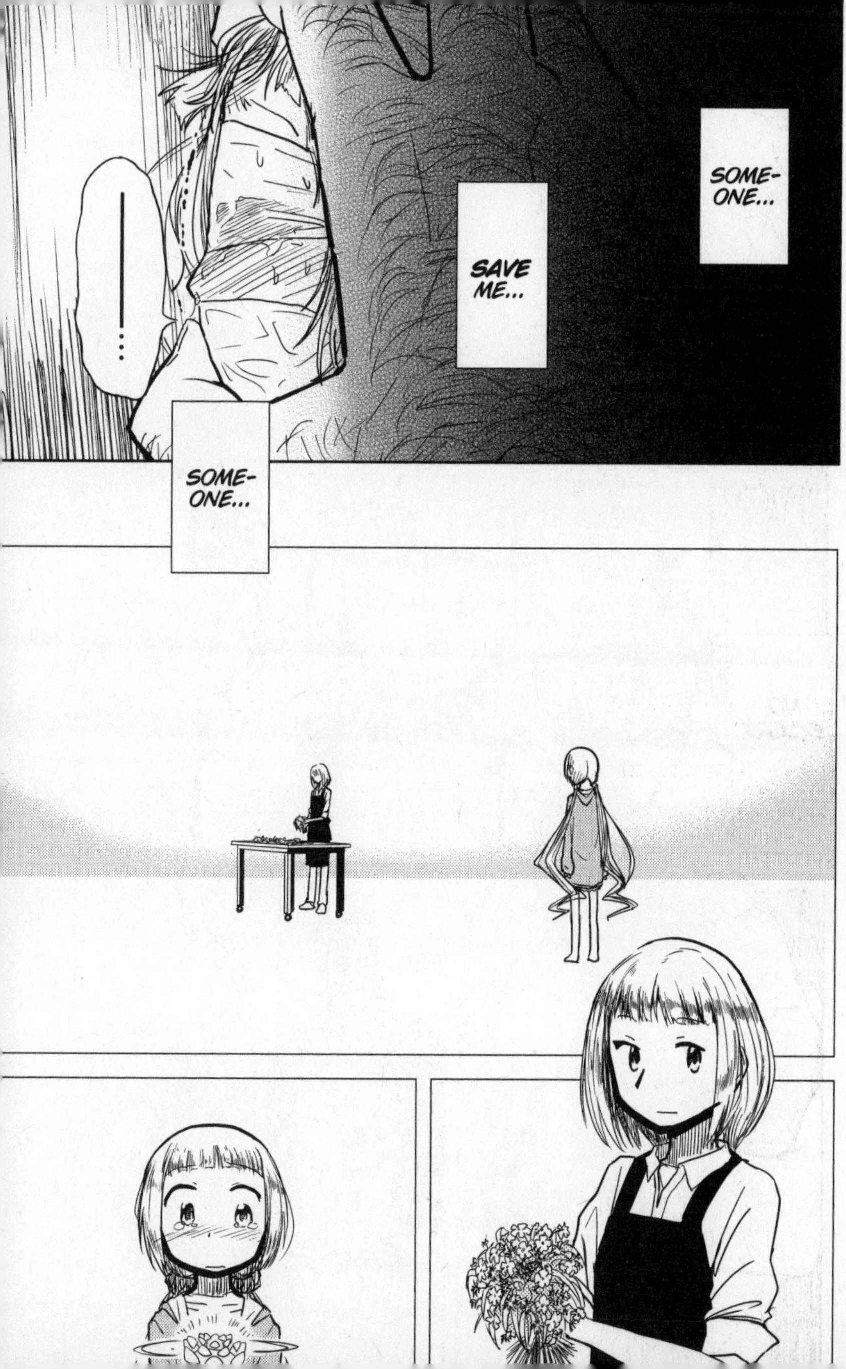
SOME-ONE...
SAVE ME...
......
SOME-ONE...

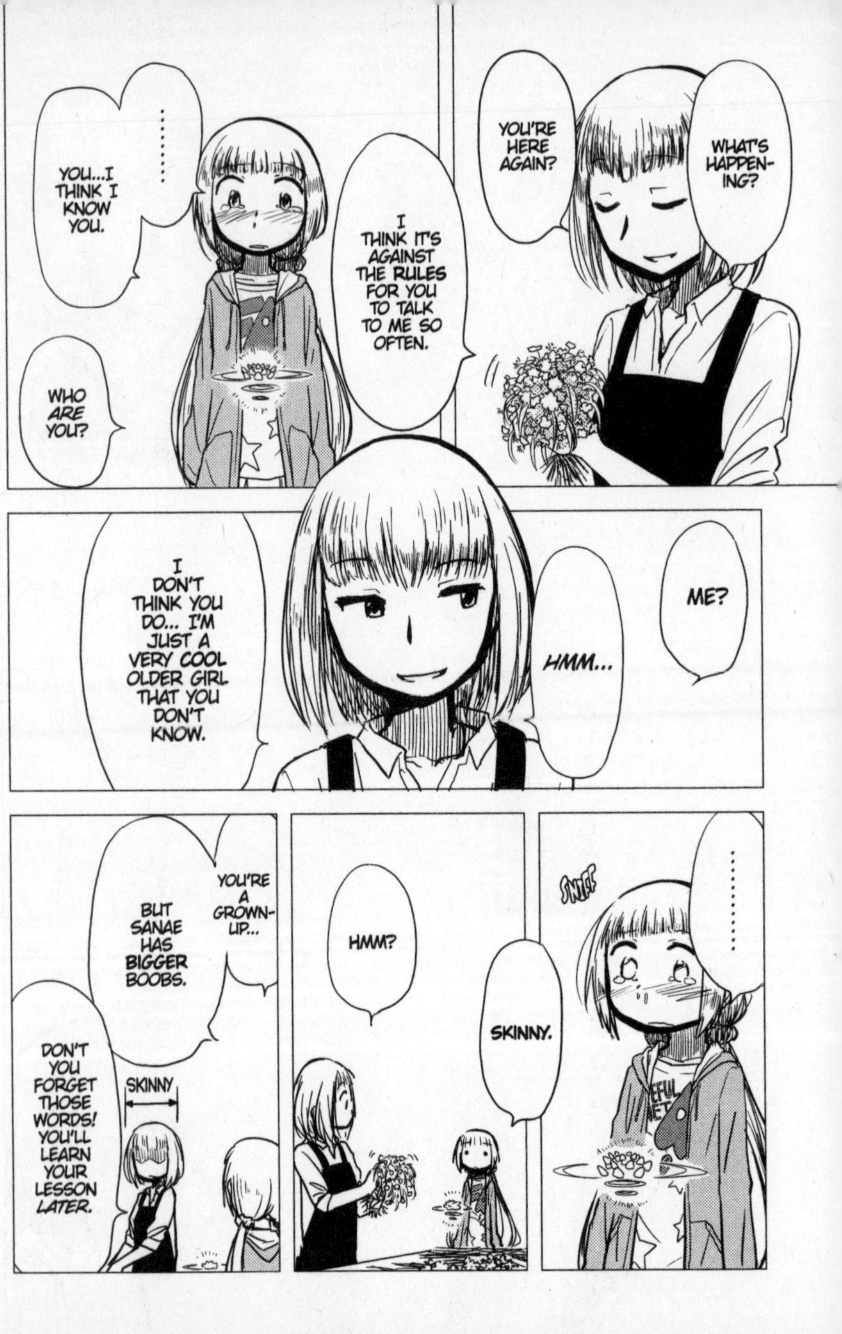
WHAT'S HAPPEN-ING?
YOU'RE HERE AGAIN?
I THINK IT'S AGAINST THE RULES FOR YOU TO TALK TO ME SO OFTEN.
......
YOU...I THINK I KNOW YOU.
WHO ARE YOU?
ME?
HMM...
I DON'T THINK YOU DO... I'M JUST A VERY COOL OLDER GIRL THAT YOU DON'T KNOW.
......
SNIFF
SKINNY.
HMM?
YOU'RE A GROWN-UP...
BUT SANAE HAS BIGGER BOOBS.
SKINNY
DON'T YOU FORGET THOSE WORDS! YOU'LL LEARN YOUR LESSON LATER.

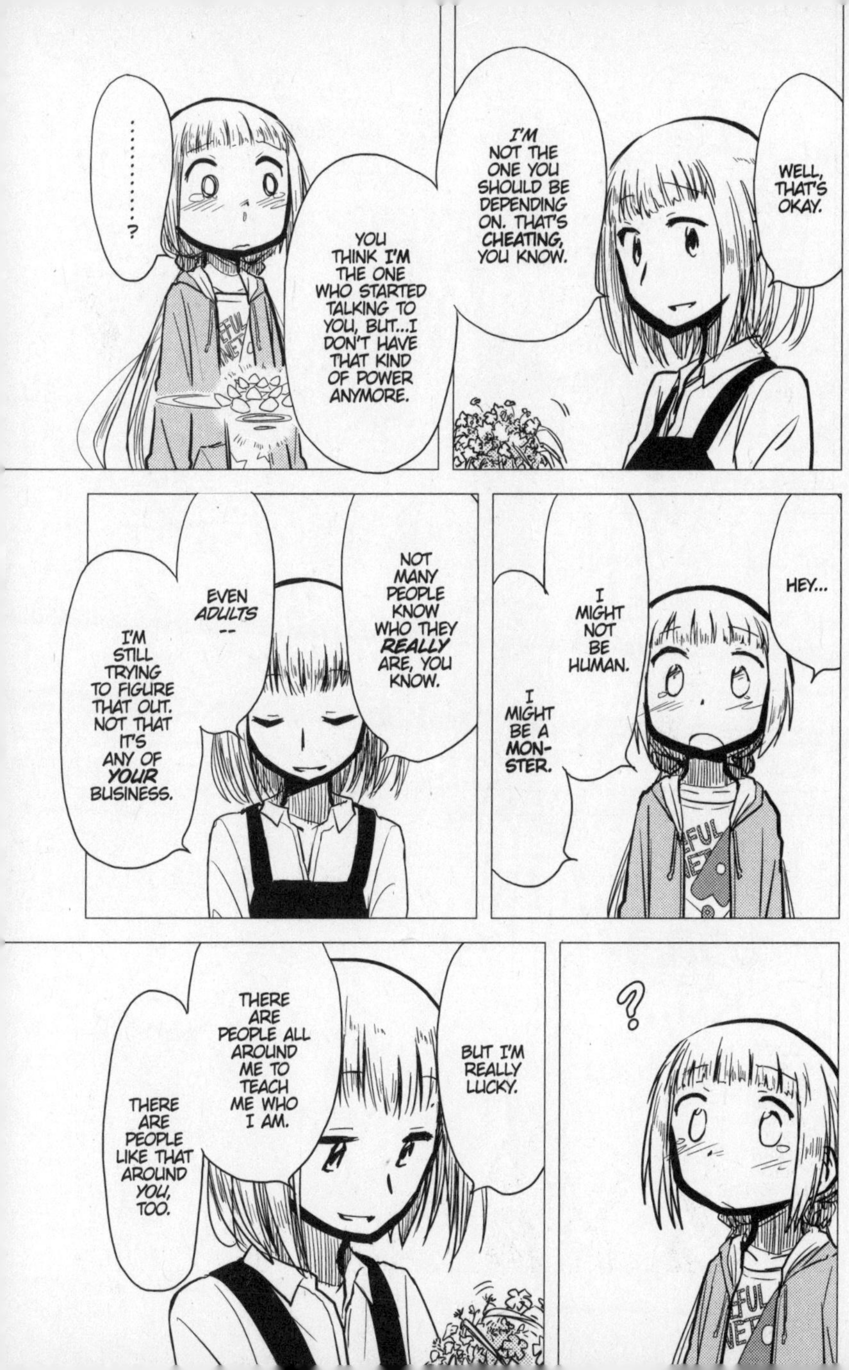
WELL, THAT'S OKAY.
*I'M* NOT THE ONE YOU SHOULD BE DEPENDING ON. THAT'S CHEATING, YOU KNOW.
YOU THINK I'M THE ONE WHO STARTED TALKING TO YOU, BUT...I DON'T HAVE THAT KIND OF POWER ANYMORE.
.........?
HEY...
I MIGHT NOT BE HUMAN.
I MIGHT BE A MON-STER.
NOT MANY PEOPLE KNOW WHO THEY *REALLY* ARE, YOU KNOW.
EVEN *ADULTS* --
I'M STILL TRYING TO FIGURE THAT OUT. NOT THAT IT'S ANY OF *YOUR* BUSINESS.
?
BUT I'M REALLY LUCKY.
THERE ARE PEOPLE ALL AROUND ME TO TEACH ME WHO I AM.
THERE ARE PEOPLE LIKE THAT AROUND *YOU*, TOO.

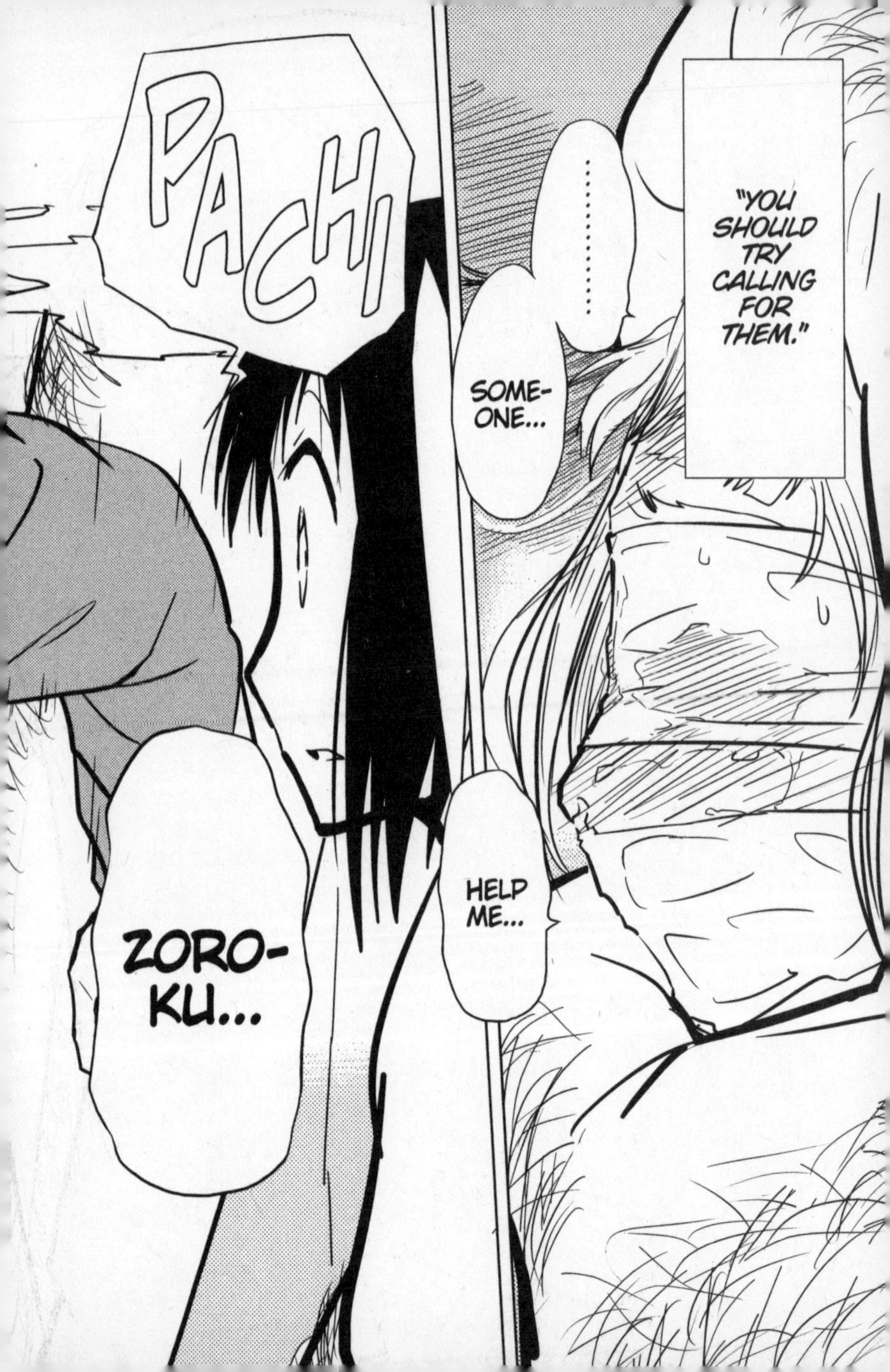
"YOU SHOULD TRY CALLING FOR THEM."
......
SOME-ONE...
HELP ME...
PACHI
ZORO-KU...

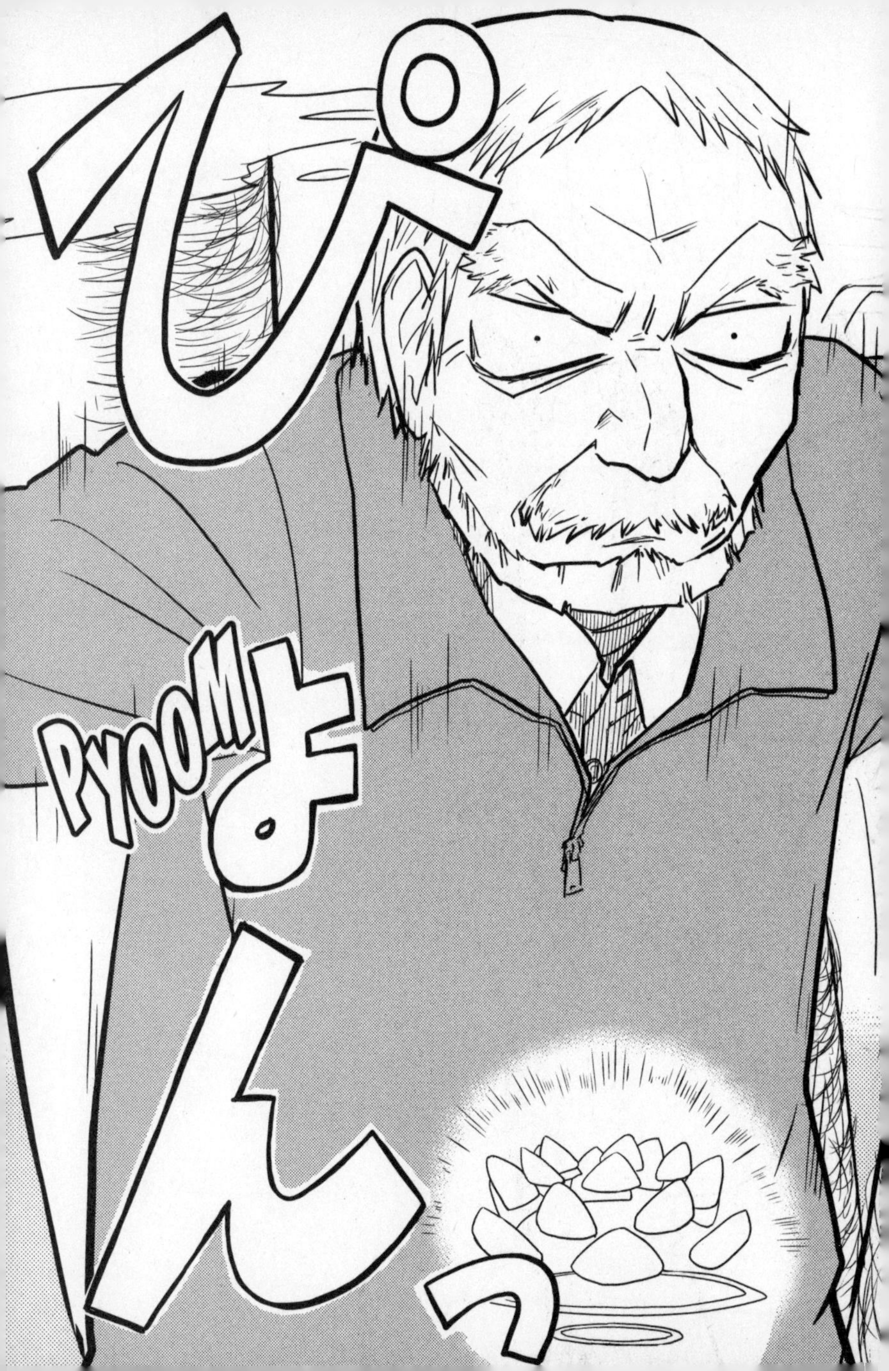
ぴょんっ
PYOOM

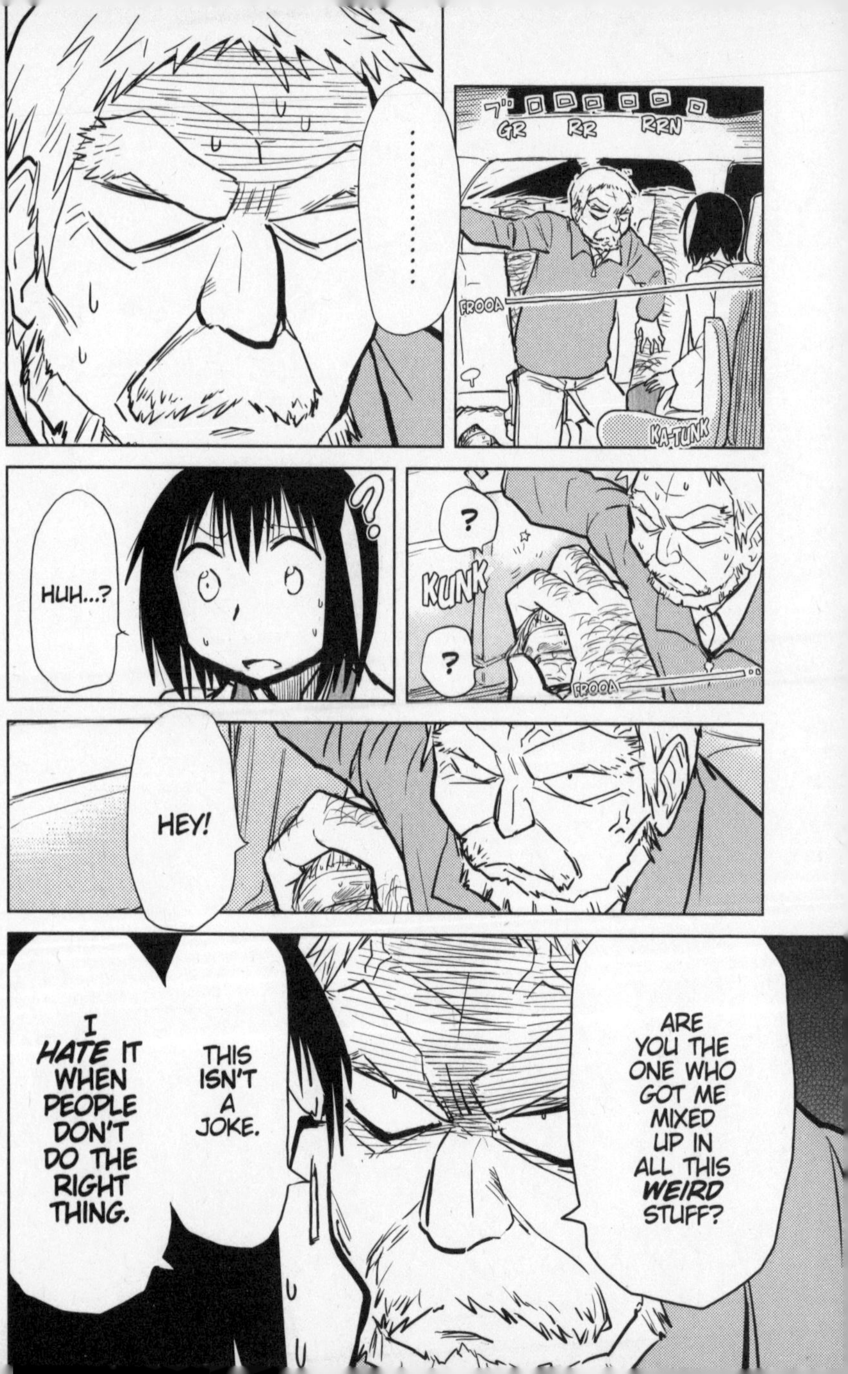
GR RR RRN
FROOA
KA-TUNK
......
?
KUNK
?
FROOA
HUH...?
HEY!
ARE YOU THE ONE WHO GOT ME MIXED UP IN ALL THIS WEIRD STUFF?
THIS ISN'T A JOKE.
I HATE IT WHEN PEOPLE DON'T DO THE RIGHT THING.

Alice & Zoroku

All this time the Guard was looking at her,

first through a telescope,

then through a microscope,

and then through an opera-glass.

At last he said, "You're traveling the wrong way,"

and shut up the window and went away.

## Chapter.6

# With Regard to the Passenger Car

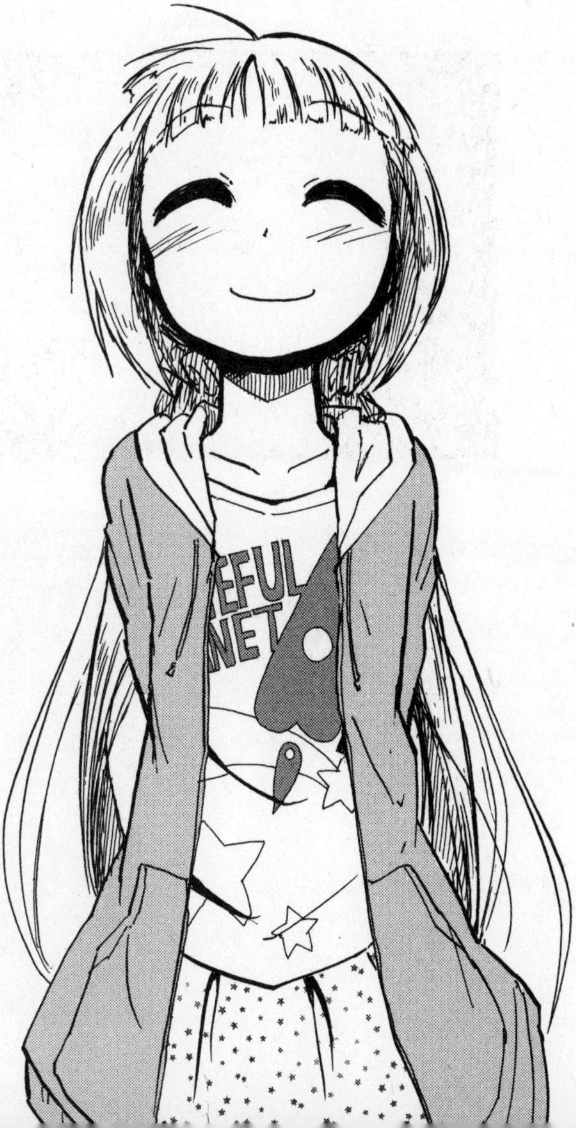

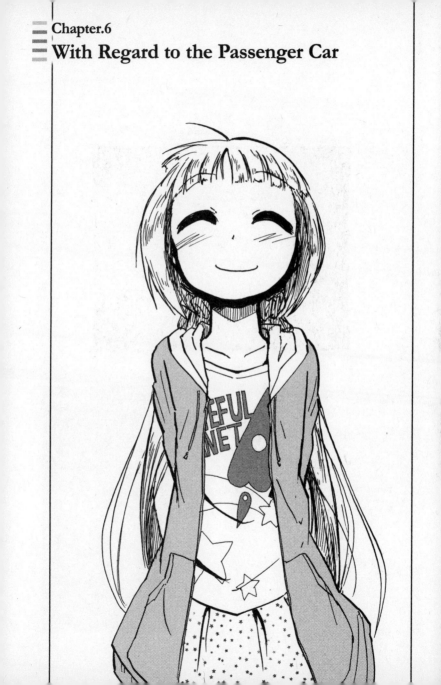

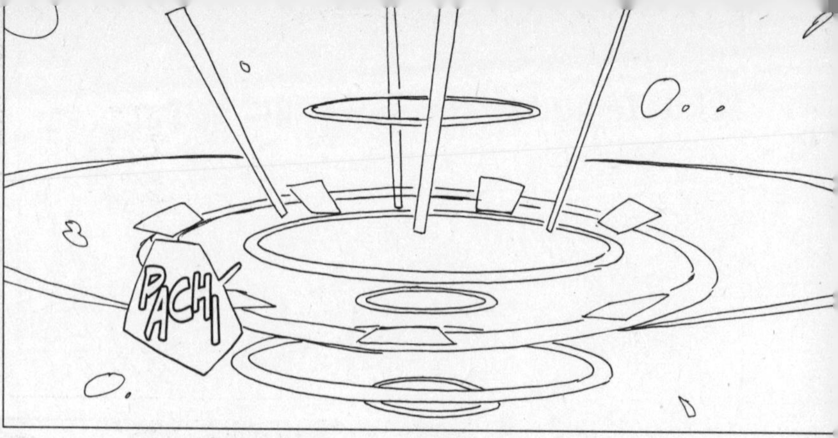
PACHI

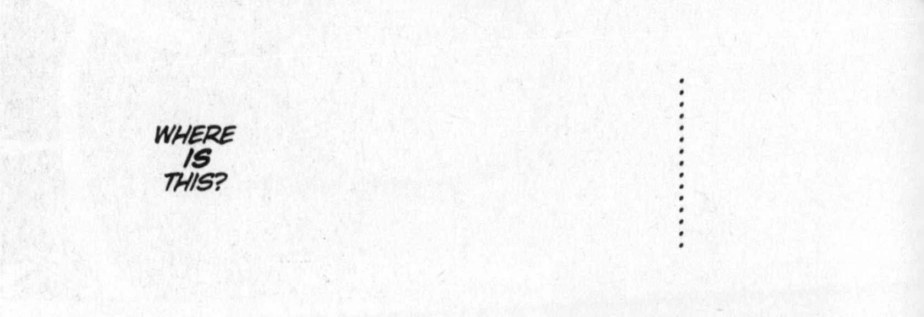
……
WHERE IS THIS?

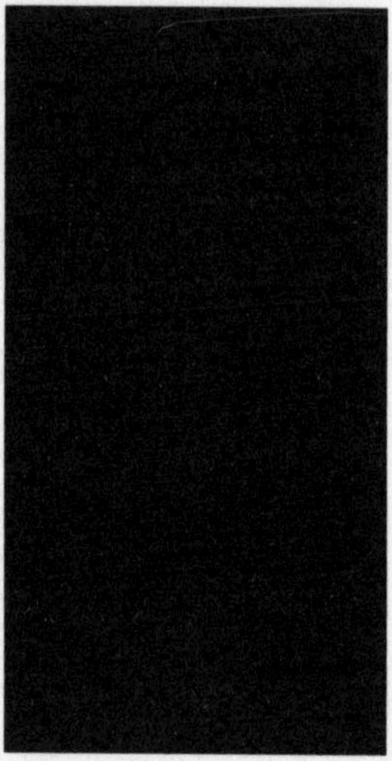

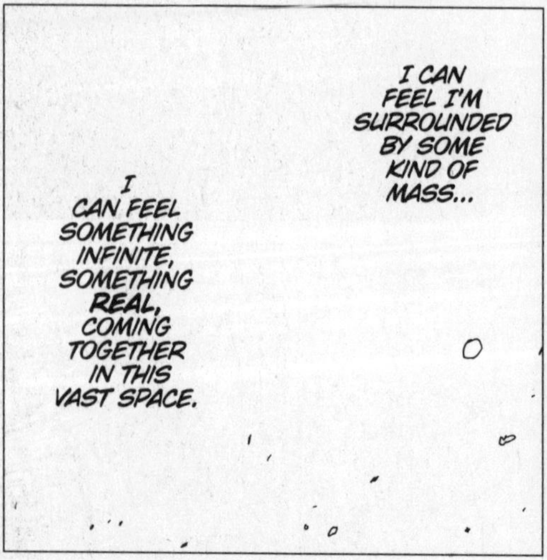
I CAN FEEL I'M SURROUNDED BY SOME KIND OF MASS...
I CAN FEEL SOMETHING INFINITE, SOMETHING REAL, COMING TOGETHER IN THIS VAST SPACE.

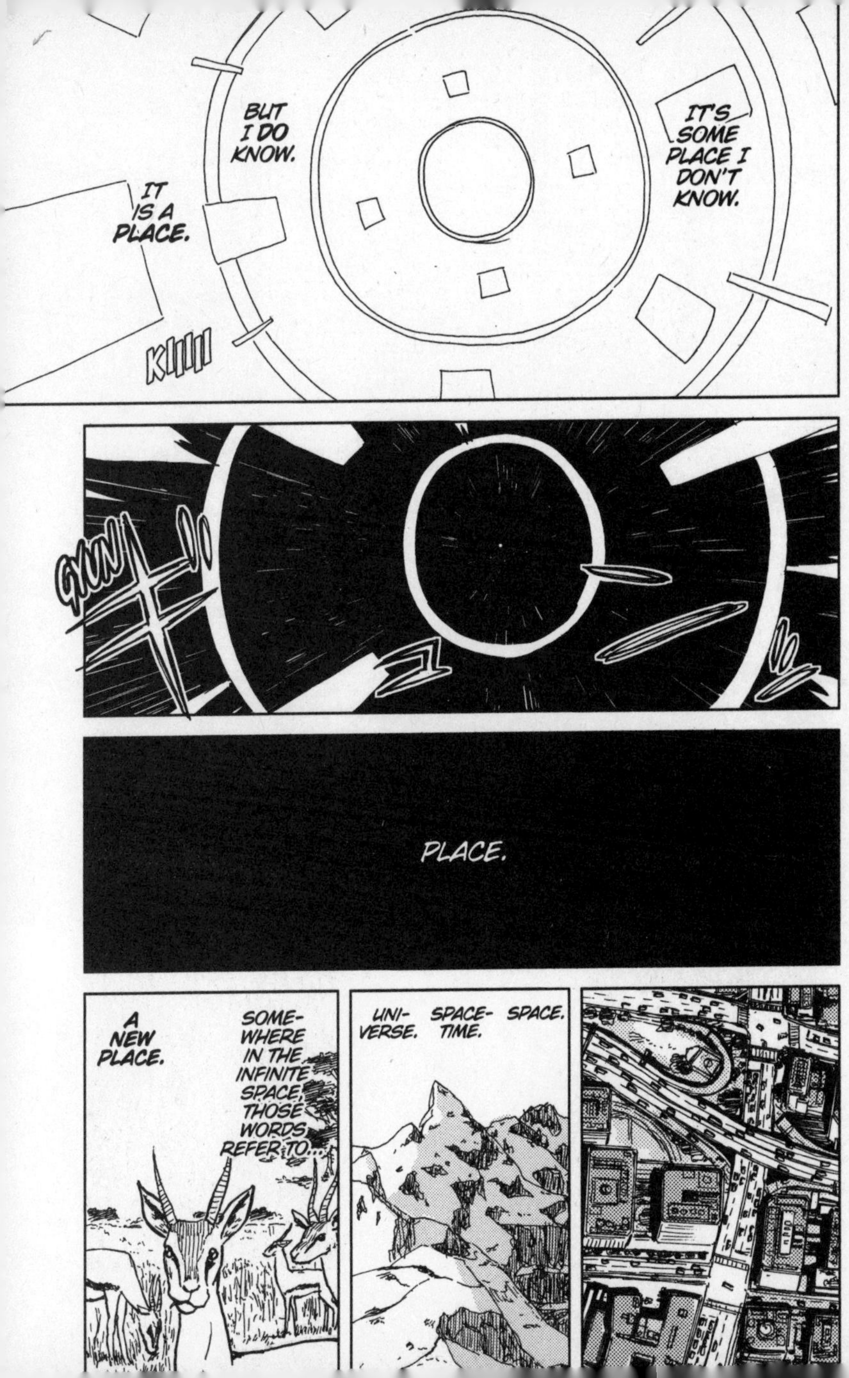
IT'S SOME PLACE I DON'T KNOW.
BUT I DO KNOW.
IT IS A PLACE.
KIIIII
GYUN
PLACE.
SPACE.
SPACE-TIME.
UNIVERSE.
SOMEWHERE IN THE INFINITE SPACE, THOSE WORDS REFER TO...
A NEW PLACE.

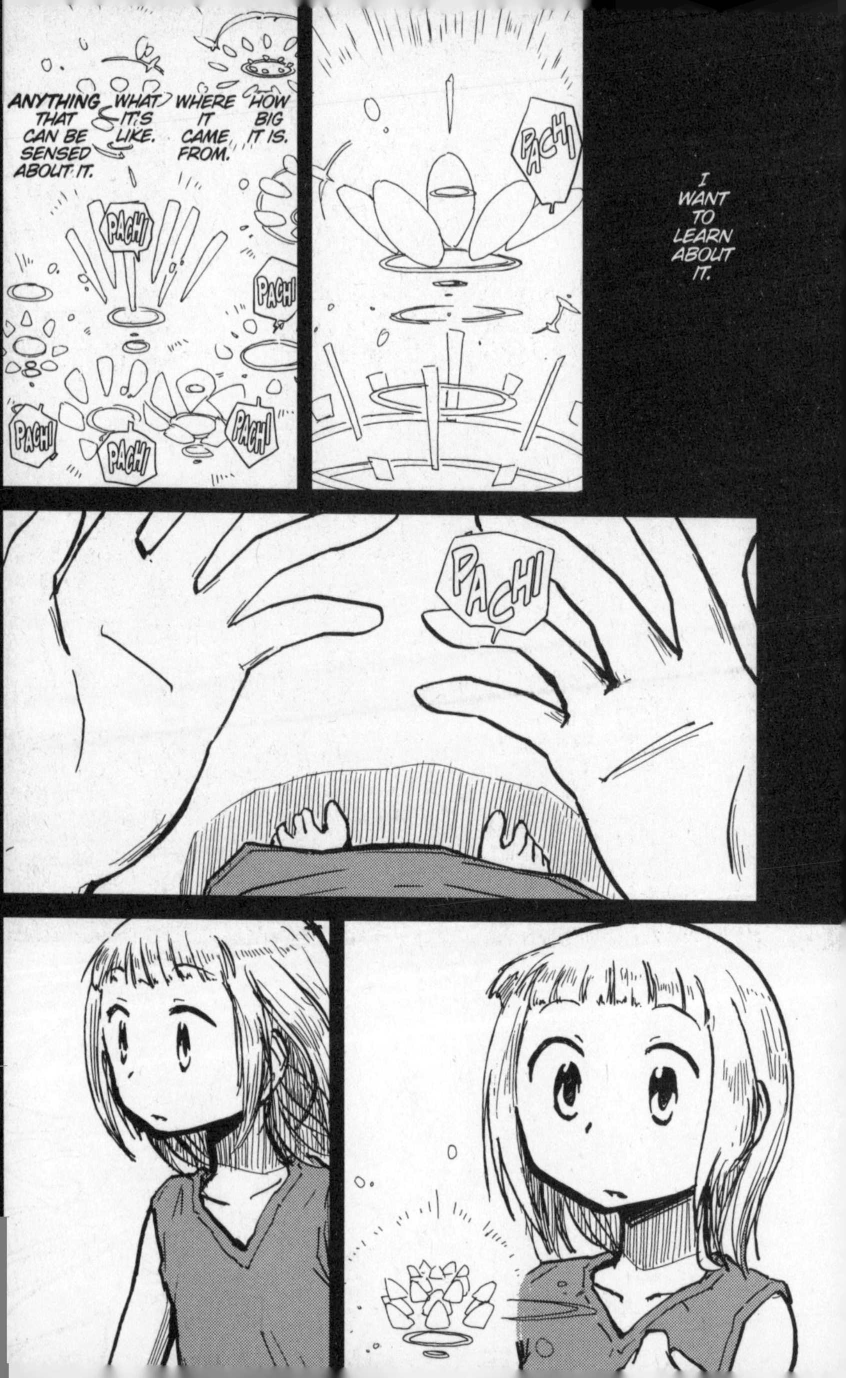
I WANT TO LEARN ABOUT IT.
PACHI
HOW BIG IT IS.
WHERE IT CAME FROM.
WHAT IT'S LIKE.
ANYTHING THAT CAN BE SENSED ABOUT IT.
PACHI
PACHI
PACHI
PACHI
PACHI
PACHI

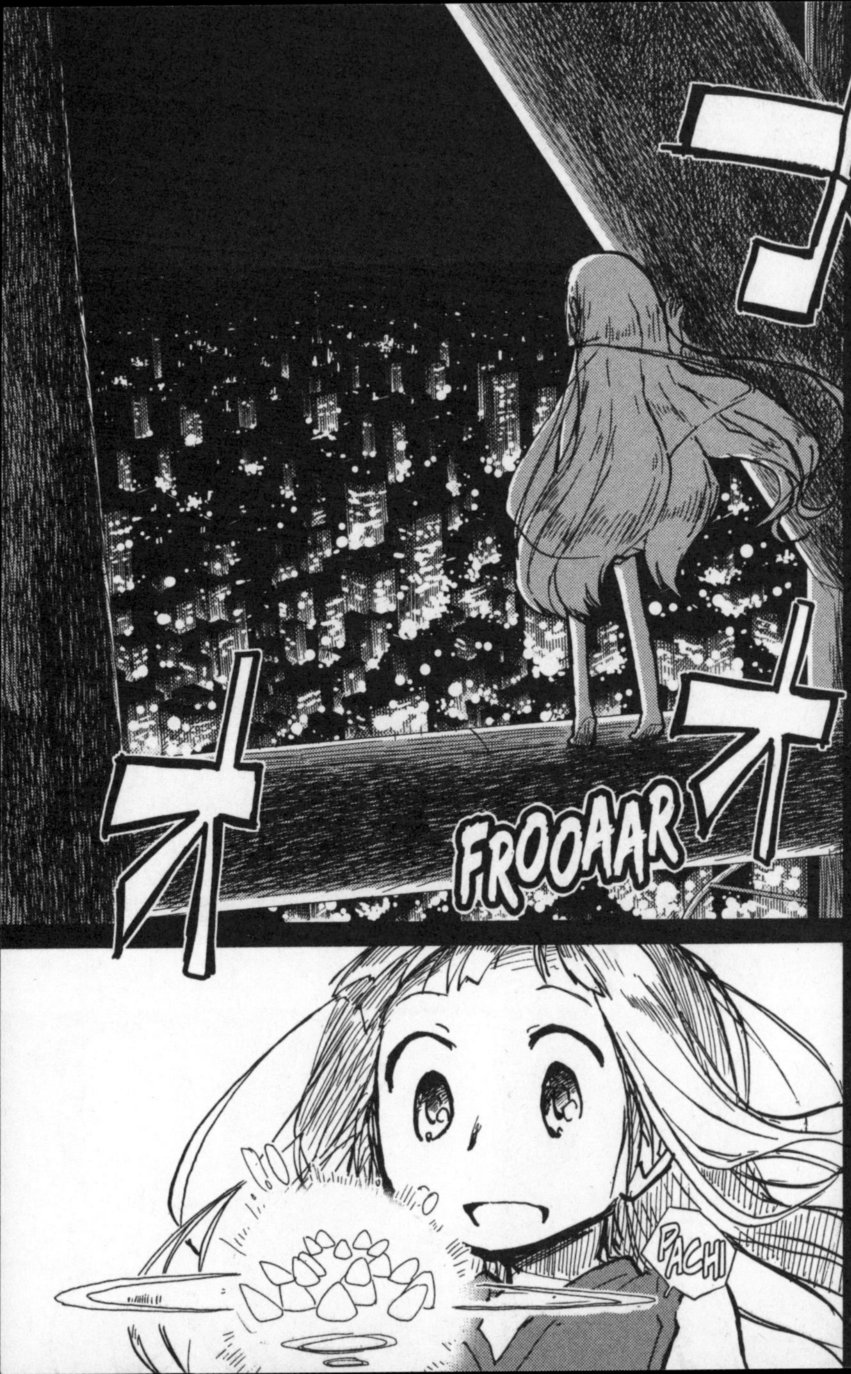
FROOAAR
PACHI

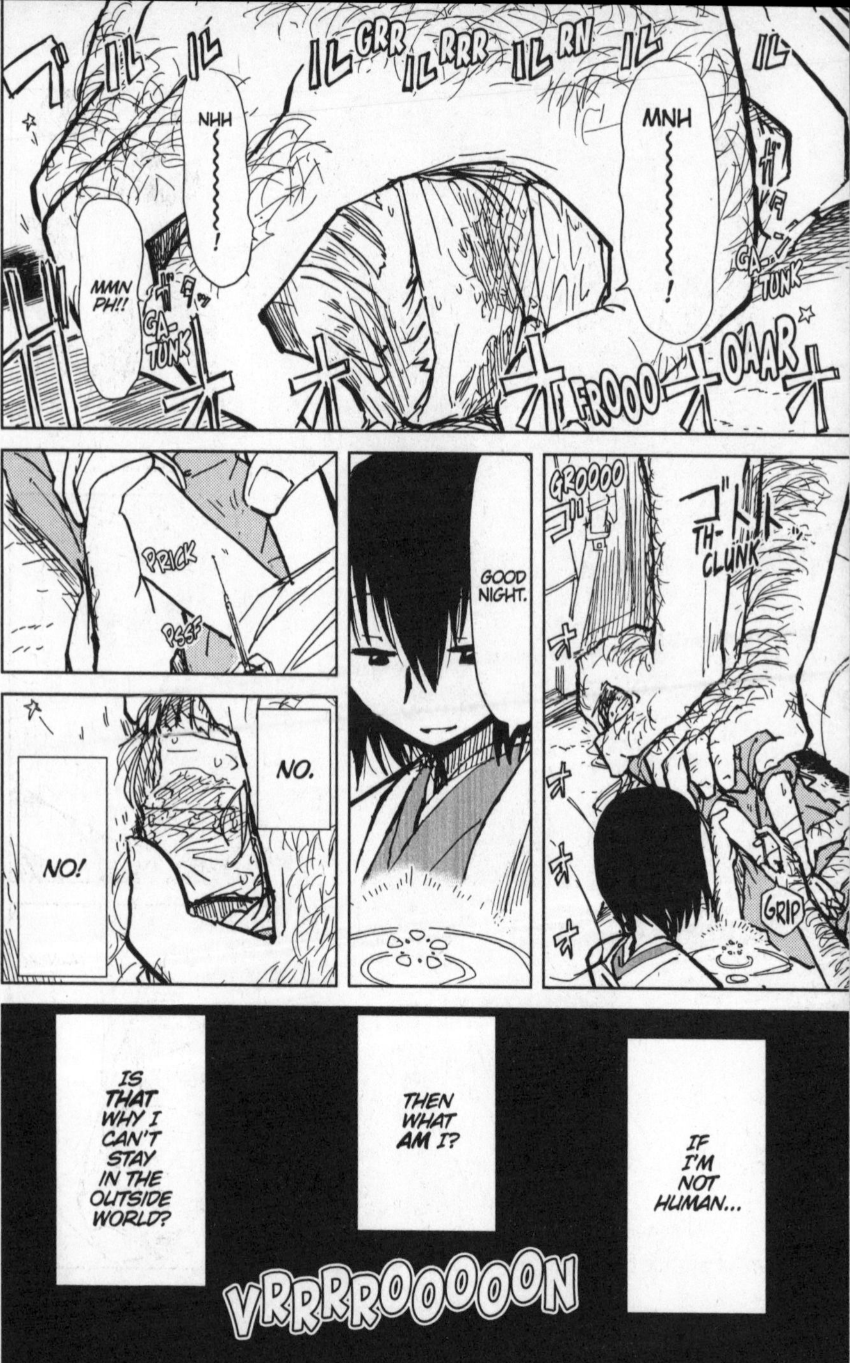
GRR
RRR
RN
MNH ~~~~~~!
NHH ~~~~~~!
GA-TUNK
MMN PH!!
GA-TUNK
FROOO-OAAR
GROOOO
TH-CLUNK
GRIP
GOOD NIGHT.
PRICK
PSSF
NO.
NO!
IF I'M NOT HUMAN...
THEN WHAT AM I?
IS THAT WHY I CAN'T STAY IN THE OUTSIDE WORLD?
VRRRROOOOOON

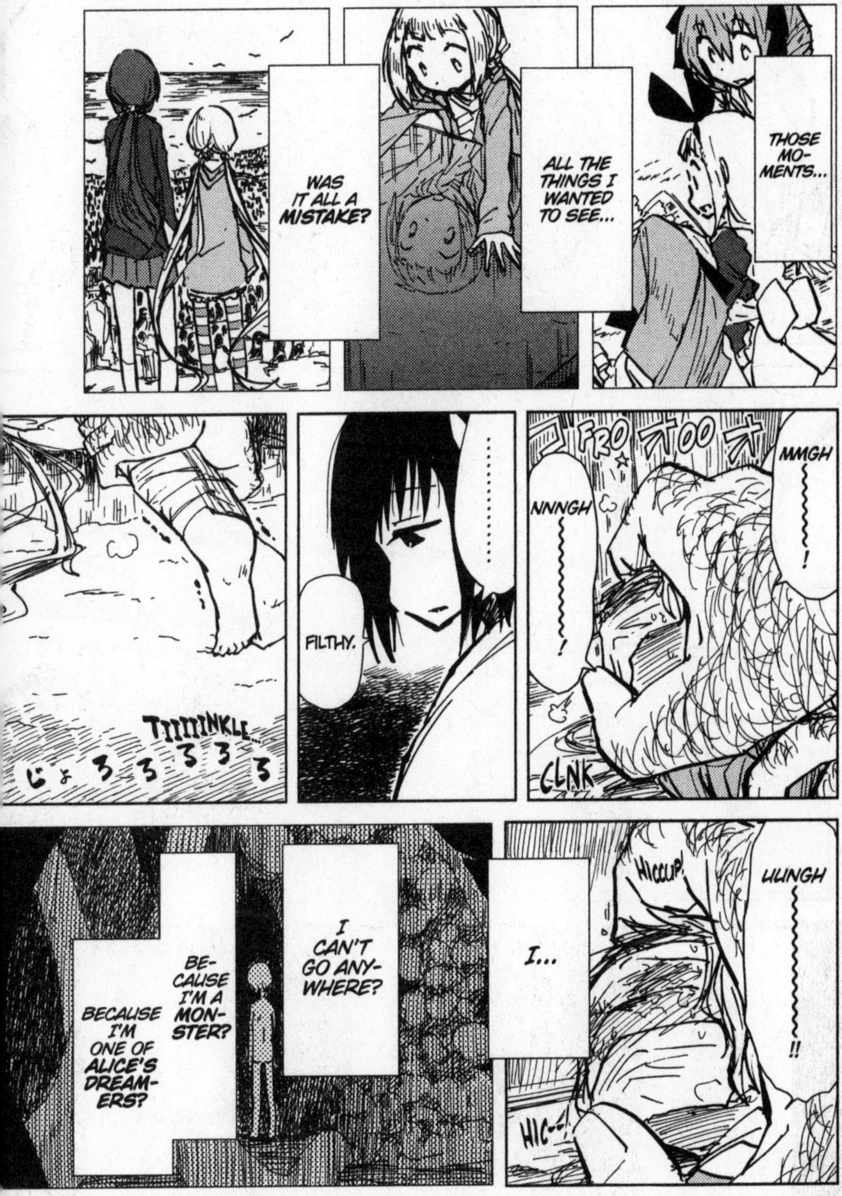
THOSE MO-MENTS...
ALL THE THINGS I WANTED TO SEE...
WAS IT ALL A MISTAKE?
FROTOO
MMGH~~~!
NNNGH~~~!
CLNK
......
FILTHY.
TIIIIINKLE...
じょろろろろろ
UUNGH~~~!!
HICCUP!
HIC--!
I...
I CAN'T GO ANY-WHERE?
BE-CAUSE I'M A MON-STER?
BECAUSE I'M ONE OF ALICE'S DREAM-ERS?

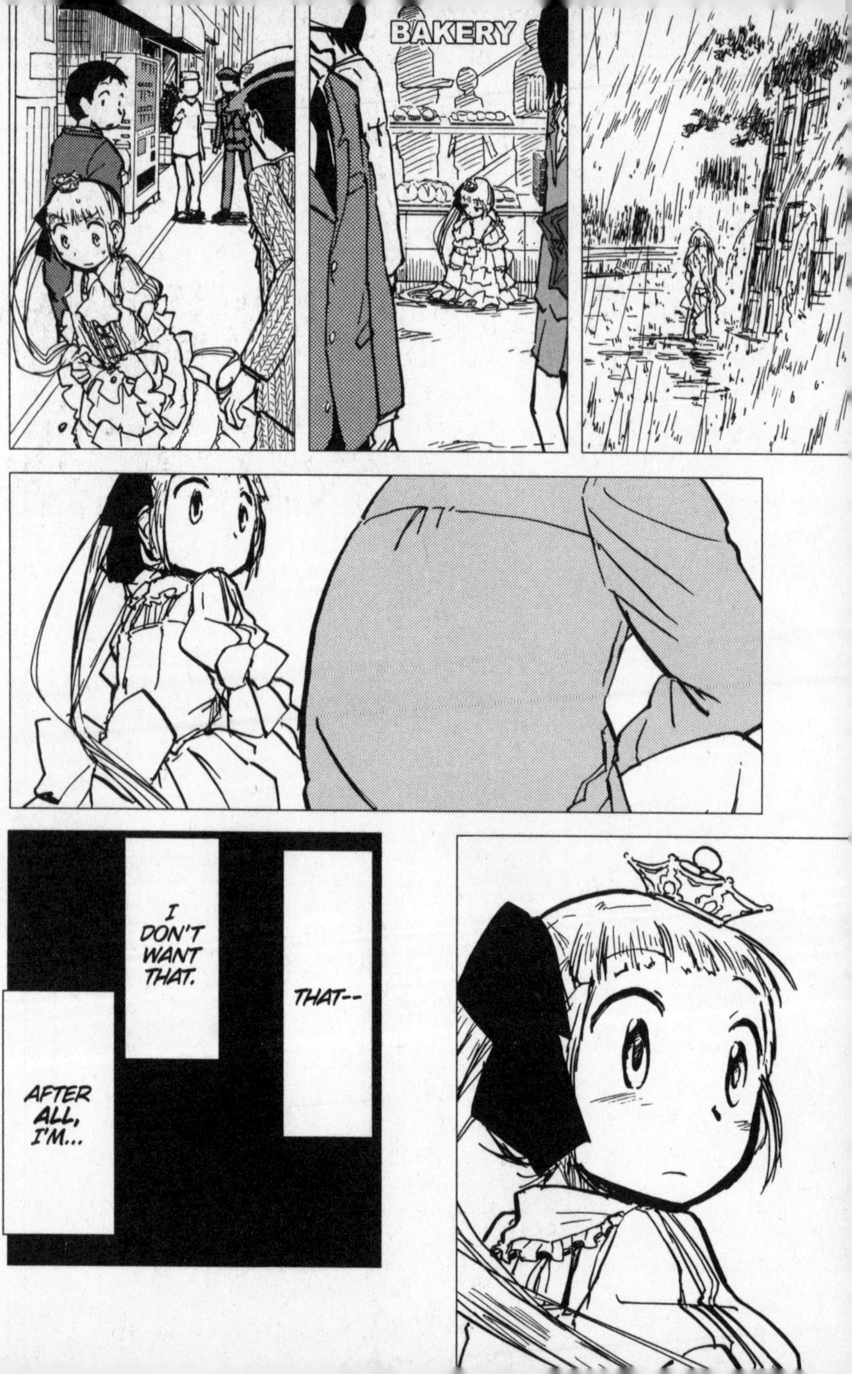
BAKERY
THAT--
I DON'T WANT THAT.
AFTER ALL, I'M...

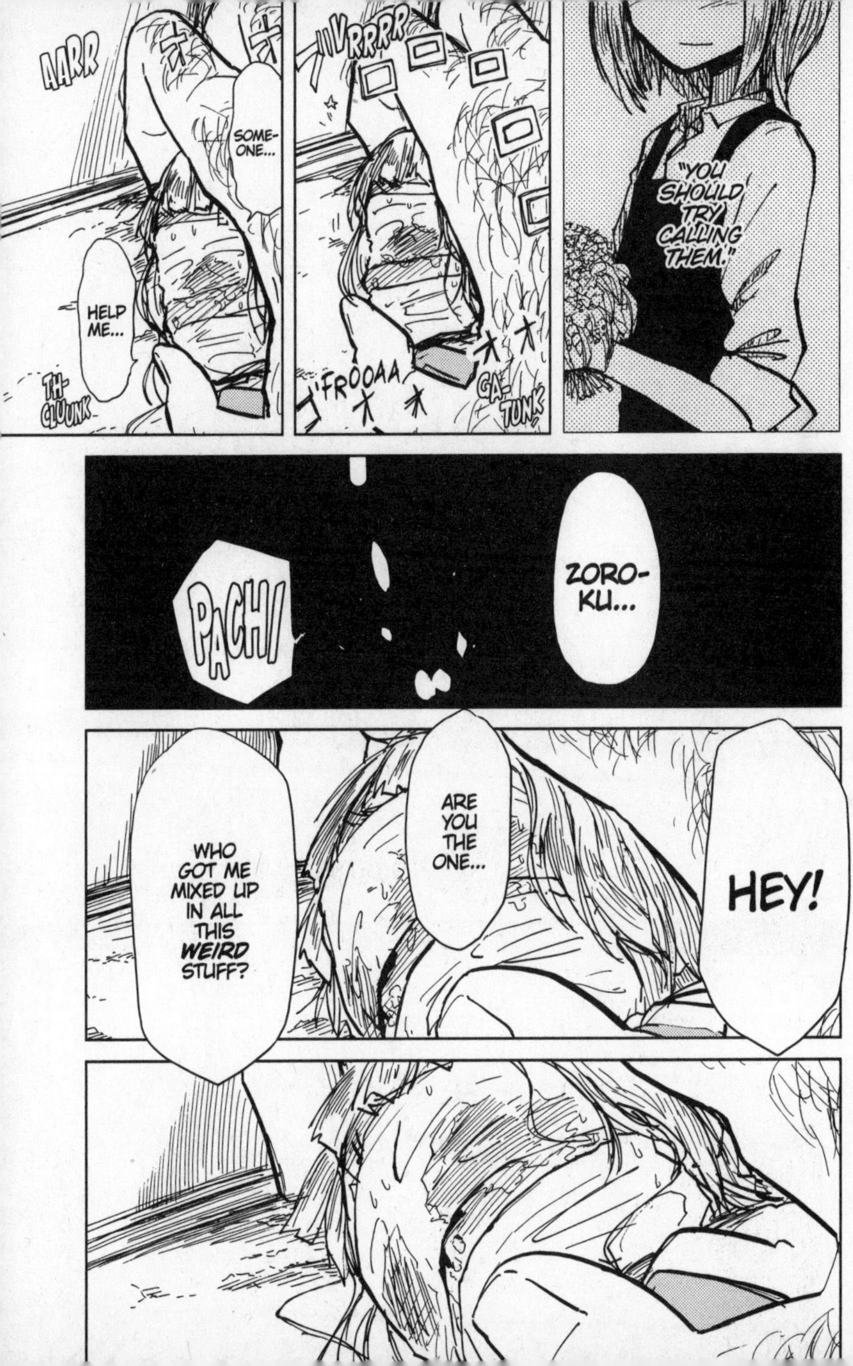
"YOU SHOULD TRY CALLING THEM."
VRRRR
GA-TUNK
FROOAA
SOME-ONE...
AARR
HELP ME...
TH-CLUUNK
ZORO-KU...
PACHI
HEY!
ARE YOU THE ONE...
WHO GOT ME MIXED UP IN ALL THIS *WEIRD* STUFF?

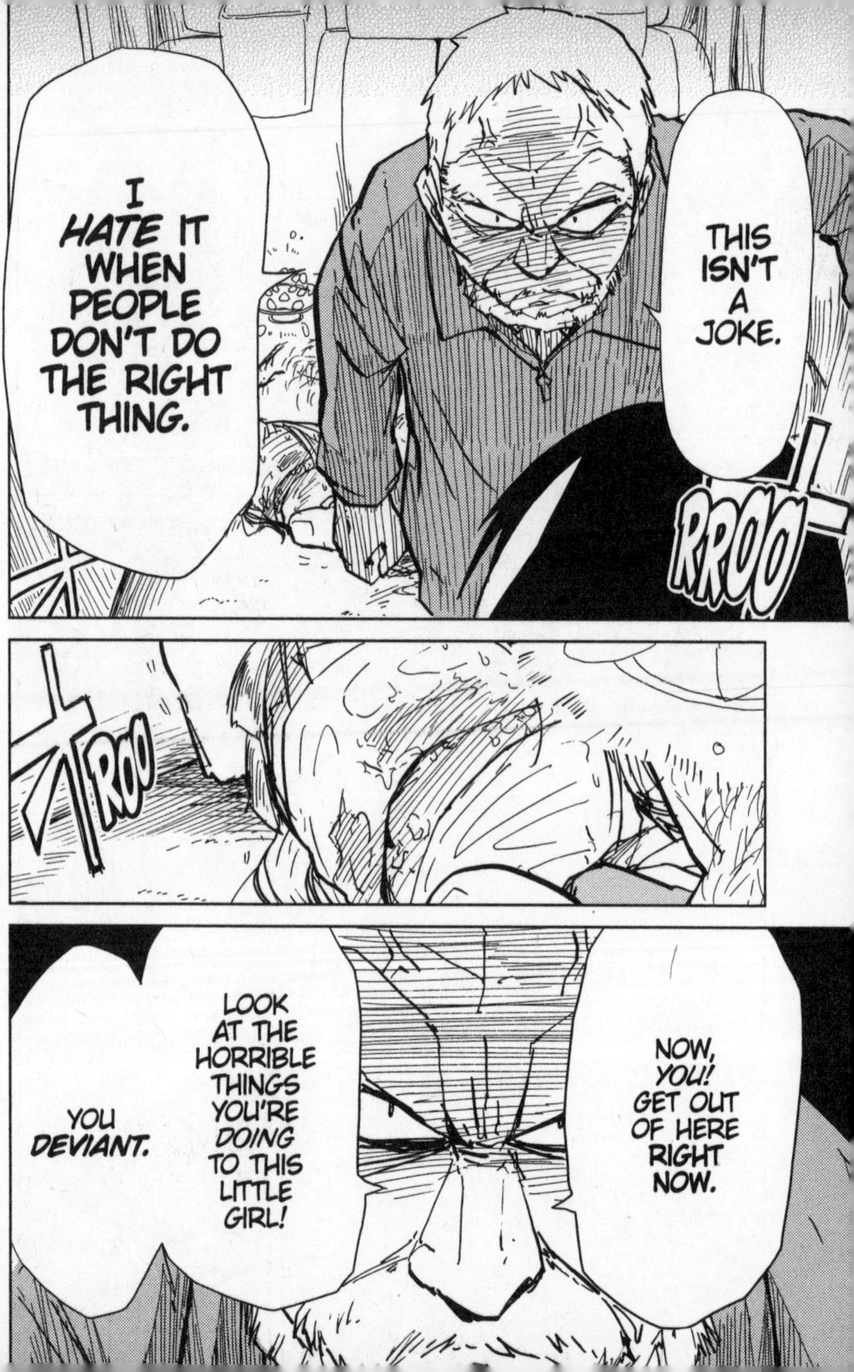
THIS ISN'T A JOKE.
I HATE IT WHEN PEOPLE DON'T DO THE RIGHT THING.
RROO
ROO
NOW, YOU! GET OUT OF HERE RIGHT NOW.
LOOK AT THE HORRIBLE THINGS YOU'RE DOING TO THIS LITTLE GIRL!
YOU DEVIANT.

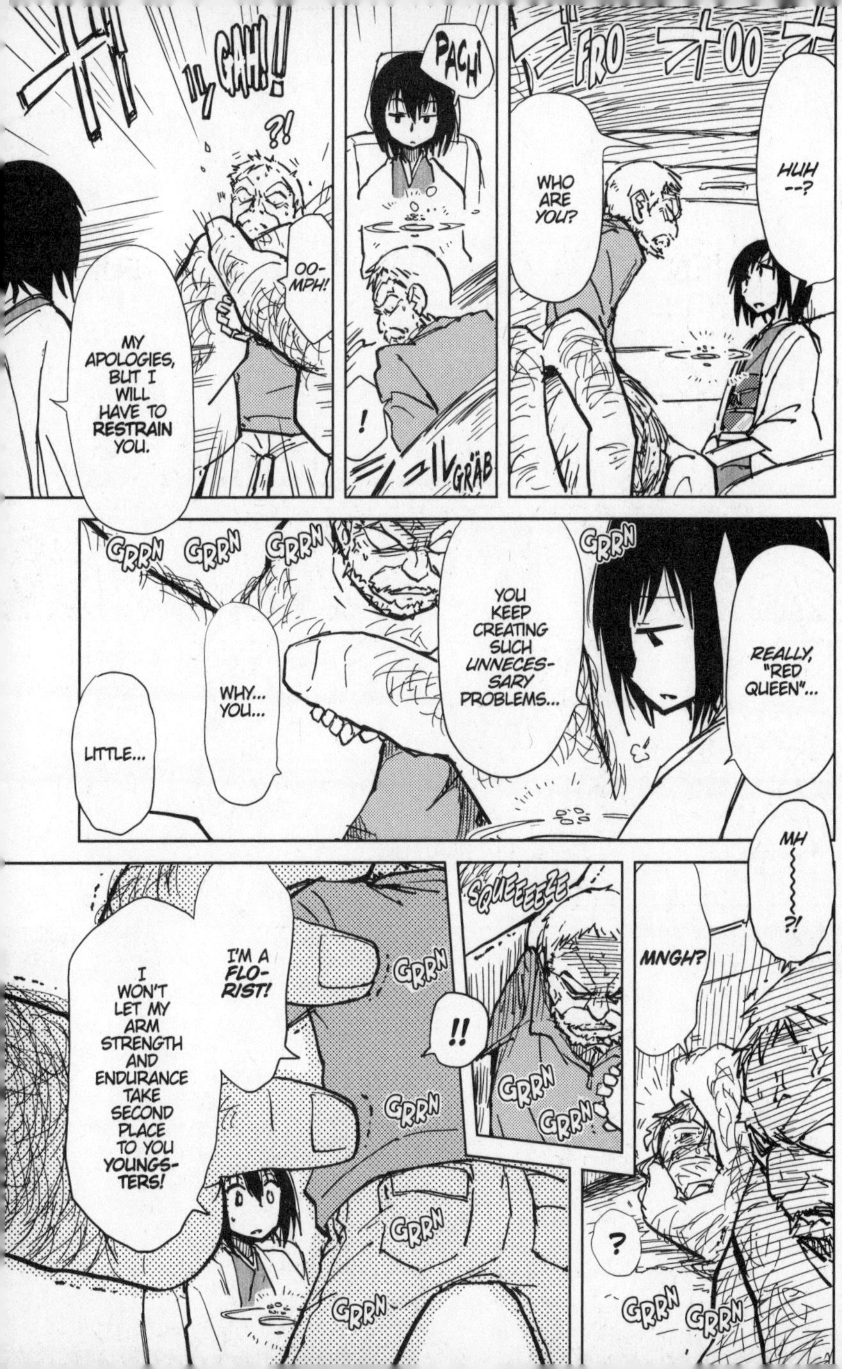
FRO OO
HUH --?
WHO ARE YOU?
PACHI
!
GRÄB
GAH!!
?!
OO-MPH!
MY APOLOGIES, BUT I WILL HAVE TO RESTRAIN YOU.
GRRN
REALLY, "RED QUEEN"...
YOU KEEP CREATING SUCH UNNECES-SARY PROBLEMS...
GRRN
GRRN
GRRN
WHY... YOU...
LITTLE...
MH~~~~?!
MNGH?
?
GRRN
GRRN
SQUEEEEEZE
GRRN
GRRN
!!
I'M A FLORIST!
I WON'T LET MY ARM STRENGTH AND ENDURANCE TAKE SECOND PLACE TO YOU YOUNGSTERS!
GRRN
GRRN
GRRN
GRRN

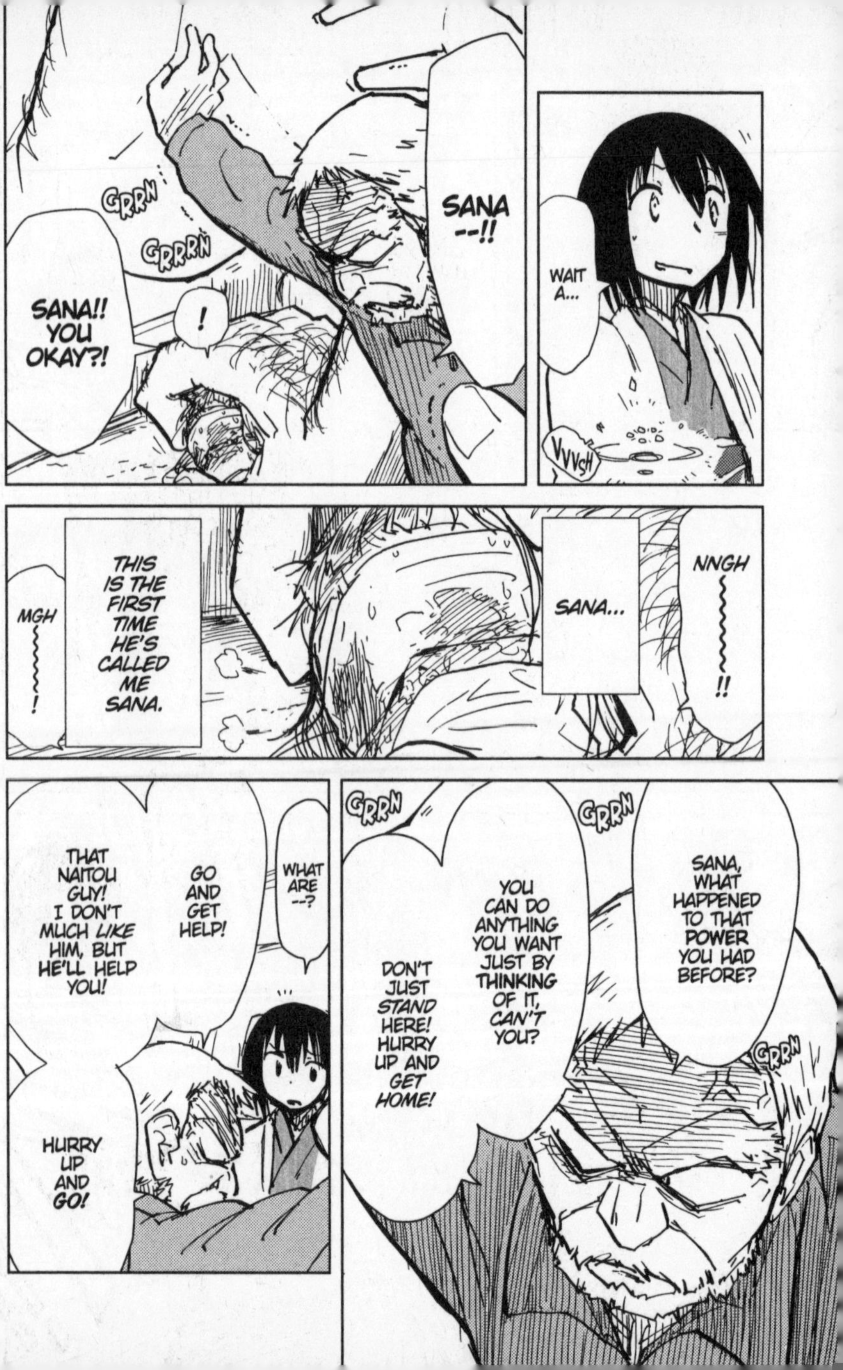
WAIT A...
VVVSH
SANA --!!
GRRN
GRRRN
!
SANA!! YOU OKAY?!
NNGH ~~!!
SANA...
THIS IS THE FIRST TIME HE'S CALLED ME SANA.
MGH ~!
GRRN
SANA, WHAT HAPPENED TO THAT POWER YOU HAD BEFORE?
YOU CAN DO ANYTHING YOU WANT JUST BY THINKING OF IT, CAN'T YOU?
GRRN
DON'T JUST STAND HERE! HURRY UP AND GET HOME!
GRRN
WHAT ARE --?
GO AND GET HELP!
THAT NAITOU GUY! I DON'T MUCH LIKE HIM, BUT HE'LL HELP YOU!
HURRY UP AND GO!

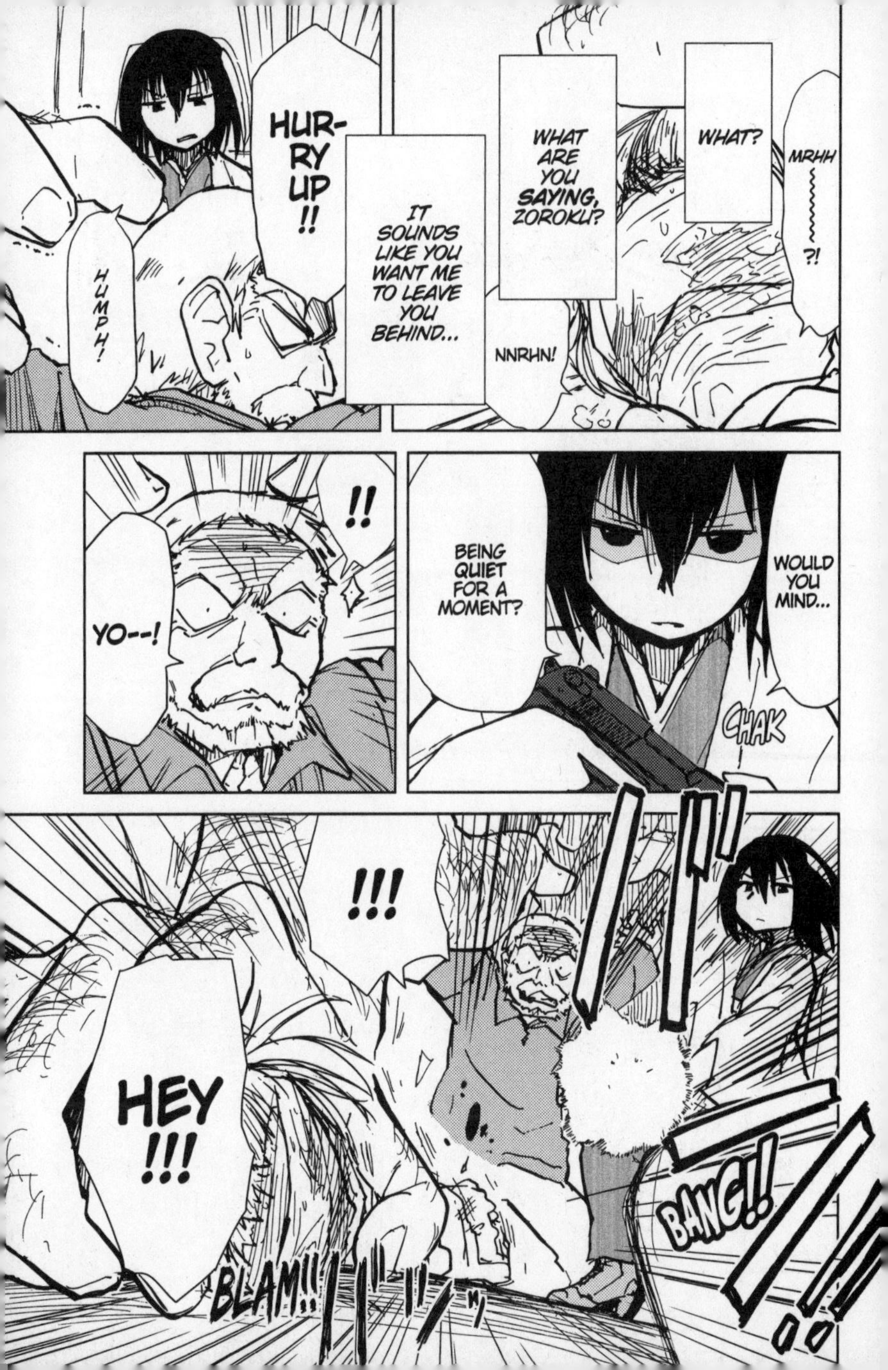
MRHH~~~?!
WHAT?
WHAT ARE YOU SAYING, ZOROKU?
NNRHN!
IT SOUNDS LIKE YOU WANT ME TO LEAVE YOU BEHIND...
HUR-RY UP!!
HUMPH!
WOULD YOU MIND...
BEING QUIET FOR A MOMENT?
CHAK
!!
YO--!
BANG!!
!!!
HEY!!!
BLAM!!

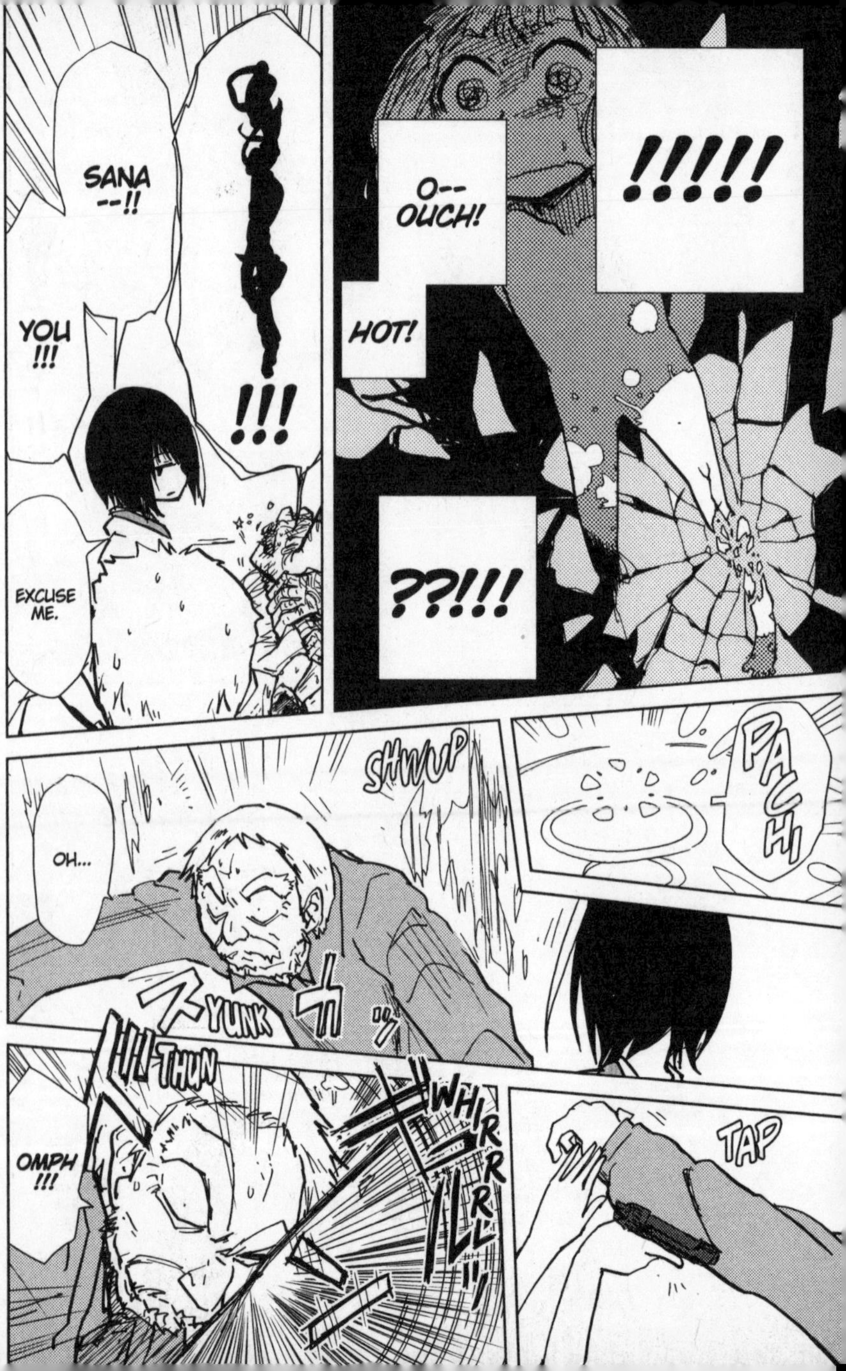
!!!!!
O-- OUCH!
HOT!
??!!!
SANA --!!
YOU !!!
!!!
EXCUSE ME.
PACHI
SHWUP
OH...
YUNK
TAP
WHIRRRLL
THUN
OMPH !!!

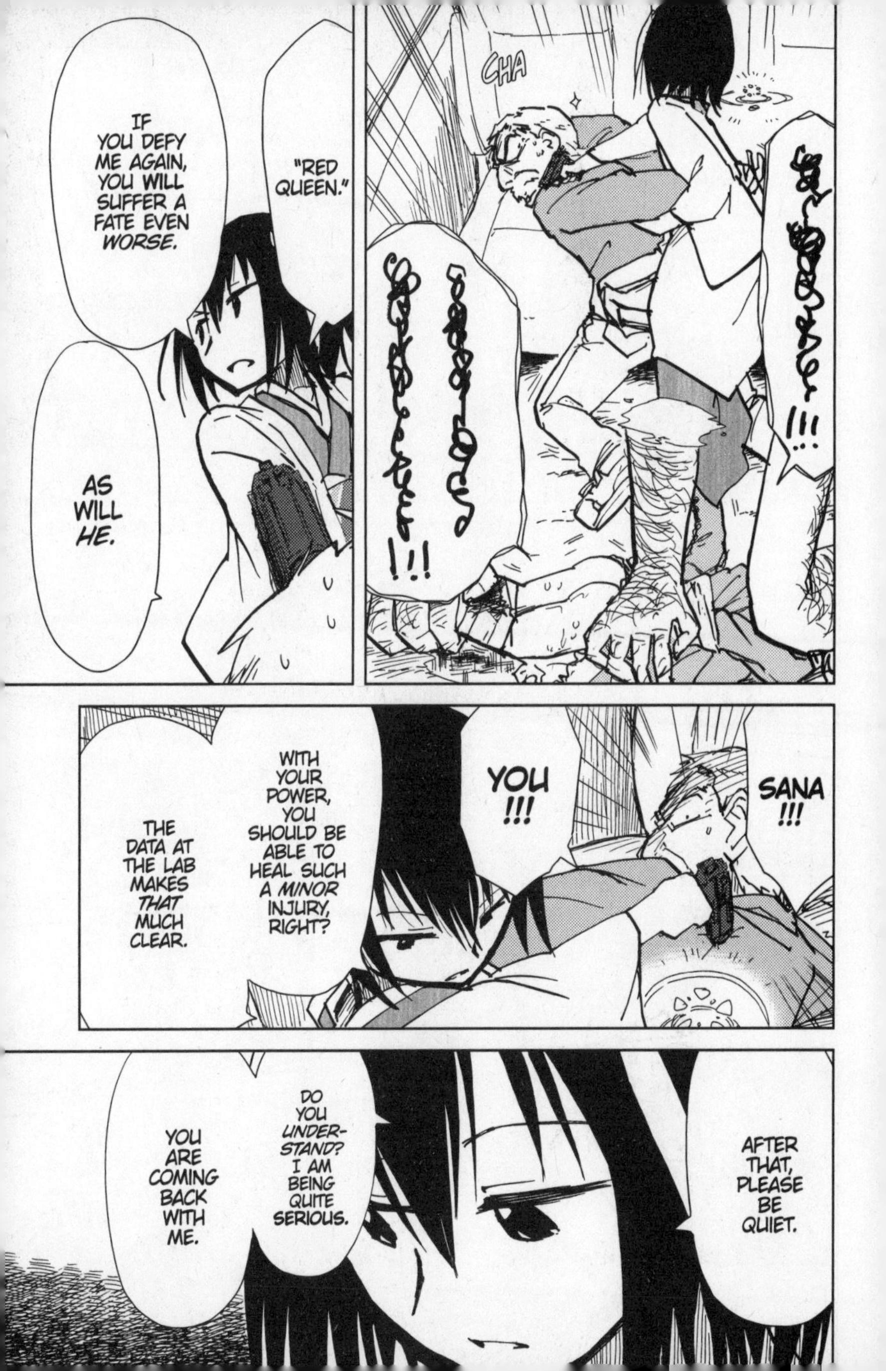
CHA
!!!...
!!!
"RED QUEEN."
IF YOU DEFY ME AGAIN, YOU WILL SUFFER A FATE EVEN *WORSE.*
AS WILL *HE.*
SANA !!!
YOU !!!
WITH YOUR POWER, YOU SHOULD BE ABLE TO HEAL SUCH A *MINOR* INJURY, RIGHT?
THE DATA AT THE LAB MAKES *THAT* MUCH CLEAR.
AFTER THAT, PLEASE BE QUIET.
DO YOU *UNDER-STAND?* I AM BEING QUITE SERIOUS.
YOU ARE COMING BACK WITH ME.

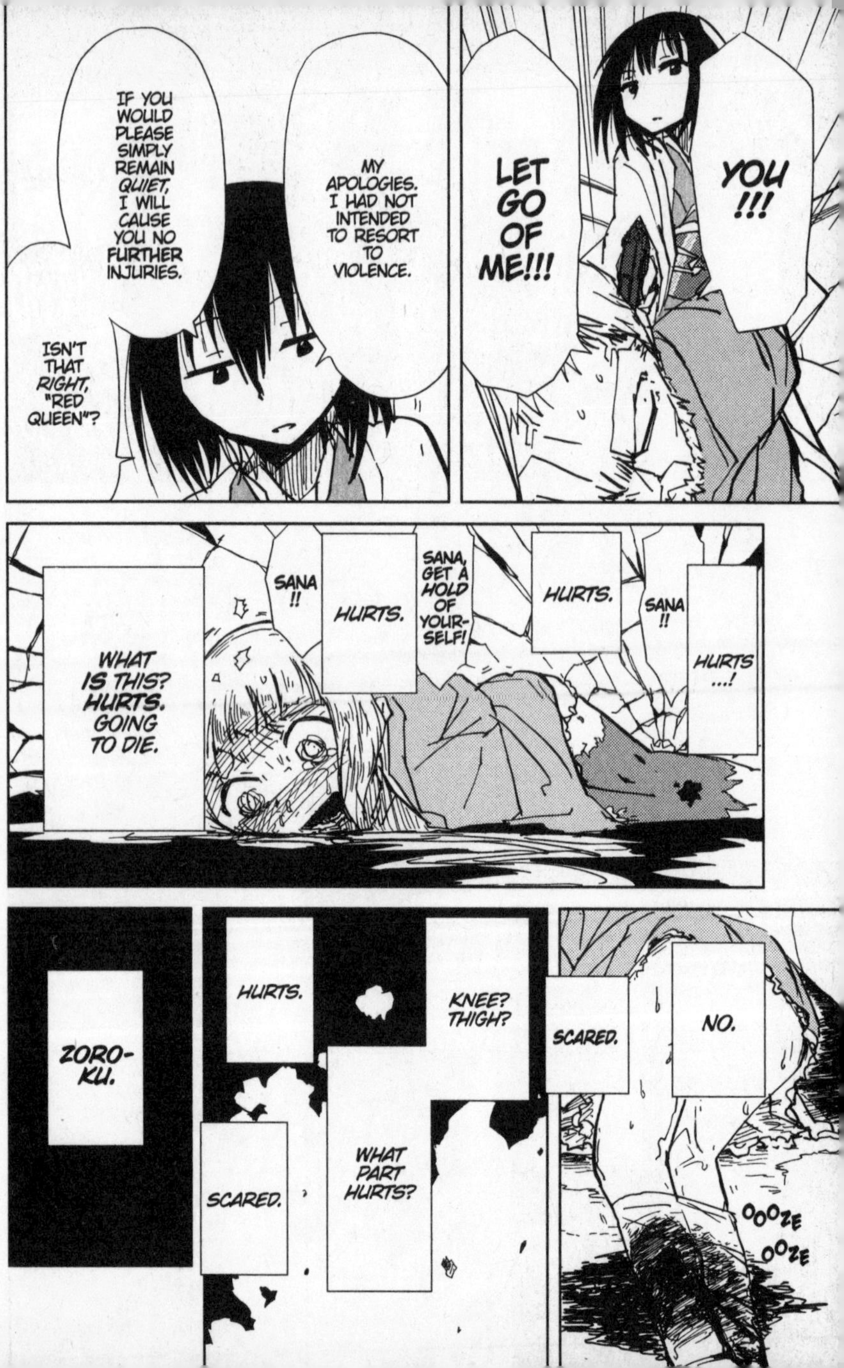
YOU !!!
LET GO OF ME!!!
MY APOLOGIES. I HAD NOT INTENDED TO RESORT TO VIOLENCE.
IF YOU WOULD PLEASE SIMPLY REMAIN *QUIET*, I WILL CAUSE YOU NO FURTHER INJURIES.
ISN'T THAT *RIGHT*, "RED QUEEN"?
*HURTS ...!*
SANA !!
*HURTS.*
SANA, GET A *HOLD* OF YOURSELF!
*HURTS.*
SANA !!
*WHAT IS THIS? HURTS. GOING TO DIE.*
*NO.*
*SCARED.*
OOOZE
OOZE
*KNEE? THIGH?*
*HURTS.*
*WHAT PART HURTS?*
*SCARED.*
*ZORO-KU.*

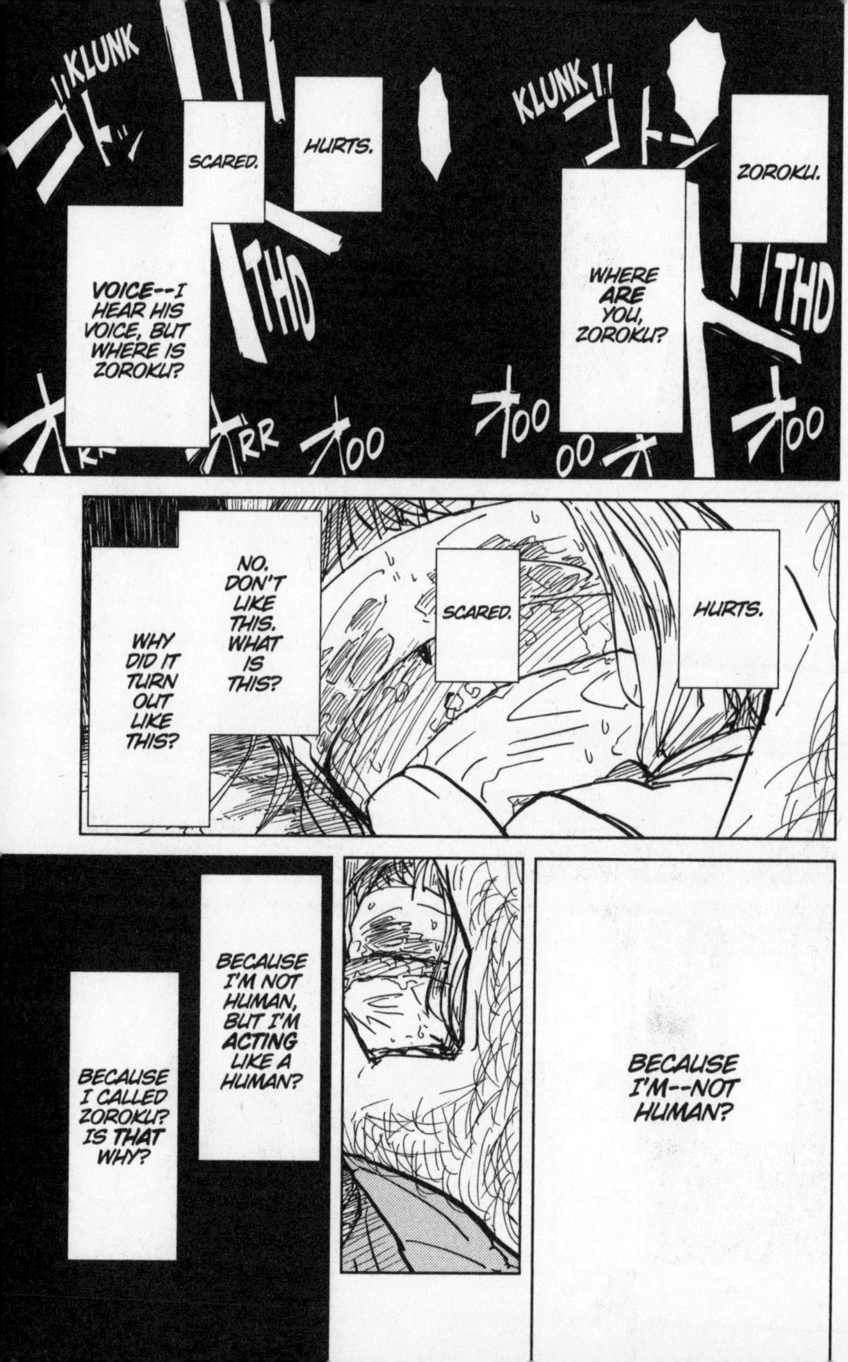
ZOROKU.
KLUNK
WHERE ARE YOU, ZOROKU?
THD
OO
OO
OO
KLUNK
HURTS.
SCARED.
THD
VOICE--I HEAR HIS VOICE, BUT WHERE IS ZOROKU?
OO
RR
HURTS.
SCARED.
NO. DON'T LIKE THIS. WHAT IS THIS?
WHY DID IT TURN OUT LIKE THIS?
BECAUSE I'M--NOT HUMAN?
BECAUSE I'M NOT HUMAN, BUT I'M ACTING LIKE A HUMAN?
BECAUSE I CALLED ZOROKU? IS THAT WHY?

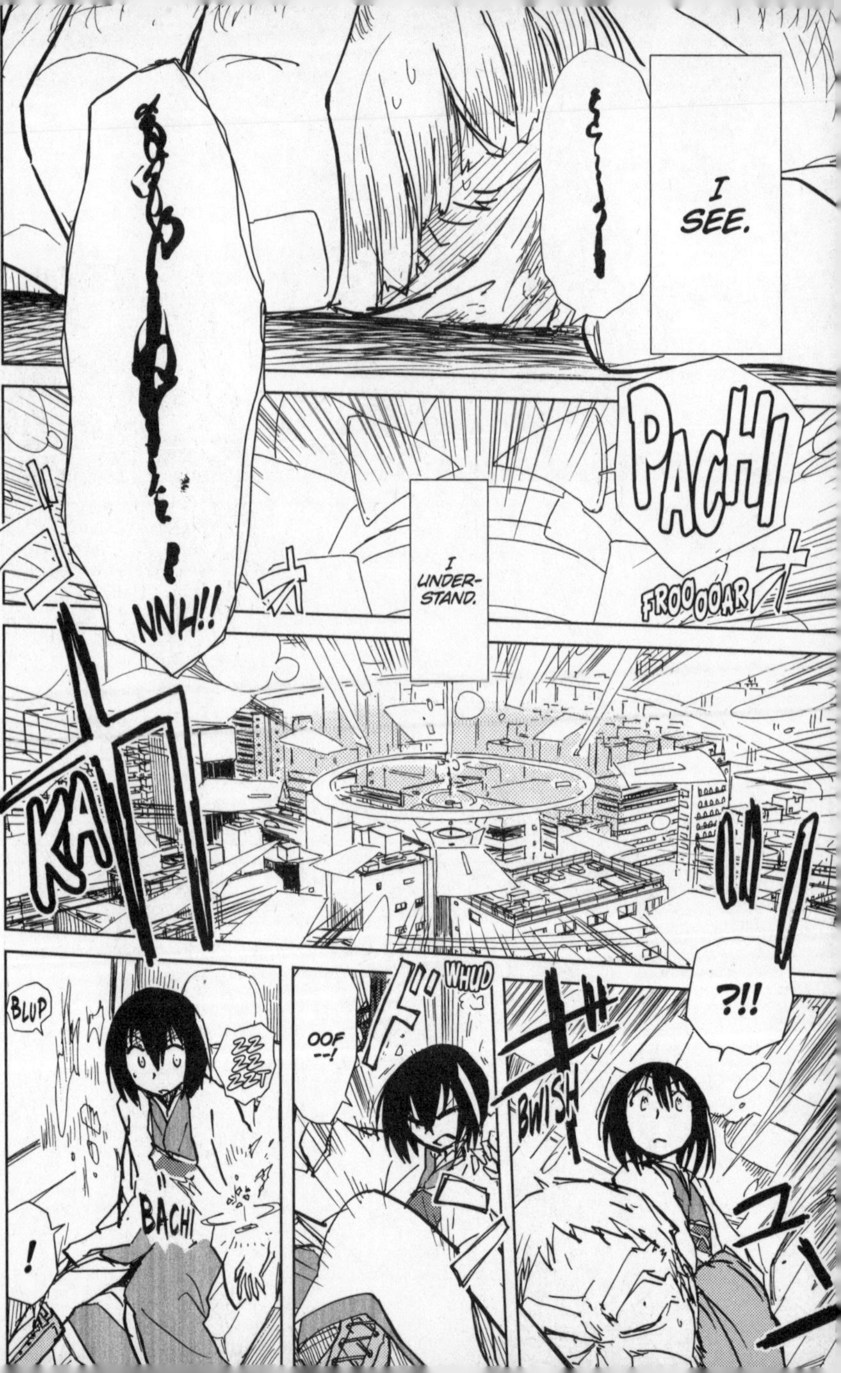
I SEE.
NNH!!
PACHI
FROOOOAR
I UNDER-STAND.
KA
?!!
BWISH
WHUD
OOF --!
BLUP
ZZZZZZT
BACHI
!

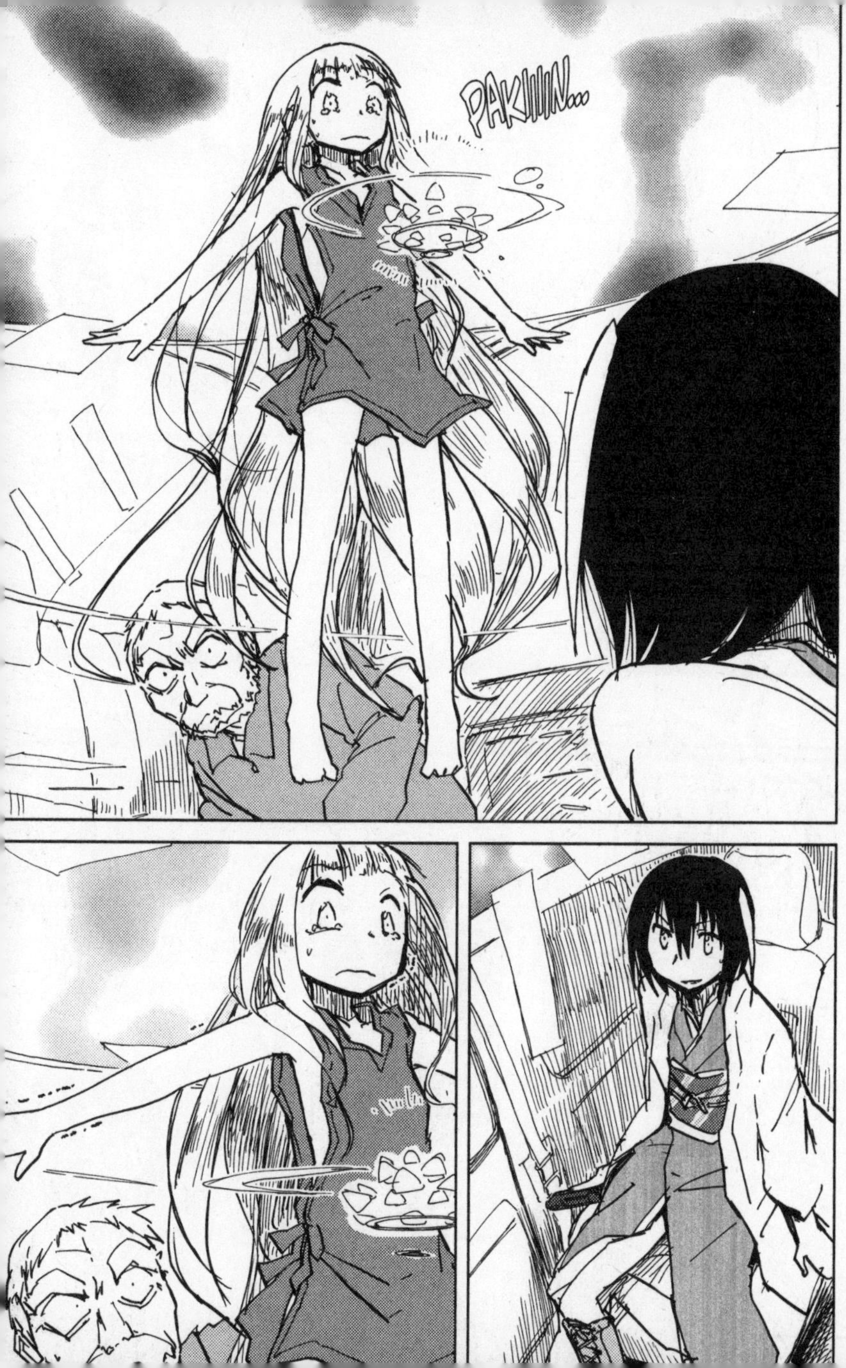
PAKIIIIN...

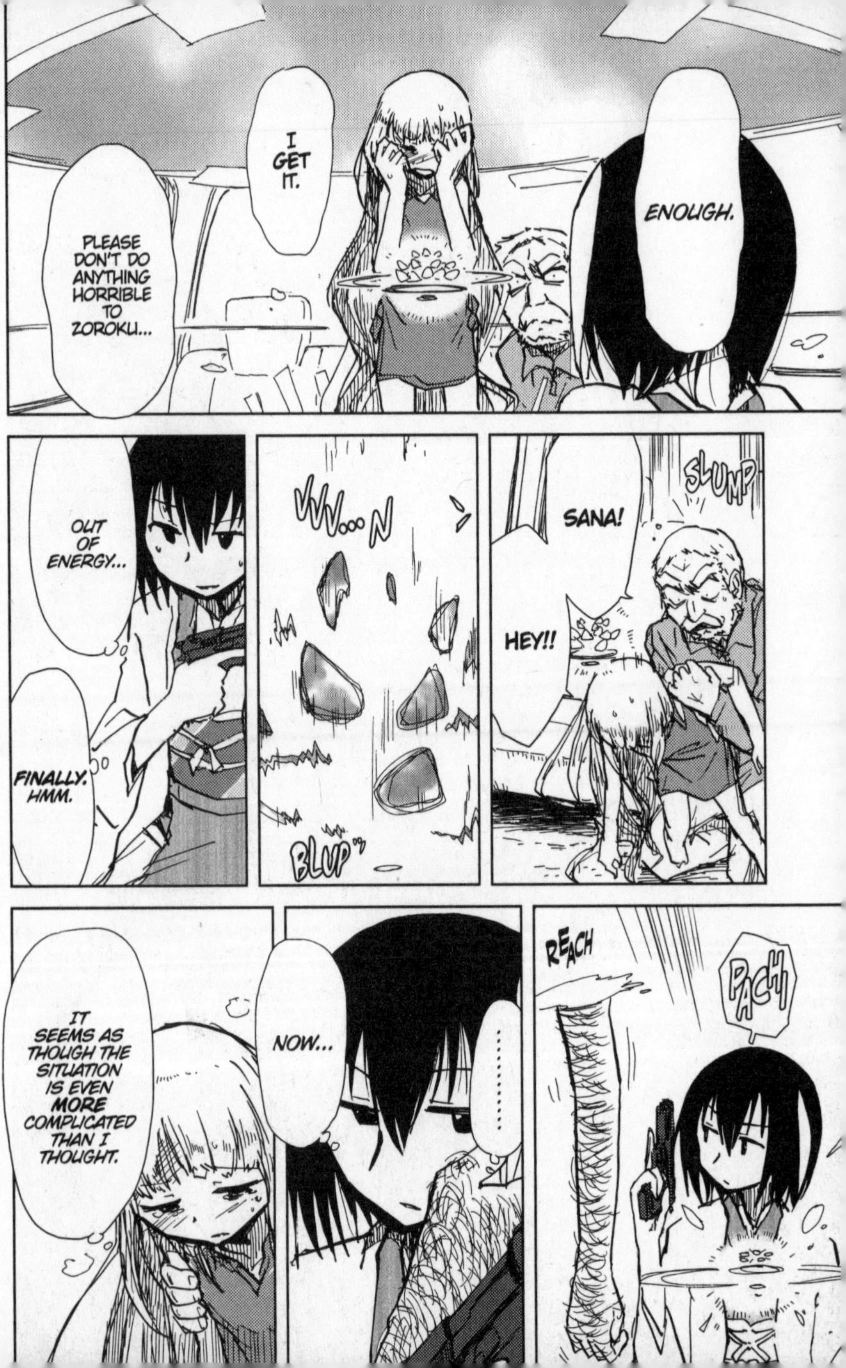
ENOUGH.
I GET IT.
PLEASE DON'T DO ANYTHING HORRIBLE TO ZOROKU...
SLUMP
SANA!
HEY!!
VVV...N
BLUP
OUT OF ENERGY...
FINALLY. HMM.
REACH
PACHI
......
NOW...
IT SEEMS AS THOUGH THE SITUATION IS EVEN MORE COMPLICATED THAN I THOUGHT.

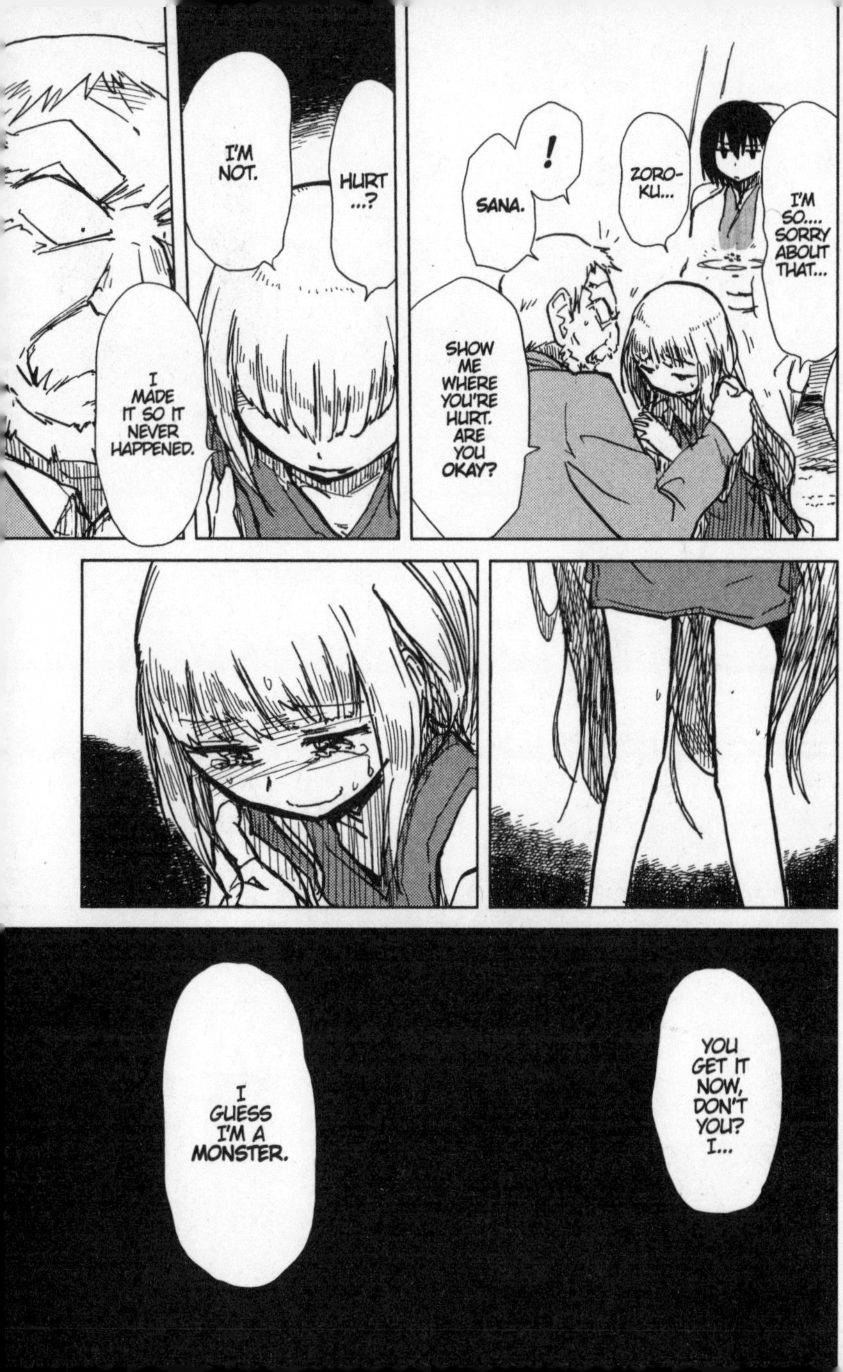
I'M SO.... SORRY ABOUT THAT...
ZORO-KU...
!
SANA.
SHOW ME WHERE YOU'RE HURT. ARE YOU OKAY?
HURT ...?
I'M NOT.
I MADE IT SO IT NEVER HAPPENED.
YOU GET IT NOW, DON'T YOU? I...
I GUESS I'M A MONSTER.

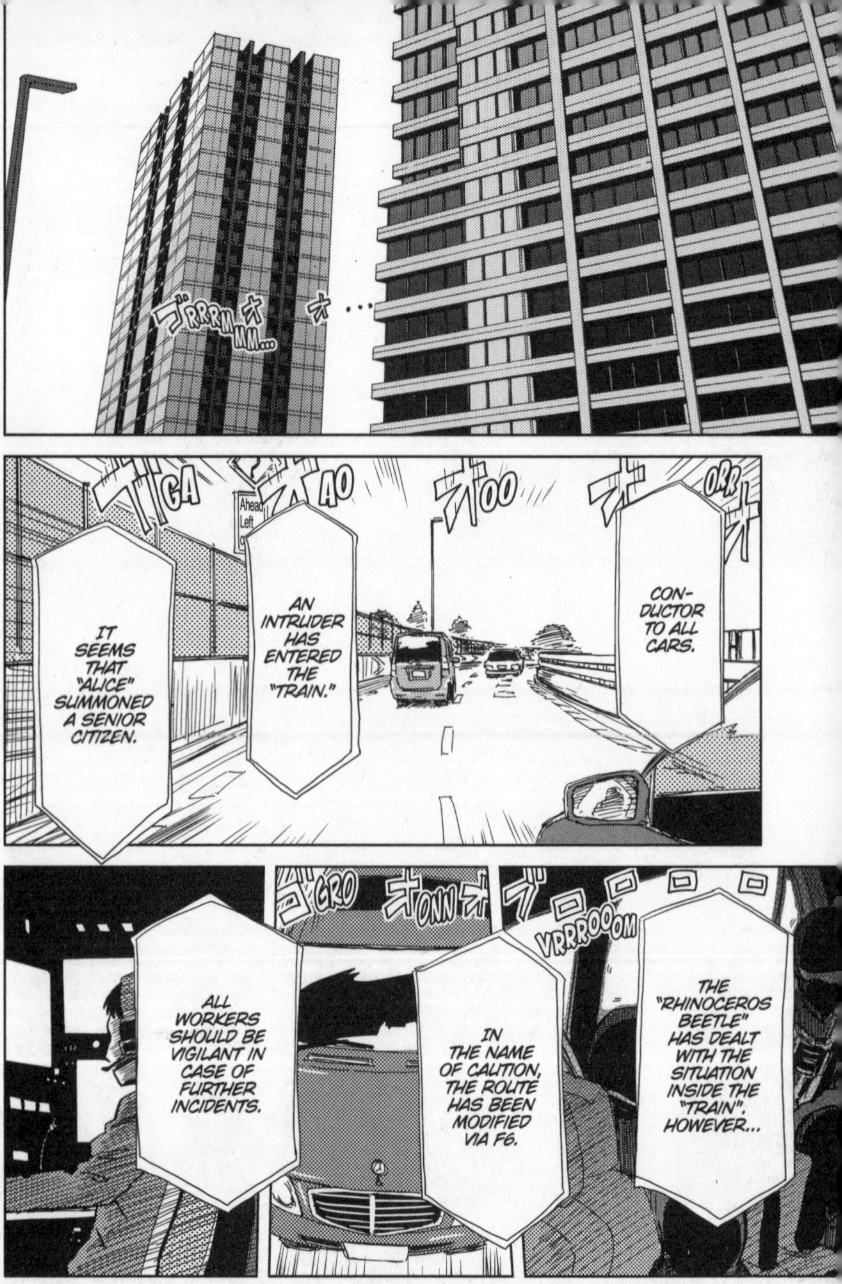
RRRMMM...
GA AO OO ORR
Ahead
Left
CON-DUCTOR TO ALL CARS.
AN INTRUDER HAS ENTERED THE "TRAIN."
IT SEEMS THAT "ALICE" SUMMONED A SENIOR CITIZEN.
GRO ONN
VRRROOOM
THE "RHINOCEROS BEETLE" HAS DEALT WITH THE SITUATION INSIDE THE "TRAIN". HOWEVER...
IN THE NAME OF CAUTION, THE ROUTE HAS BEEN MODIFIED VIA F6.
ALL WORKERS SHOULD BE VIGILANT IN CASE OF FURTHER INCIDENTS.

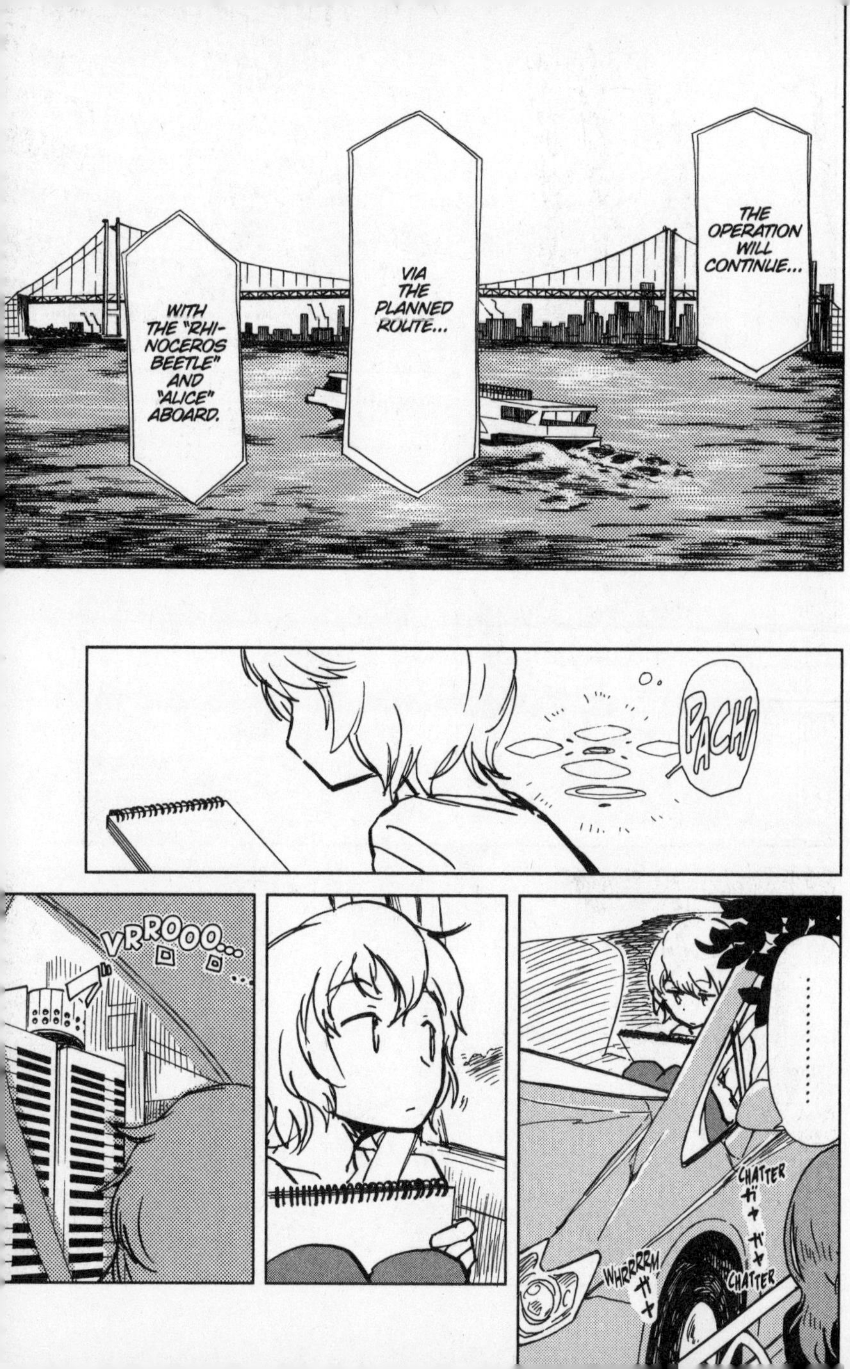
THE OPERATION WILL CONTINUE...
VIA THE PLANNED ROUTE...
WITH THE "RHINOCEROS BEETLE" AND "ALICE" ABOARD.
PACHI
......
CHATTER
WHRRRM
CHATTER
VRROOO...

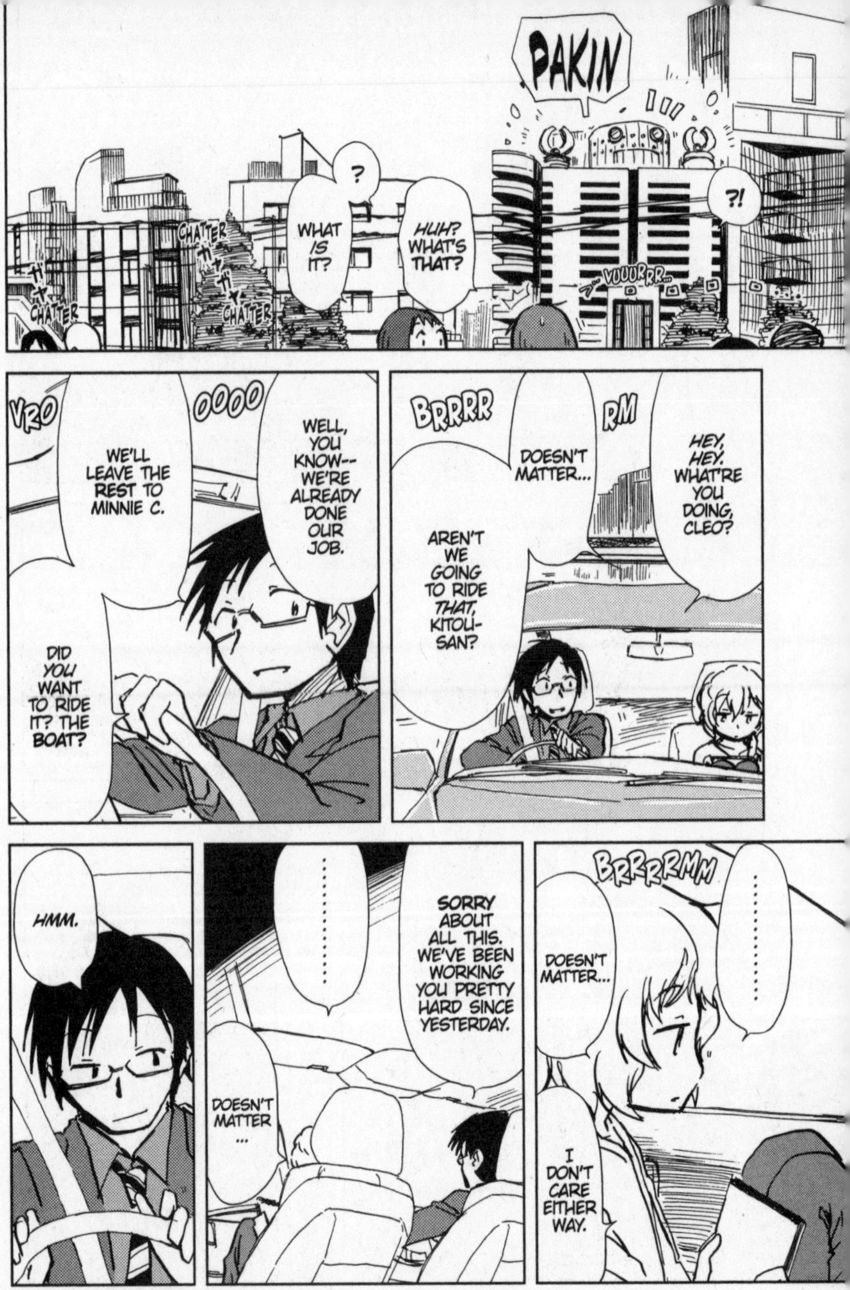
PAKIN
?!
HUH? WHAT'S THAT?
?
WHAT IS IT?
VUUURRR...
CHATTER
CHATTER
CHATTER
BRRRR
RM
HEY, HEY. WHAT'RE YOU DOING, CLEO?
DOESN'T MATTER...
AREN'T WE GOING TO RIDE THAT, KITOU-SAN?
VRO
OOOO
WELL, YOU KNOW-- WE'RE ALREADY DONE OUR JOB.
WE'LL LEAVE THE REST TO MINNIE C.
DID YOU WANT TO RIDE IT? THE BOAT?
BRRRRMM
......
DOESN'T MATTER...
I DON'T CARE EITHER WAY.
......
SORRY ABOUT ALL THIS. WE'VE BEEN WORKING YOU PRETTY HARD SINCE YESTERDAY.
DOESN'T MATTER ...
HMM.

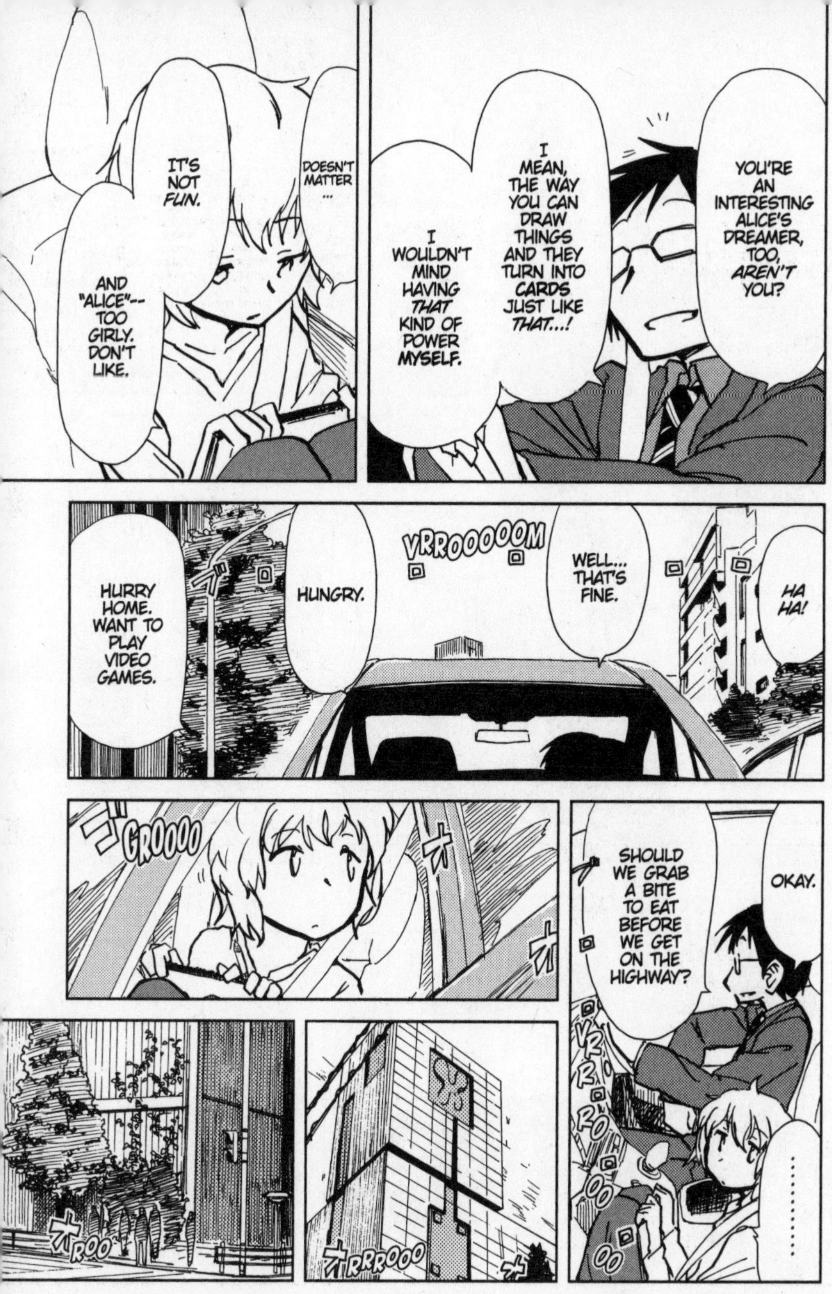
YOU'RE AN INTERESTING ALICE'S DREAMER, TOO, *AREN'T* YOU?
I MEAN, THE WAY YOU CAN DRAW THINGS AND THEY TURN INTO CARDS JUST LIKE *THAT...!*
I WOULDN'T MIND HAVING *THAT* KIND OF POWER MYSELF.
DOESN'T MATTER ...
IT'S NOT *FUN.*
AND "ALICE"-- TOO GIRLY. DON'T LIKE.
HA HA!
WELL... THAT'S FINE.
VRROOOOOOM
HUNGRY.
HURRY HOME. WANT TO PLAY VIDEO GAMES.
OKAY.
SHOULD WE GRAB A BITE TO EAT BEFORE WE GET ON THE HIGHWAY?
......
GROOOO
TRRROOO
TROO

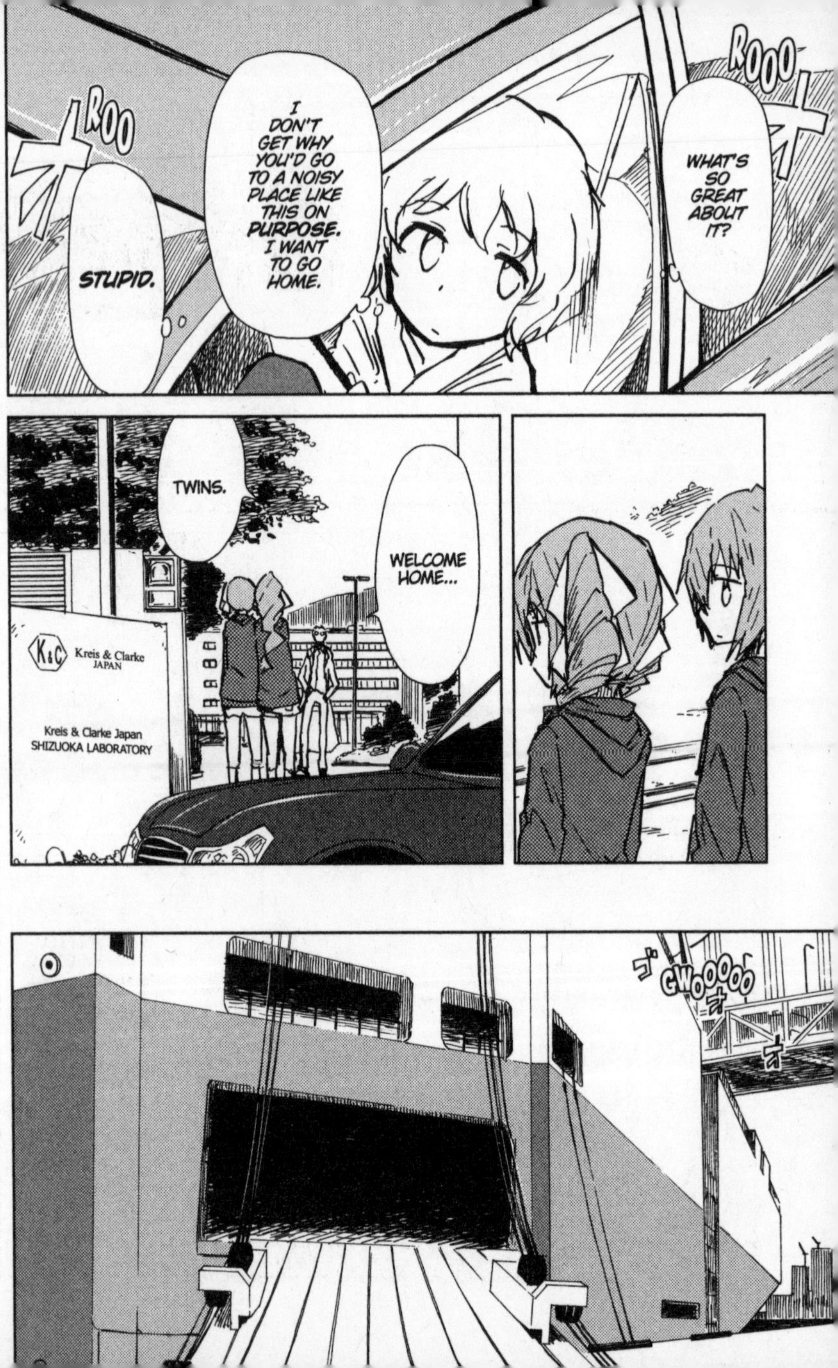

ROOO
WHAT'S SO GREAT ABOUT IT?
I DON'T GET WHY YOU'D GO TO A NOISY PLACE LIKE THIS ON PURPOSE. I WANT TO GO HOME.
ROO
STUPID.
WELCOME HOME...
TWINS.
K&C Kreis & Clarke JAPAN
Kreis & Clarke Japan SHIZUOKA LABORATORY
GWOOOOO

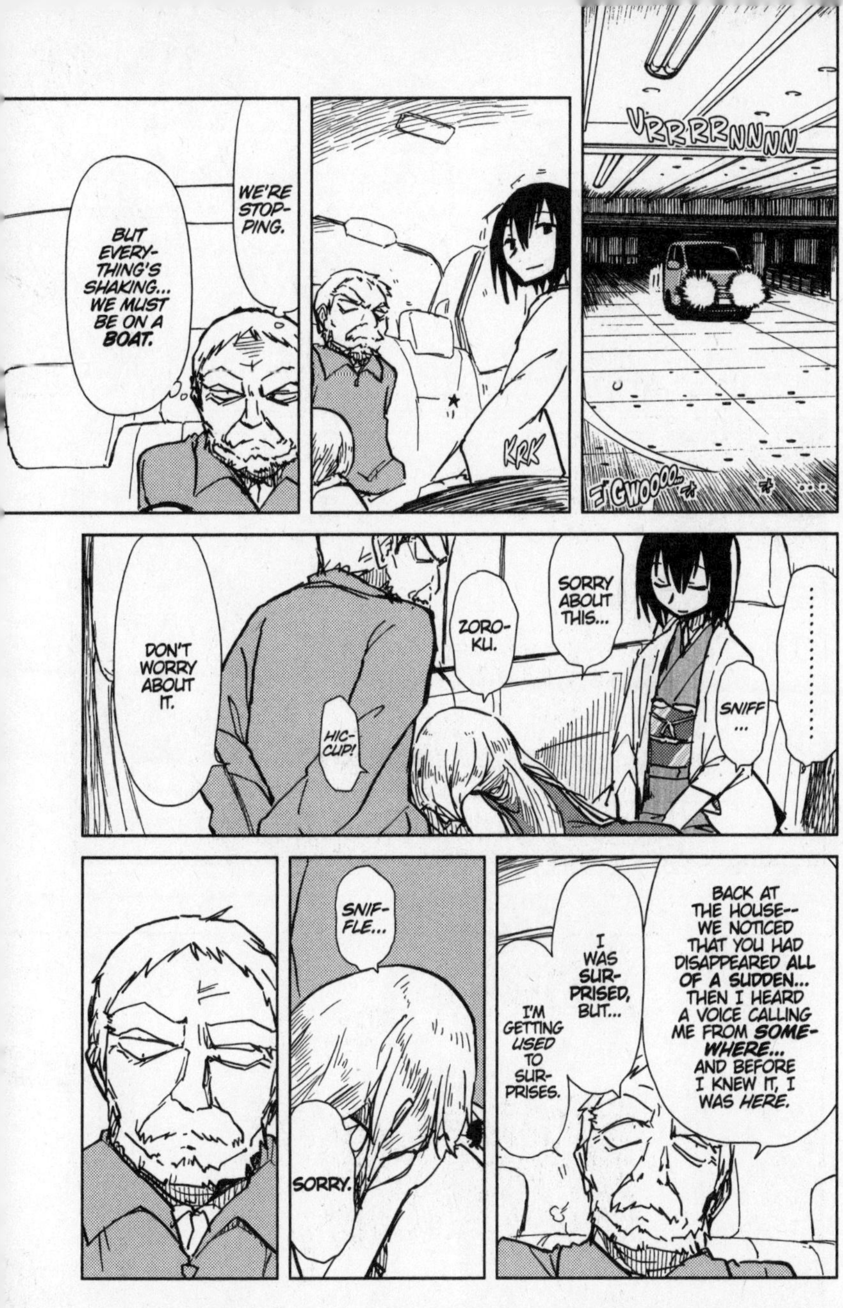
VRRRRNNNNN
GWOOOO...
...
KRK
WE'RE STOP-PING.
BUT EVERY-THING'S SHAKING... WE MUST BE ON A BOAT.
......
SNIFF...
SORRY ABOUT THIS...
ZORO-KU.
HIC-CUP!
DON'T WORRY ABOUT IT.
BACK AT THE HOUSE-- WE NOTICED THAT YOU HAD DISAPPEARED ALL OF A SUDDEN... THEN I HEARD A VOICE CALLING ME FROM SOME-WHERE... AND BEFORE I KNEW IT, I WAS HERE.
I WAS SUR-PRISED, BUT...
I'M GETTING USED TO SUR-PRISES.
SNIF-FLE...
SORRY.

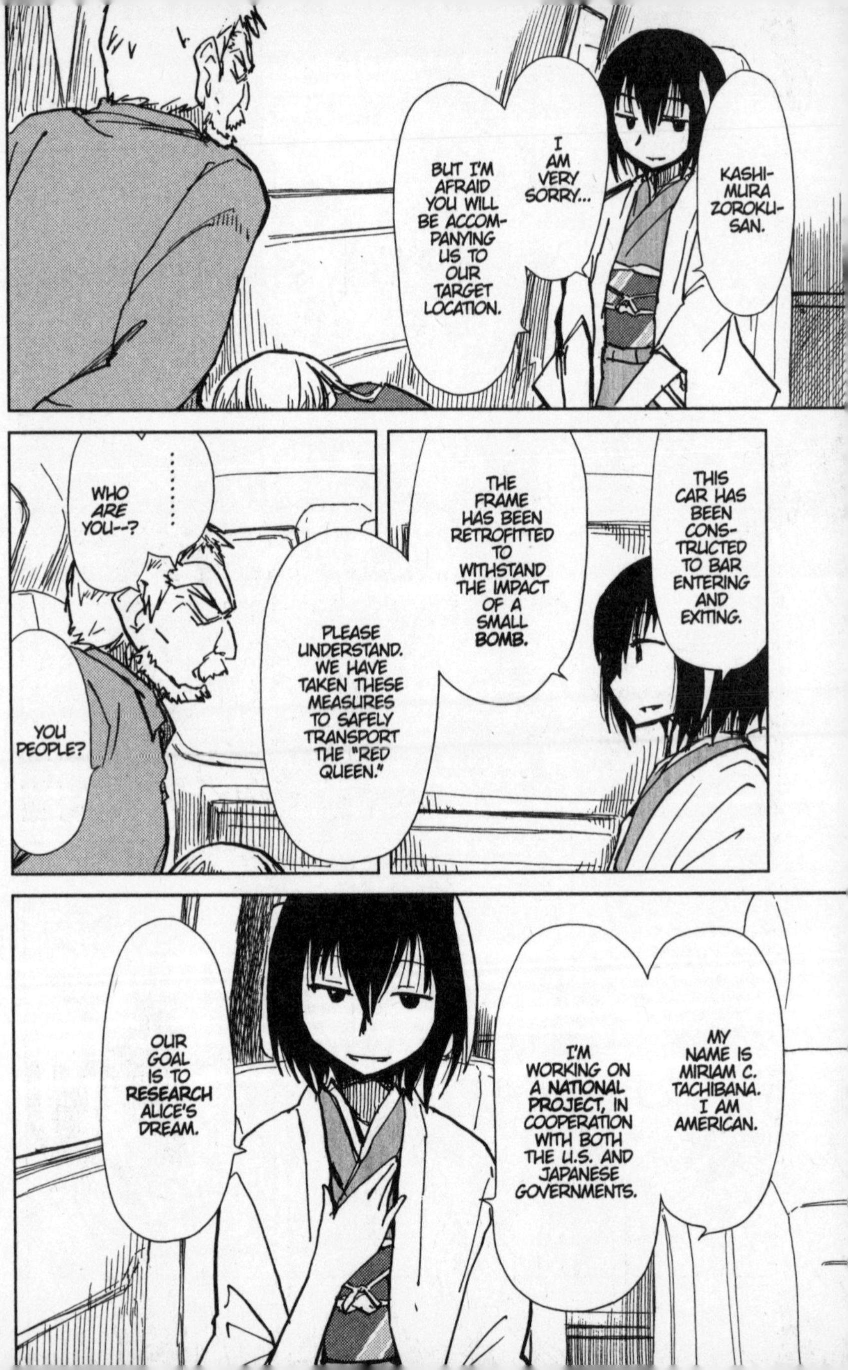
KASHI-MURA ZOROKU-SAN.
I AM VERY SORRY...
BUT I'M AFRAID YOU WILL BE ACCOM-PANYING US TO OUR TARGET LOCATION.
THIS CAR HAS BEEN CONS-TRUCTED TO BAR ENTERING AND EXITING.
THE FRAME HAS BEEN RETROFITTED TO WITHSTAND THE IMPACT OF A SMALL BOMB.
PLEASE UNDERSTAND. WE HAVE TAKEN THESE MEASURES TO SAFELY TRANSPORT THE "RED QUEEN."
......
WHO ARE YOU--?
YOU PEOPLE?
MY NAME IS MIRIAM C. TACHIBANA. I AM AMERICAN.
I'M WORKING ON A NATIONAL PROJECT, IN COOPERATION WITH BOTH THE U.S. AND JAPANESE GOVERNMENTS.
OUR GOAL IS TO RESEARCH ALICE'S DREAM.

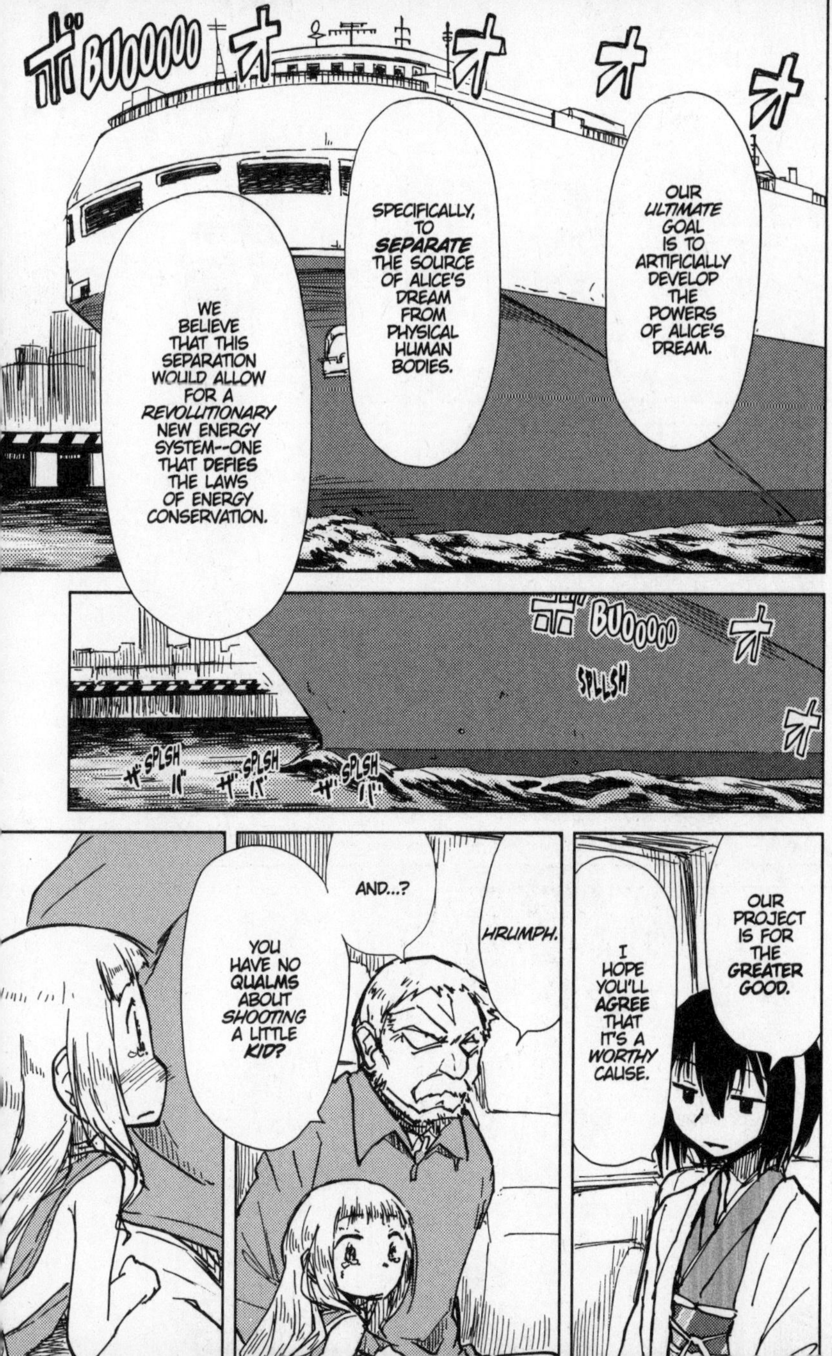
ボBUOOOOO オ オ オ オ
OUR *ULTIMATE* GOAL IS TO ARTIFICIALLY DEVELOP THE POWERS OF ALICE'S DREAM.
SPECIFICALLY, TO ***SEPARATE*** THE SOURCE OF ALICE'S DREAM FROM PHYSICAL HUMAN BODIES.
WE BELIEVE THAT THIS SEPARATION WOULD ALLOW FOR A *REVOLUTIONARY* NEW ENERGY SYSTEM--ONE THAT DEFIES THE LAWS OF ENERGY CONSERVATION.
ボBUOOOOOO オ オ
SPLLSH
ザ SPLSH バ
ザ SPLSH バ
ザ SPLSH バ
OUR PROJECT IS FOR THE GREATER GOOD.
I HOPE YOU'LL AGREE THAT IT'S A *WORTHY* CAUSE.
AND...?
*HRUMPH.*
YOU HAVE NO QUALMS ABOUT *SHOOTING* A LITTLE *KID?*

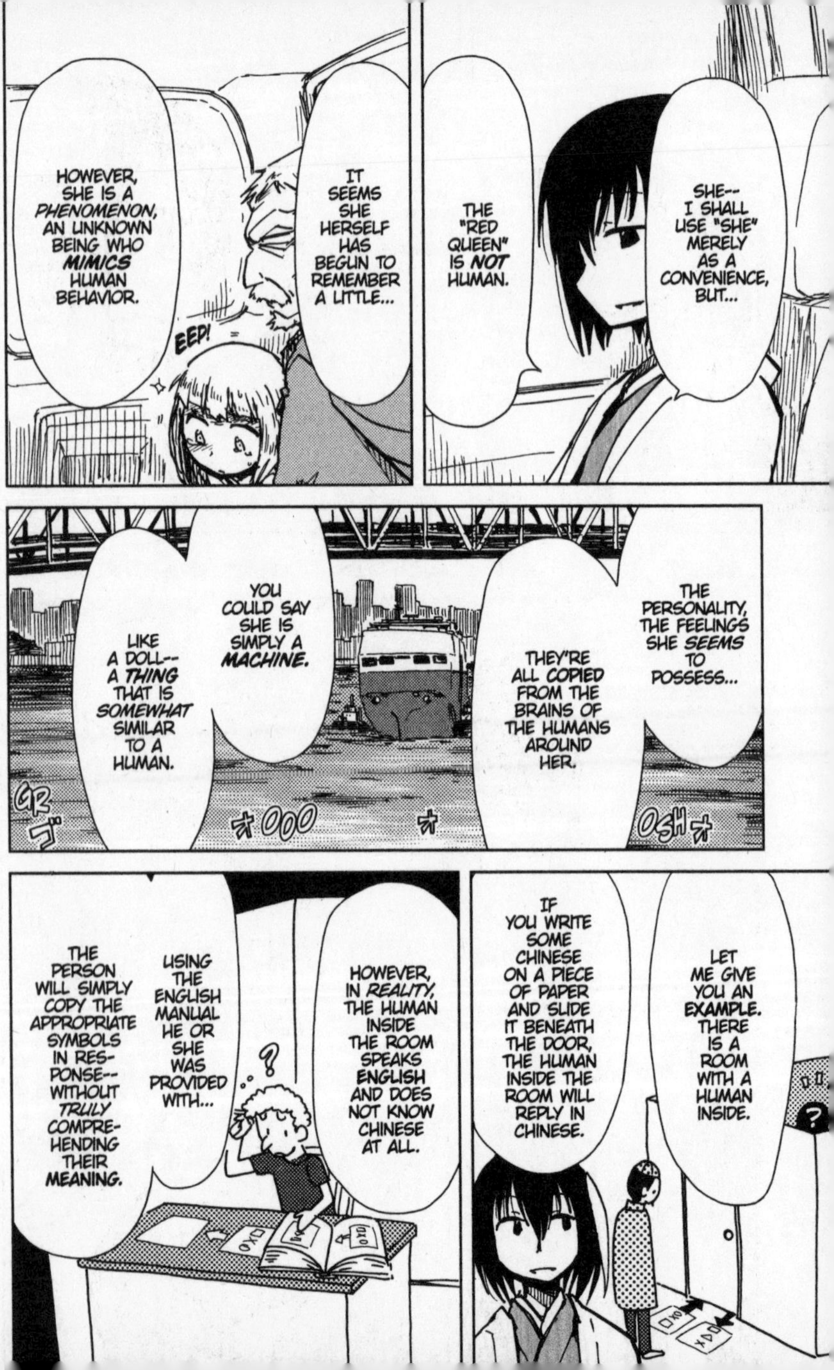
SHE-- I SHALL USE "SHE" MERELY AS A CONVENIENCE, BUT...
THE "RED QUEEN" IS *NOT* HUMAN.
IT SEEMS SHE HERSELF HAS BEGUN TO REMEMBER A LITTLE...
HOWEVER, SHE IS A *PHENOMENON*, AN UNKNOWN BEING WHO ***MIMICS*** HUMAN BEHAVIOR.
EEP!
THE PERSONALITY, THE FEELINGS SHE *SEEMS* TO POSSESS...
THEY'RE ALL COPIED FROM THE BRAINS OF THE HUMANS AROUND HER.
YOU COULD SAY SHE IS SIMPLY A ***MACHINE.***
LIKE A DOLL-- A *THING* THAT IS *SOMEWHAT* SIMILAR TO A HUMAN.
GRゴ OOOオ オ OSHオ
LET ME GIVE YOU AN **EXAMPLE.** THERE IS A ROOM WITH A HUMAN INSIDE.
?
IF YOU WRITE SOME CHINESE ON A PIECE OF PAPER AND SLIDE IT BENEATH THE DOOR, THE HUMAN INSIDE THE ROOM WILL REPLY IN CHINESE.
HOWEVER, IN *REALITY*, THE HUMAN INSIDE THE ROOM SPEAKS ENGLISH AND DOES NOT KNOW CHINESE AT ALL.
?
USING THE ENGLISH MANUAL HE OR SHE WAS PROVIDED WITH...
THE PERSON WILL SIMPLY COPY THE APPROPRIATE SYMBOLS IN RESPONSE-- WITHOUT *TRULY* COMPREHENDING THEIR **MEANING.**

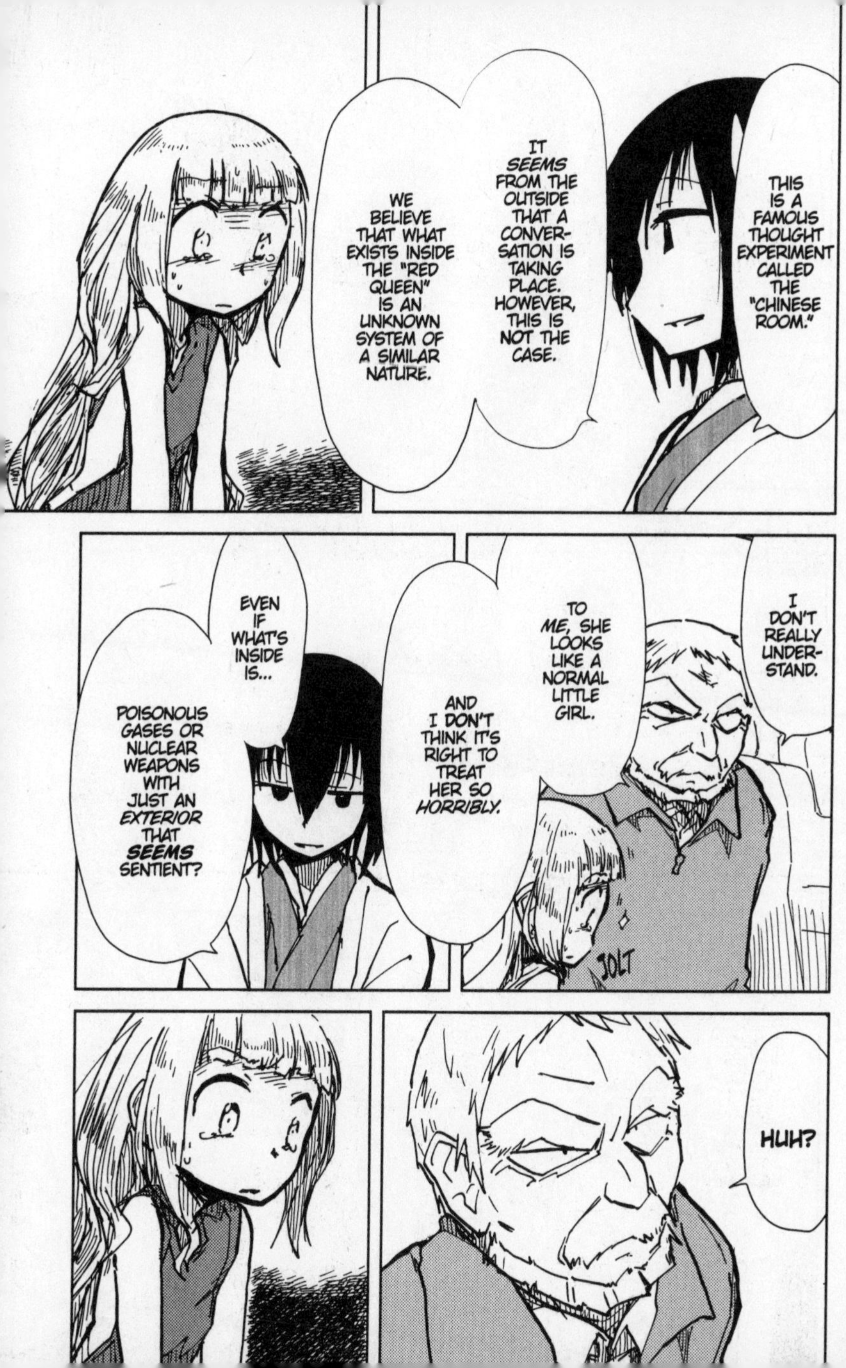
THIS IS A FAMOUS THOUGHT EXPERIMENT CALLED THE "CHINESE ROOM."
IT *SEEMS* FROM THE OUTSIDE THAT A CONVERSATION IS TAKING PLACE. HOWEVER, THIS IS NOT THE CASE.
WE BELIEVE THAT WHAT EXISTS INSIDE THE "RED QUEEN" IS AN UNKNOWN SYSTEM OF A SIMILAR NATURE.
I DON'T REALLY UNDERSTAND.
TO *ME*, SHE LOOKS LIKE A NORMAL LITTLE GIRL.
AND I DON'T THINK IT'S RIGHT TO TREAT HER SO *HORRIBLY.*
JOLT
EVEN IF WHAT'S INSIDE IS...
POISONOUS GASES OR NUCLEAR WEAPONS WITH JUST AN *EXTERIOR* THAT ***SEEMS*** SENTIENT?
HUH?

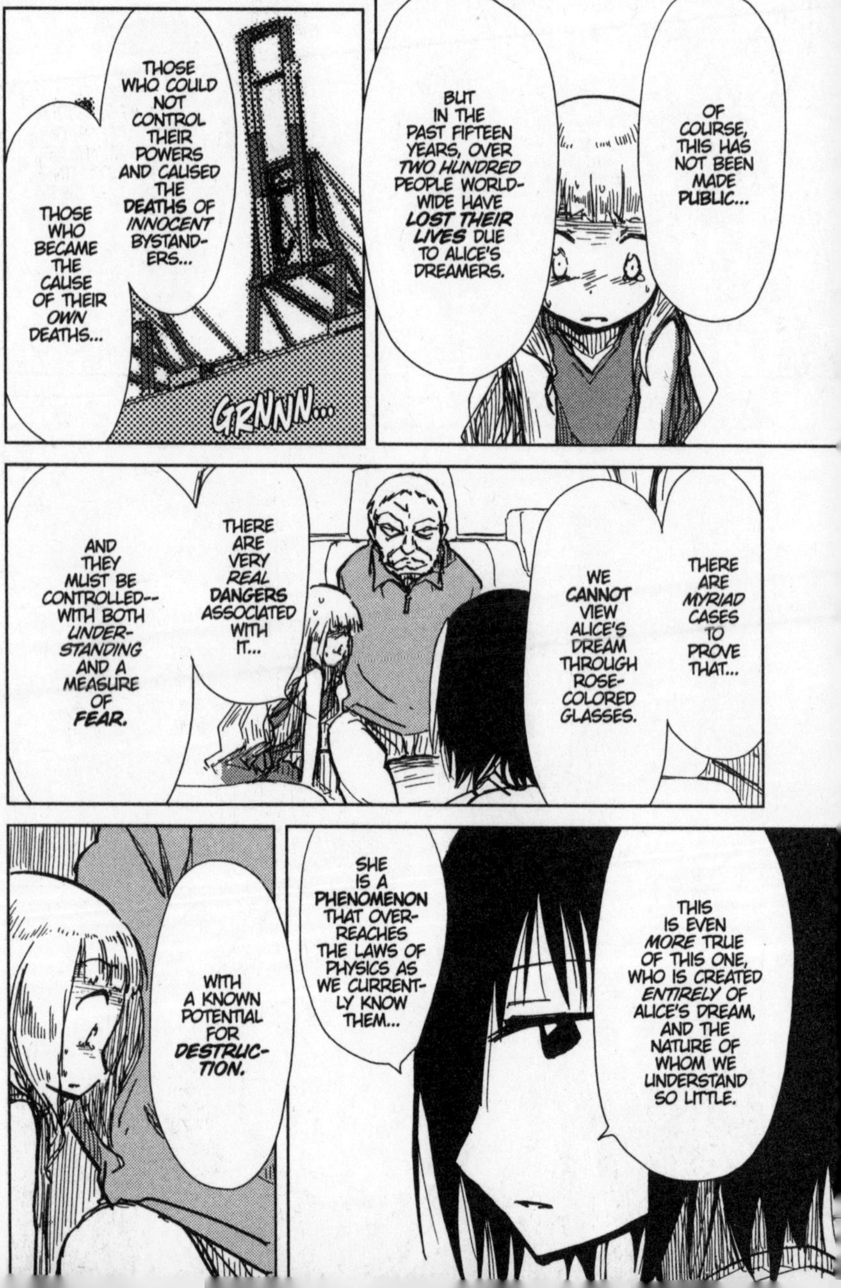
OF COURSE, THIS HAS NOT BEEN MADE PUBLIC...
BUT IN THE PAST FIFTEEN YEARS, OVER TWO HUNDRED PEOPLE WORLD-WIDE HAVE LOST THEIR LIVES DUE TO ALICE'S DREAMERS.
THOSE WHO COULD NOT CONTROL THEIR POWERS AND CAUSED THE DEATHS OF INNOCENT BYSTANDERS...
THOSE WHO BECAME THE CAUSE OF THEIR OWN DEATHS...
GRNNN...
THERE ARE MYRIAD CASES TO PROVE THAT...
WE CANNOT VIEW ALICE'S DREAM THROUGH ROSE-COLORED GLASSES.
THERE ARE VERY REAL DANGERS ASSOCIATED WITH IT...
AND THEY MUST BE CONTROLLED-- WITH BOTH UNDERSTANDING AND A MEASURE OF FEAR.
THIS IS EVEN MORE TRUE OF THIS ONE, WHO IS CREATED ENTIRELY OF ALICE'S DREAM, AND THE NATURE OF WHOM WE UNDERSTAND SO LITTLE.
SHE IS A PHENOMENON THAT OVER-REACHES THE LAWS OF PHYSICS AS WE CURRENTLY KNOW THEM...
WITH A KNOWN POTENTIAL FOR DESTRUCTION.

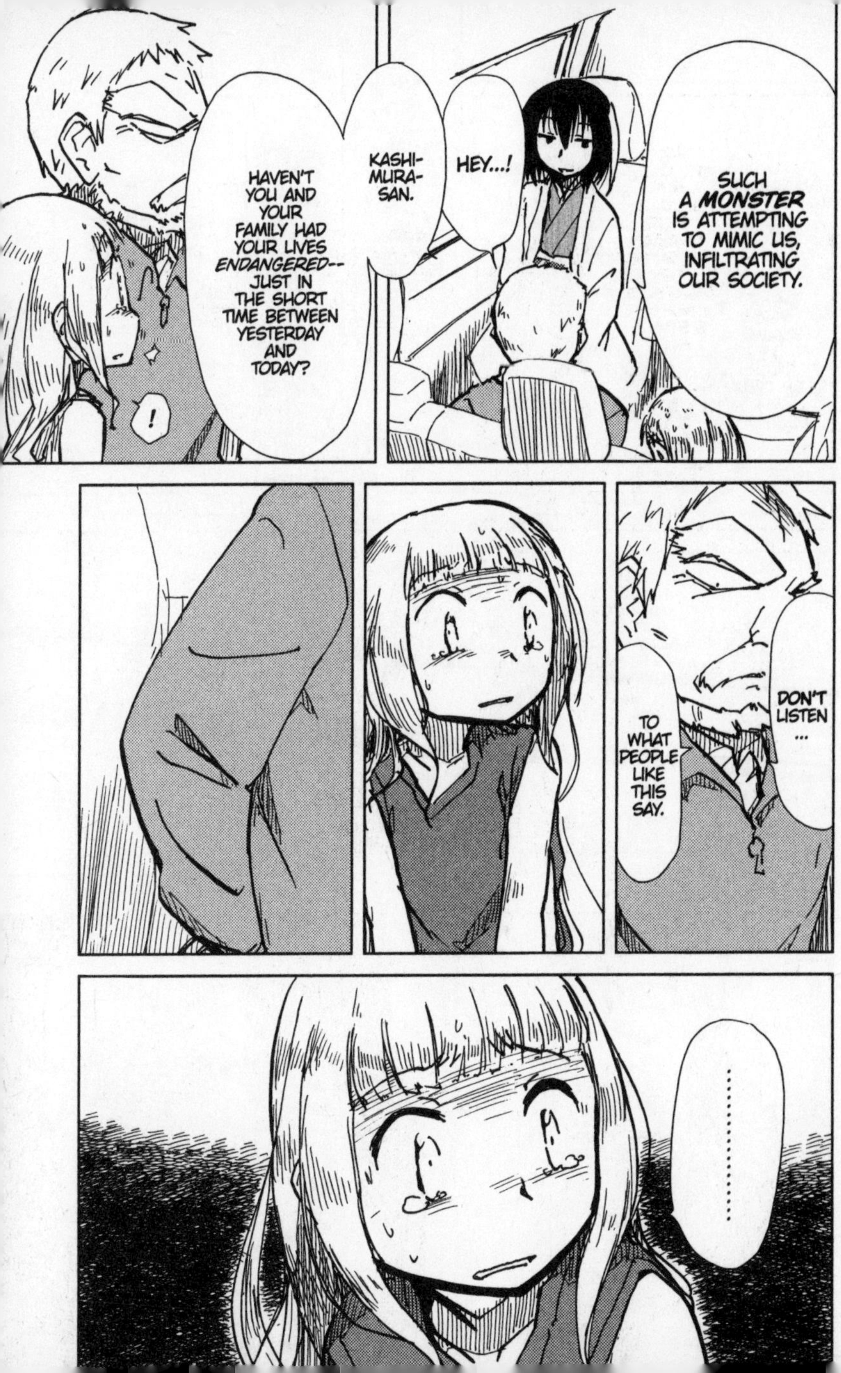
SUCH A MONSTER IS ATTEMPTING TO MIMIC US, INFILTRATING OUR SOCIETY.
HEY...!
KASHIMURA-SAN.
HAVEN'T YOU AND YOUR FAMILY HAD YOUR LIVES ENDANGERED-- JUST IN THE SHORT TIME BETWEEN YESTERDAY AND TODAY?
!
DON'T LISTEN ...
TO WHAT PEOPLE LIKE THIS SAY.
......

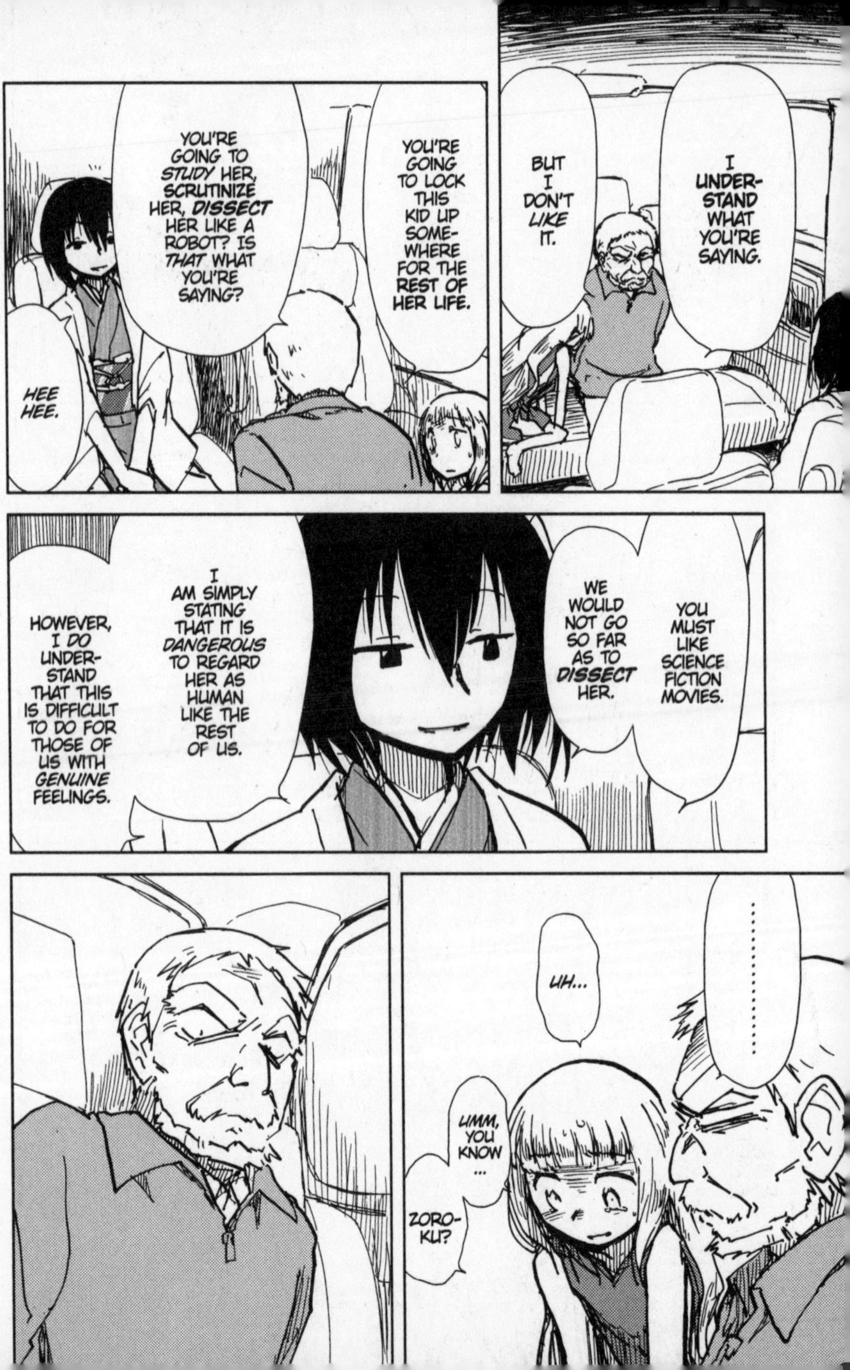
I UNDERSTAND WHAT YOU'RE SAYING.
BUT I DON'T *LIKE* IT.
YOU'RE GOING TO LOCK THIS KID UP SOMEWHERE FOR THE REST OF HER LIFE.
YOU'RE GOING TO *STUDY* HER, SCRUTINIZE HER, ***DISSECT*** HER LIKE A ROBOT? IS *THAT* WHAT YOU'RE SAYING?
HEE HEE.
YOU MUST LIKE SCIENCE FICTION MOVIES.
WE WOULD NOT GO SO FAR AS TO ***DISSECT*** HER.
I AM SIMPLY STATING THAT IT IS *DANGEROUS* TO REGARD HER AS HUMAN LIKE THE REST OF US.
HOWEVER, I *DO* UNDERSTAND THAT THIS IS DIFFICULT TO DO FOR THOSE OF US WITH *GENUINE* FEELINGS.
......
UH...
UMM, YOU KNOW...
ZOROKU?

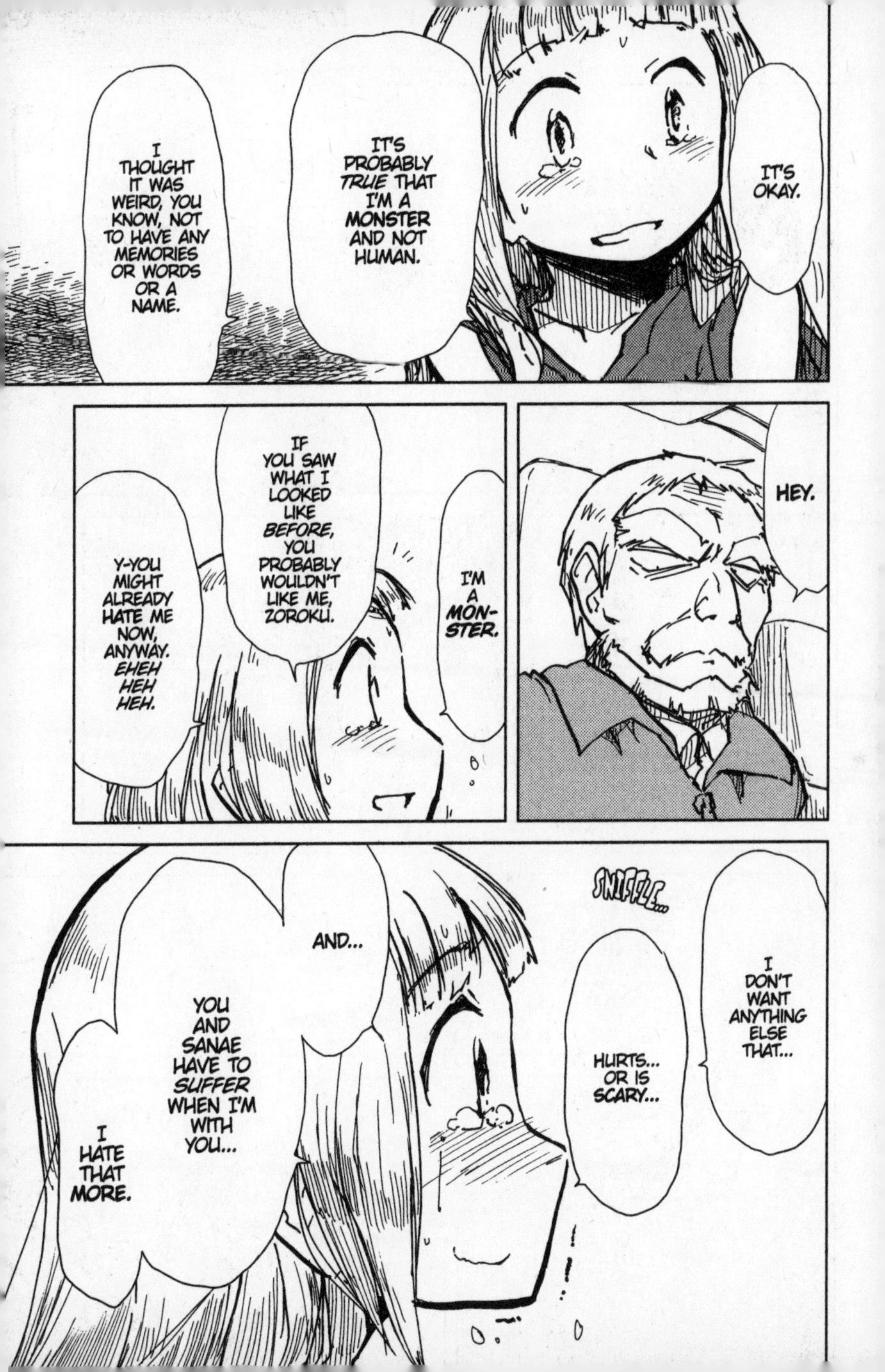
IT'S OKAY.
IT'S PROBABLY TRUE THAT I'M A MONSTER AND NOT HUMAN.
I THOUGHT IT WAS WEIRD, YOU KNOW, NOT TO HAVE ANY MEMORIES OR WORDS OR A NAME.
HEY.
I'M A MON-STER.
IF YOU SAW WHAT I LOOKED LIKE BEFORE, YOU PROBABLY WOULDN'T LIKE ME, ZOROKU.
Y-YOU MIGHT ALREADY HATE ME NOW, ANYWAY. EHEH HEH HEH.
SNIFFLE...
I DON'T WANT ANYTHING ELSE THAT...
HURTS... OR IS SCARY...
AND...
YOU AND SANAE HAVE TO SUFFER WHEN I'M WITH YOU...
I HATE THAT MORE.

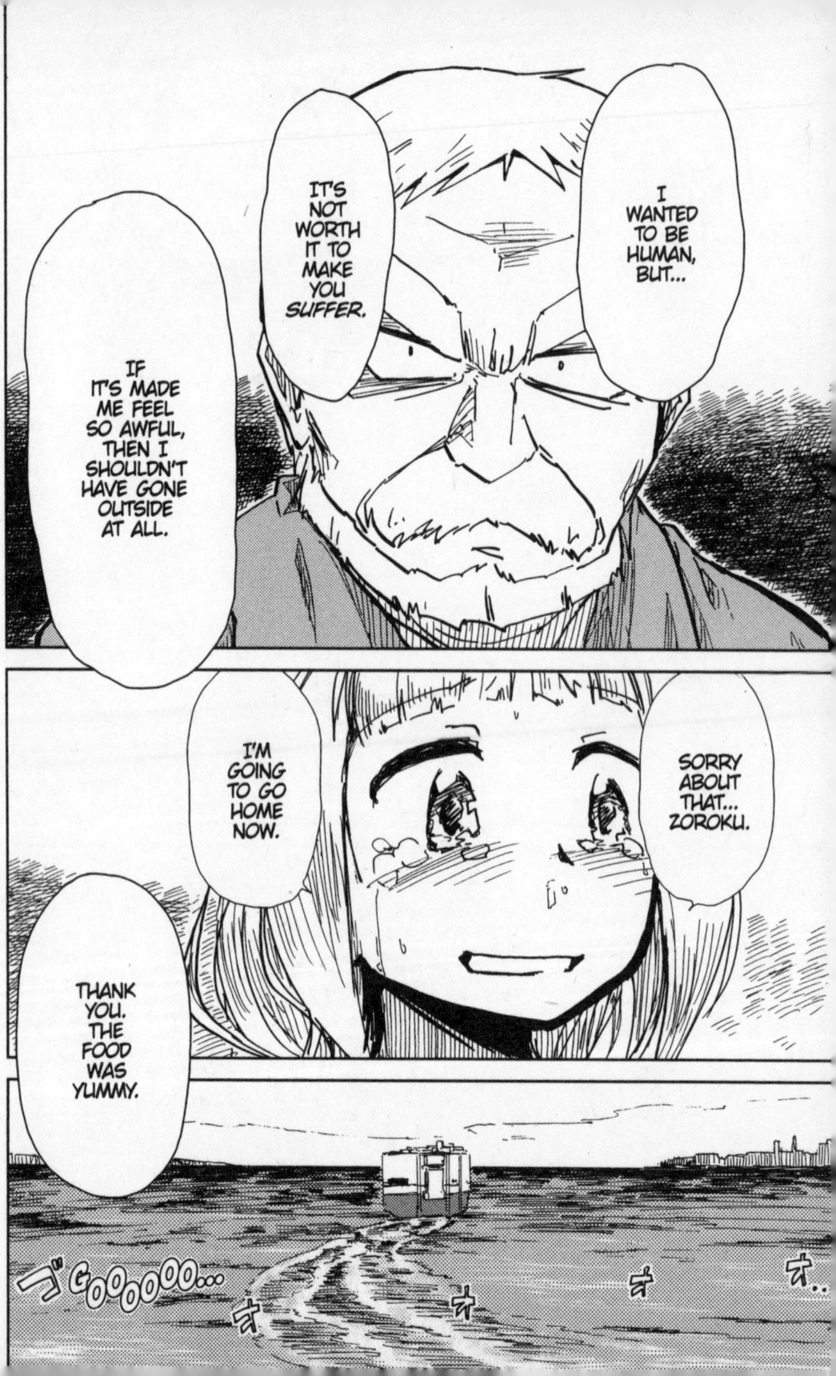
I WANTED TO BE HUMAN, BUT...
IT'S NOT WORTH IT TO MAKE YOU SUFFER.
IF IT'S MADE ME FEEL SO AWFUL, THEN I SHOULDN'T HAVE GONE OUTSIDE AT ALL.
SORRY ABOUT THAT... ZOROKU.
I'M GOING TO GO HOME NOW.
THANK YOU. THE FOOD WAS YUMMY.
オ..
オ
オ
オ
ゴGOOOOOO...

Alice & Zoroku

•◆•

It was like this.

## JABBERWOCKY.

'Twas brillig, and the slithy toves
Did gyre and gimble in the wabe;
All mimsy were the borogoves,
And the mome raths outgrabe.

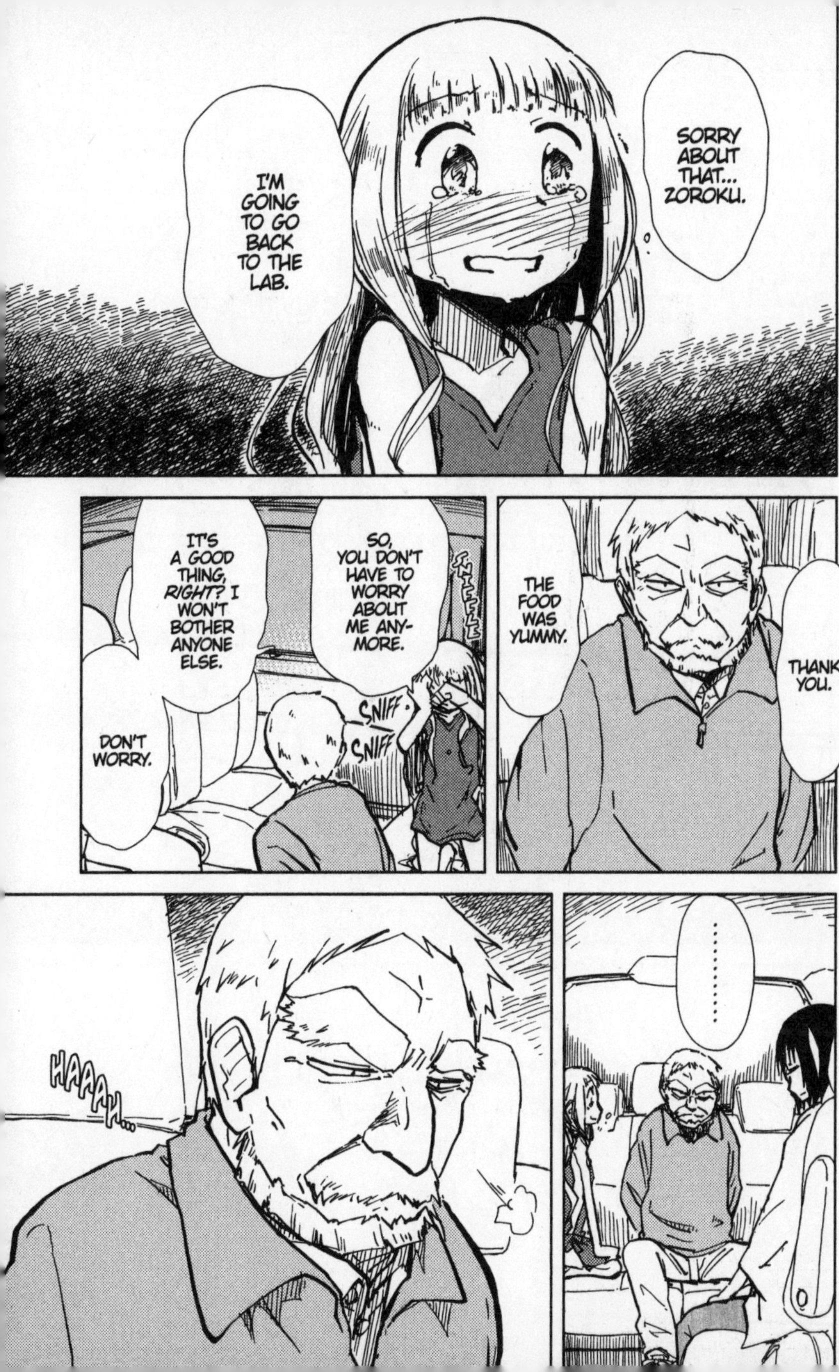
SORRY ABOUT THAT... ZOROKU.
I'M GOING TO GO BACK TO THE LAB.
THANK YOU.
THE FOOD WAS YUMMY.
SNIFFLE
SO, YOU DON'T HAVE TO WORRY ABOUT ME ANY-MORE.
IT'S A GOOD THING, *RIGHT?* I WON'T BOTHER ANYONE ELSE.
SNIFF
SNIFF
DON'T WORRY.
......
HAAAH...

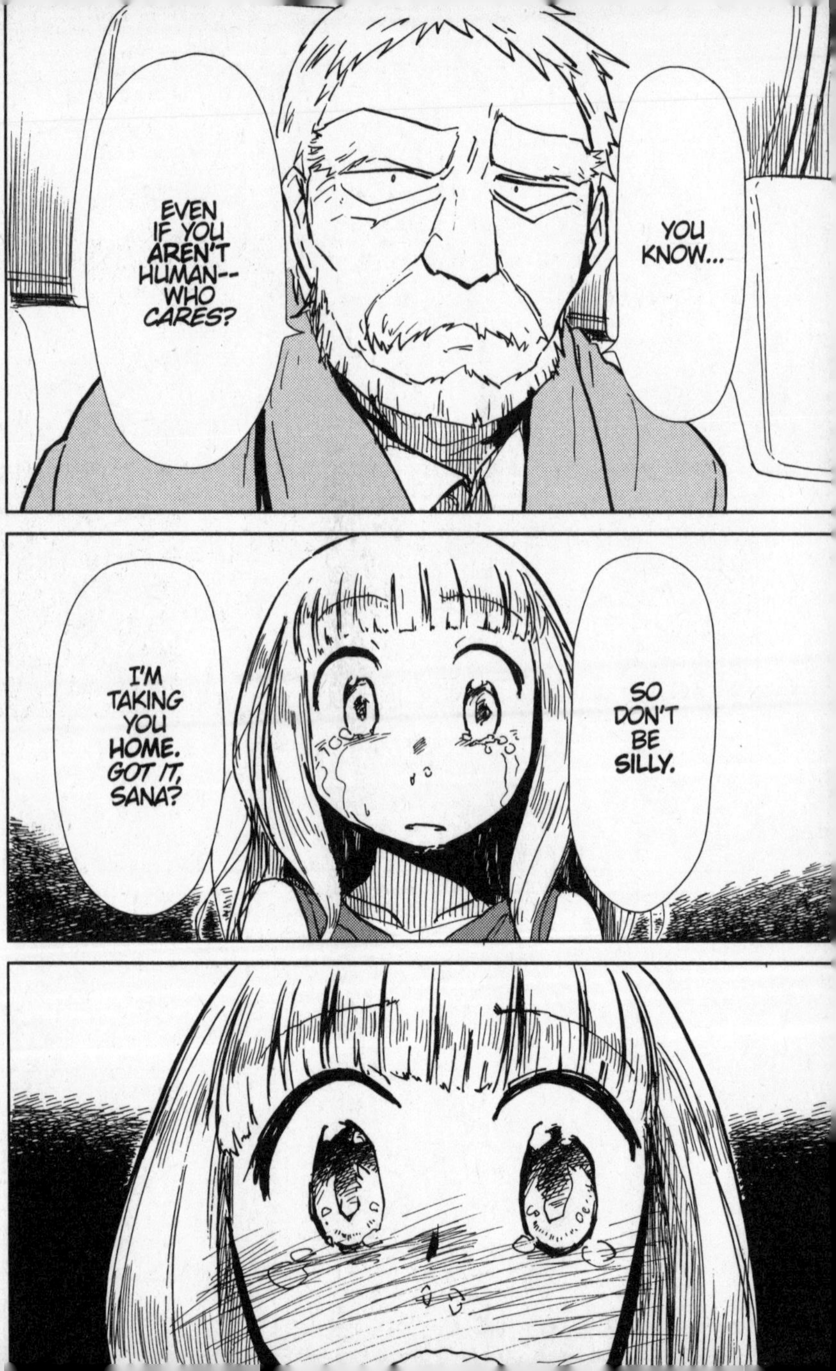
YOU KNOW...
EVEN IF YOU AREN'T HUMAN-- WHO CARES?
SO DON'T BE SILLY.
I'M TAKING YOU HOME. GOT IT, SANA?

## Chapter.7
# The Dream of the Triangular Room (reprise)

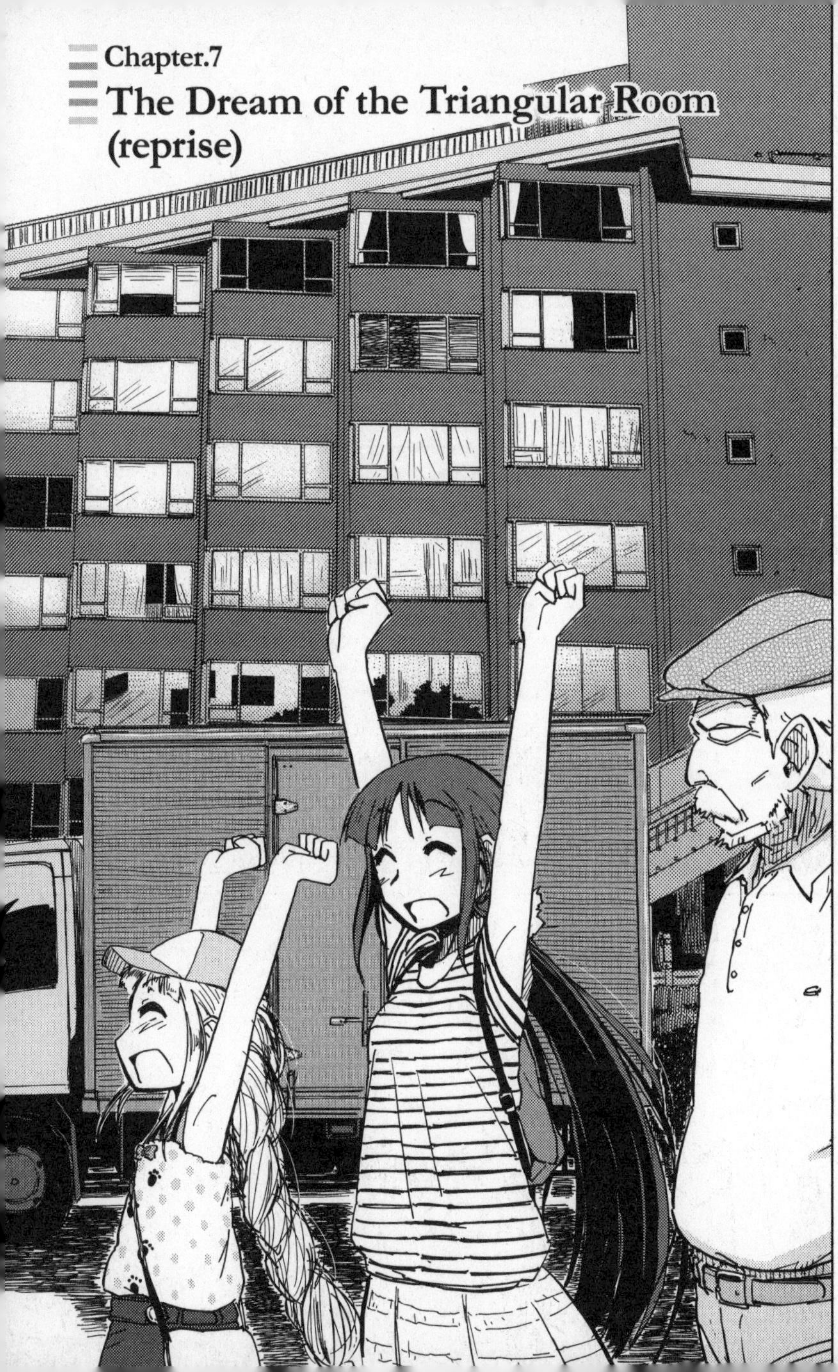

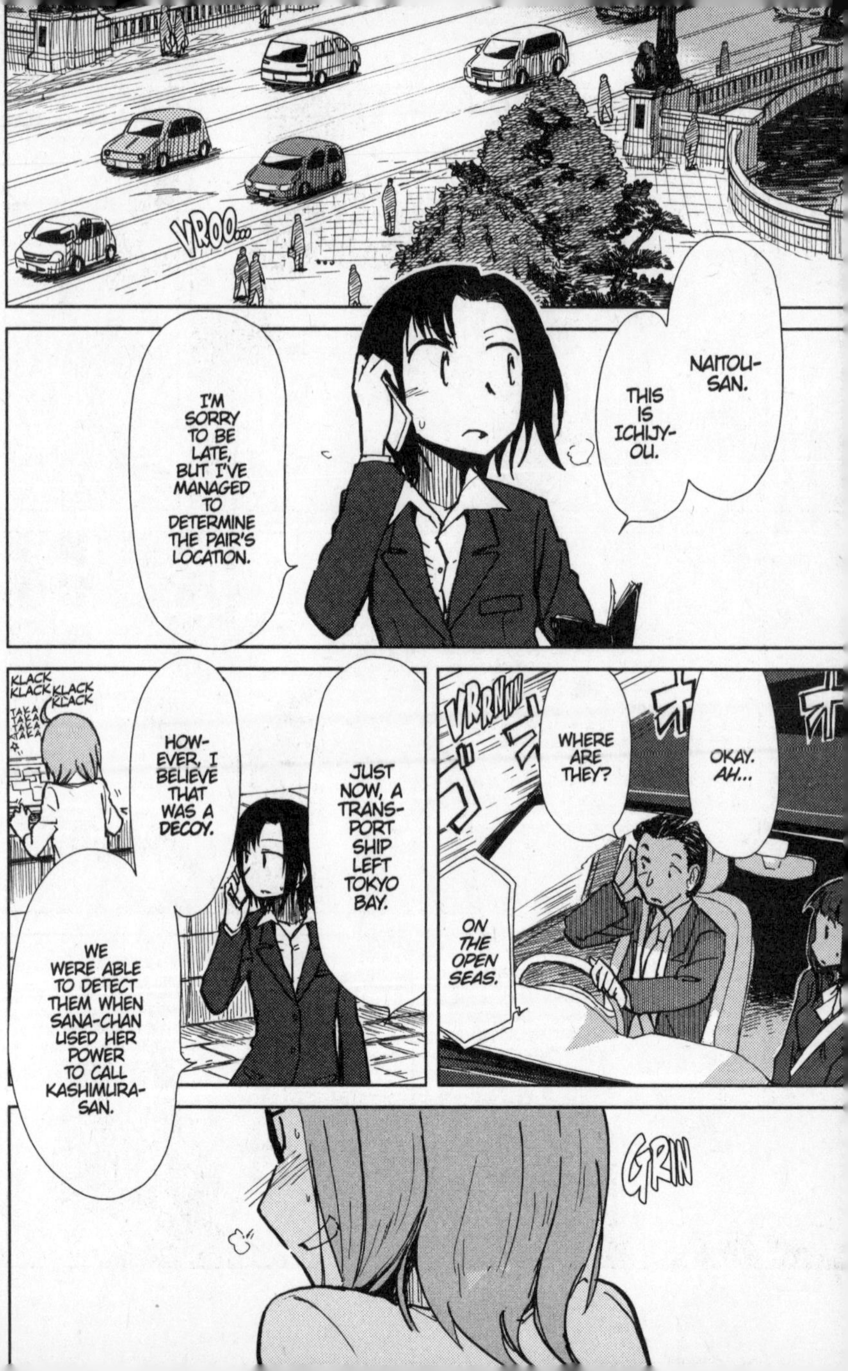
VROO...
NAITOU-SAN.
THIS IS ICHIJYOU.
I'M SORRY TO BE LATE, BUT I'VE MANAGED TO DETERMINE THE PAIR'S LOCATION.
OKAY. AH...
WHERE ARE THEY?
VRRNNN
ON THE OPEN SEAS.
JUST NOW, A TRANSPORT SHIP LEFT TOKYO BAY.
HOWEVER, I BELIEVE THAT WAS A DECOY.
KLACK KLACK KLACK KLACK
TAKA TAKA TAKA TAKA
WE WERE ABLE TO DETECT THEM WHEN SANA-CHAN USED HER POWER TO CALL KASHIMURA-SAN.
GRIN

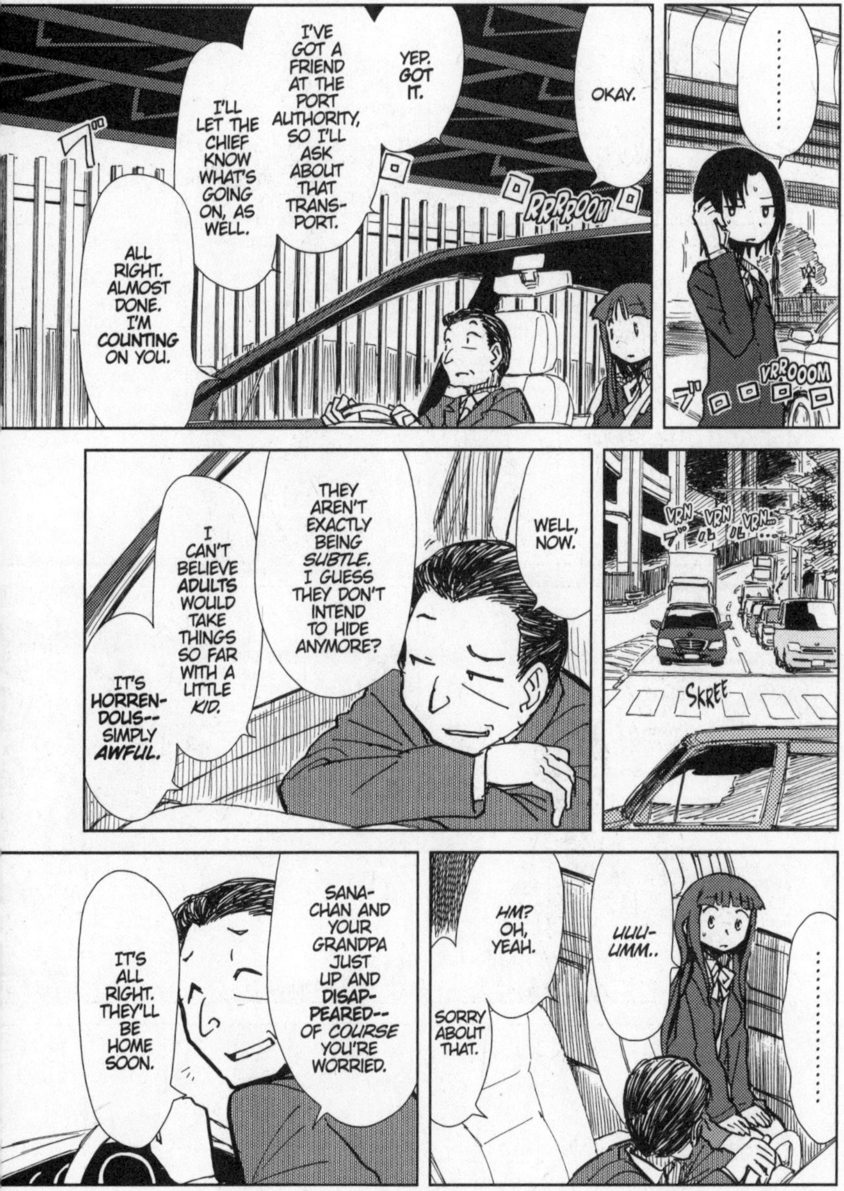

......
VRROOOM
OKAY.
YEP. GOT IT.
I'VE GOT A FRIEND AT THE PORT AUTHORITY, SO I'LL ASK ABOUT THAT TRANSPORT.
I'LL LET THE CHIEF KNOW WHAT'S GOING ON, AS WELL.
RRRROOM
ALL RIGHT. ALMOST DONE. I'M COUNTING ON YOU.
VRN VRN VRN...
SKREE
WELL, NOW.
THEY AREN'T EXACTLY BEING *SUBTLE.* I GUESS THEY DON'T INTEND TO HIDE ANYMORE?
I CAN'T BELIEVE ADULTS WOULD TAKE THINGS SO FAR WITH A LITTLE *KID.*
IT'S HORRENDOUS-- SIMPLY ***AWFUL.***
......
*UUU-UMM..*
*HM?* OH, YEAH.
SORRY ABOUT THAT.
SANA-CHAN AND YOUR GRANDPA JUST UP AND DISAPPEARED-- OF *COURSE* YOU'RE WORRIED.
IT'S ALL RIGHT. THEY'LL BE HOME SOON.

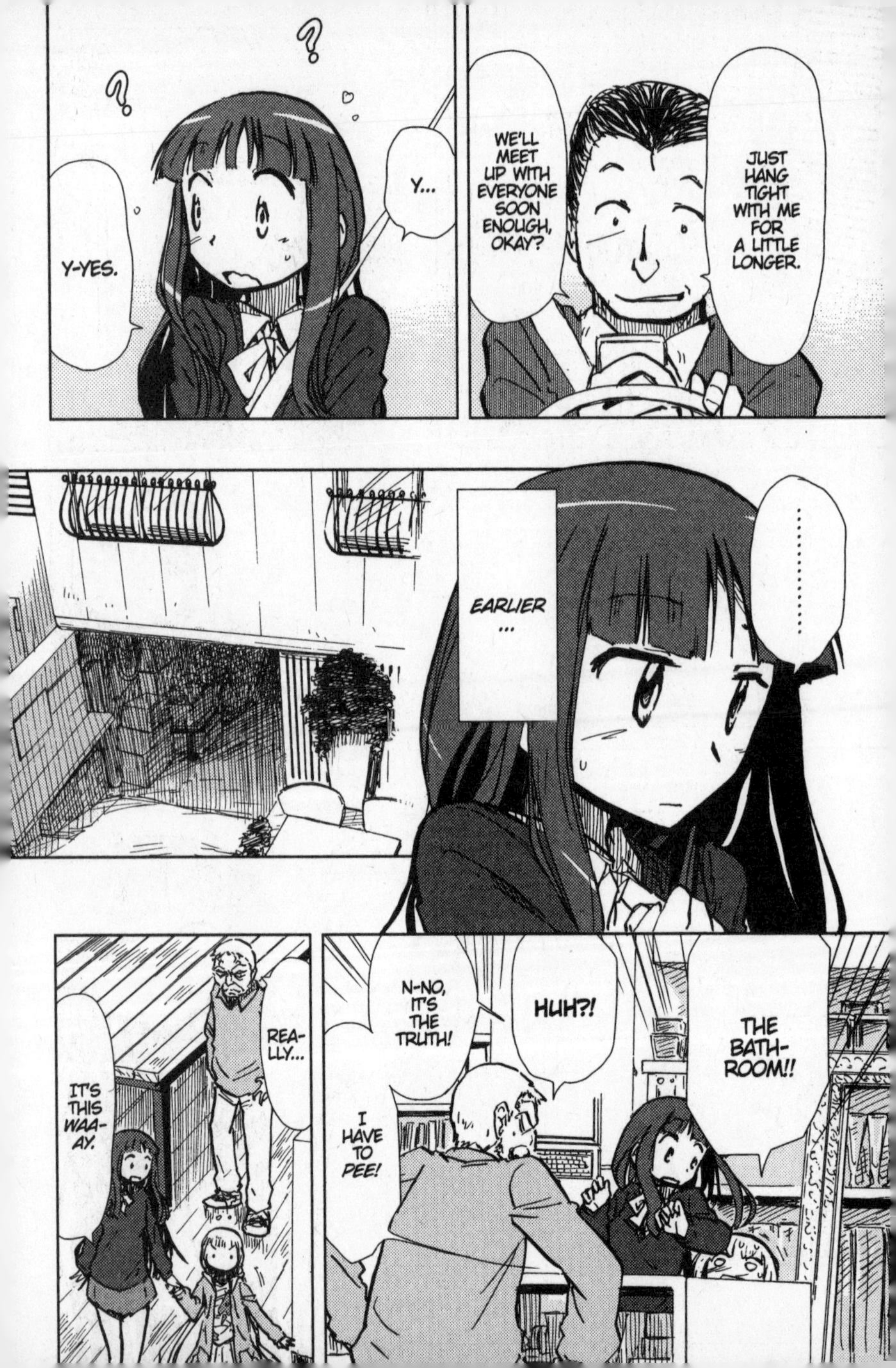
JUST HANG TIGHT WITH ME FOR A LITTLE LONGER.
WE'LL MEET UP WITH EVERYONE SOON ENOUGH, OKAY?
Y...
Y-YES.
......
EARLIER ...
THE BATH-ROOM!!
HUH?!
N-NO, IT'S THE TRUTH!
I HAVE TO PEE!
REA-LLY...
IT'S THIS WAA-AY.

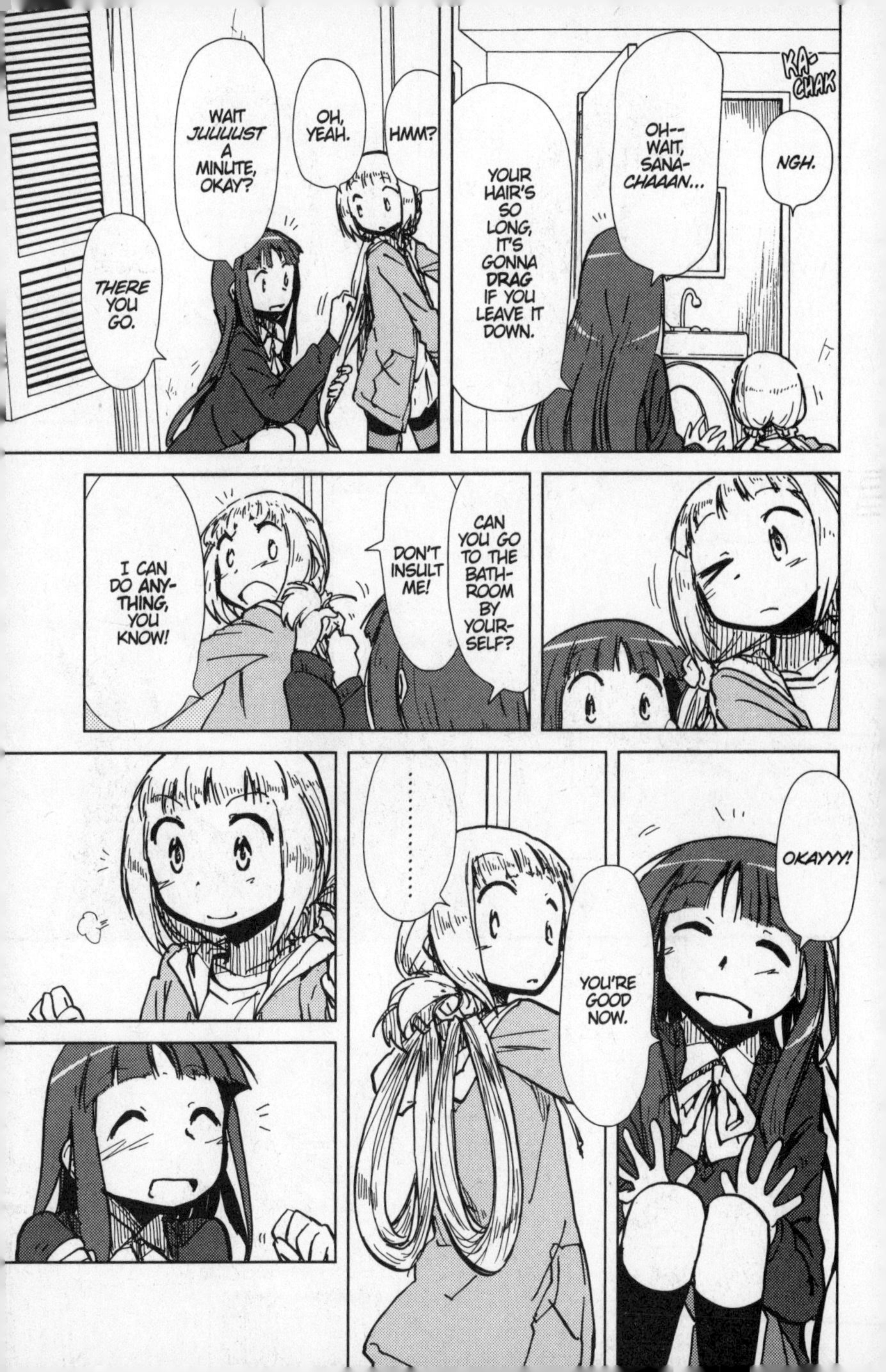
KA-CHAK
NGH.
OH-- WAIT, SANA-CHAAAN...
YOUR HAIR'S SO LONG, IT'S GONNA DRAG IF YOU LEAVE IT DOWN.
HMM?
OH, YEAH.
WAIT JUUUUST A MINUTE, OKAY?
THERE YOU GO.
CAN YOU GO TO THE BATH-ROOM BY YOUR-SELF?
DON'T INSULT ME!
I CAN DO ANY-THING, YOU KNOW!
OKAYYY!
YOU'RE GOOD NOW.
......

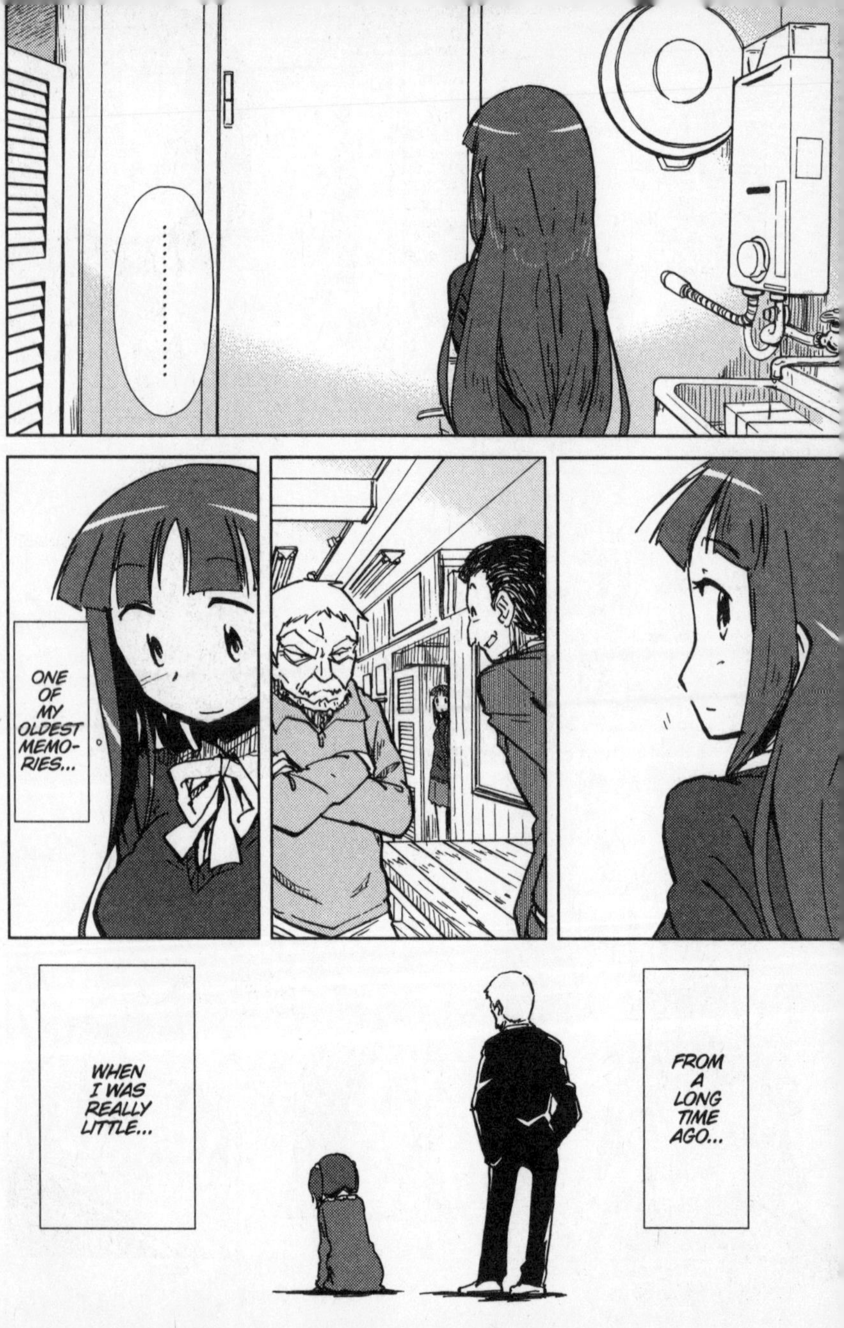
……
ONE OF MY OLDEST MEMORIES...
FROM A LONG TIME AGO...
WHEN I WAS REALLY LITTLE...

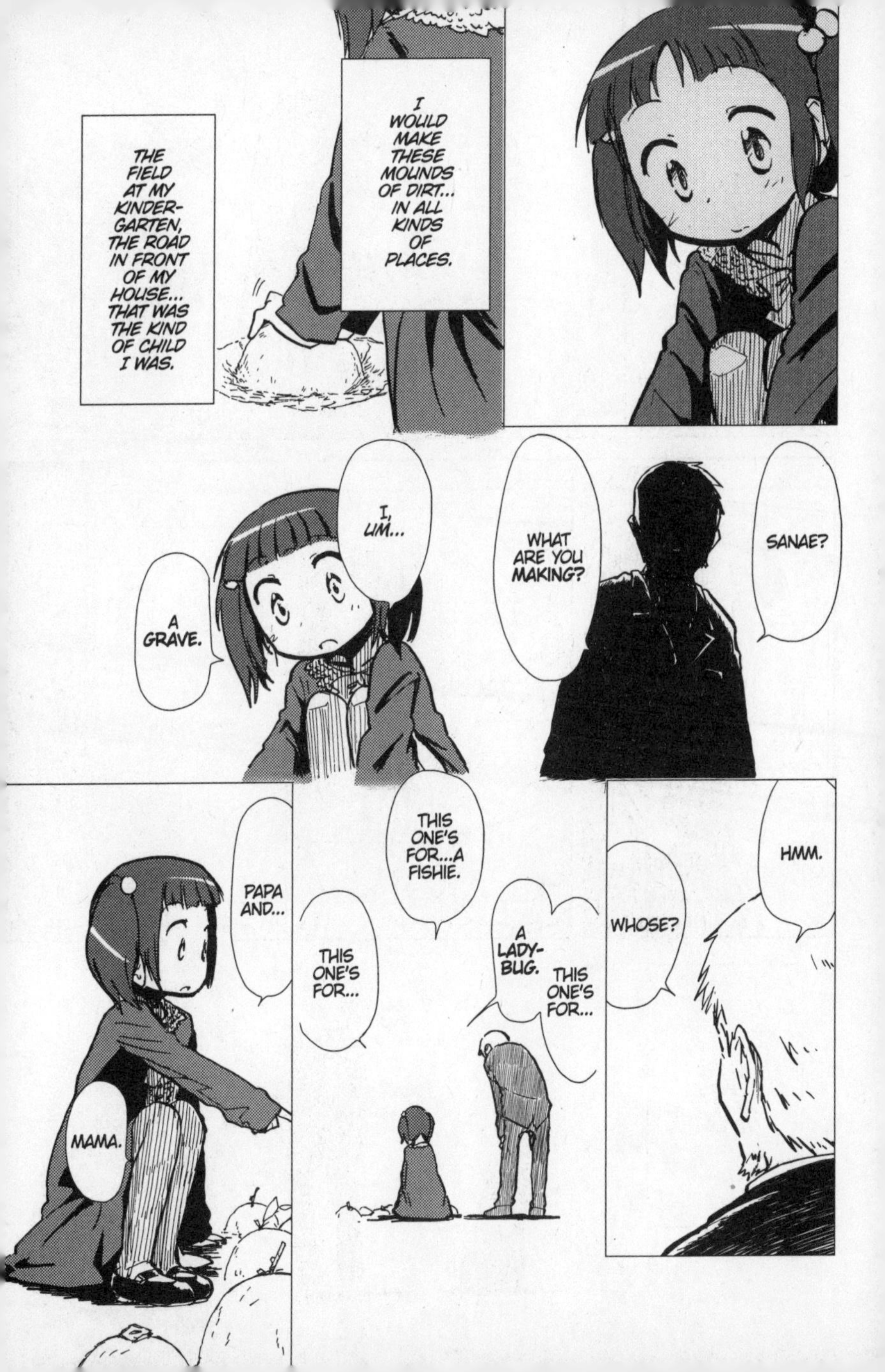
I WOULD MAKE THESE MOUNDS OF DIRT... IN ALL KINDS OF PLACES.
THE FIELD AT MY KINDER-GARTEN, THE ROAD IN FRONT OF MY HOUSE... THAT WAS THE KIND OF CHILD I WAS.
SANAE?
WHAT ARE YOU MAKING?
I, UM...
A GRAVE.
HMM.
WHOSE?
THIS ONE'S FOR...A FISHIE.
THIS ONE'S FOR...
A LADY-BUG.
THIS ONE'S FOR...
PAPA AND...
MAMA.

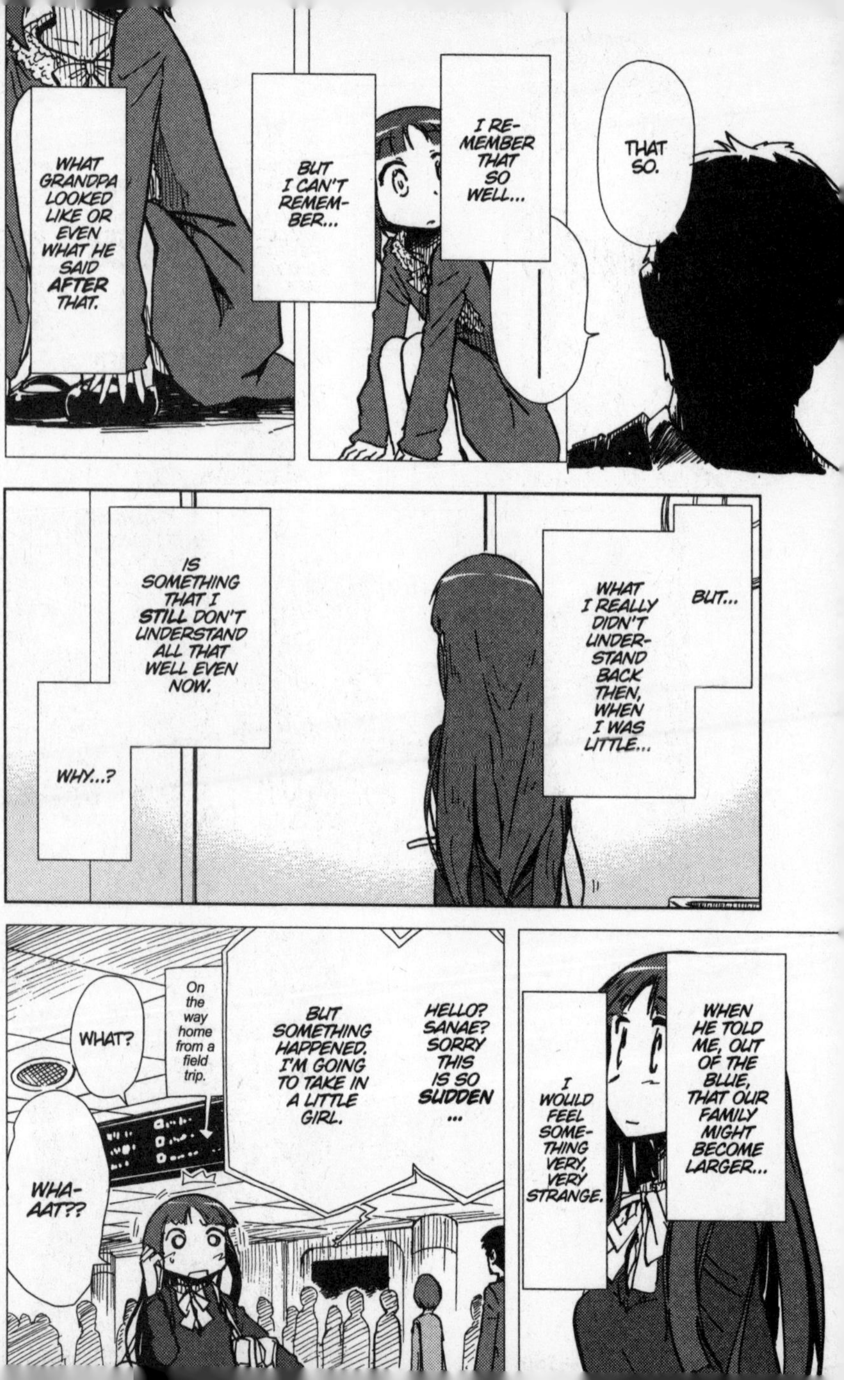
THAT SO.
—
I REMEMBER THAT SO WELL...
BUT I CAN'T REMEMBER...
WHAT GRANDPA LOOKED LIKE OR EVEN WHAT HE SAID AFTER THAT.
BUT...
WHAT I REALLY DIDN'T UNDERSTAND BACK THEN, WHEN I WAS LITTLE...
IS SOMETHING THAT I STILL DON'T UNDERSTAND ALL THAT WELL EVEN NOW.
WHY...?
WHEN HE TOLD ME, OUT OF THE BLUE, THAT OUR FAMILY MIGHT BECOME LARGER...
I WOULD FEEL SOMETHING VERY, VERY STRANGE.
HELLO? SANAE? SORRY THIS IS SO SUDDEN...
BUT SOMETHING HAPPENED. I'M GOING TO TAKE IN A LITTLE GIRL.
On the way home from a field trip.
WHAT?
WHA-AAT??

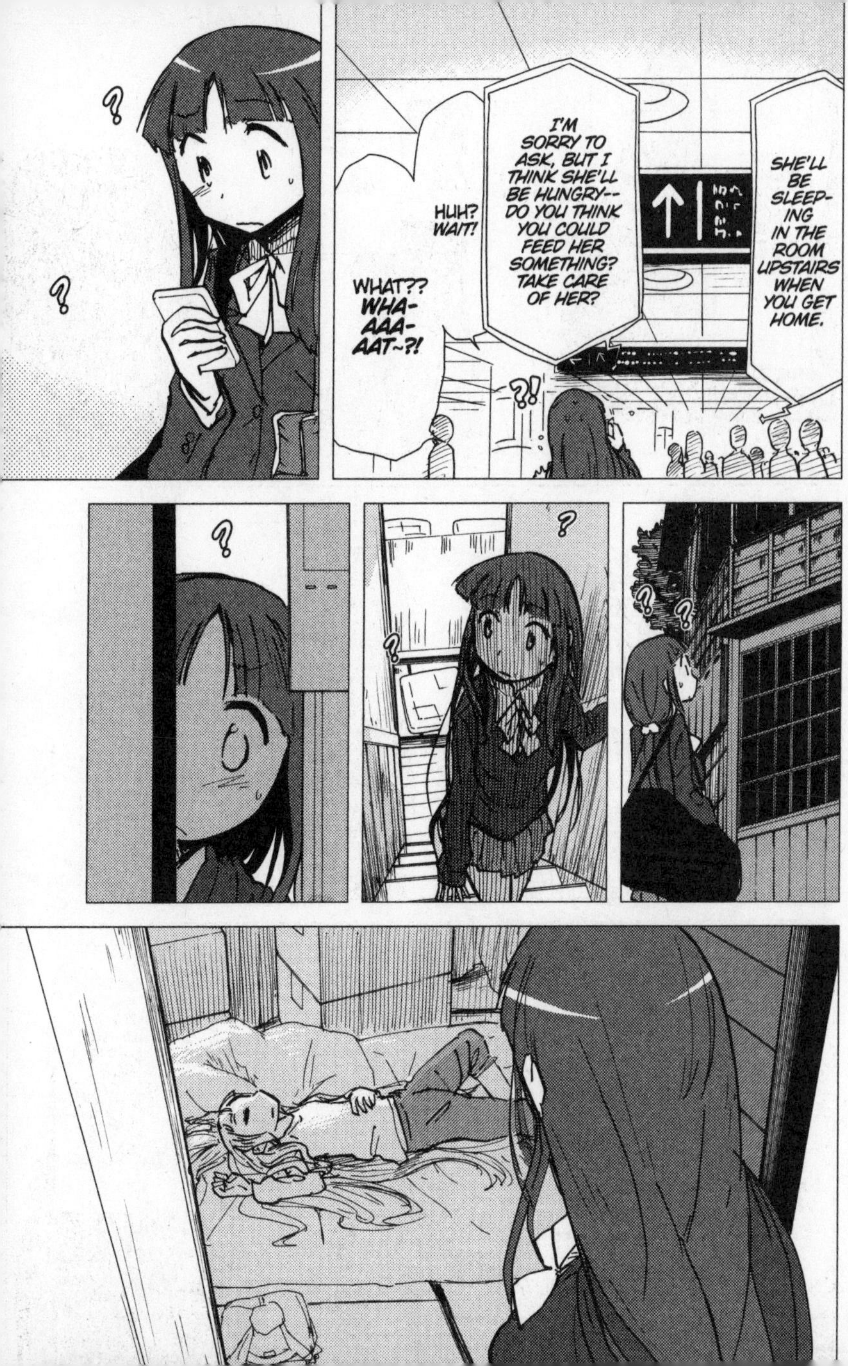
SHE'LL BE SLEEPING IN THE ROOM UPSTAIRS WHEN YOU GET HOME.
I'M SORRY TO ASK, BUT I THINK SHE'LL BE HUNGRY-- DO YOU THINK YOU COULD FEED HER SOMETHING? TAKE CARE OF HER?
HUH? WAIT!
WHAT?? WHA-AAA-AAT~?!
?!

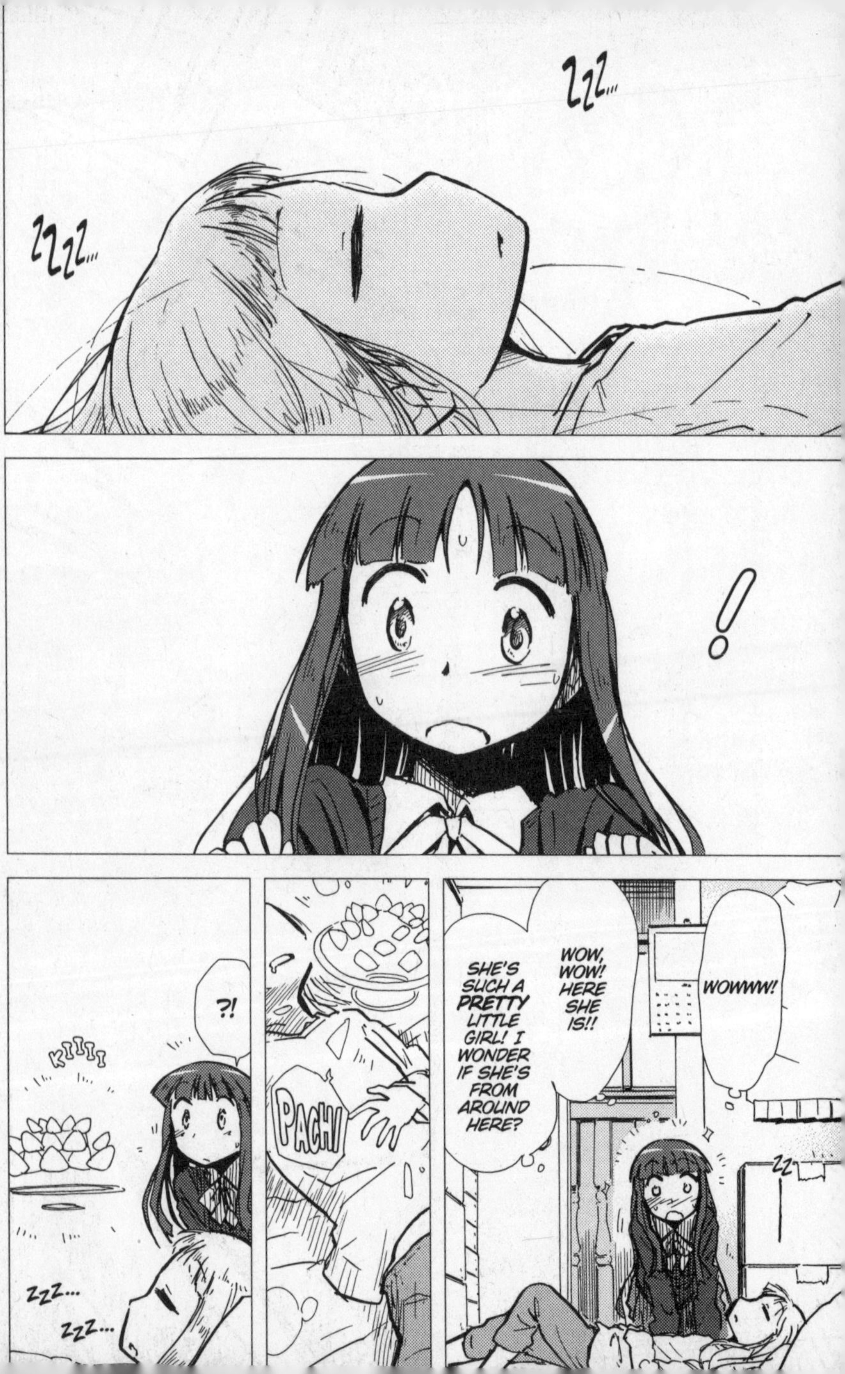
ZZZ...
ZZZZ...
!
WOWWW!
WOW, WOW! HERE SHE IS!!
SHE'S SUCH A PRETTY LITTLE GIRL! I WONDER IF SHE'S FROM AROUND HERE?
ZZ
PACHI
?!
KIIII
ZZZ...
ZZZ...

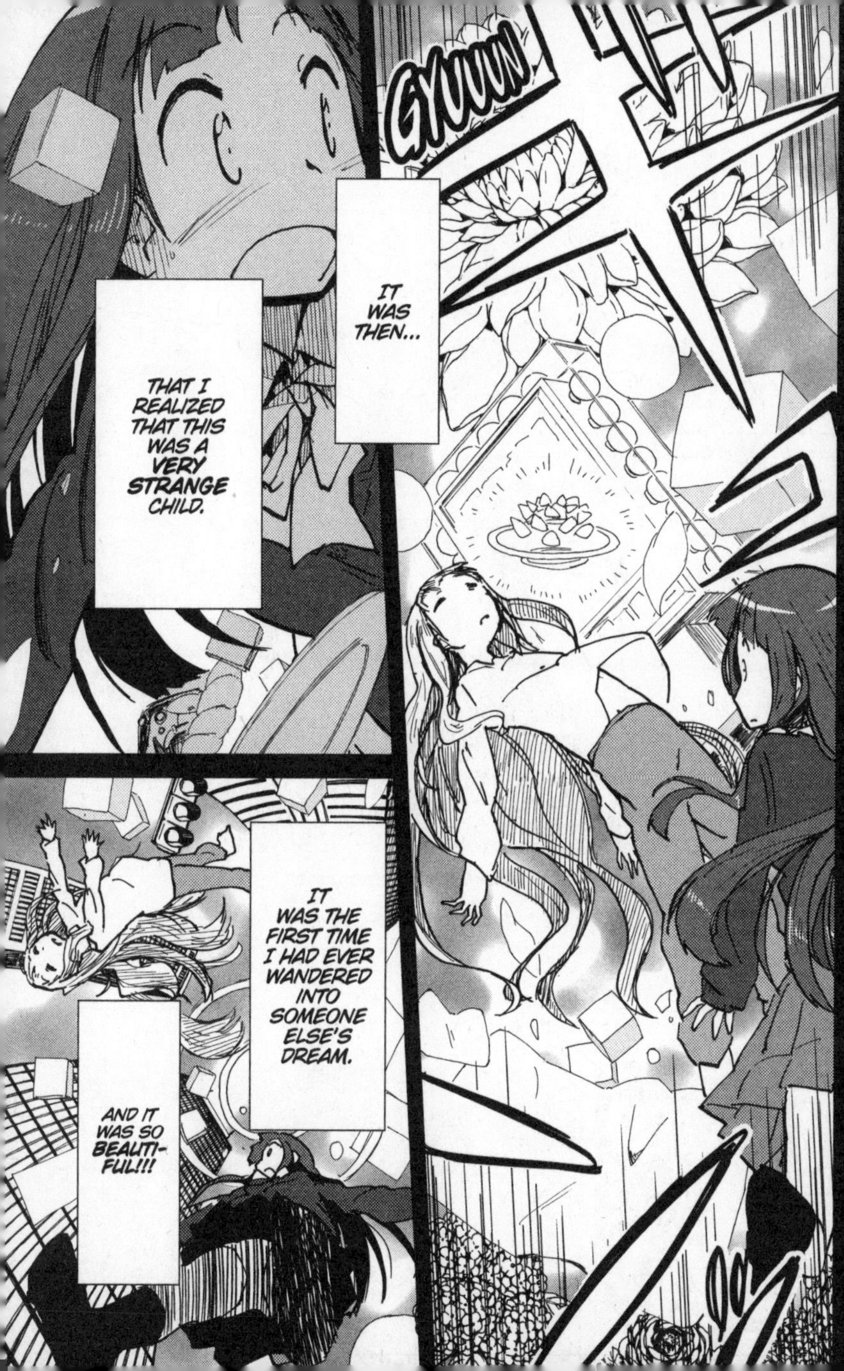
GYUUUN
IT WAS THEN...
THAT I REALIZED THAT THIS WAS A VERY STRANGE CHILD.
IT WAS THE FIRST TIME I HAD EVER WANDERED INTO SOMEONE ELSE'S DREAM.
AND IT WAS SO BEAUTI-FUL!!!

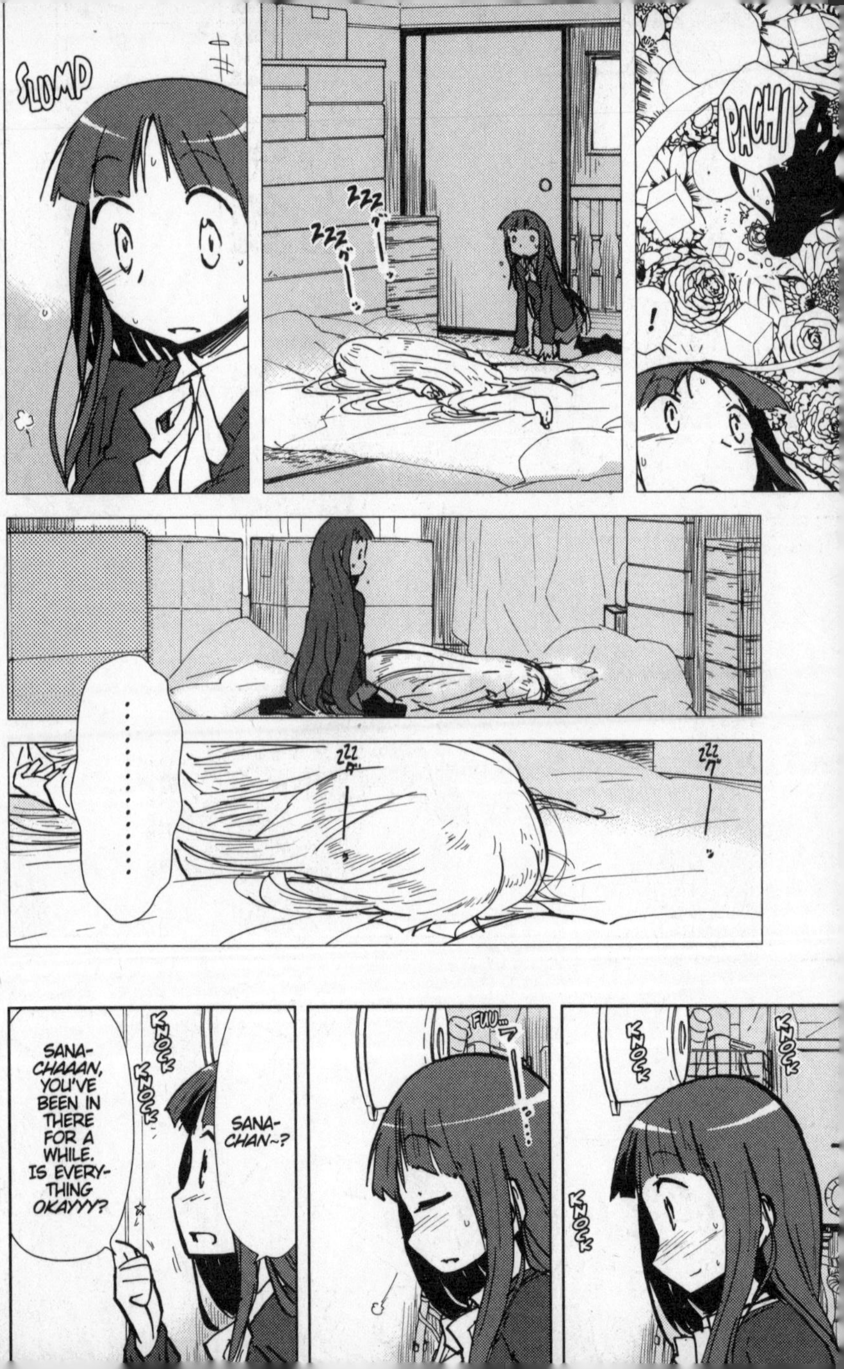
PACHI
!
ZZZ
ZZZ
SLUMP
......
ZZZ
ZZZ
KNOCK
KNOCK
KNOCK
FUU...
SANA-CHAAAN, YOU'VE BEEN IN THERE FOR A WHILE. IS EVERYTHING OKAYYY?
KNOCK
KNOCK
SANA-CHAN~?

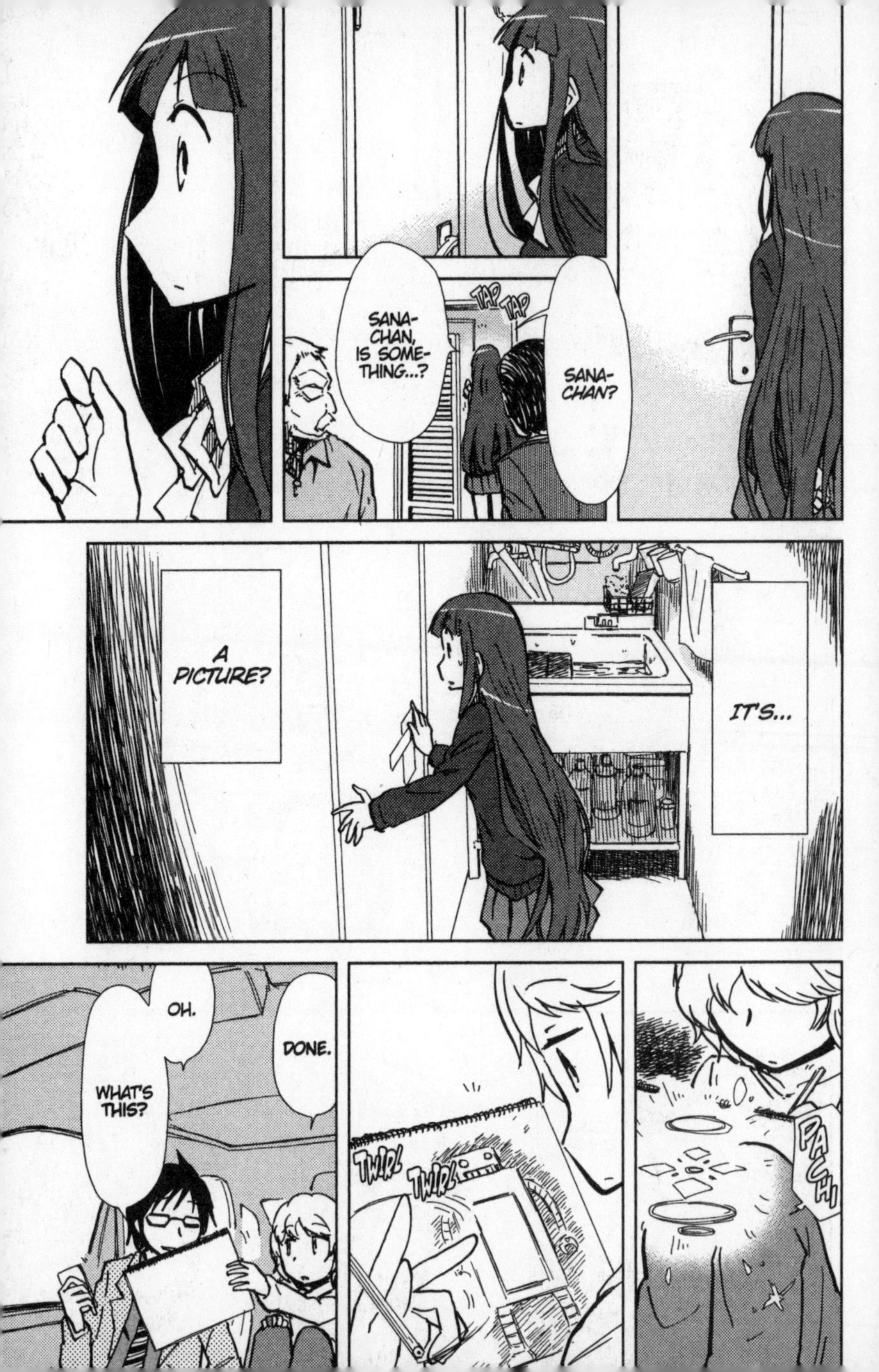
SANA-CHAN?
TAP TAP
SANA-CHAN, IS SOMETHING...?
IT'S...
A PICTURE?
PACHI
TWIRL TWIRL
DONE.
OH.
WHAT'S THIS?

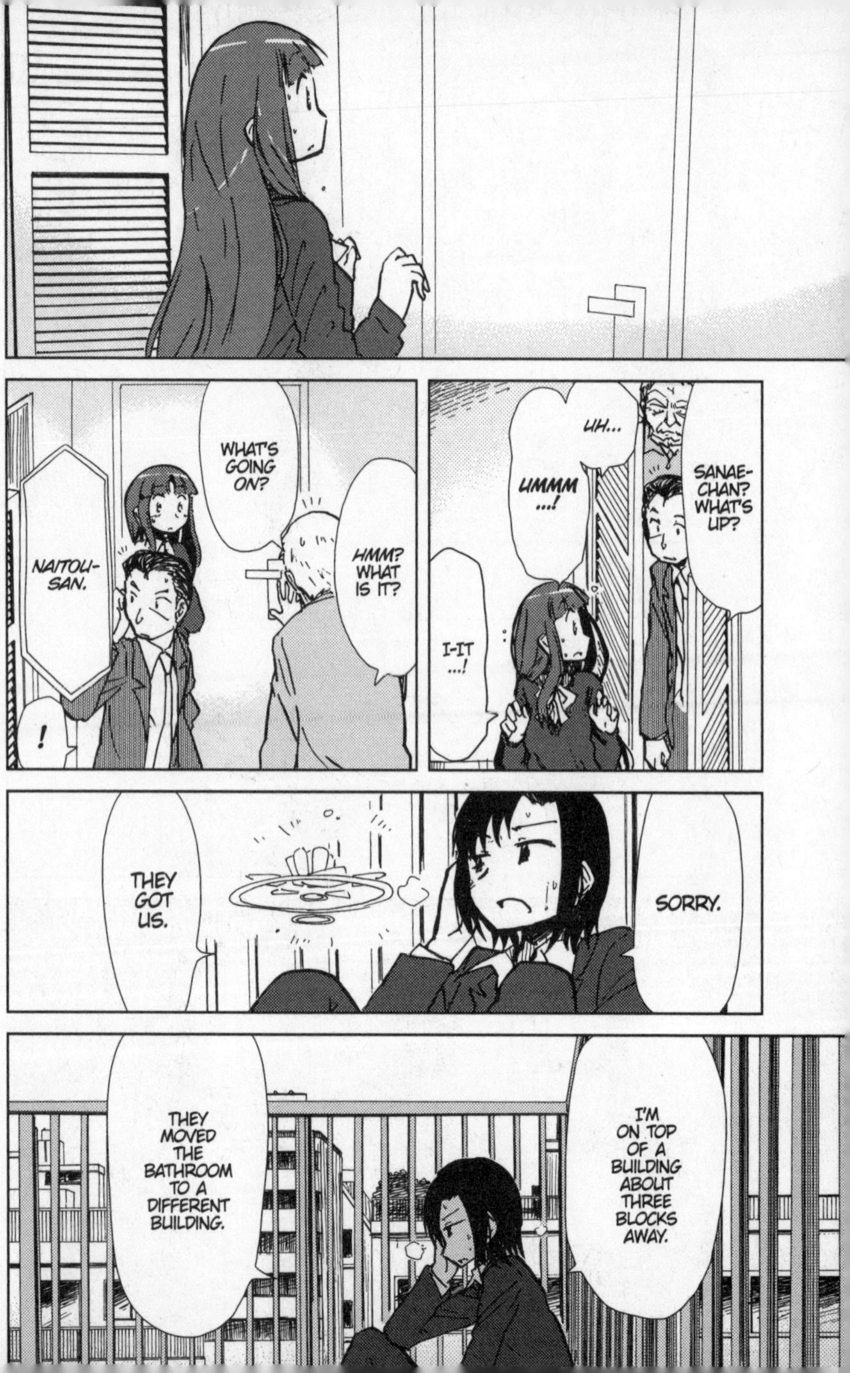
SANAE-CHAN? WHAT'S UP?
UH...
UMMM ...!
I-IT ...!
WHAT'S GOING ON?
HMM? WHAT IS IT?
NAITOU-SAN.
!
SORRY.
THEY GOT US.
I'M ON TOP OF A BUILDING ABOUT THREE BLOCKS AWAY.
THEY MOVED THE BATHROOM TO A DIFFERENT BUILDING.

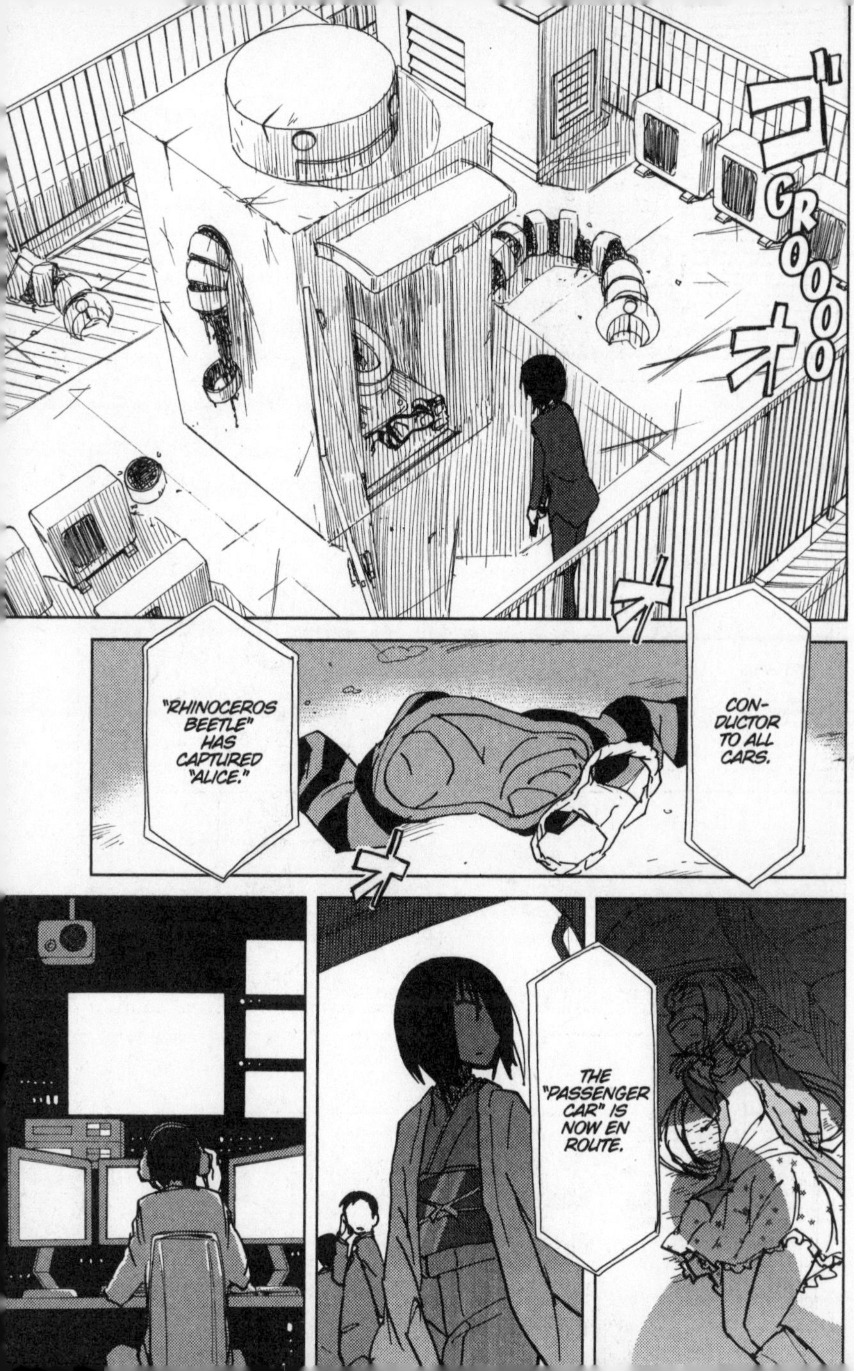
ゴ
GROOOOO
オ
CON-DUCTOR TO ALL CARS.
"RHINOCEROS BEETLE" HAS CAPTURED "ALICE."
THE "PASSENGER CAR" IS NOW EN ROUTE.

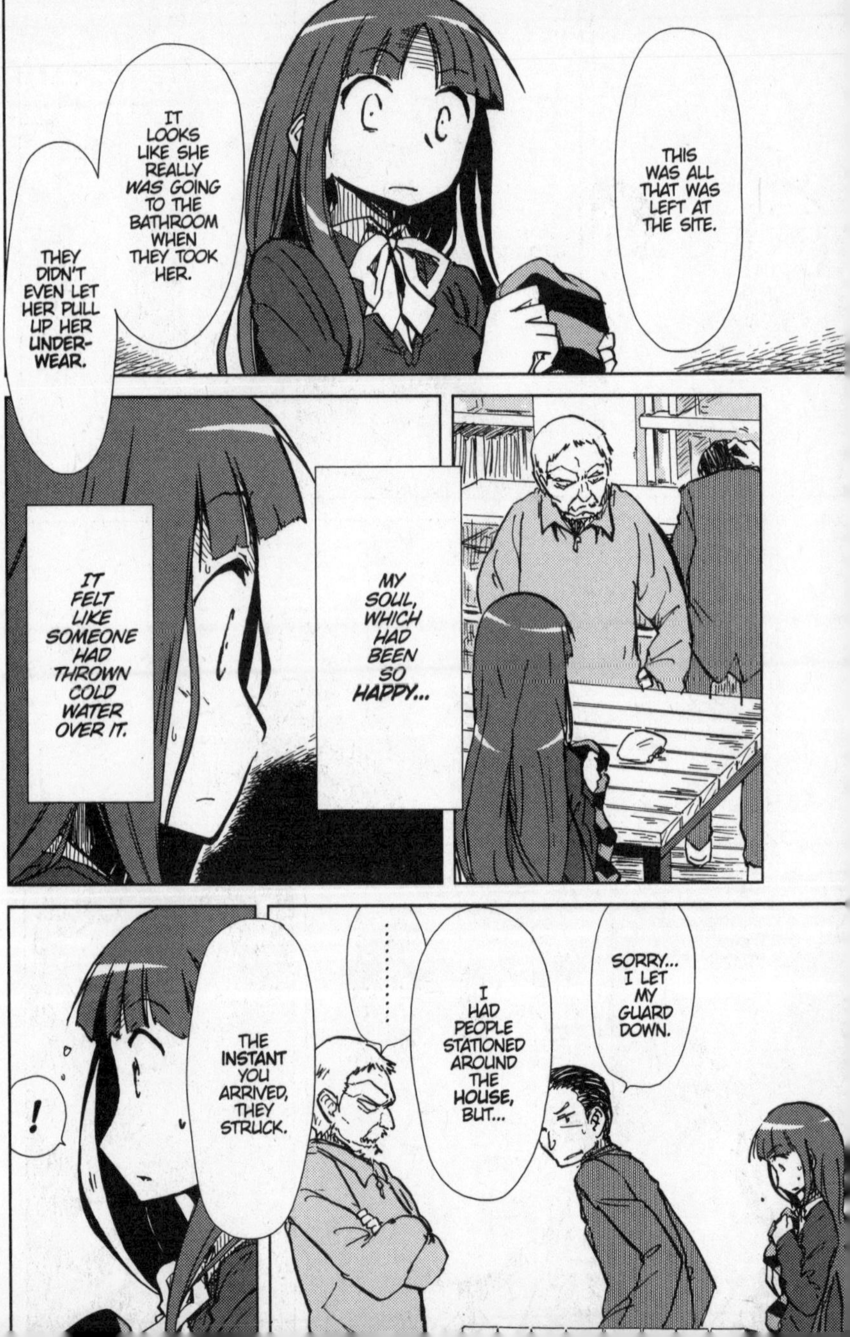
THIS WAS ALL THAT WAS LEFT AT THE SITE.
IT LOOKS LIKE SHE REALLY WAS GOING TO THE BATHROOM WHEN THEY TOOK HER.
THEY DIDN'T EVEN LET HER PULL UP HER UNDER-WEAR.
MY SOUL, WHICH HAD BEEN SO HAPPY...
IT FELT LIKE SOMEONE HAD THROWN COLD WATER OVER IT.
SORRY... I LET MY GUARD DOWN.
I HAD PEOPLE STATIONED AROUND THE HOUSE, BUT...
......
THE INSTANT YOU ARRIVED, THEY STRUCK.
!

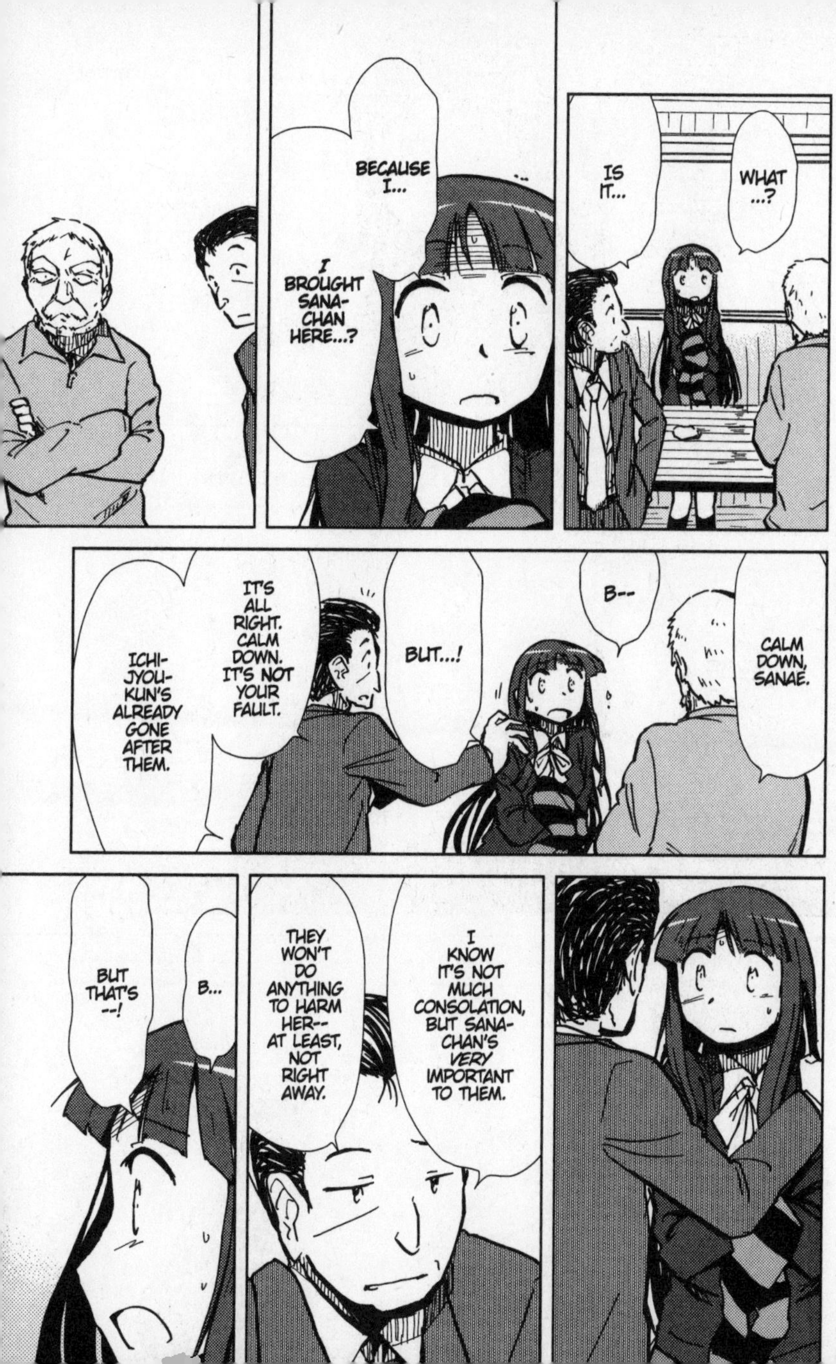
WHAT ...?
IS IT...
BECAUSE I...
I BROUGHT SANA-CHAN HERE...?
CALM DOWN, SANAE.
B--
BUT...!
IT'S ALL RIGHT. CALM DOWN. IT'S NOT YOUR FAULT.
ICHIJYOU-KUN'S ALREADY GONE AFTER THEM.
I KNOW IT'S NOT MUCH CONSOLATION, BUT SANA-CHAN'S *VERY* IMPORTANT TO THEM.
THEY WON'T DO ANYTHING TO HARM HER-- AT LEAST, NOT RIGHT AWAY.
B...
BUT THAT'S --!

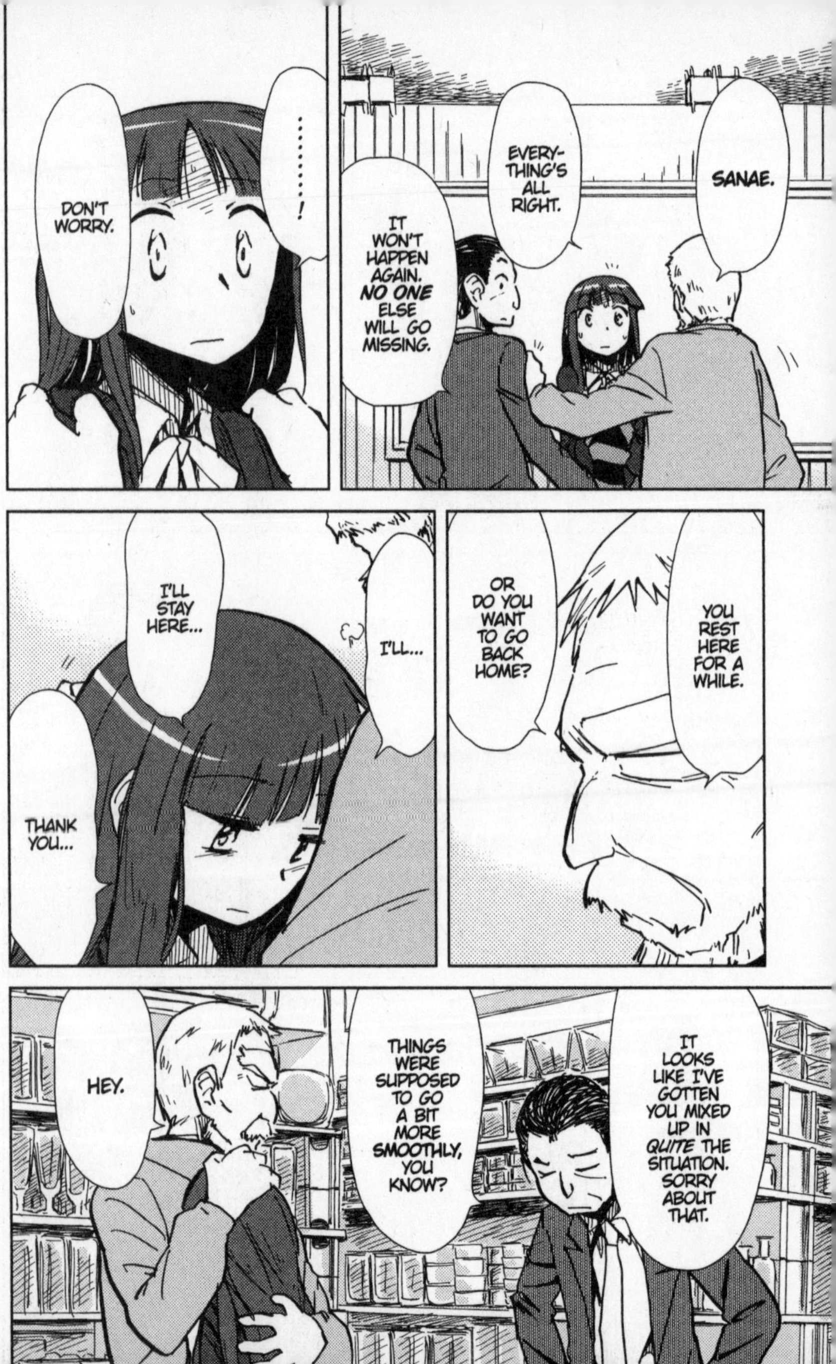
SANAE.
EVERY-THING'S ALL RIGHT.
IT WON'T HAPPEN AGAIN. *NO ONE* ELSE WILL GO MISSING.
......!
DON'T WORRY.
YOU REST HERE FOR A WHILE.
OR DO YOU WANT TO GO BACK HOME?
I'LL...
I'LL STAY HERE...
THANK YOU...
IT LOOKS LIKE I'VE GOTTEN YOU MIXED UP IN *QUITE* THE SITUATION. SORRY ABOUT THAT.
THINGS WERE SUPPOSED TO GO A BIT MORE SMOOTHLY, YOU KNOW?
HEY.

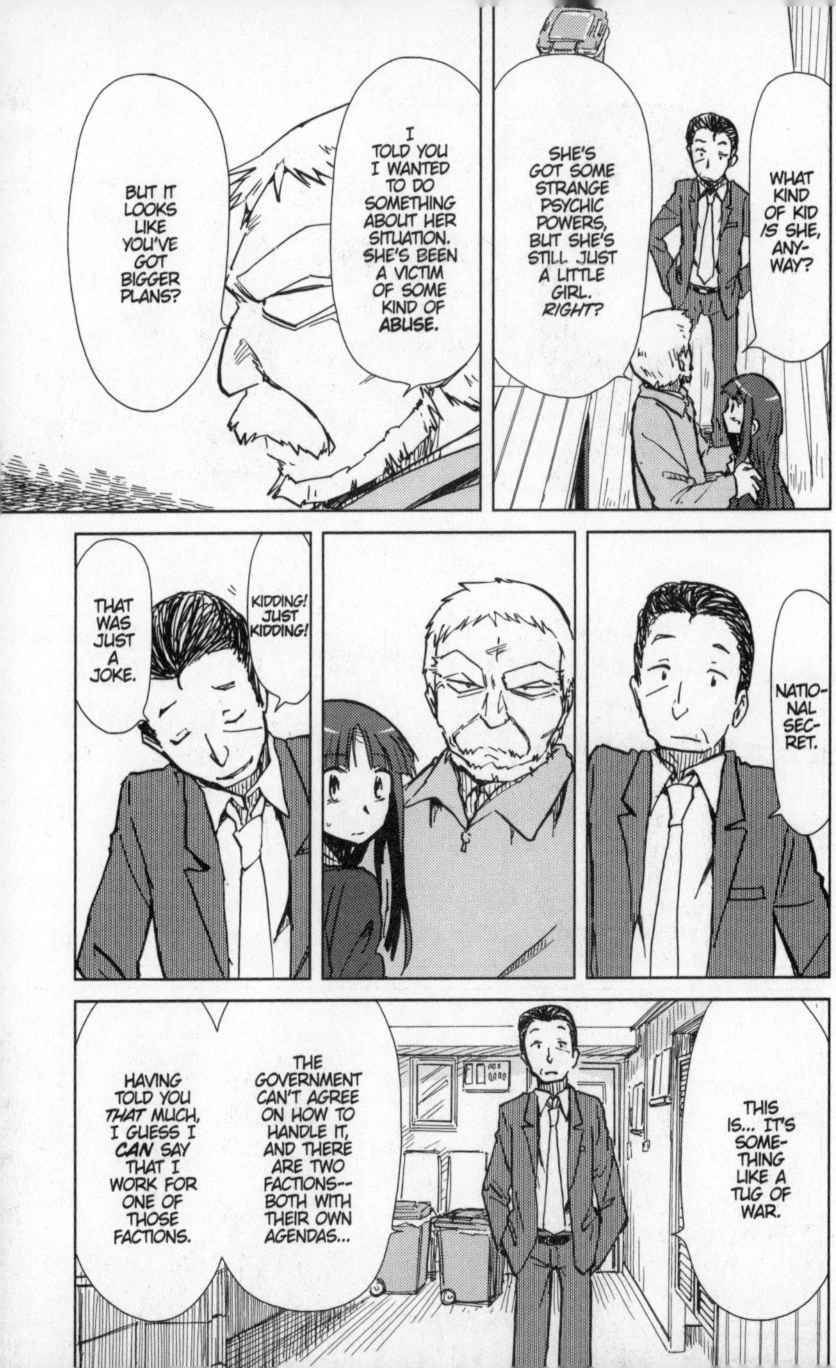
WHAT KIND OF KID *IS* SHE, ANYWAY?
SHE'S GOT SOME STRANGE PSYCHIC POWERS, BUT SHE'S STILL JUST A LITTLE GIRL. *RIGHT?*
I TOLD YOU I WANTED TO DO SOMETHING ABOUT HER SITUATION. SHE'S BEEN A VICTIM OF SOME KIND OF **ABUSE.**
BUT IT LOOKS LIKE YOU'VE GOT BIGGER PLANS?
NATIONAL SECRET.
KIDDING! JUST KIDDING!
THAT WAS JUST A JOKE.
THIS IS... IT'S SOMETHING LIKE A TUG OF WAR.
THE GOVERNMENT CAN'T AGREE ON HOW TO HANDLE IT, AND THERE ARE TWO FACTIONS--BOTH WITH THEIR OWN AGENDAS...
HAVING TOLD YOU *THAT* MUCH, I GUESS I ***CAN*** SAY THAT I WORK FOR ONE OF THOSE FACTIONS.

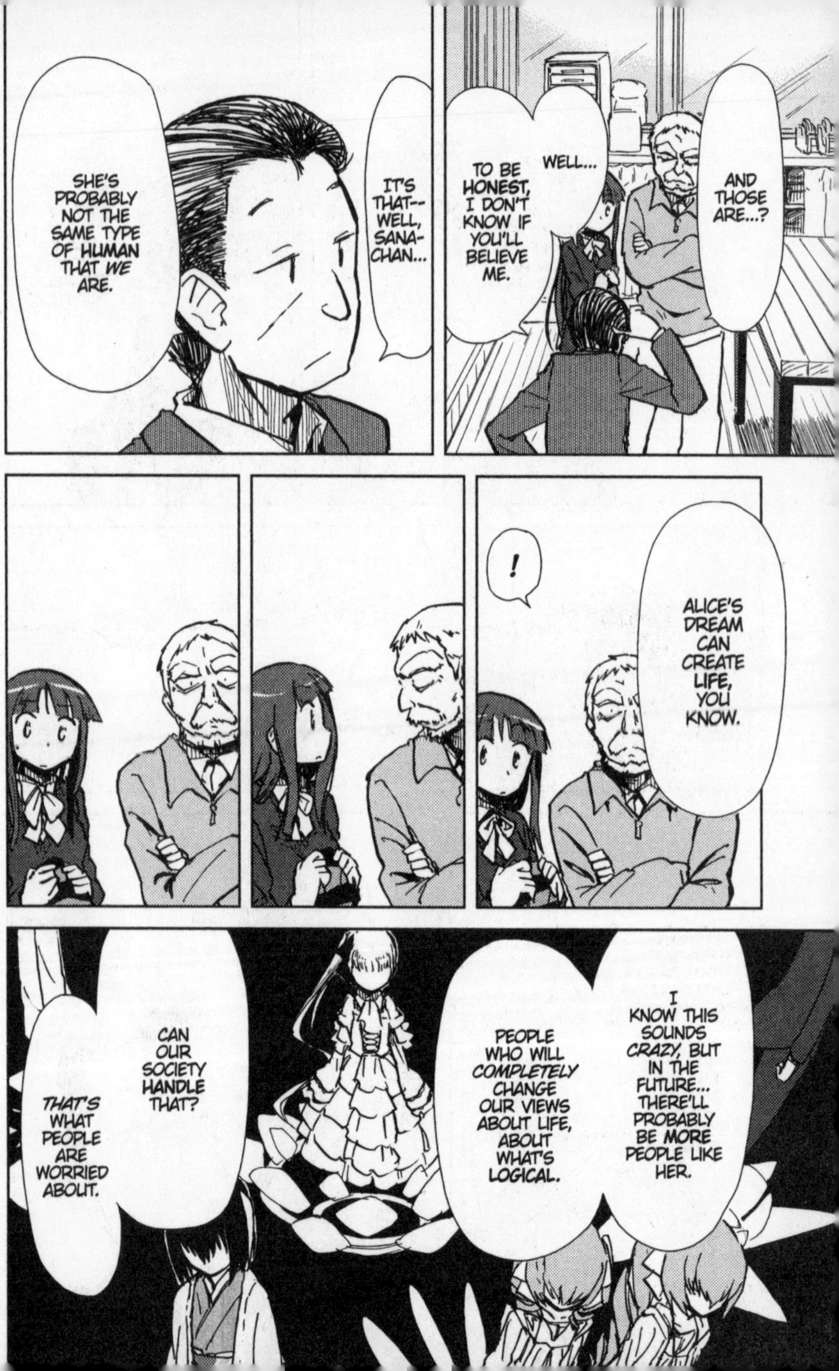
AND THOSE ARE...?
WELL...
TO BE HONEST, I DON'T KNOW IF YOU'LL BELIEVE ME.
IT'S THAT-- WELL, SANA-CHAN...
SHE'S PROBABLY NOT THE SAME TYPE OF HUMAN THAT *WE* ARE.
ALICE'S DREAM CAN CREATE LIFE, YOU KNOW.
!
I KNOW THIS SOUNDS *CRAZY*, BUT IN THE FUTURE... THERE'LL PROBABLY BE *MORE* PEOPLE LIKE HER.
PEOPLE WHO WILL *COMPLETELY* CHANGE OUR VIEWS ABOUT LIFE, ABOUT WHAT'S LOGICAL.
CAN OUR SOCIETY HANDLE THAT?
*THAT'S* WHAT PEOPLE ARE WORRIED ABOUT.

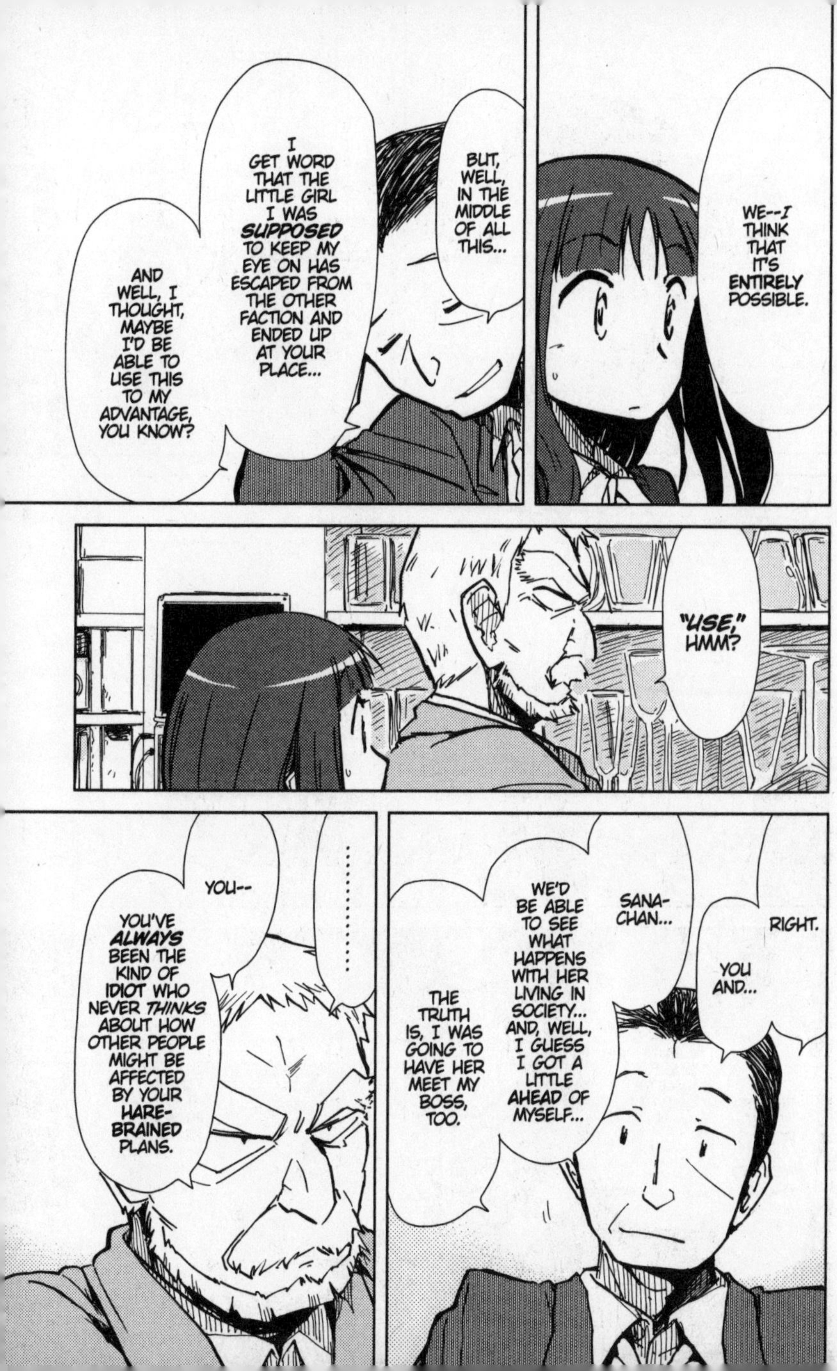
WE--*I* THINK THAT IT'S ENTIRELY POSSIBLE.
BUT, WELL, IN THE MIDDLE OF ALL THIS...
I GET WORD THAT THE LITTLE GIRL I WAS ***SUPPOSED*** TO KEEP MY EYE ON HAS ESCAPED FROM THE OTHER FACTION AND ENDED UP AT YOUR PLACE...
AND WELL, I THOUGHT, MAYBE I'D BE ABLE TO USE THIS TO MY ADVANTAGE, YOU KNOW?
***"USE,"*** HMM?
RIGHT.
YOU AND...
SANA-CHAN...
WE'D BE ABLE TO SEE WHAT HAPPENS WITH HER LIVING IN SOCIETY... AND, WELL, I GUESS I GOT A LITTLE AHEAD OF MYSELF...
THE TRUTH IS, I WAS GOING TO HAVE HER MEET MY BOSS, TOO.
......
YOU--
YOU'VE ***ALWAYS*** BEEN THE KIND OF IDIOT WHO NEVER *THINKS* ABOUT HOW OTHER PEOPLE MIGHT BE AFFECTED BY YOUR HARE-BRAINED PLANS.

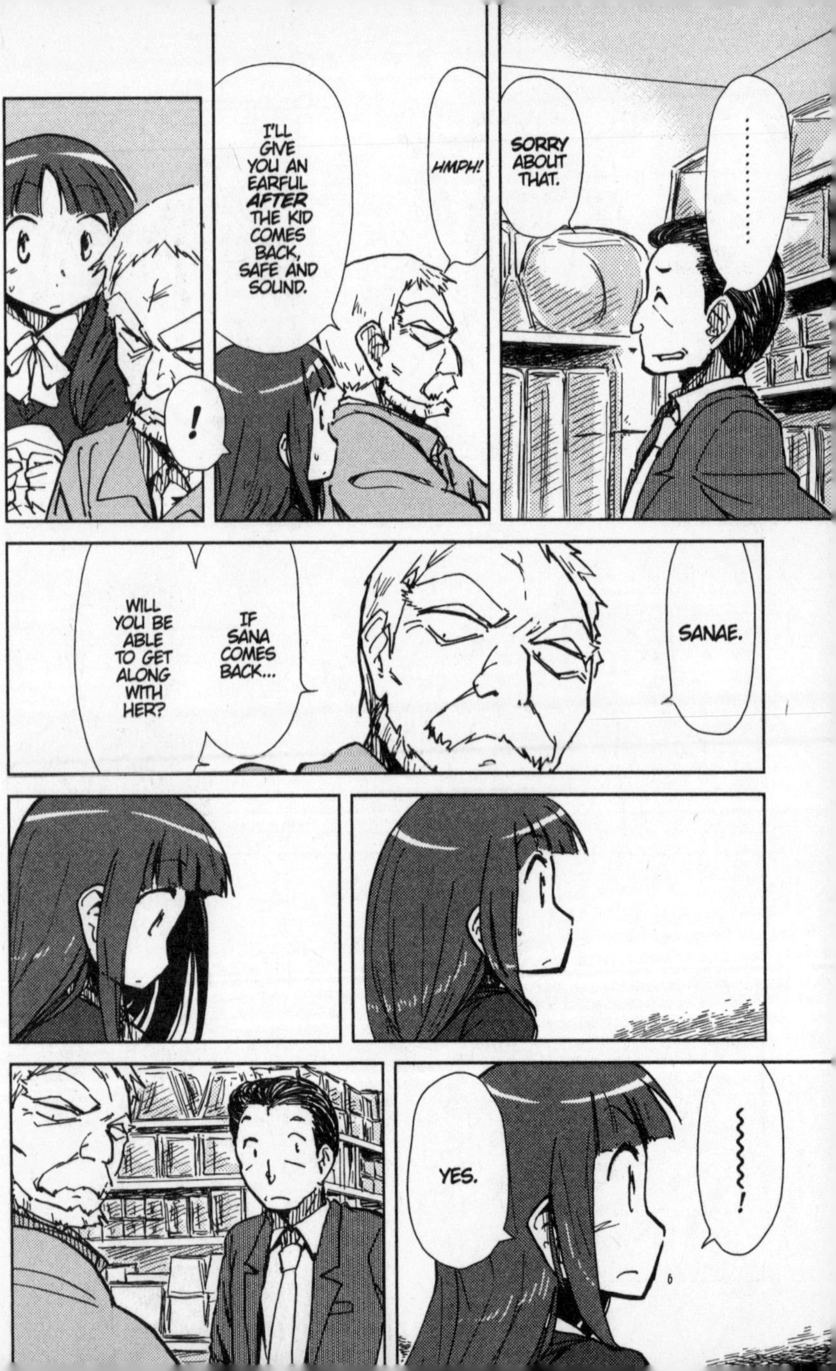
......
SORRY ABOUT THAT.
HMPH!
I'LL GIVE YOU AN EARFUL ***AFTER*** THE KID COMES BACK, SAFE AND SOUND.
!
SANAE.
IF SANA COMES BACK...
WILL YOU BE ABLE TO GET ALONG WITH HER?
YES.

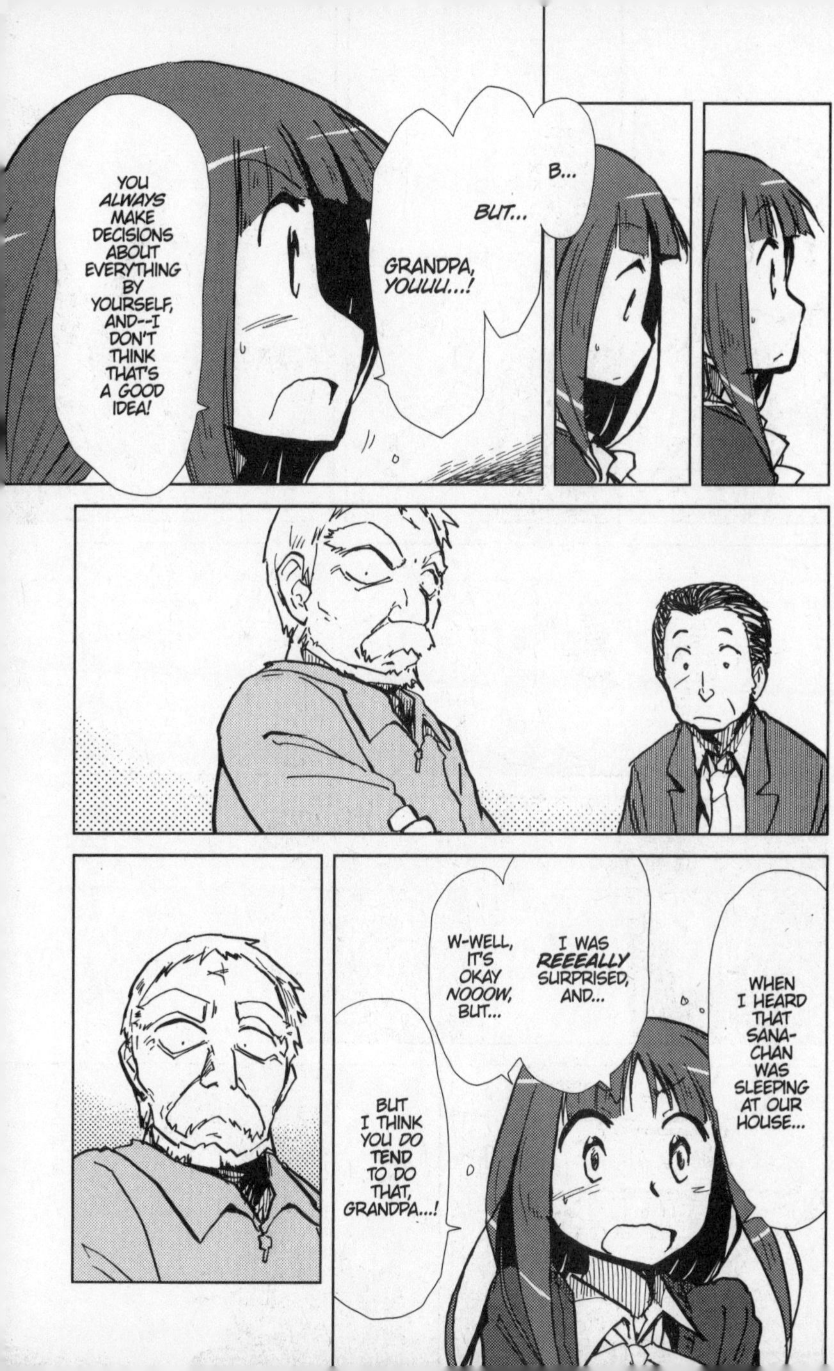
B...
BUT...
GRANDPA, YOUUU...!
YOU ALWAYS MAKE DECISIONS ABOUT EVERYTHING BY YOURSELF, AND--I DON'T THINK THAT'S A GOOD IDEA!
WHEN I HEARD THAT SANA-CHAN WAS SLEEPING AT OUR HOUSE...
I WAS REEEALLY SURPRISED, AND...
W-WELL, IT'S OKAY NOOOW, BUT...
BUT I THINK YOU DO TEND TO DO THAT, GRANDPA...!

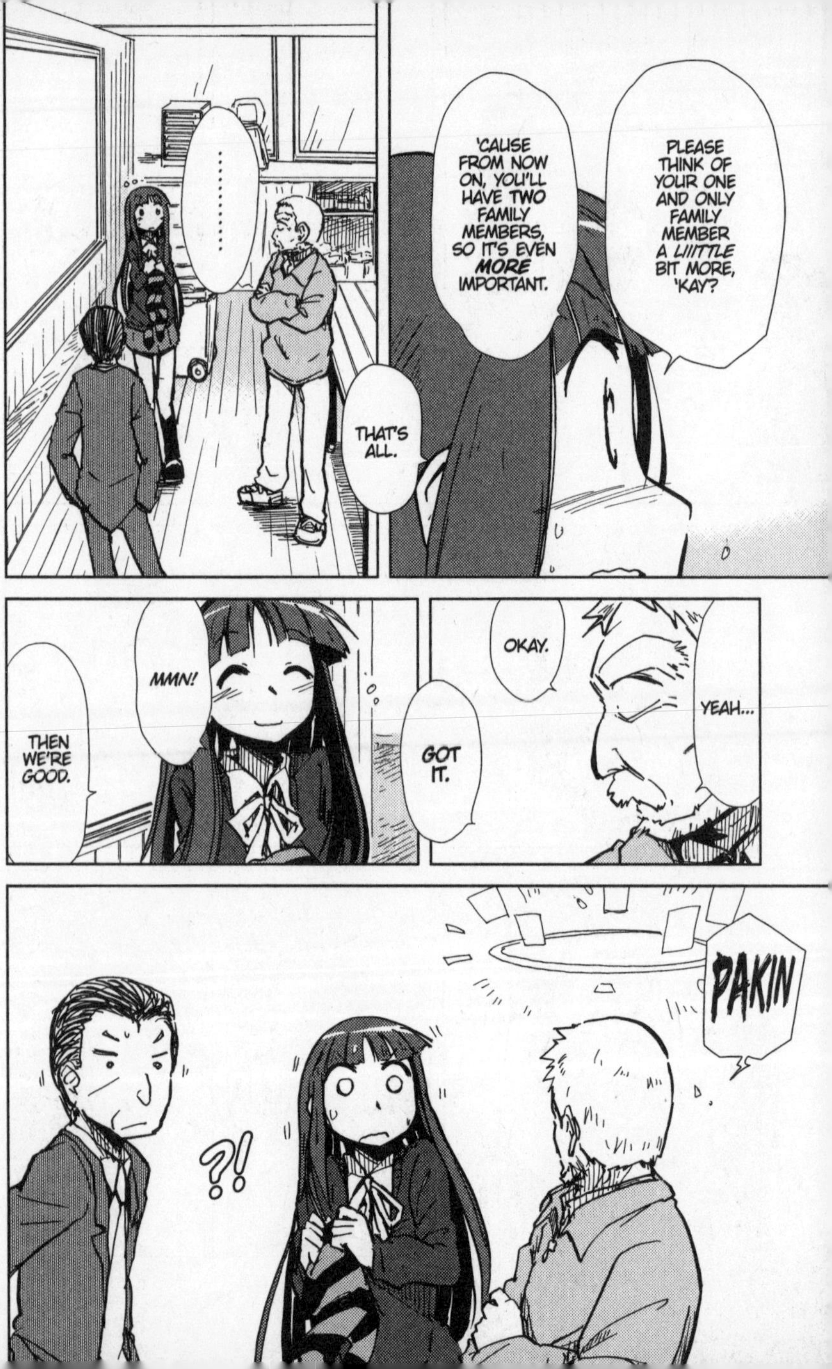
PLEASE THINK OF YOUR ONE AND ONLY FAMILY MEMBER A LIIIITTLE BIT MORE, 'KAY?
'CAUSE FROM NOW ON, YOU'LL HAVE TWO FAMILY MEMBERS, SO IT'S EVEN MORE IMPORTANT.
THAT'S ALL.
......
YEAH...
OKAY.
GOT IT.
MMN!
THEN WE'RE GOOD.
PAKIN
?!

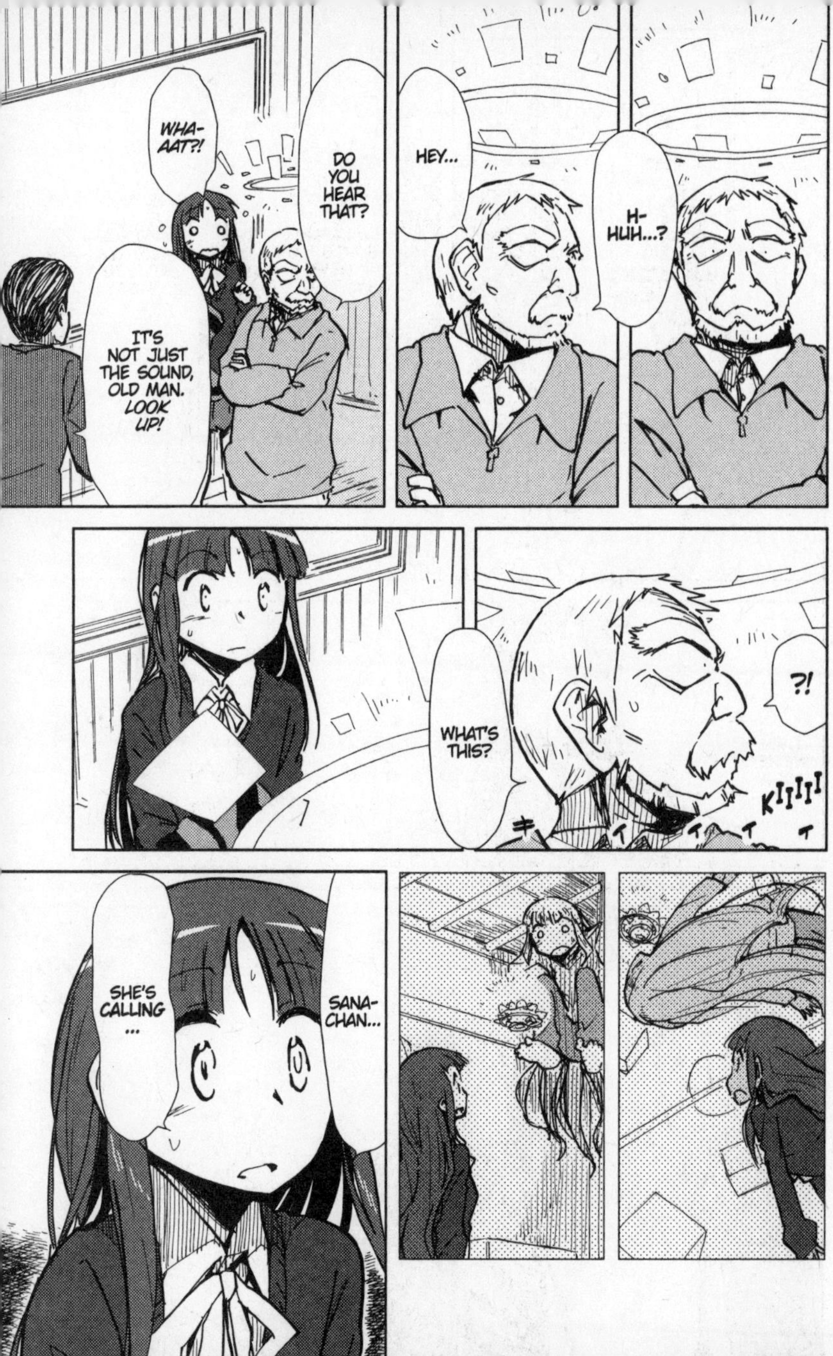
H-HUH...?
HEY...
DO YOU HEAR THAT?
WHA-AAT?!
IT'S NOT JUST THE SOUND, OLD MAN. LOOK UP!
?!
WHAT'S THIS?
KIIIII
SANA-CHAN...
SHE'S CALLING ...

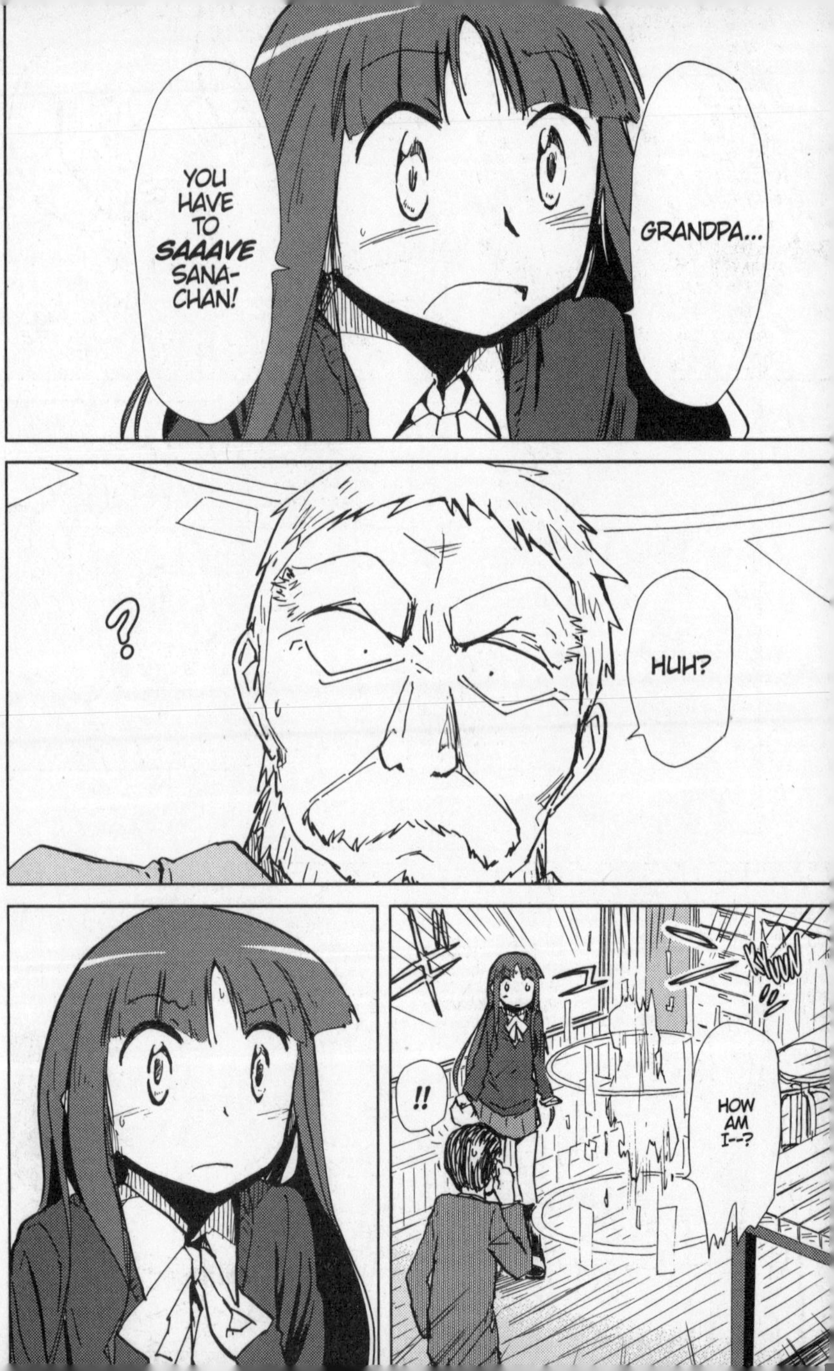
GRANDPA...
YOU HAVE TO SAAAVE SANA-CHAN!
HUH?
?
KYUUN
HOW AM I--?
!!

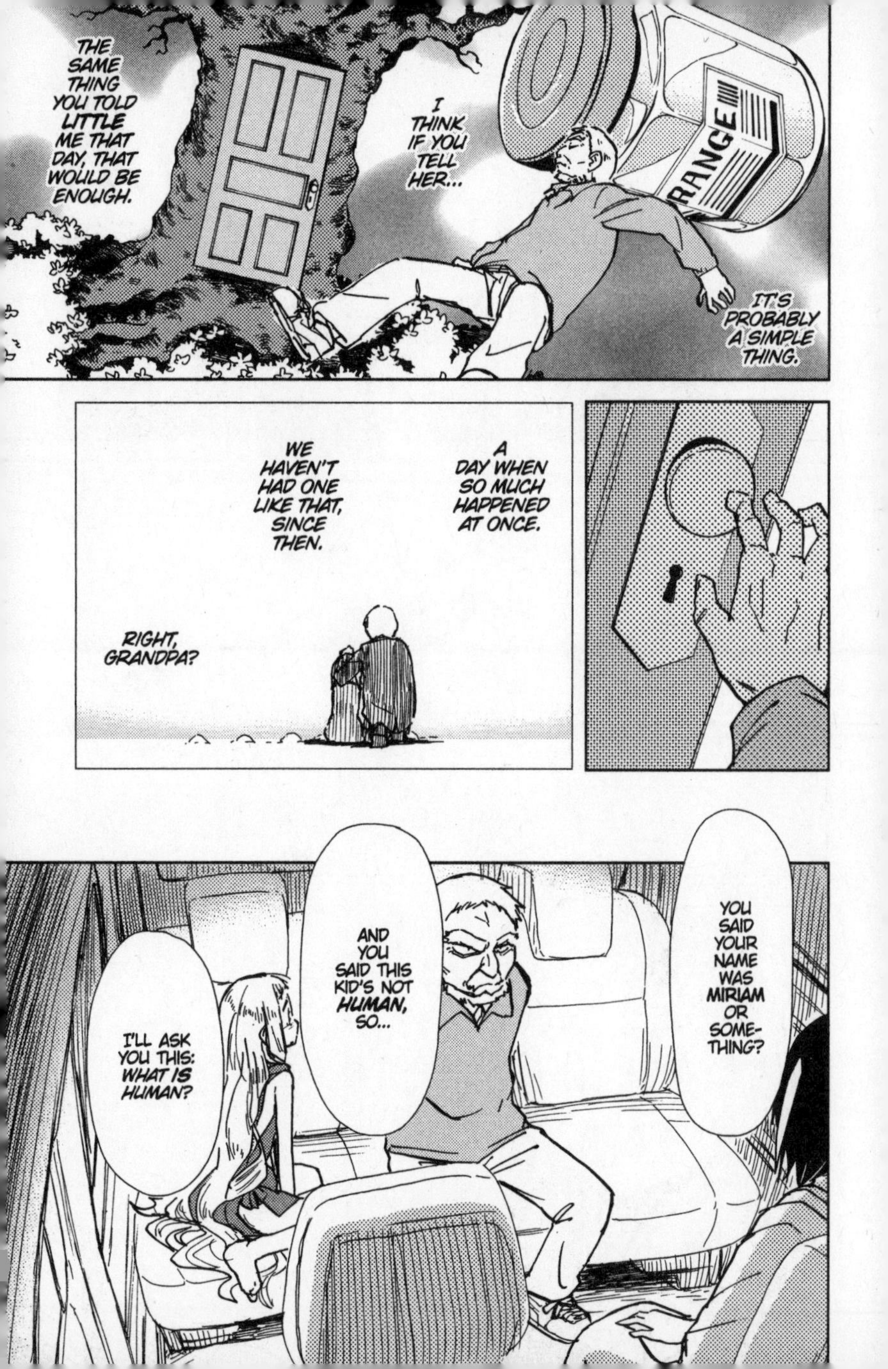
I THINK IF YOU TELL HER...
THE SAME THING YOU TOLD *LITTLE* ME THAT DAY, THAT WOULD BE ENOUGH.
IT'S PROBABLY A SIMPLE THING.
A DAY WHEN SO MUCH HAPPENED AT ONCE.
WE HAVEN'T HAD ONE LIKE THAT, SINCE THEN.
RIGHT, GRANDPA?
YOU SAID YOUR NAME WAS MIRIAM OR SOME-THING?
AND YOU SAID THIS KID'S NOT *HUMAN*, SO...
I'LL ASK YOU THIS: *WHAT IS HUMAN?*

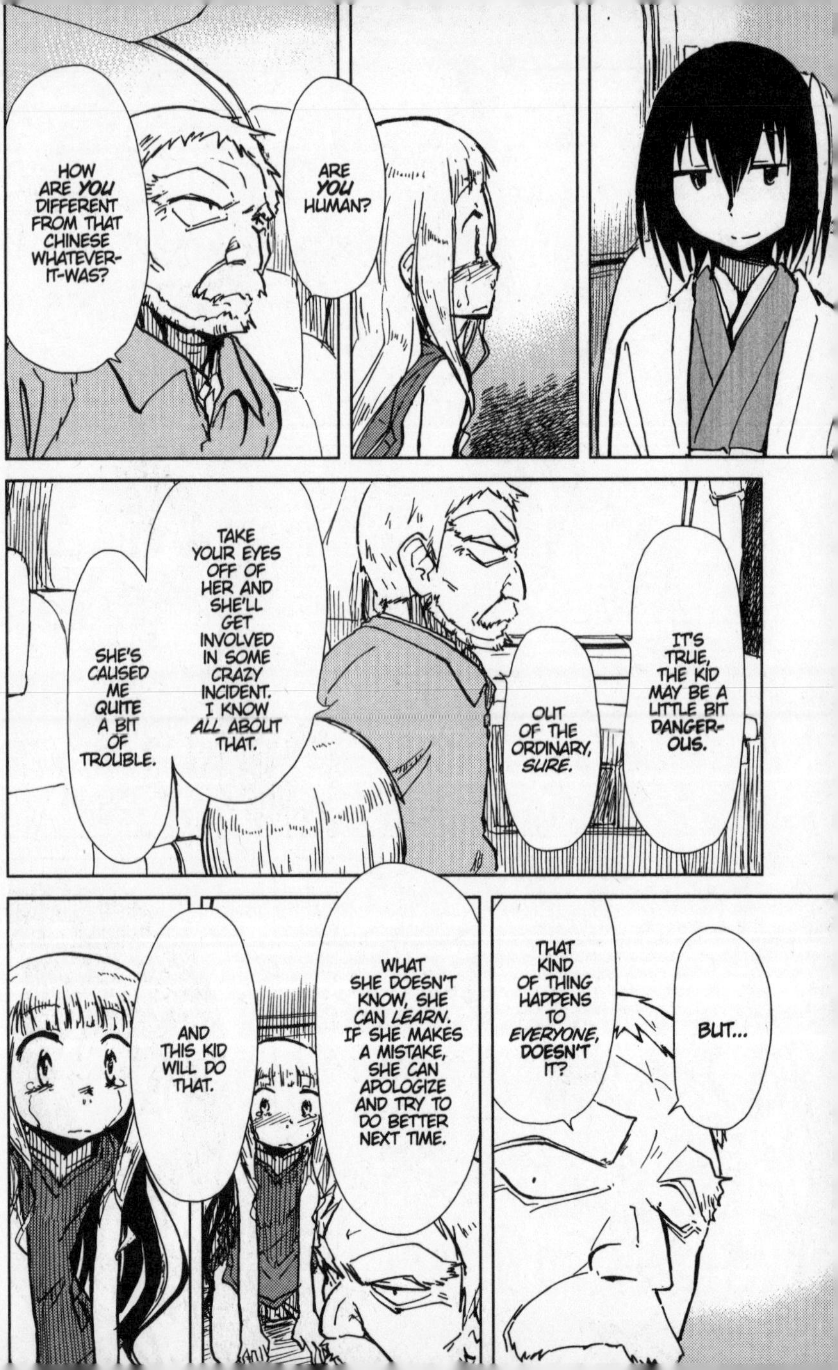
ARE YOU HUMAN?
HOW ARE YOU DIFFERENT FROM THAT CHINESE WHATEVER-IT-WAS?
IT'S TRUE, THE KID MAY BE A LITTLE BIT DANGER-OUS.
OUT OF THE ORDINARY, SURE.
TAKE YOUR EYES OFF OF HER AND SHE'LL GET INVOLVED IN SOME CRAZY INCIDENT. I KNOW ALL ABOUT THAT.
SHE'S CAUSED ME QUITE A BIT OF TROUBLE.
BUT...
THAT KIND OF THING HAPPENS TO EVERYONE, DOESN'T IT?
WHAT SHE DOESN'T KNOW, SHE CAN LEARN. IF SHE MAKES A MISTAKE, SHE CAN APOLOGIZE AND TRY TO DO BETTER NEXT TIME.
AND THIS KID WILL DO THAT.

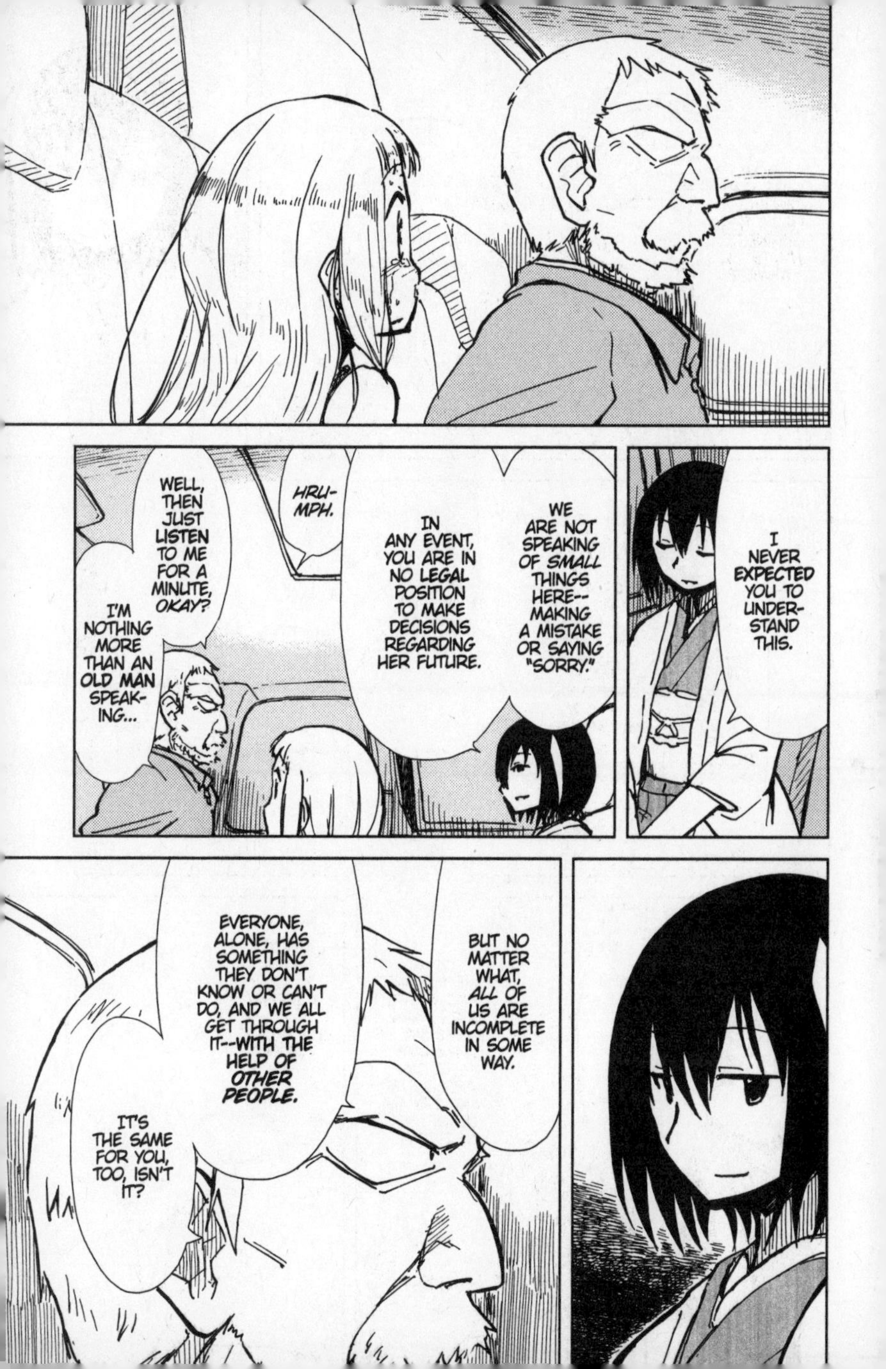
I NEVER EXPECTED YOU TO UNDER-STAND THIS.
WE ARE NOT SPEAKING OF *SMALL* THINGS HERE--MAKING A MISTAKE OR SAYING "SORRY."
IN ANY EVENT, YOU ARE IN NO LEGAL POSITION TO MAKE DECISIONS REGARDING HER FUTURE.
*HRU-MPH.*
WELL, THEN JUST LISTEN TO ME FOR A MINUTE, *OKAY?*
I'M NOTHING MORE THAN AN OLD MAN SPEAKING...
BUT NO MATTER WHAT, *ALL* OF US ARE INCOMPLETE IN SOME WAY.
EVERYONE, ALONE, HAS SOMETHING THEY DON'T KNOW OR CAN'T DO, AND WE ALL GET THROUGH IT--WITH THE HELP OF ***OTHER PEOPLE.***
IT'S THE SAME FOR YOU, TOO, ISN'T IT?

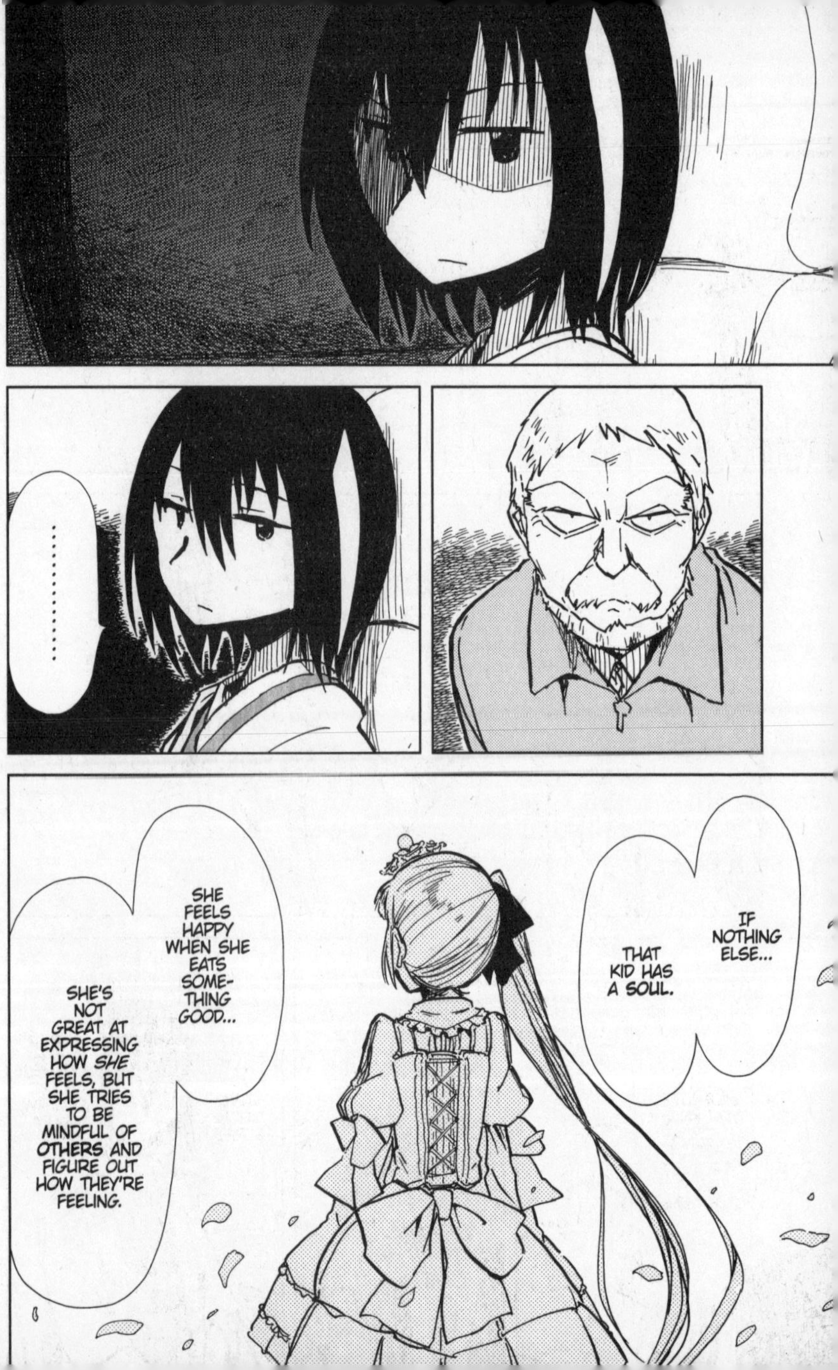
......
IF NOTHING ELSE...
THAT KID HAS A SOUL.
SHE FEELS HAPPY WHEN SHE EATS SOMETHING GOOD...
SHE'S NOT GREAT AT EXPRESSING HOW *SHE* FEELS, BUT SHE TRIES TO BE MINDFUL OF OTHERS AND FIGURE OUT HOW THEY'RE FEELING.

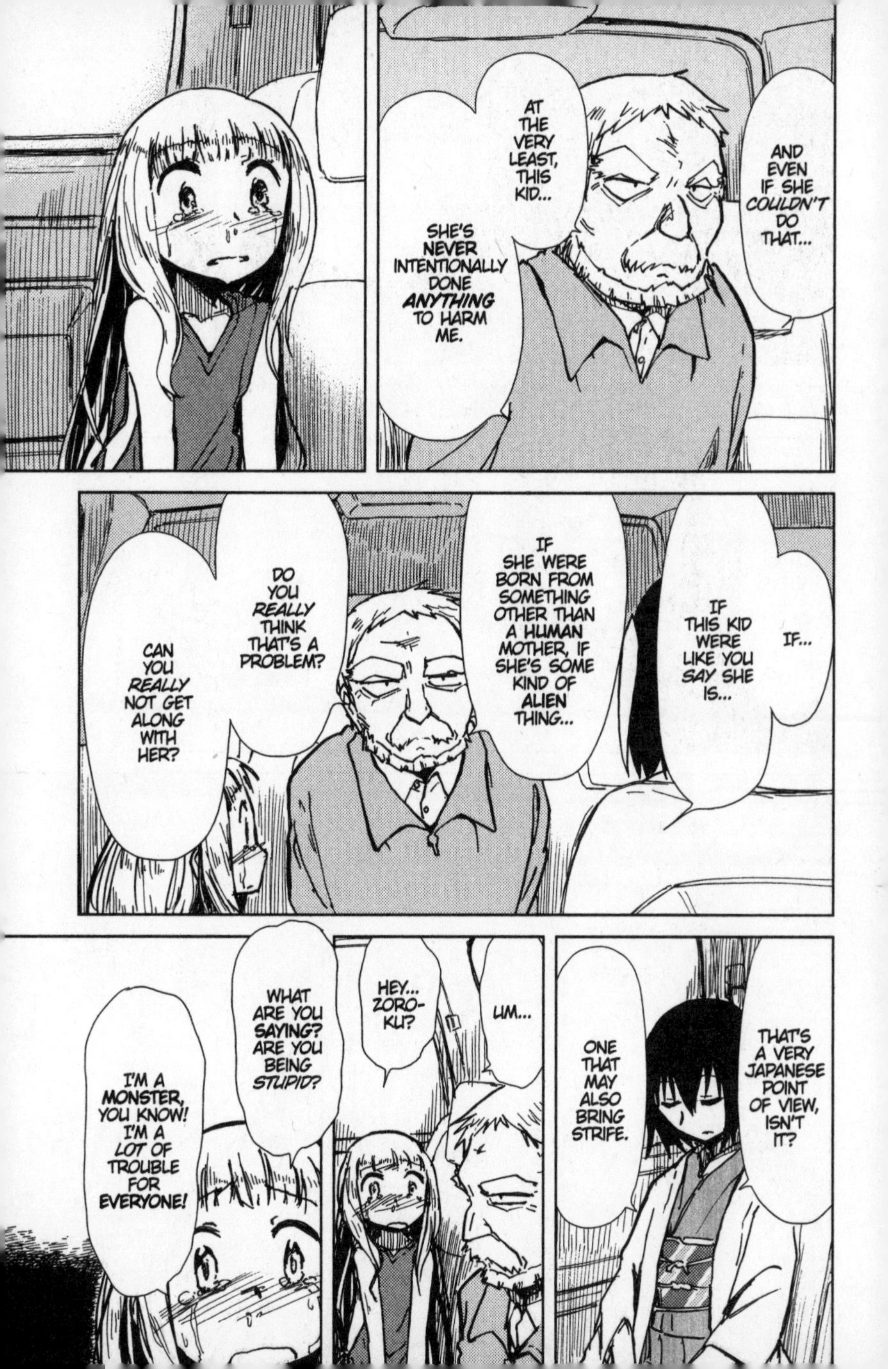

AT THE VERY LEAST, THIS KID...
SHE'S NEVER INTENTIONALLY DONE *ANYTHING* TO HARM ME.
AND EVEN IF SHE *COULDN'T* DO THAT...
IF...
IF THIS KID WERE LIKE YOU *SAY* SHE IS...
IF SHE WERE BORN FROM SOMETHING OTHER THAN A HUMAN MOTHER, IF SHE'S SOME KIND OF ALIEN THING...
DO YOU *REALLY* THINK THAT'S A PROBLEM?
CAN YOU *REALLY* NOT GET ALONG WITH HER?
THAT'S A VERY JAPANESE POINT OF VIEW, ISN'T IT?
ONE THAT MAY ALSO BRING STRIFE.
UM...
HEY... ZORO-KU?
WHAT ARE YOU SAYING? ARE YOU BEING *STUPID*?
I'M A MONSTER, YOU KNOW! I'M A *LOT* OF TROUBLE FOR EVERYONE!

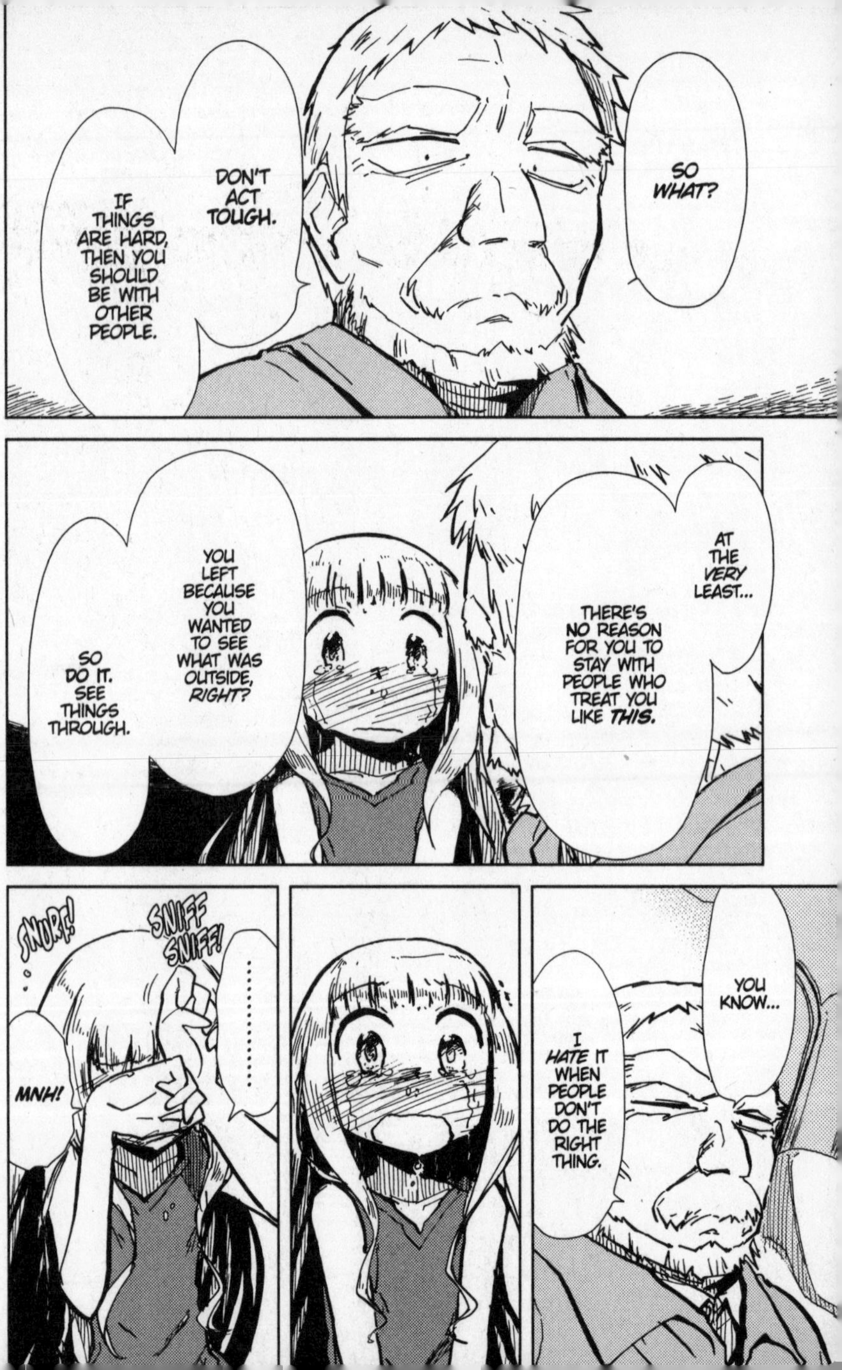
SO WHAT?
DON'T ACT TOUGH.
IF THINGS ARE HARD, THEN YOU SHOULD BE WITH OTHER PEOPLE.
AT THE VERY LEAST...
THERE'S NO REASON FOR YOU TO STAY WITH PEOPLE WHO TREAT YOU LIKE THIS.
YOU LEFT BECAUSE YOU WANTED TO SEE WHAT WAS OUTSIDE, RIGHT?
SO DO IT. SEE THINGS THROUGH.
YOU KNOW...
I HATE IT WHEN PEOPLE DON'T DO THE RIGHT THING.
......
SNIFF SNIFF!
SNORF!
MNH!

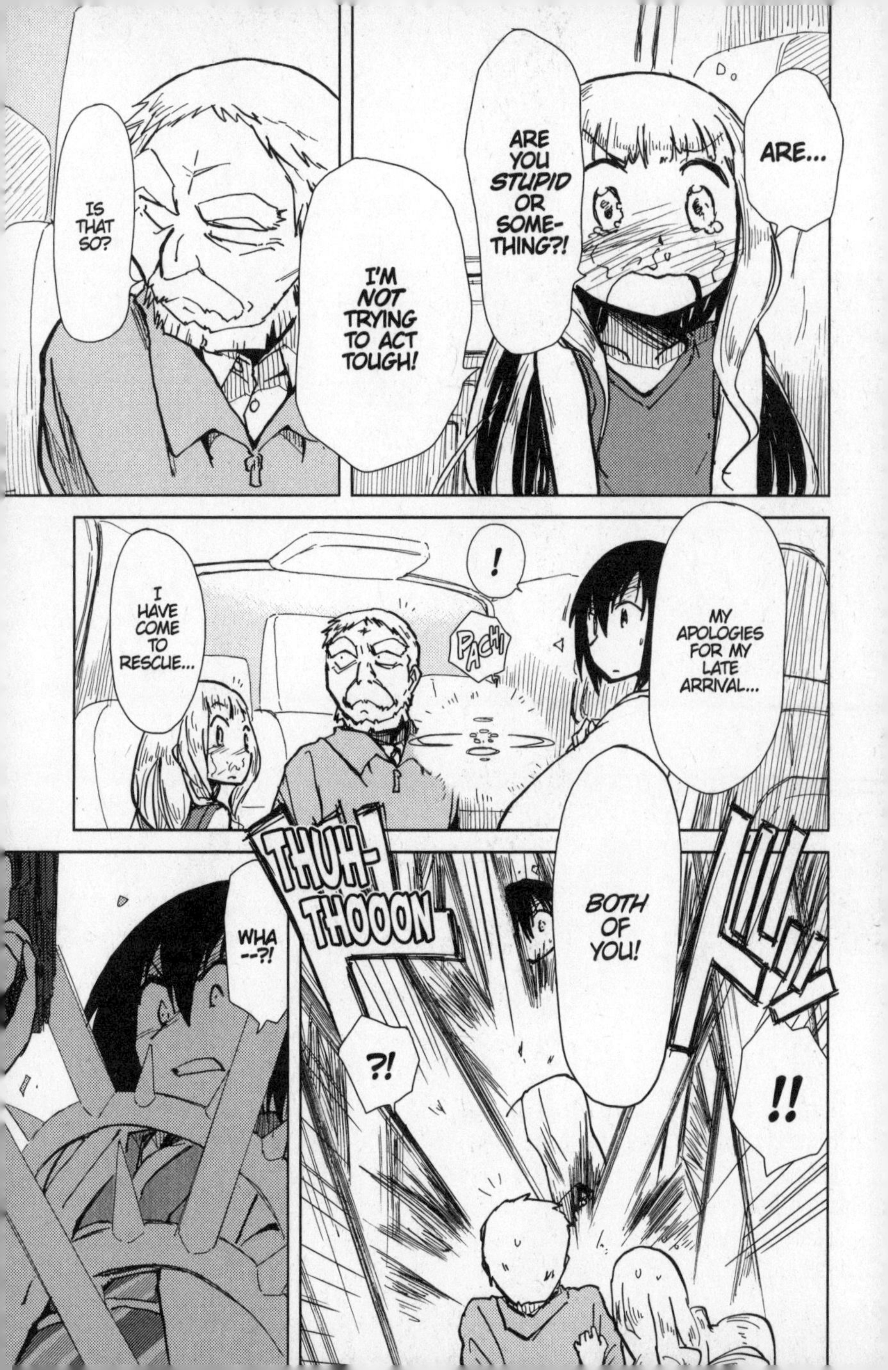
Do
ARE...
ARE YOU STUPID OR SOME-THING?!
I'M NOT TRYING TO ACT TOUGH!
IS THAT SO?
MY APOLOGIES FOR MY LATE ARRIVAL...
!
PACHI
I HAVE COME TO RESCUE...
BOTH OF YOU!
THUH-THOOON
!!
?!
WHA--?!

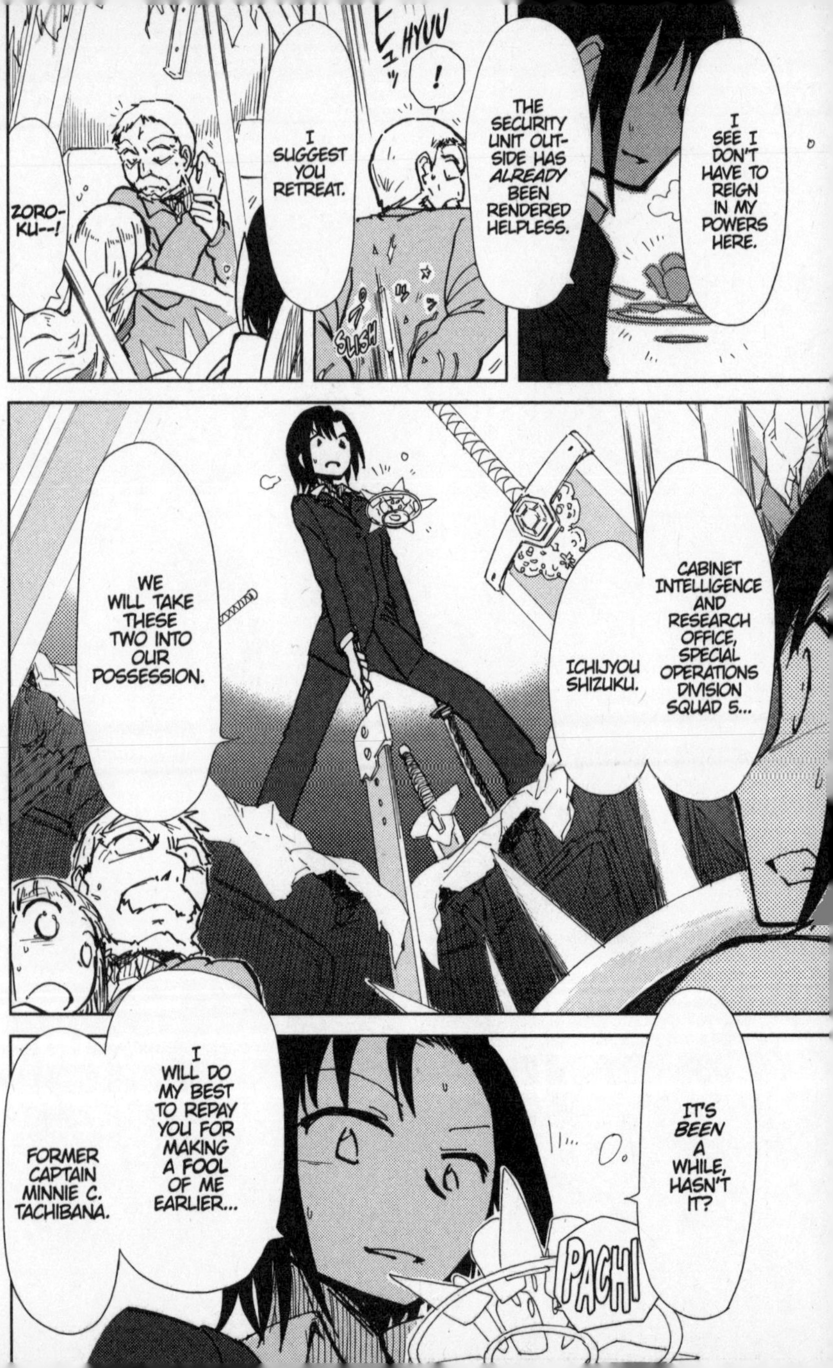
I SEE I DON'T HAVE TO REIGN IN MY POWERS HERE.
THE SECURITY UNIT OUTSIDE HAS *ALREADY* BEEN RENDERED HELPLESS.
HYUU
!
SLISH
I SUGGEST YOU RETREAT.
ZOROKU--!
CABINET INTELLIGENCE AND RESEARCH OFFICE, SPECIAL OPERATIONS DIVISION SQUAD 5...
ICHIJYOU SHIZUKU.
WE WILL TAKE THESE TWO INTO OUR POSSESSION.
IT'S *BEEN* A WHILE, HASN'T IT?
PACHI
I WILL DO MY BEST TO REPAY YOU FOR MAKING A FOOL OF ME EARLIER...
FORMER CAPTAIN MINNIE C. TACHIBANA.

Alice & Zoroku

"She's *my* prisoner, you know!"
the Red Knight said at last.

"Yes, but then *I* came and rescued her!"
the White Knight replied.

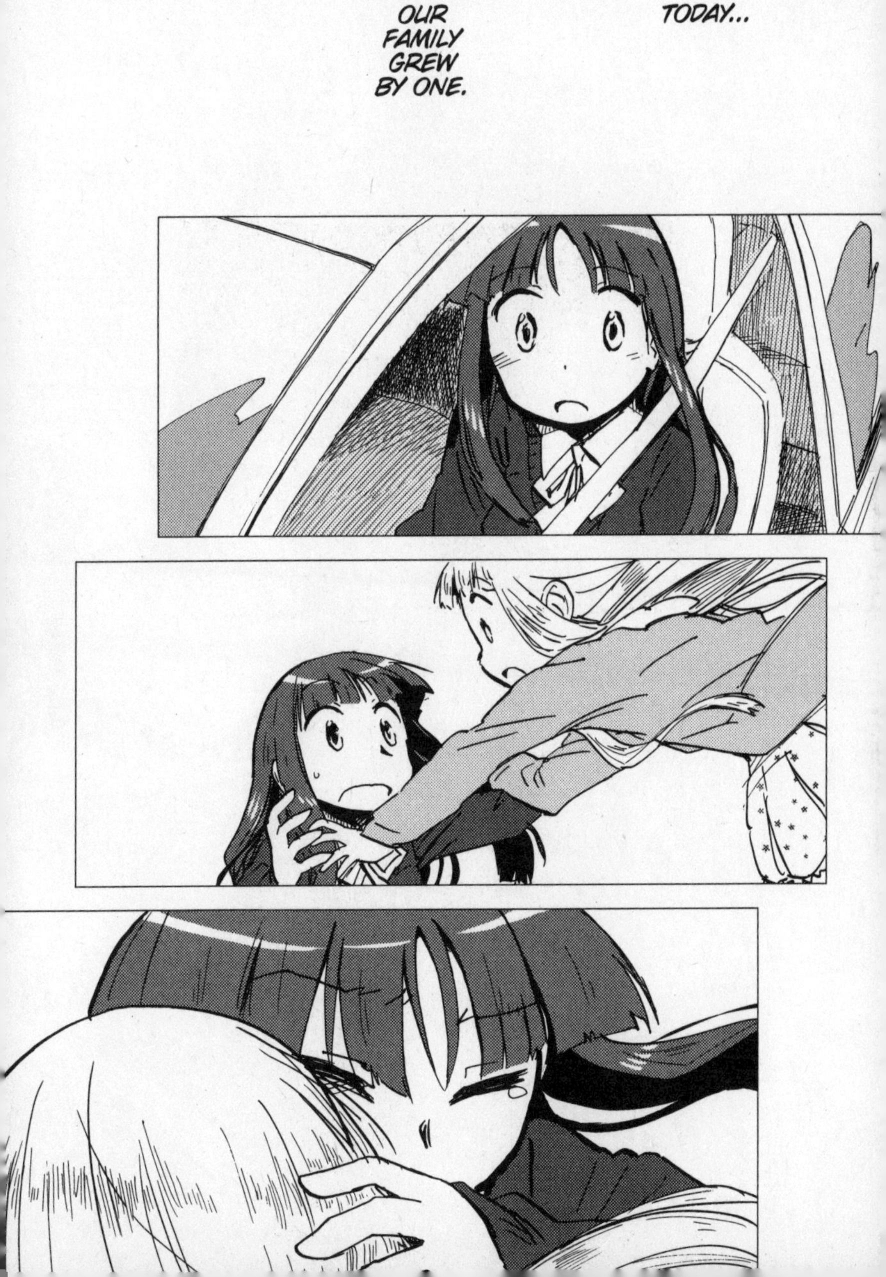
TODAY...
OUR FAMILY GREW BY ONE.

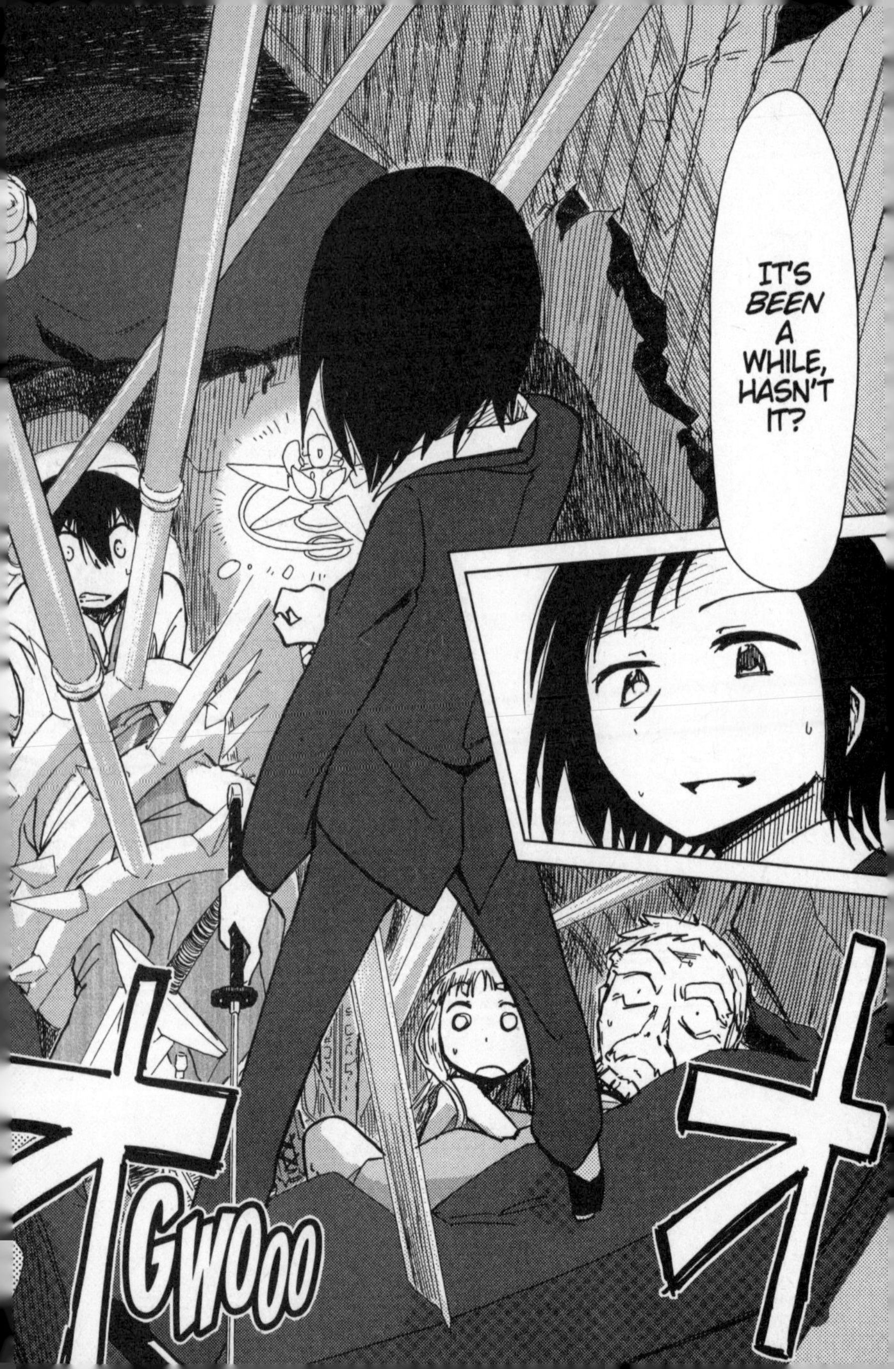
IT'S BEEN A WHILE, HASN'T IT?
GWOOO

# Chapter.8
# Fly High in the Sky

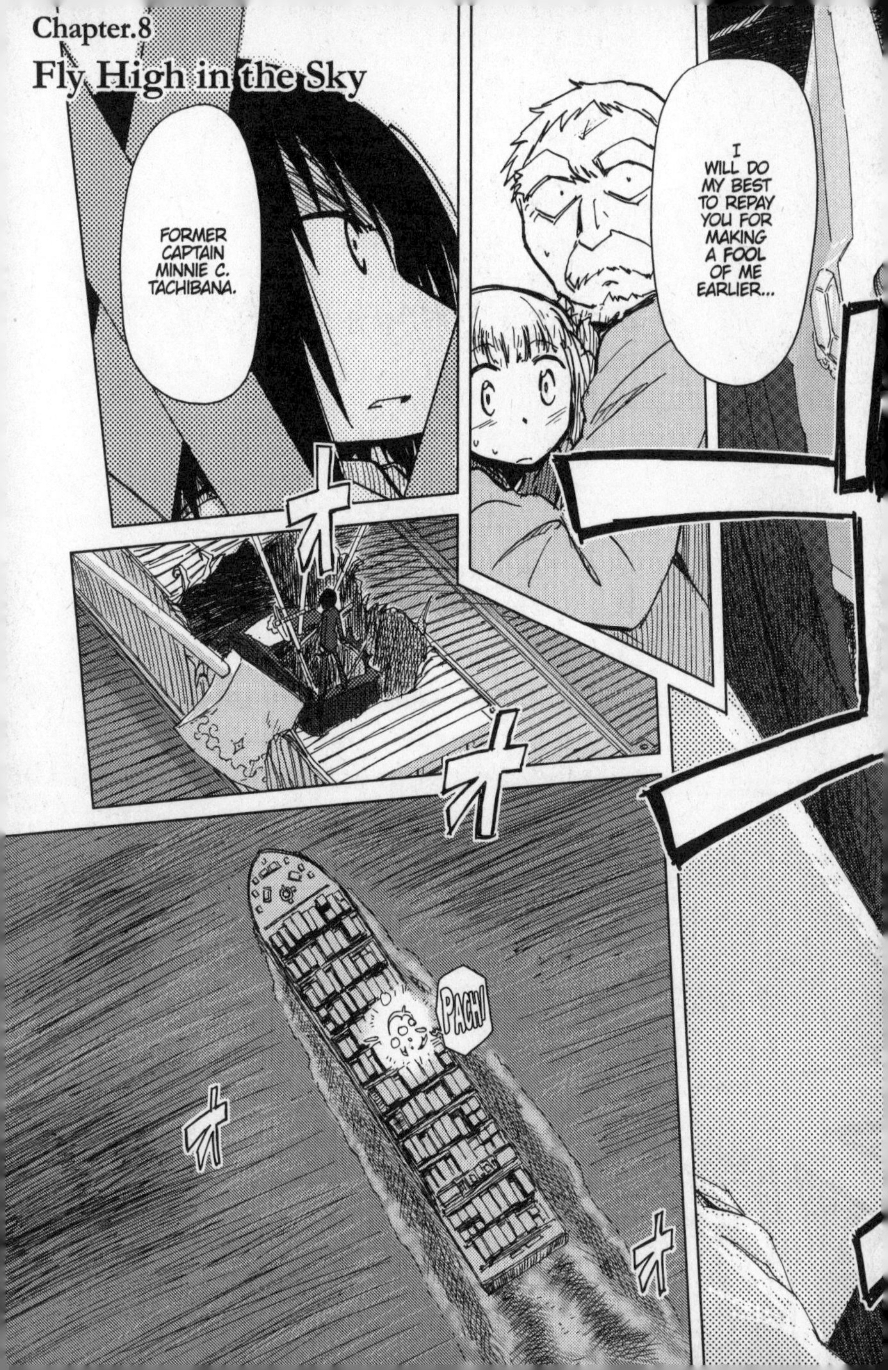
I WILL DO MY BEST TO REPAY YOU FOR MAKING A FOOL OF ME EARLIER...
FORMER CAPTAIN MINNIE C. TACHIBANA.
PACHI

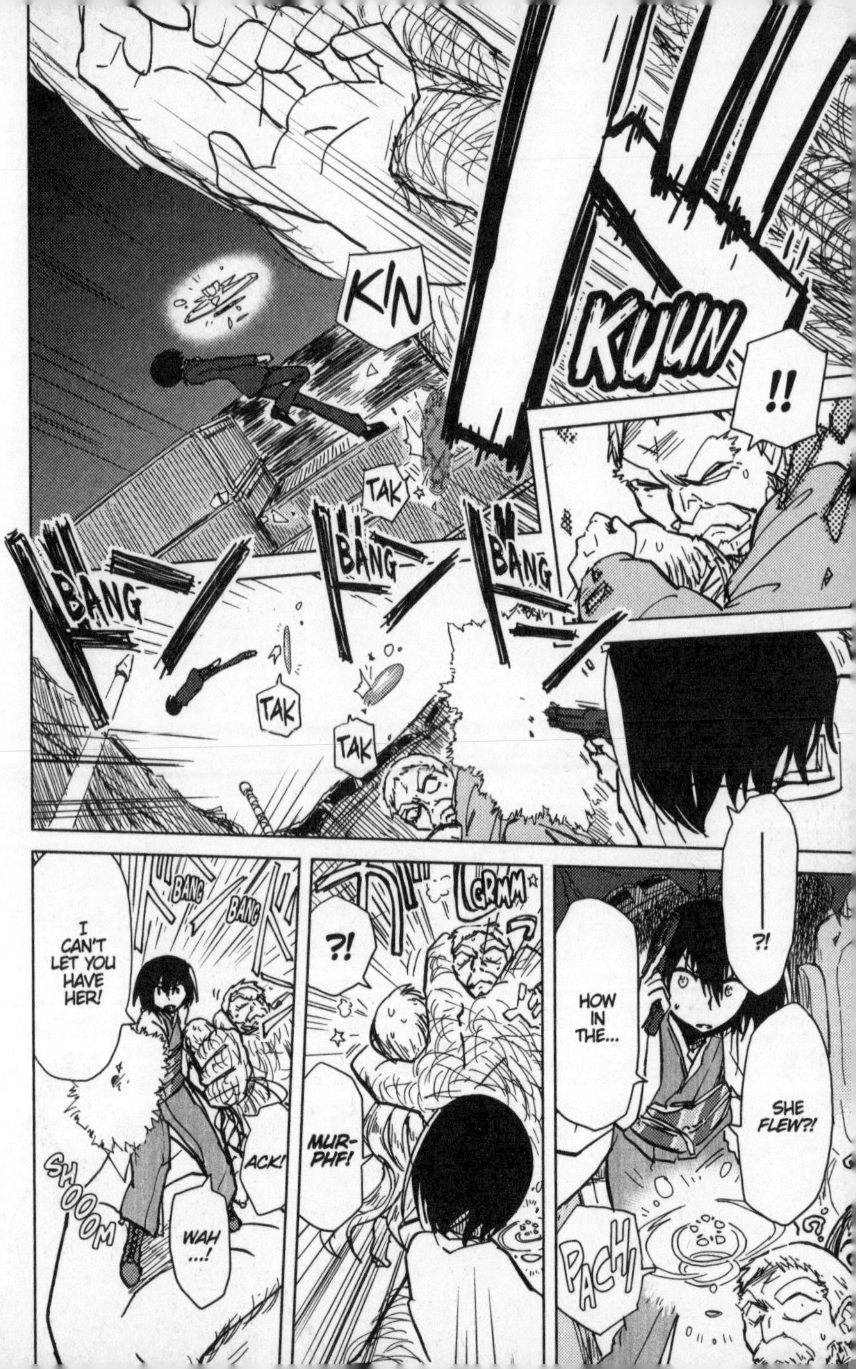

KUUN
!!
KIN
TAK
BANG
BANG
BANG
TAK
TAK
—?!
SHE FLEW?!
HOW IN THE...
PACHI
?!
GRMM
MUR-PHF!
BANG
BANG
I CAN'T LET YOU HAVE HER!
ACK!
WAH ...!
SHOOOM

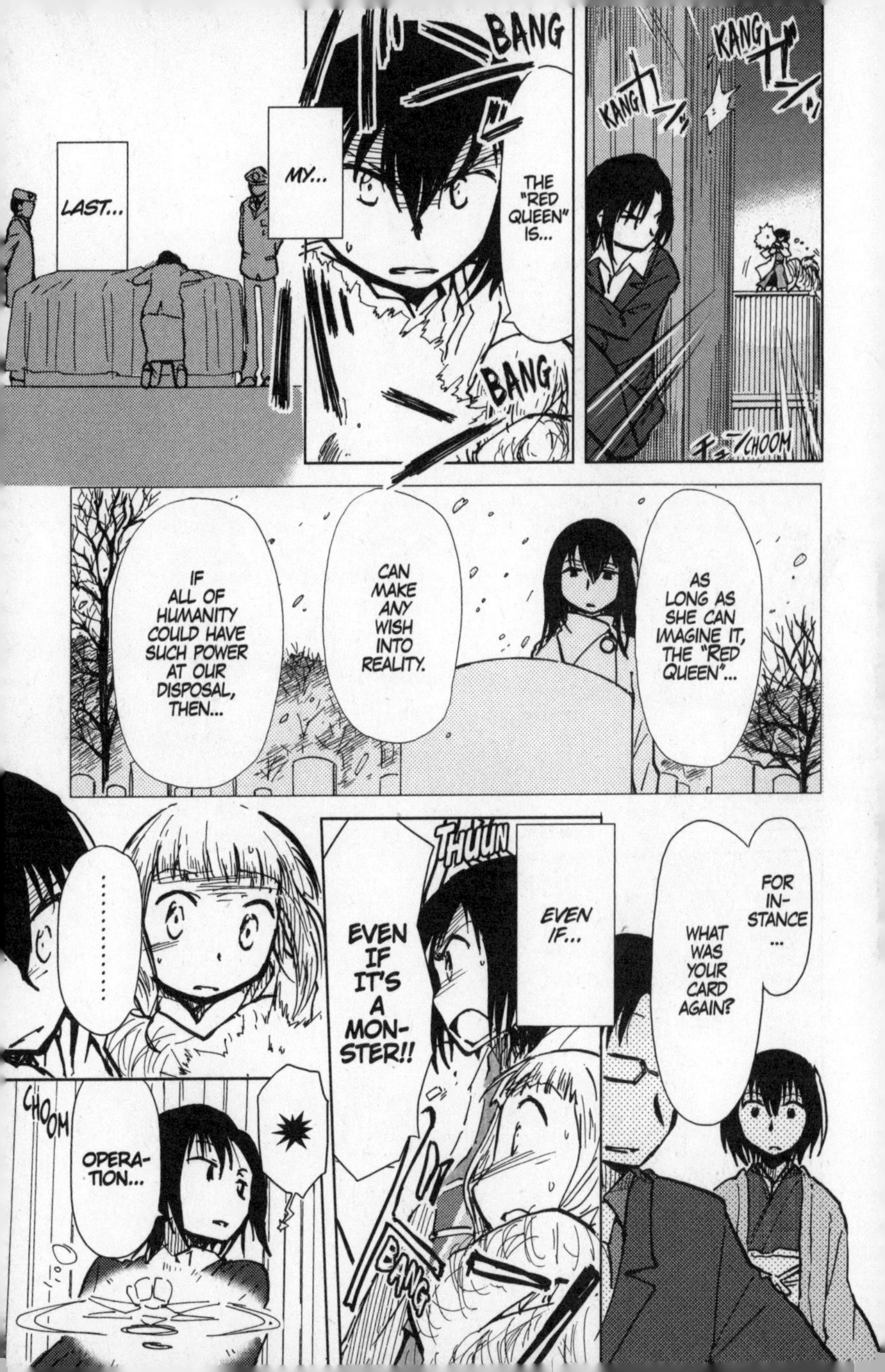
KANG
KANG
CHOOM
BANG
THE "RED QUEEN" IS...
MY...
BANG
LAST...
AS LONG AS SHE CAN IMAGINE IT, THE "RED QUEEN"...
CAN MAKE ANY WISH INTO REALITY.
IF ALL OF HUMANITY COULD HAVE SUCH POWER AT OUR DISPOSAL, THEN...
FOR INSTANCE...
WHAT WAS YOUR CARD AGAIN?
THUUN
EVEN IF...
EVEN IF IT'S A MONSTER!!
BANG
.........
CHOOM
OPERATION...

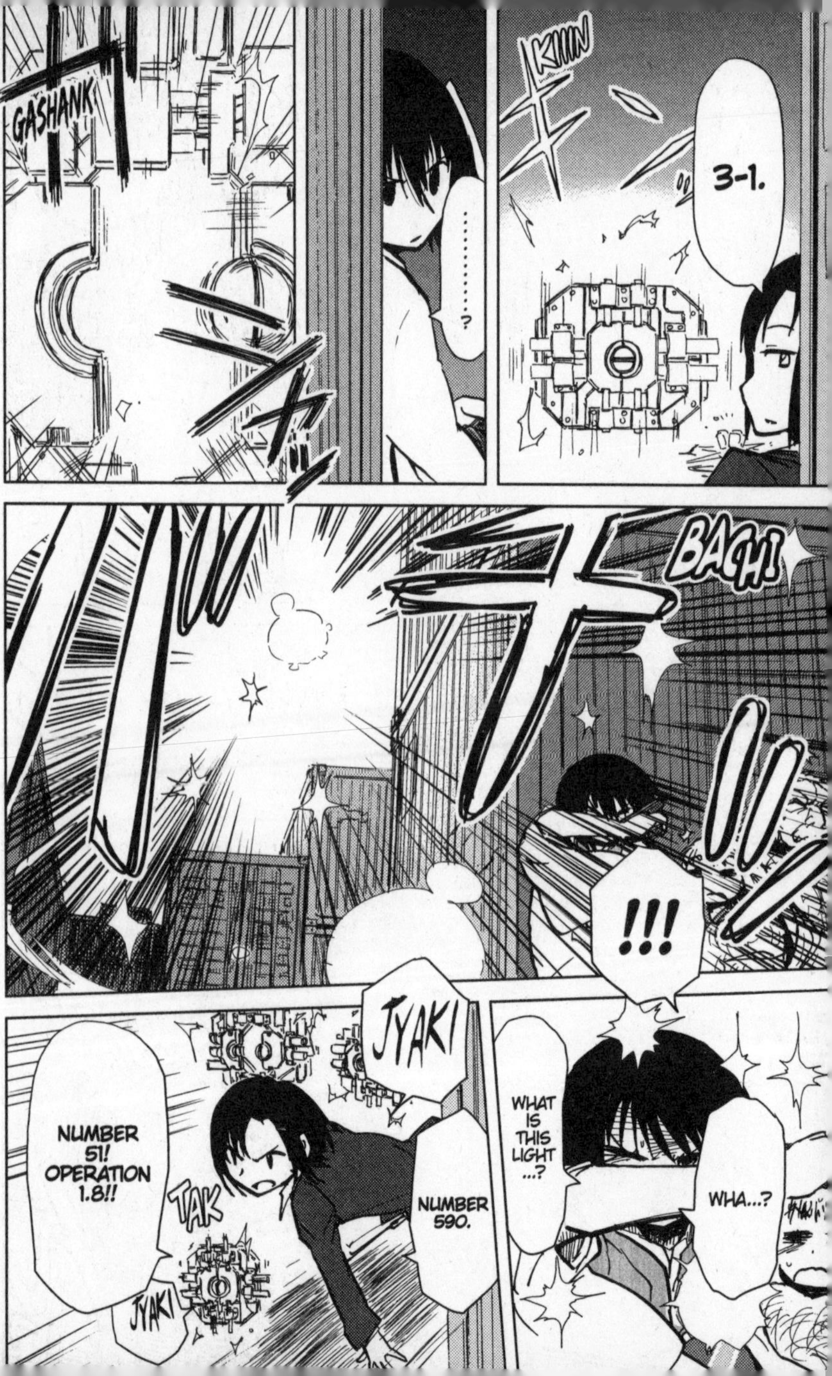
KIIIN
3-1.
......?
GASHANK
BACHI
!!!
WHAT IS THIS LIGHT ...?
WHA...?
JYAKI
NUMBER 590.
NUMBER 51! OPERATION 1.8!!
TAK
JYAKI

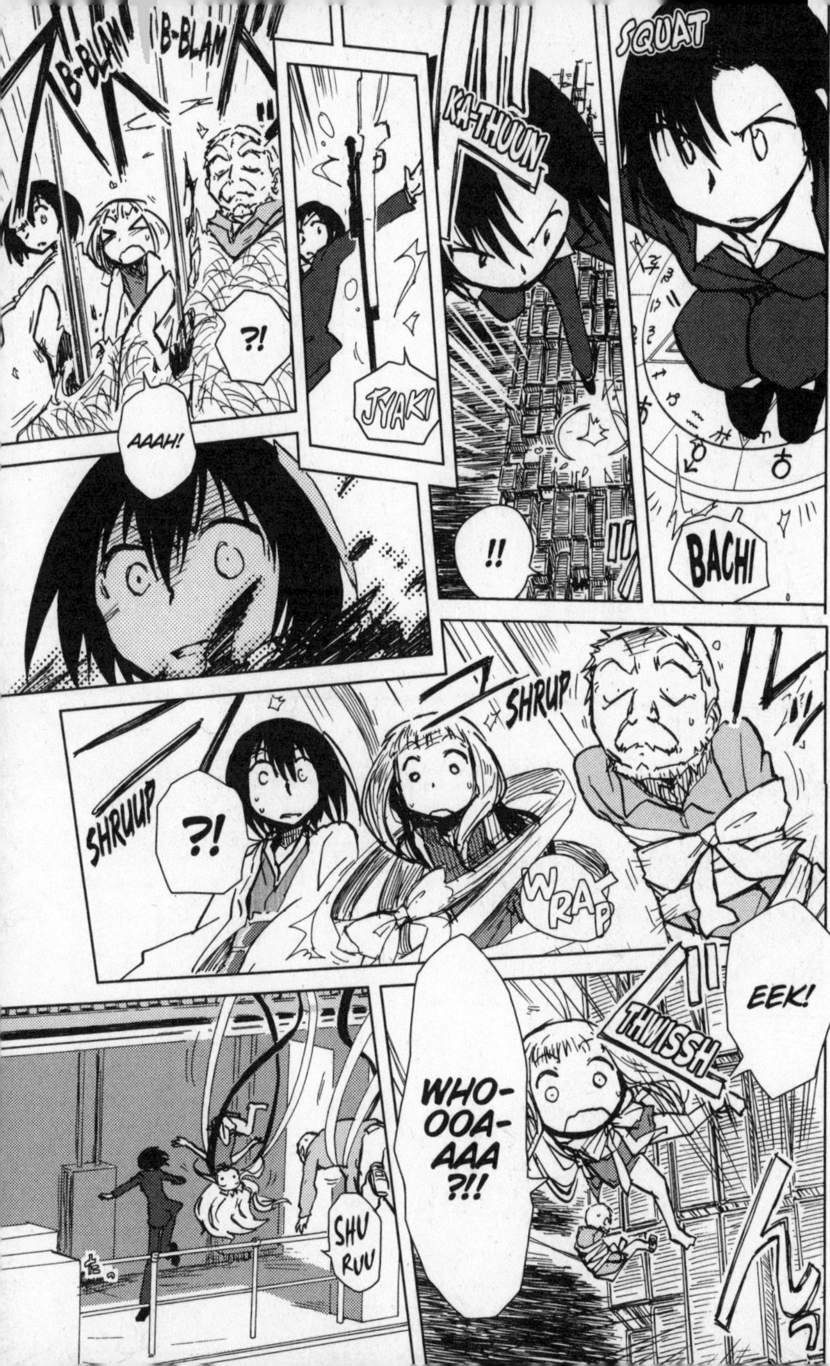
SQUAT
BACHI
KA-THUUN
!!
JYAKI
B-BLAM
B-BLAM
?!
AAAH!
SHRUP
WRAP
?!
SHRUUP
EEK!
THWISSH
WHOO-OOA-AAA?!!
SHU RUU

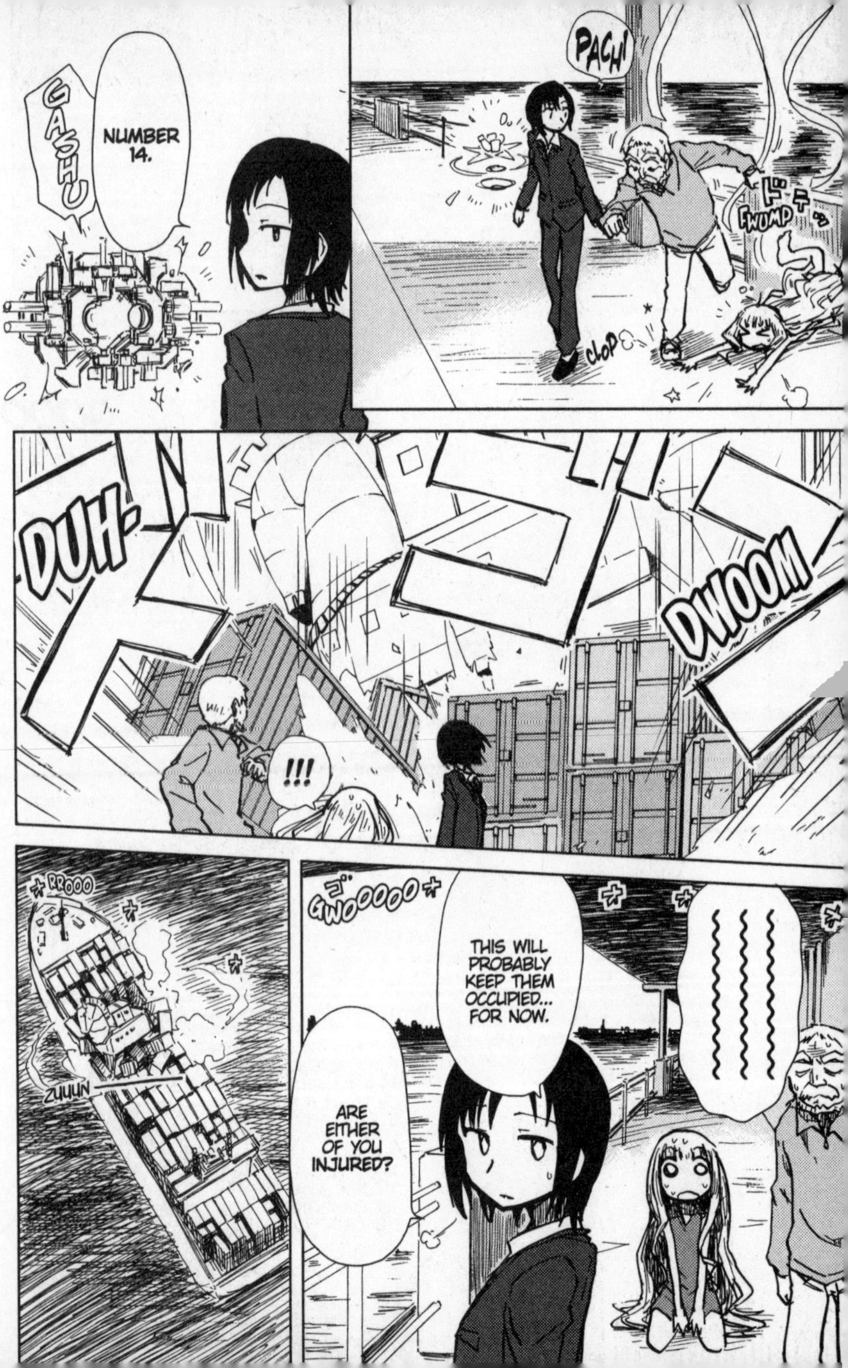
PACHI
FWUMP
CLOP
NUMBER 14.
GASHU
DUH-
DWOOM
!!!
GWOOOOO
THIS WILL PROBABLY KEEP THEM OCCUPIED... FOR NOW.
ARE EITHER OF YOU INJURED?
RROOO
ZUUUN

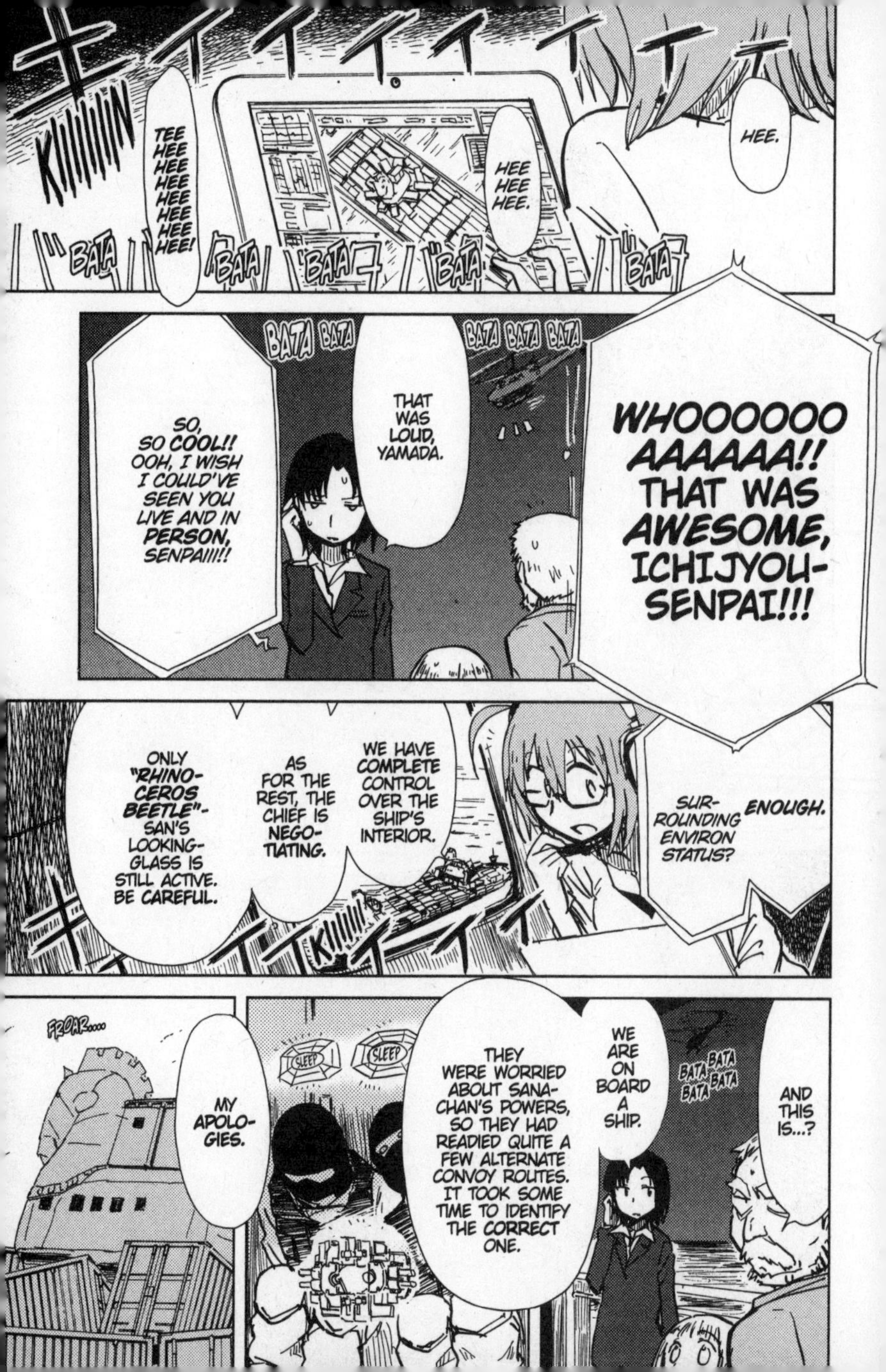
HEE.
HEE HEE HEE.
TEE HEE HEE HEE HEE HEE HEE HEE!
KIIIIIIIN
BATA
BATA
BATA
BATA
BATA
WHOOOOOOO AAAAAA!! THAT WAS AWESOME, ICHIJYOU-SENPAI!!!
BATA BATA BATA
THAT WAS LOUD, YAMADA.
BATA BATA
SO, SO COOL!! OOH, I WISH I COULD'VE SEEN YOU LIVE AND IN PERSON, SENPAIII!!
ENOUGH.
SUR-ROUNDING ENVIRON STATUS?
WE HAVE COMPLETE CONTROL OVER THE SHIP'S INTERIOR.
AS FOR THE REST, THE CHIEF IS NEGO-TIATING.
ONLY "RHINO-CEROS BEETLE"-SAN'S LOOKING-GLASS IS STILL ACTIVE. BE CAREFUL.
KIIIIIIN
AND THIS IS...?
BATA BATA BATA BATA
WE ARE ON BOARD A SHIP.
THEY WERE WORRIED ABOUT SANA-CHAN'S POWERS, SO THEY HAD READIED QUITE A FEW ALTERNATE CONVOY ROUTES. IT TOOK SOME TIME TO IDENTIFY THE CORRECT ONE.
SLEEP
SLEEP
MY APOLO-GIES.
FROAR....

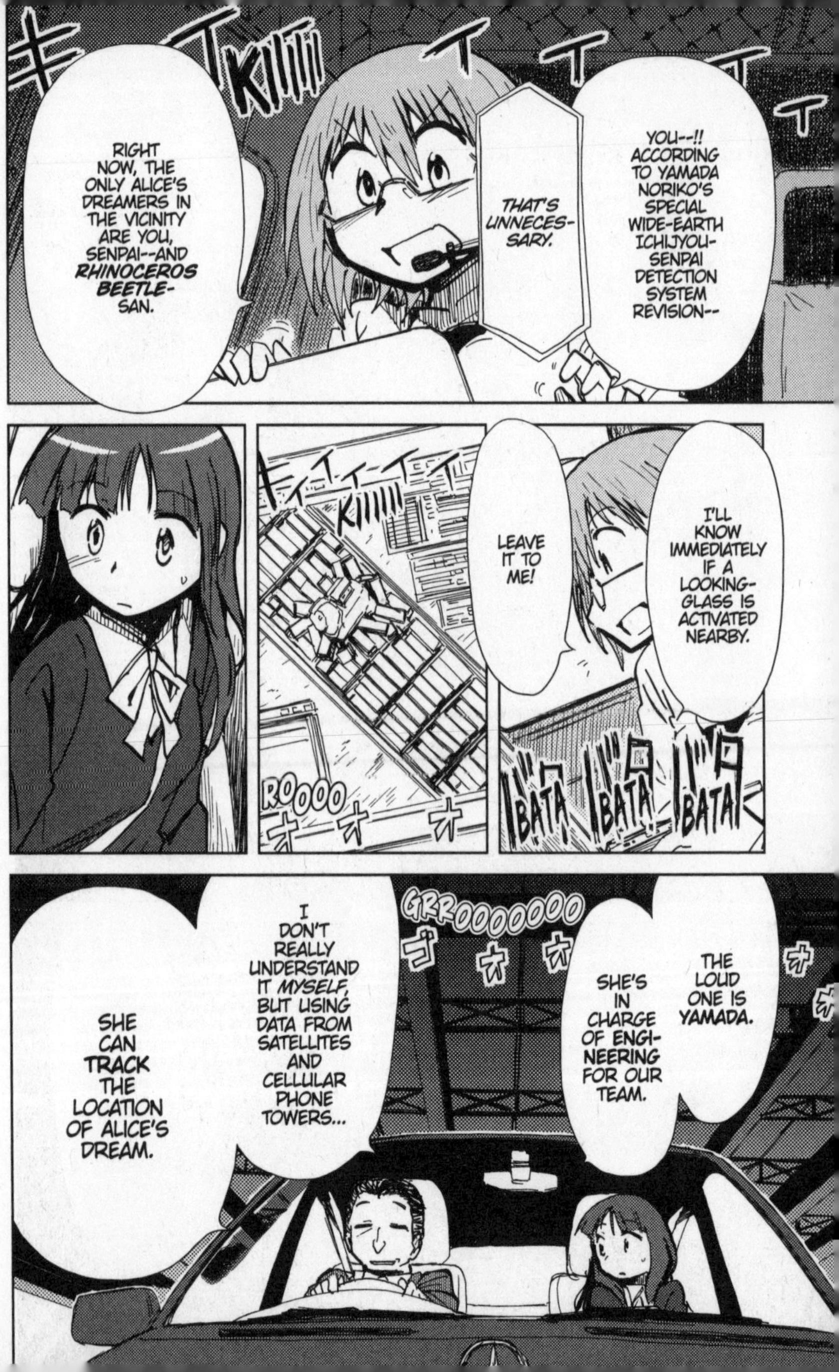
KIIIII
YOU--!! ACCORDING TO YAMADA NORIKO'S SPECIAL WIDE-EARTH ICHIJYOU-SENPAI DETECTION SYSTEM REVISION--
THAT'S UNNECESSARY.
RIGHT NOW, THE ONLY ALICE'S DREAMERS IN THE VICINITY ARE YOU, SENPAI--AND RHINOCEROS BEETLE-SAN.
I'LL KNOW IMMEDIATELY IF A LOOKING-GLASS IS ACTIVATED NEARBY.
LEAVE IT TO ME!
BATA BATA BATA
KIIIII
ROOOO
THE LOUD ONE IS YAMADA.
SHE'S IN CHARGE OF ENGINEERING FOR OUR TEAM.
GRROOOOOOOO
I DON'T REALLY UNDERSTAND IT MYSELF, BUT USING DATA FROM SATELLITES AND CELLULAR PHONE TOWERS...
SHE CAN TRACK THE LOCATION OF ALICE'S DREAM.

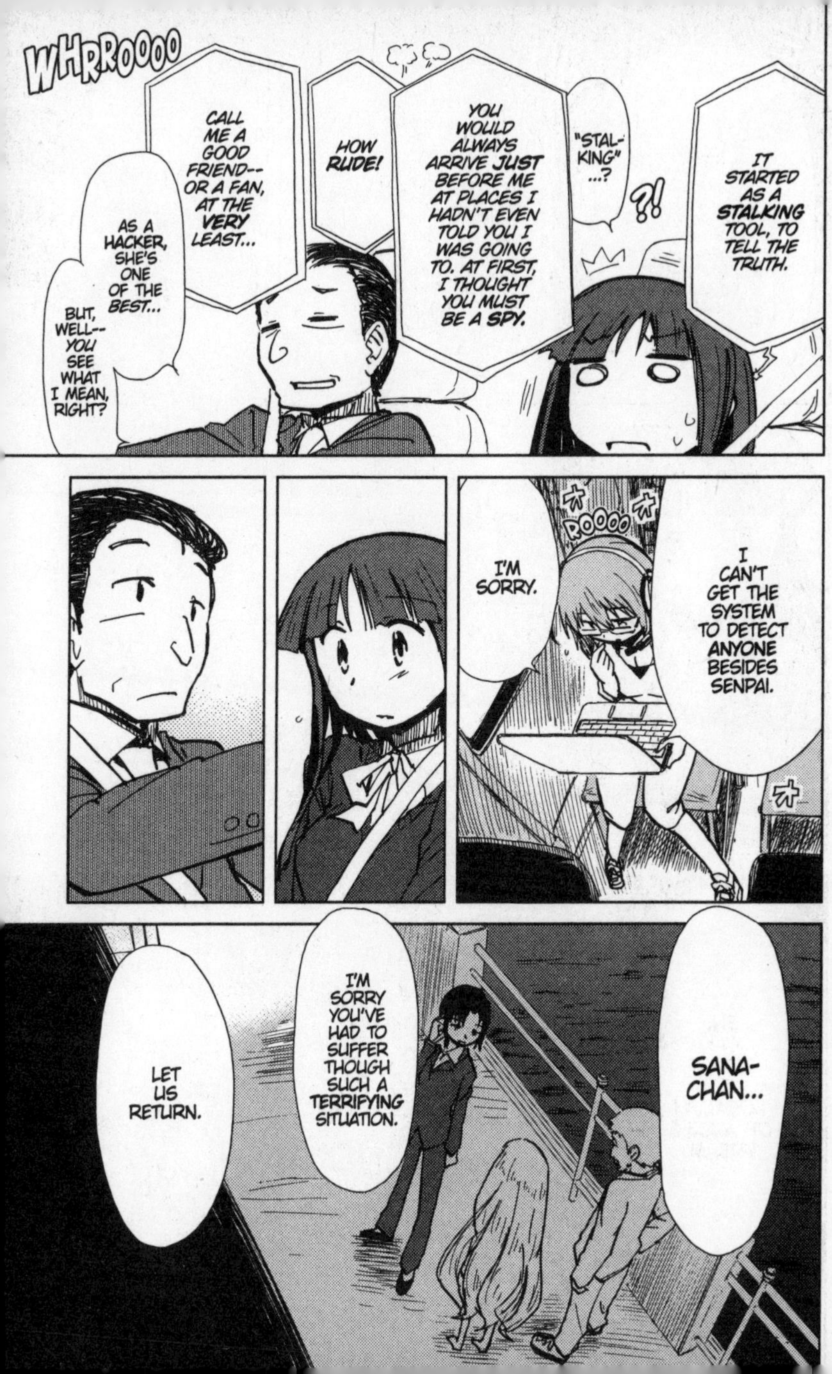
WHRROOOO
IT STARTED AS A STALKING TOOL, TO TELL THE TRUTH.
"STAL-KING" ...?
?!
YOU WOULD ALWAYS ARRIVE JUST BEFORE ME AT PLACES I HADN'T EVEN TOLD YOU I WAS GOING TO. AT FIRST, I THOUGHT YOU MUST BE A SPY.
HOW RUDE!
CALL ME A GOOD FRIEND--OR A FAN, AT THE VERY LEAST...
AS A HACKER, SHE'S ONE OF THE BEST...
BUT, WELL--YOU SEE WHAT I MEAN, RIGHT?
ROOOO
I CAN'T GET THE SYSTEM TO DETECT ANYONE BESIDES SENPAI.
I'M SORRY.
SANA-CHAN...
I'M SORRY YOU'VE HAD TO SUFFER THOUGH SUCH A TERRIFYING SITUATION.
LET US RETURN.

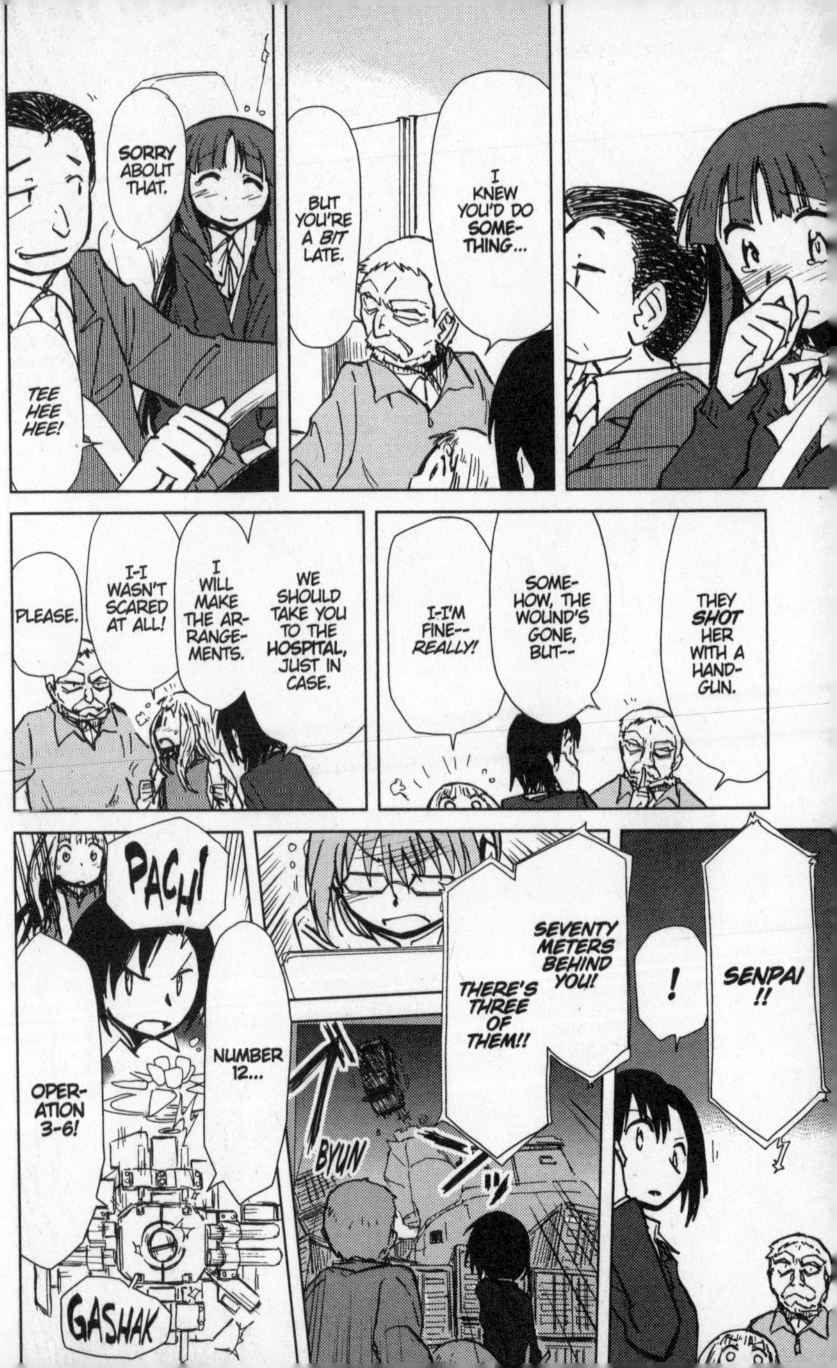
I KNEW YOU'D DO SOME-THING...
BUT YOU'RE A *BIT* LATE.
SORRY ABOUT THAT.
TEE HEE HEE!
THEY *SHOT* HER WITH A HAND-GUN.
SOME-HOW, THE WOUND'S GONE, BUT--
I-I'M FINE-- *REALLY!*
WE SHOULD TAKE YOU TO THE HOSPITAL, JUST IN CASE.
I WILL MAKE THE AR-RANGE-MENTS.
I-I WASN'T SCARED AT ALL!
PLEASE.
SENPAI!!
!
SEVENTY METERS BEHIND YOU!
THERE'S THREE OF THEM!!
BYUN
PACHI
NUMBER 12...
OPER-ATION 3-6!
GASHAK

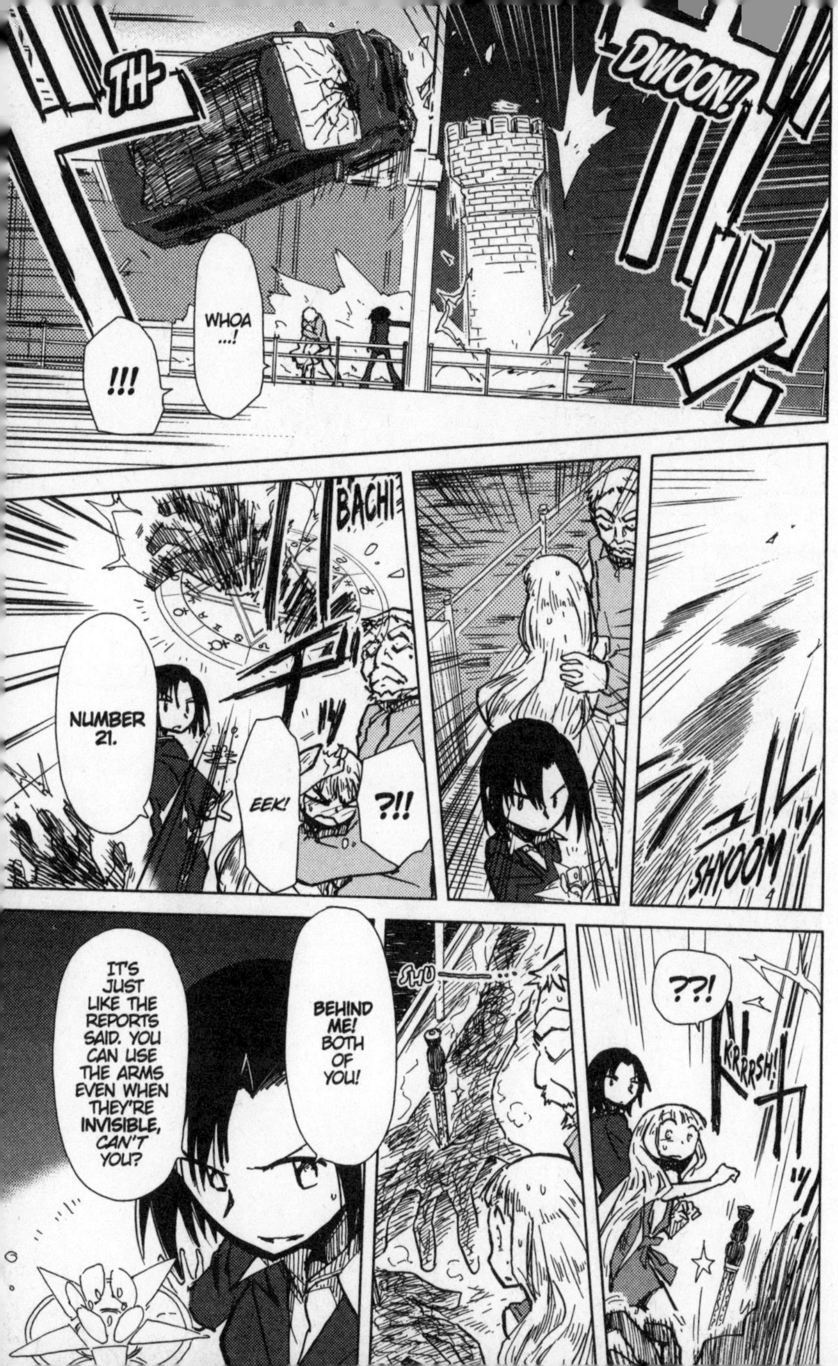
DWOON!
TH-
WHOA ...!
!!!
SHYOOM
BACHI
?!!
EEK!
NUMBER 21.
??!
KRRRSH!
SHU—...
BEHIND ME! BOTH OF YOU!
IT'S JUST LIKE THE REPORTS SAID. YOU CAN USE THE ARMS EVEN WHEN THEY'RE INVISIBLE, CAN'T YOU?

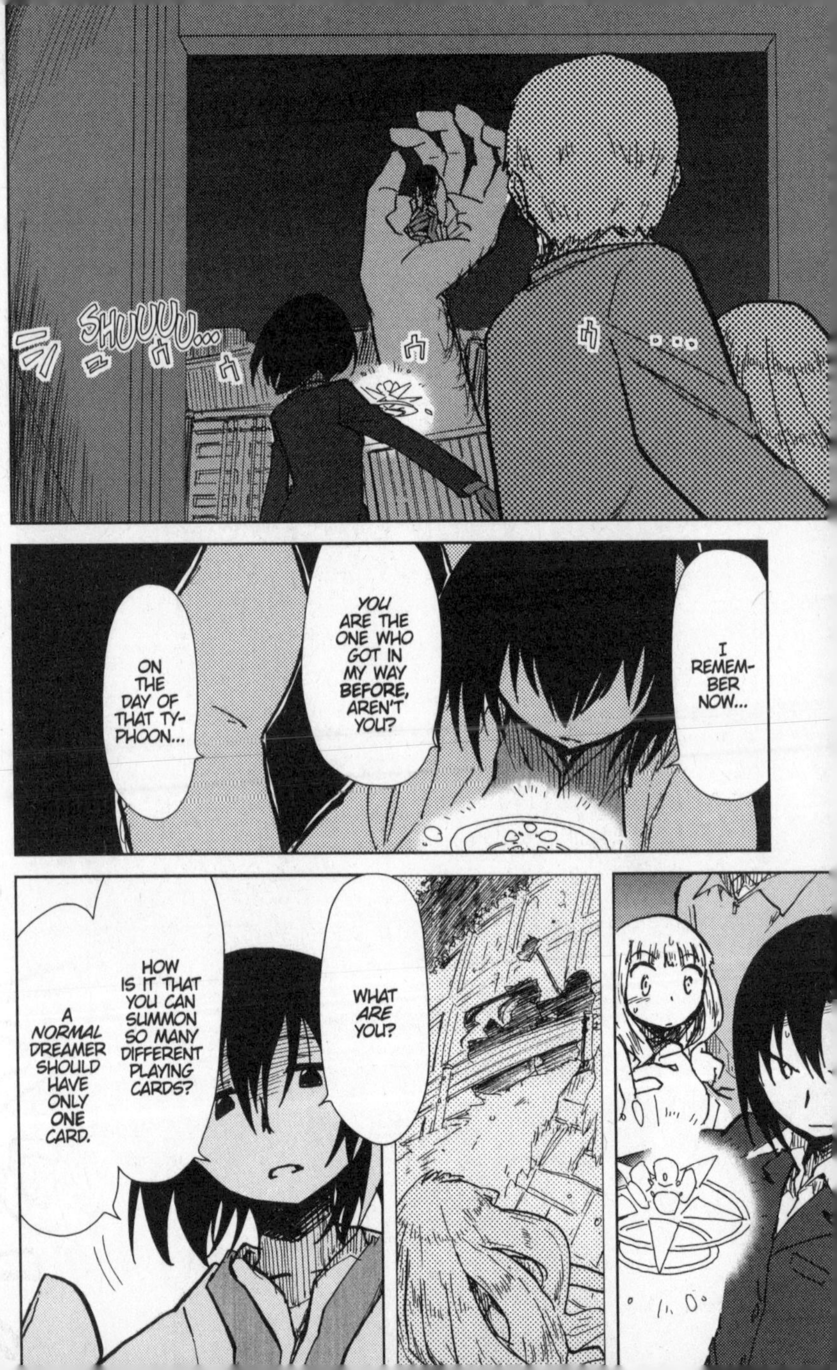
SHUUUU...
I REMEMBER NOW...
YOU ARE THE ONE WHO GOT IN MY WAY BEFORE, AREN'T YOU?
ON THE DAY OF THAT TYPHOON...
WHAT ARE YOU?
HOW IS IT THAT YOU CAN SUMMON SO MANY DIFFERENT PLAYING CARDS?
A NORMAL DREAMER SHOULD HAVE ONLY ONE CARD.

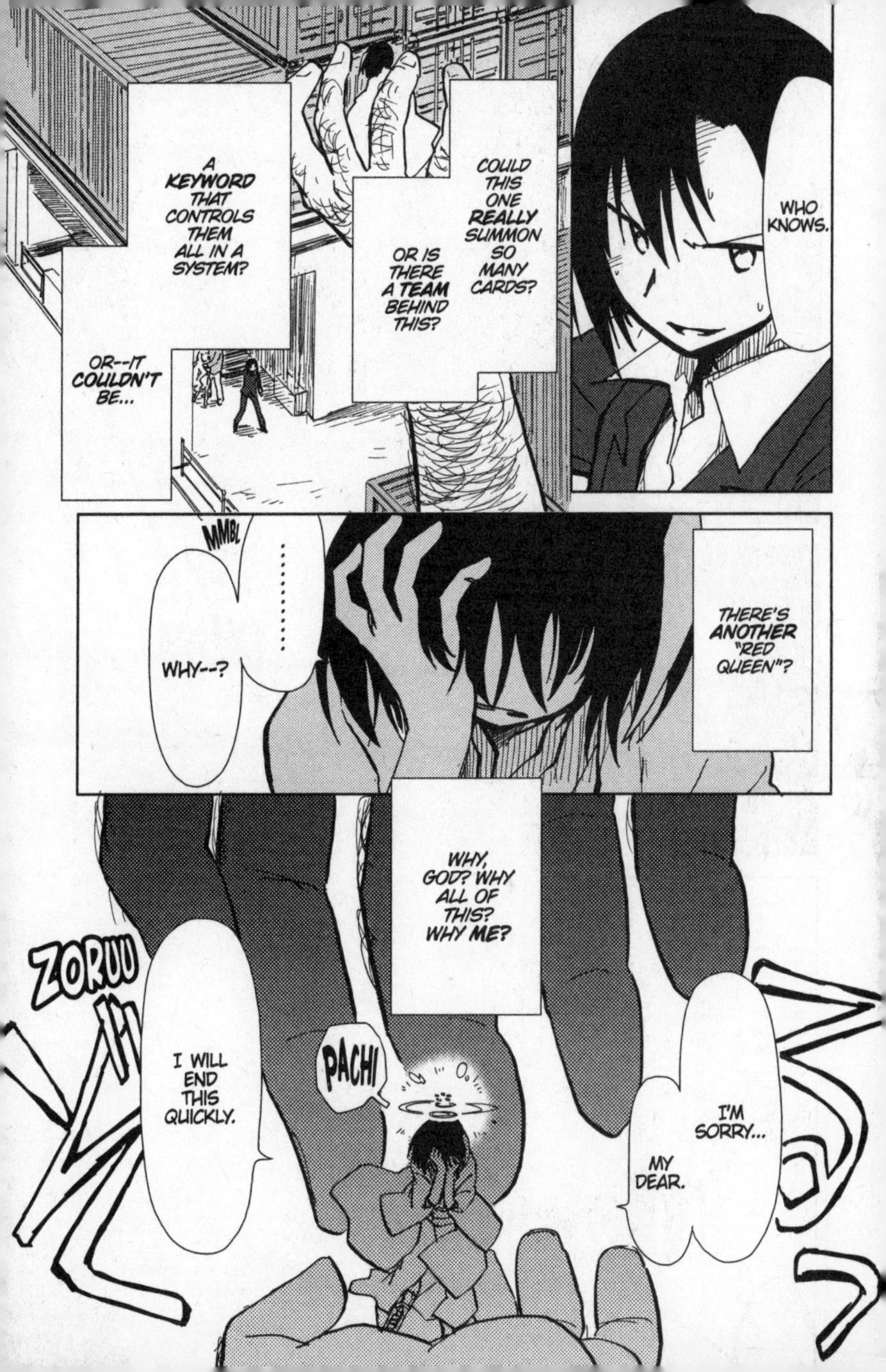
WHO KNOWS.
COULD THIS ONE REALLY SUMMON SO MANY CARDS?
OR IS THERE A TEAM BEHIND THIS?
A KEYWORD THAT CONTROLS THEM ALL IN A SYSTEM?
OR--IT COULDN'T BE...
THERE'S ANOTHER "RED QUEEN"?
MMBL
......
WHY--?
WHY, GOD? WHY ALL OF THIS? WHY ME?
I'M SORRY...
MY DEAR.
PACHI
I WILL END THIS QUICKLY.
ZORUU

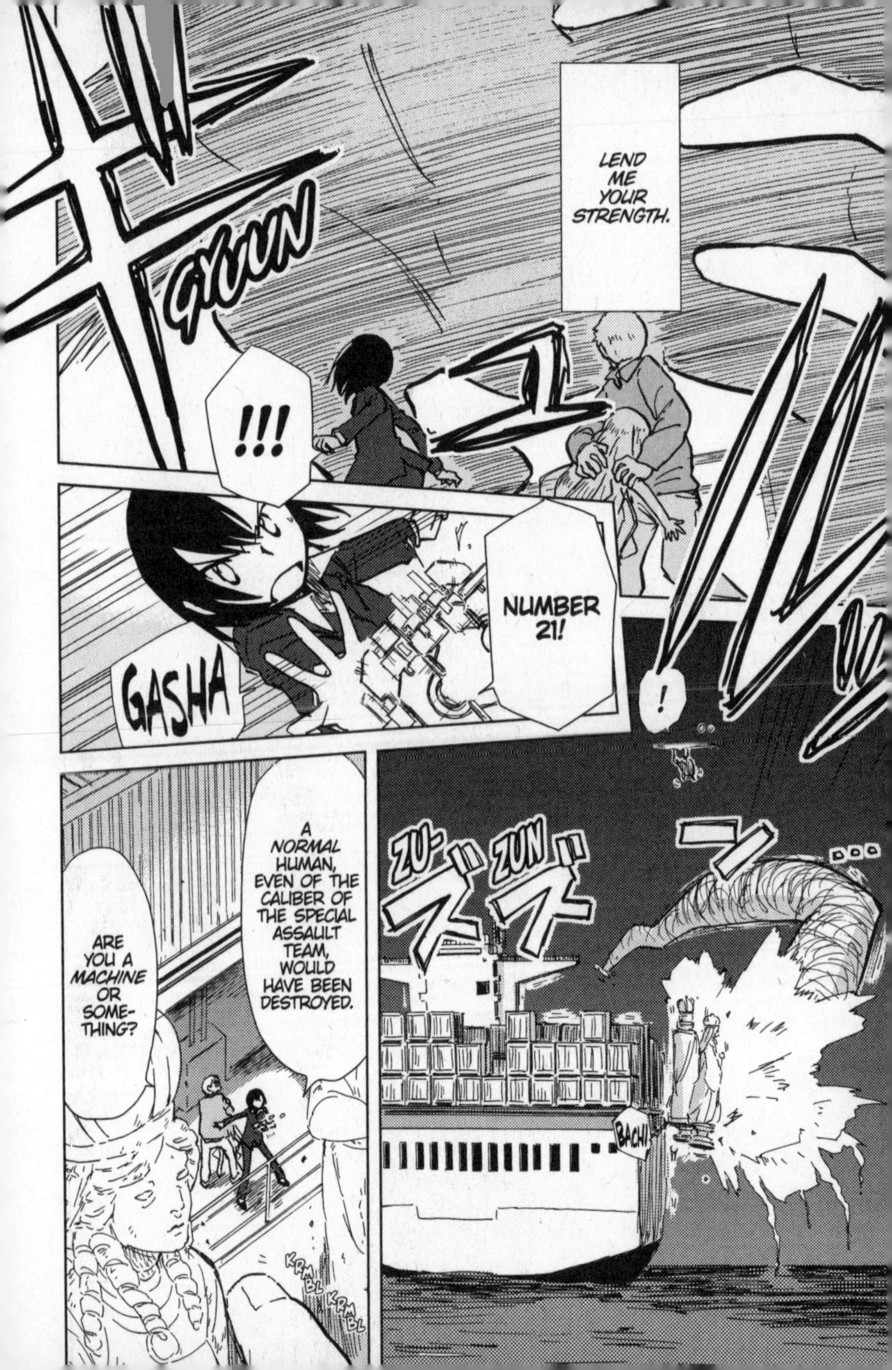

LEND ME YOUR STRENGTH.
GYUUN
!!!
!
NUMBER 21!
GASHA
ZU- ZUN
BACHI!
A *NORMAL* HUMAN, EVEN OF THE CALIBER OF THE SPECIAL ASSAULT TEAM, WOULD HAVE BEEN DESTROYED.
ARE YOU A *MACHINE* OR SOME-THING?
KRMBL KRMBL

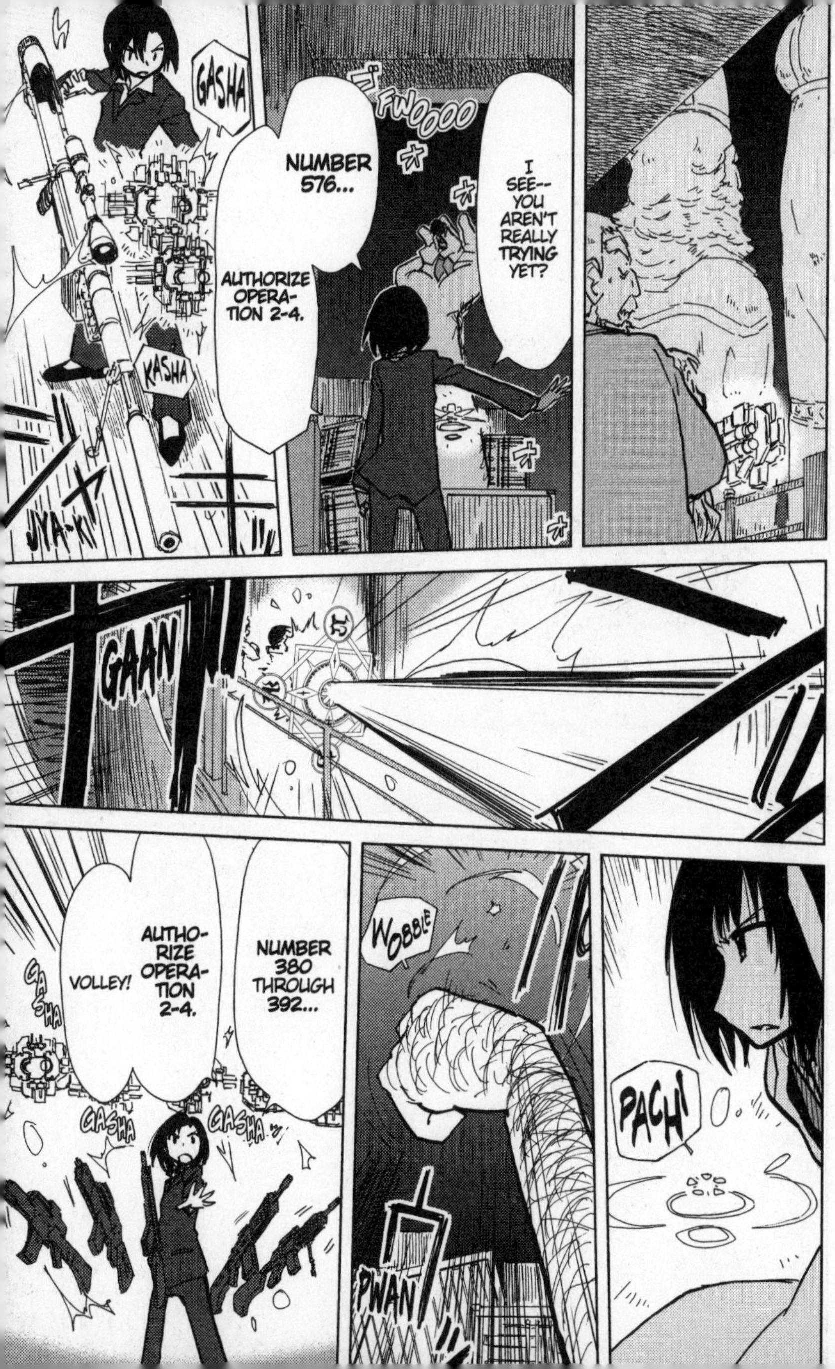
FWOOOO
I SEE-- YOU AREN'T REALLY TRYING YET?
NUMBER 576...
AUTHORIZE OPERATION 2-4.
GASHA
KASHA
JIYA-KI
GAAN
PACHI
WOBBLE
PWAN
NUMBER 380 THROUGH 392...
AUTHORIZE OPERATION 2-4.
VOLLEY!
GASHA
GASHA
GASHA

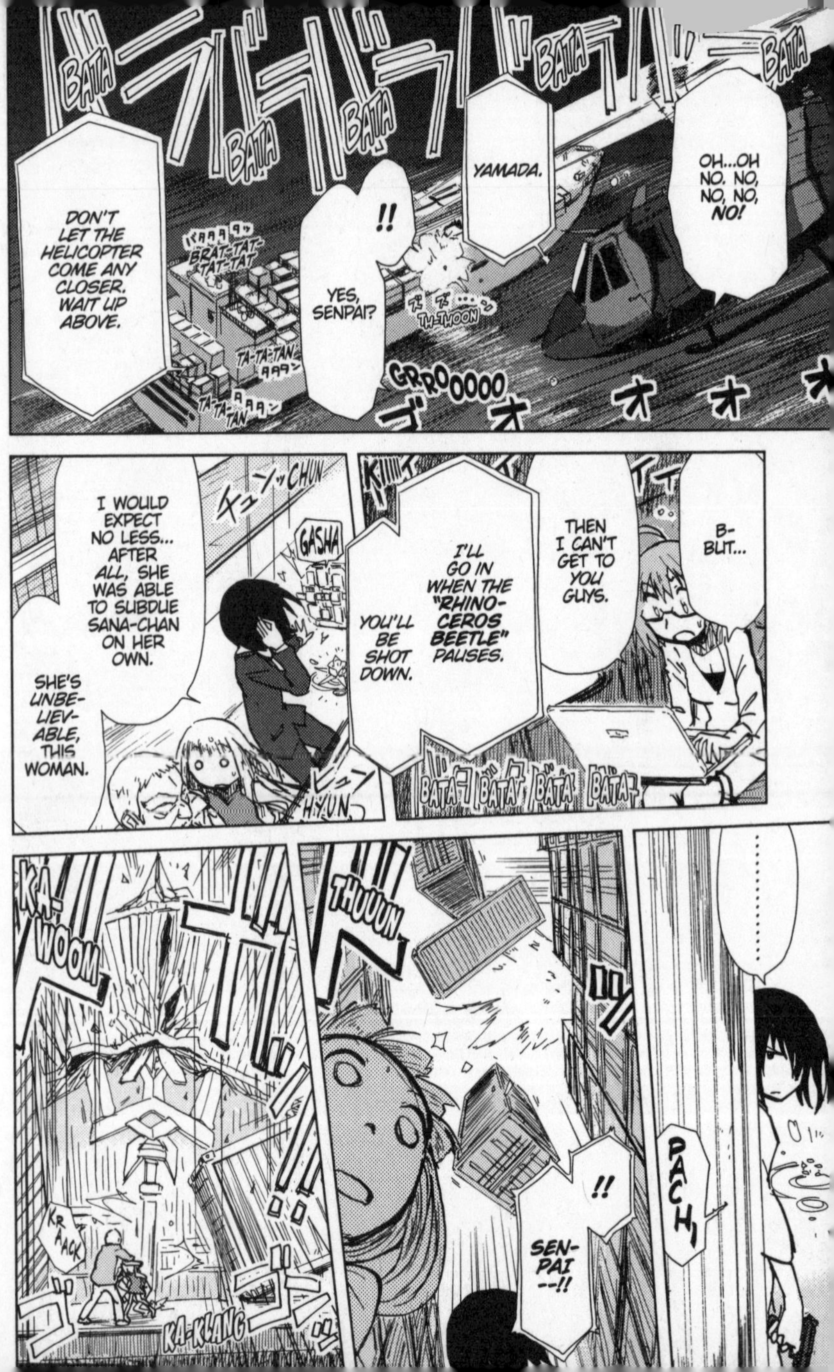
BATA BATA BATA BATA BATA BATA
OH...OH NO. NO, NO, NO, NO!
YAMADA.
!!
YES, SENPAI?
TH-THOON
BRAT-TAT-TAT-TAT
DON'T LET THE HELICOPTER COME ANY CLOSER. WAIT UP ABOVE.
TA-TA-TAN
TA-TA-TAN
GRROOOOO
B-BUT...
THEN I CAN'T GET TO YOU GUYS.
I'LL GO IN WHEN THE "RHINOCEROS BEETLE" PAUSES.
YOU'LL BE SHOT DOWN.
BATA BATA BATA BATA
CHUN
GASHA
I WOULD EXPECT NO LESS... AFTER ALL, SHE WAS ABLE TO SUBDUE SANA-CHAN ON HER OWN.
SHE'S UNBELIEVABLE, THIS WOMAN.
HYUN
......
PACHI
THUUUN
!!
SEN-PAI--!!
KA-WOOM
KRAACK
KA-KLANG

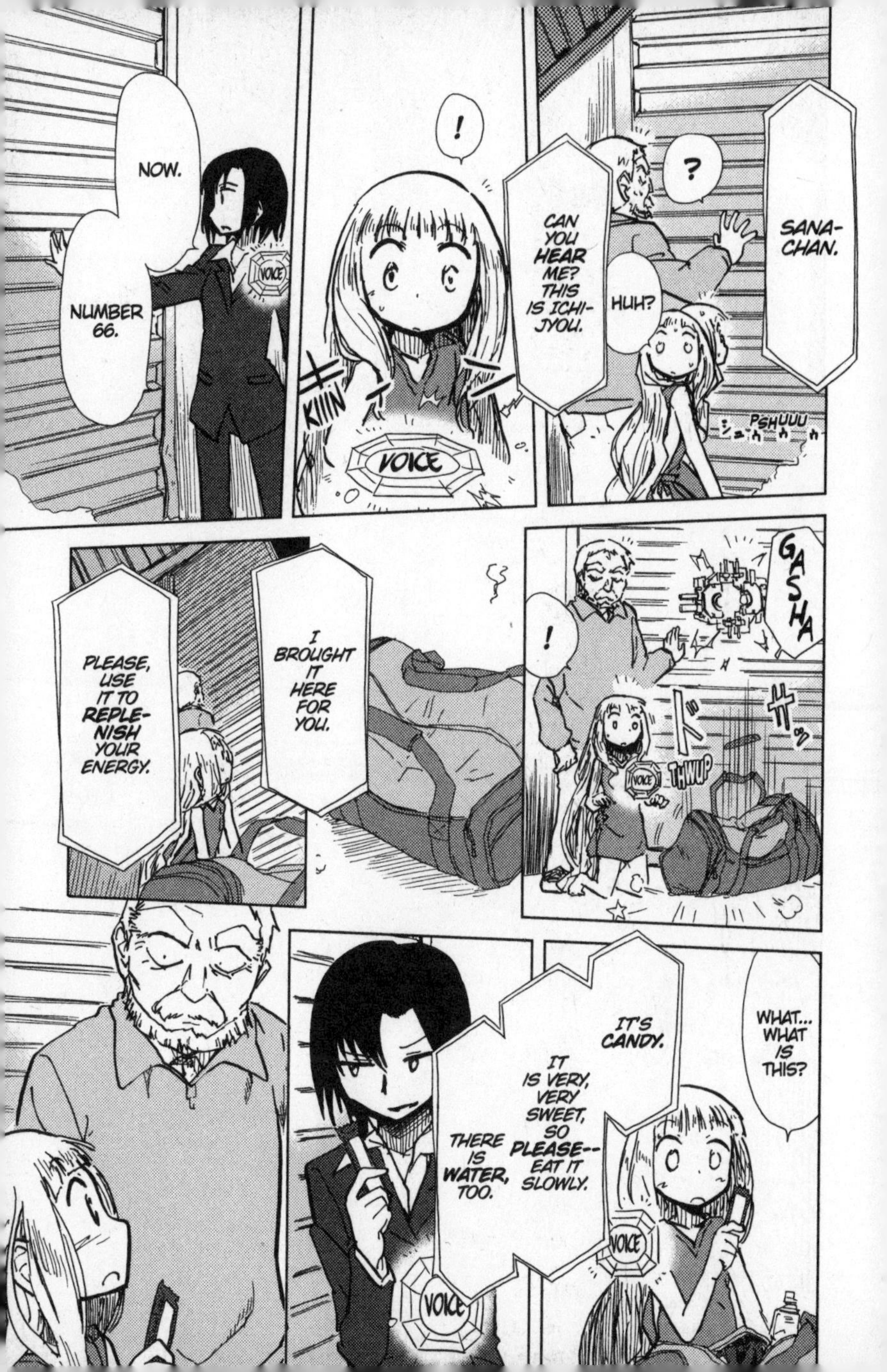
SANA-CHAN.
?
HUH?
PSHUUU
CAN YOU HEAR ME? THIS IS ICHIJYOU.
!
KIIIN
VOICE
NOW.
NUMBER 66.
VOICE
GASHA
!
THWUP
VOICE
I BROUGHT IT HERE FOR YOU.
PLEASE, USE IT TO REPLENISH YOUR ENERGY.
WHAT... WHAT IS THIS?
VOICE
IT'S CANDY.
IT IS VERY, VERY SWEET, SO PLEASE-- EAT IT SLOWLY.
THERE IS WATER, TOO.
VOICE

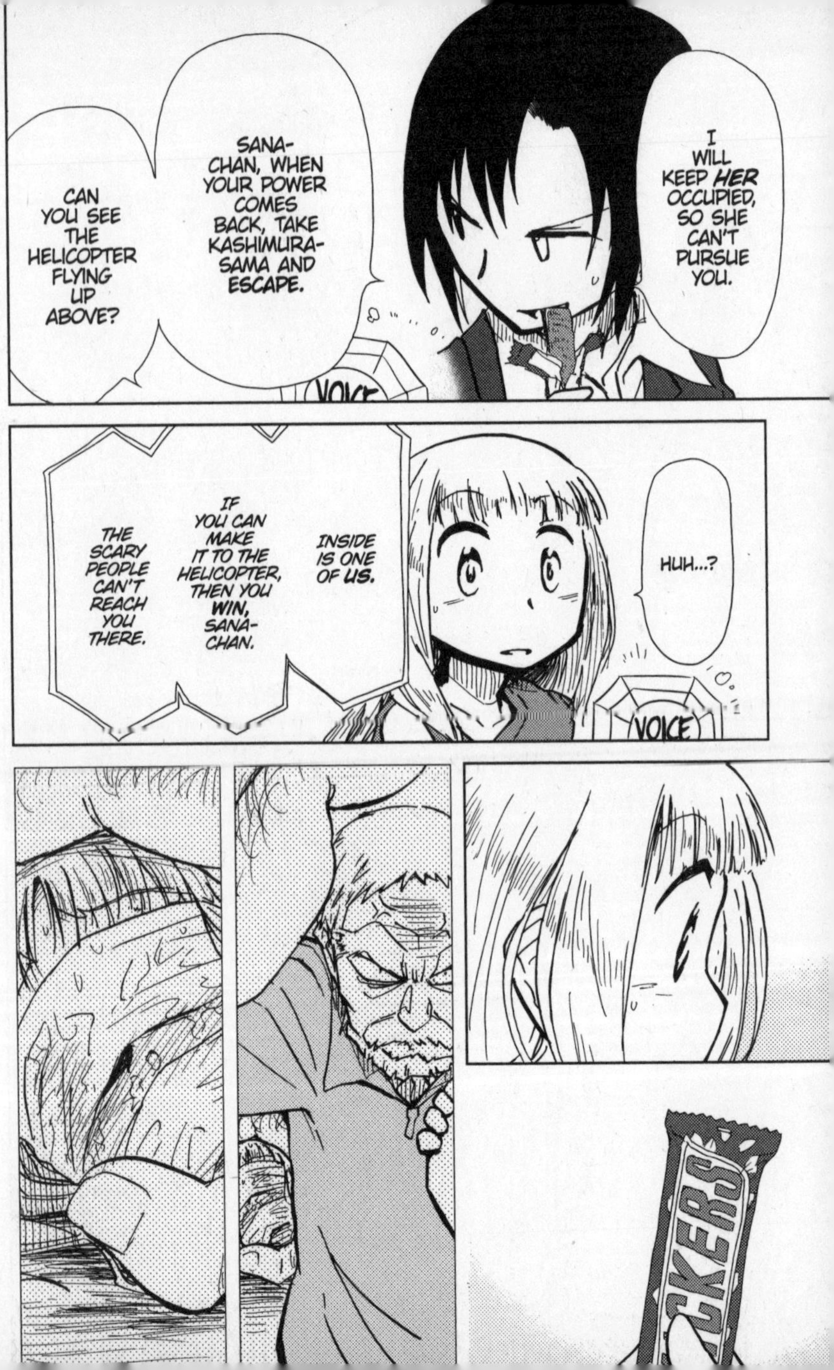
I WILL KEEP HER OCCUPIED, SO SHE CAN'T PURSUE YOU.
SANA-CHAN, WHEN YOUR POWER COMES BACK, TAKE KASHIMURA-SAMA AND ESCAPE.
CAN YOU SEE THE HELICOPTER FLYING UP ABOVE?
VOICE
HUH...?
VOICE
INSIDE IS ONE OF US.
IF YOU CAN MAKE IT TO THE HELICOPTER, THEN YOU WIN, SANA-CHAN.
THE SCARY PEOPLE CAN'T REACH YOU THERE.
CKERS

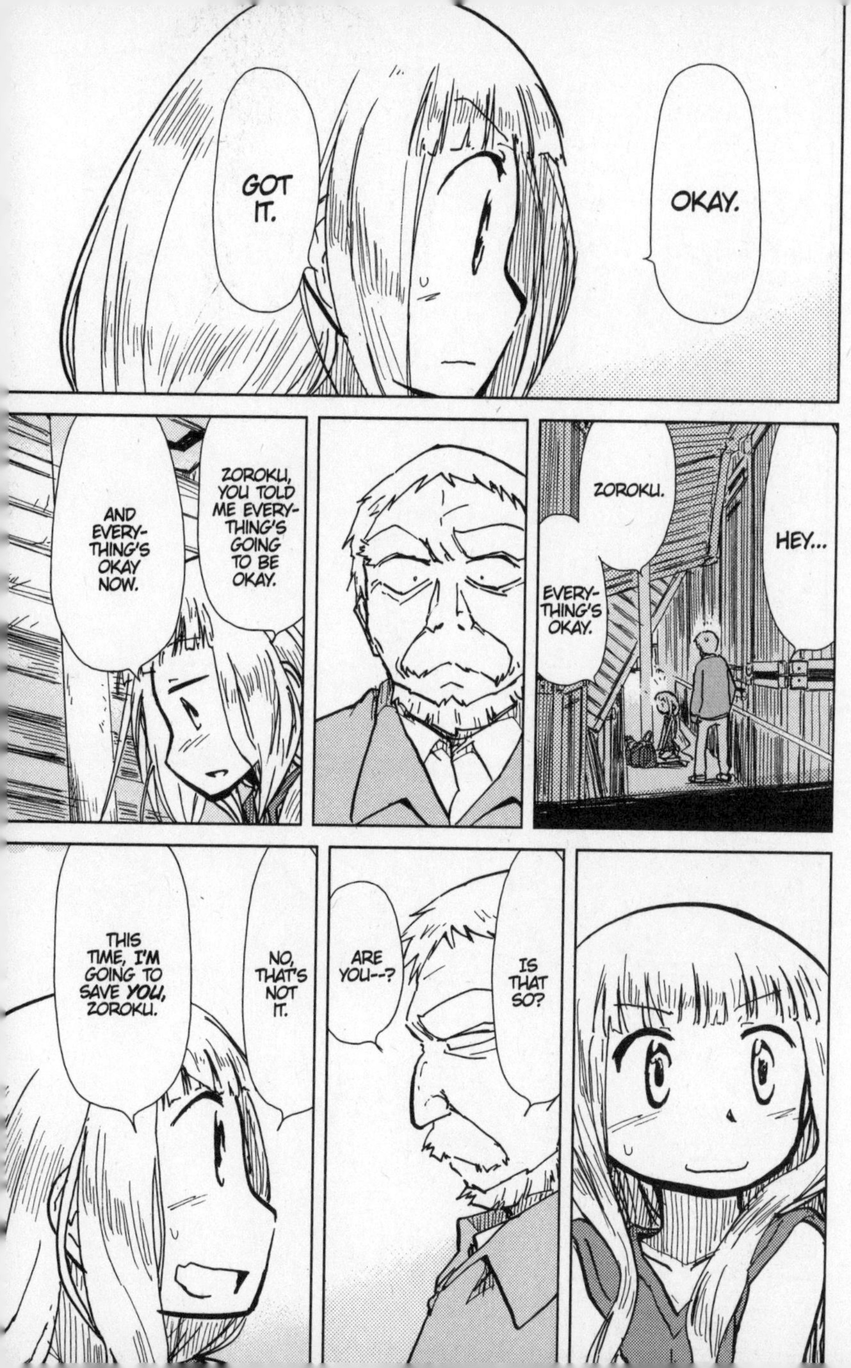
OKAY.
GOT IT.
HEY...
ZOROKU.
EVERYTHING'S OKAY.
ZOROKU, YOU TOLD ME EVERYTHING'S GOING TO BE OKAY.
AND EVERYTHING'S OKAY NOW.
IS THAT SO?
ARE YOU--?
NO, THAT'S NOT IT.
THIS TIME, I'M GOING TO SAVE *YOU*, ZOROKU.

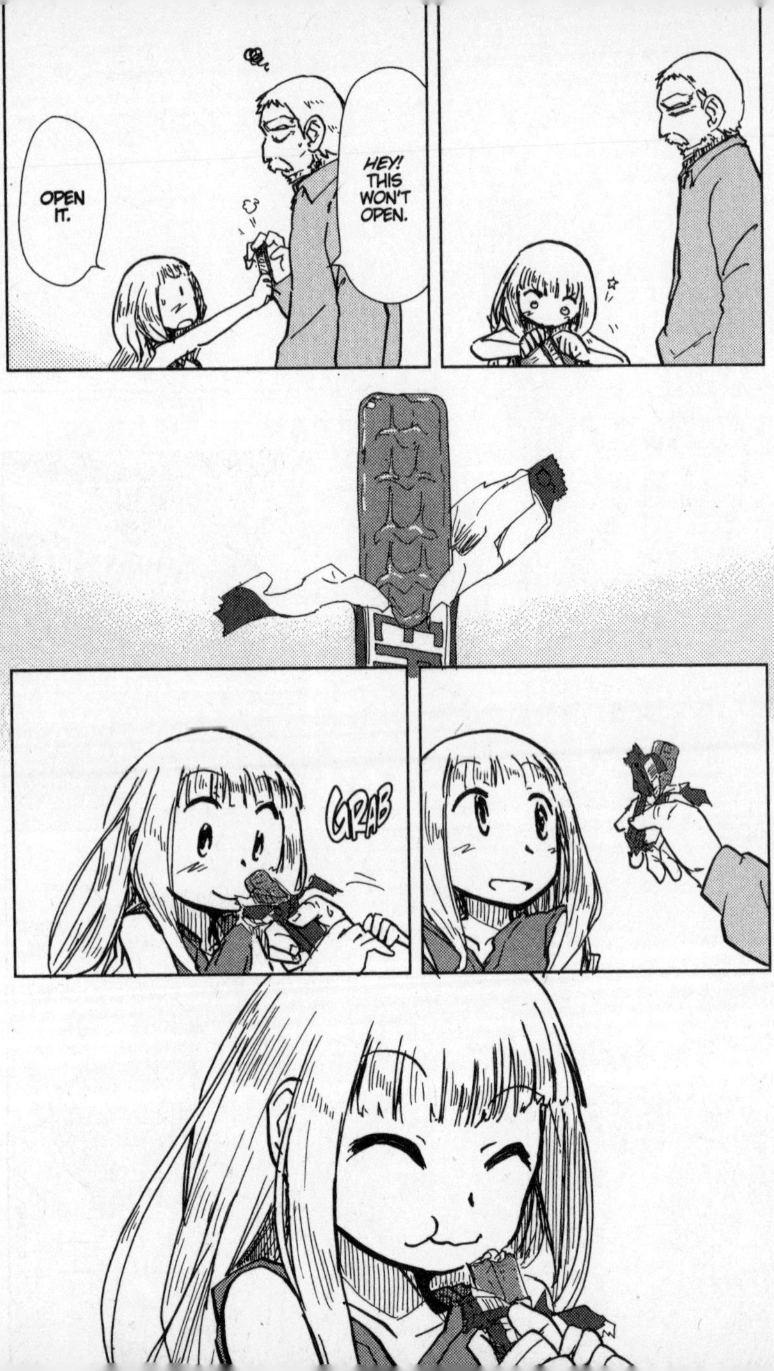
HEY! THIS WON'T OPEN.
OPEN IT.
GRAB

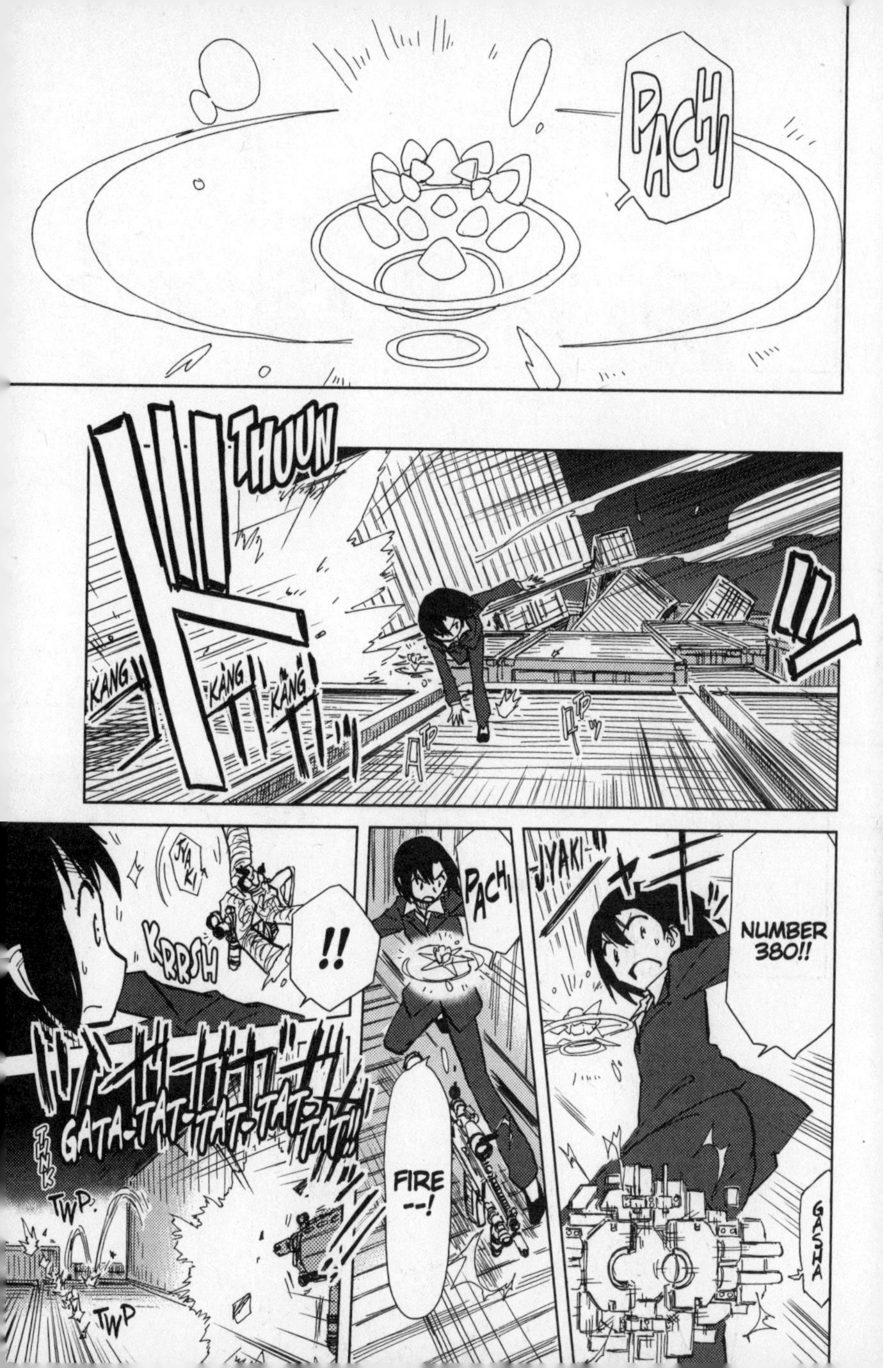
PACHI
!!
THUUN
KANG
KANG
KANG
JYAKI
NUMBER 380!!
GASHA
PACH
FIRE --!
JYAKI
!!
KRRSH
GATA-TAT-TAT-TAT-TAT!!
THUNK
TWP
TWP

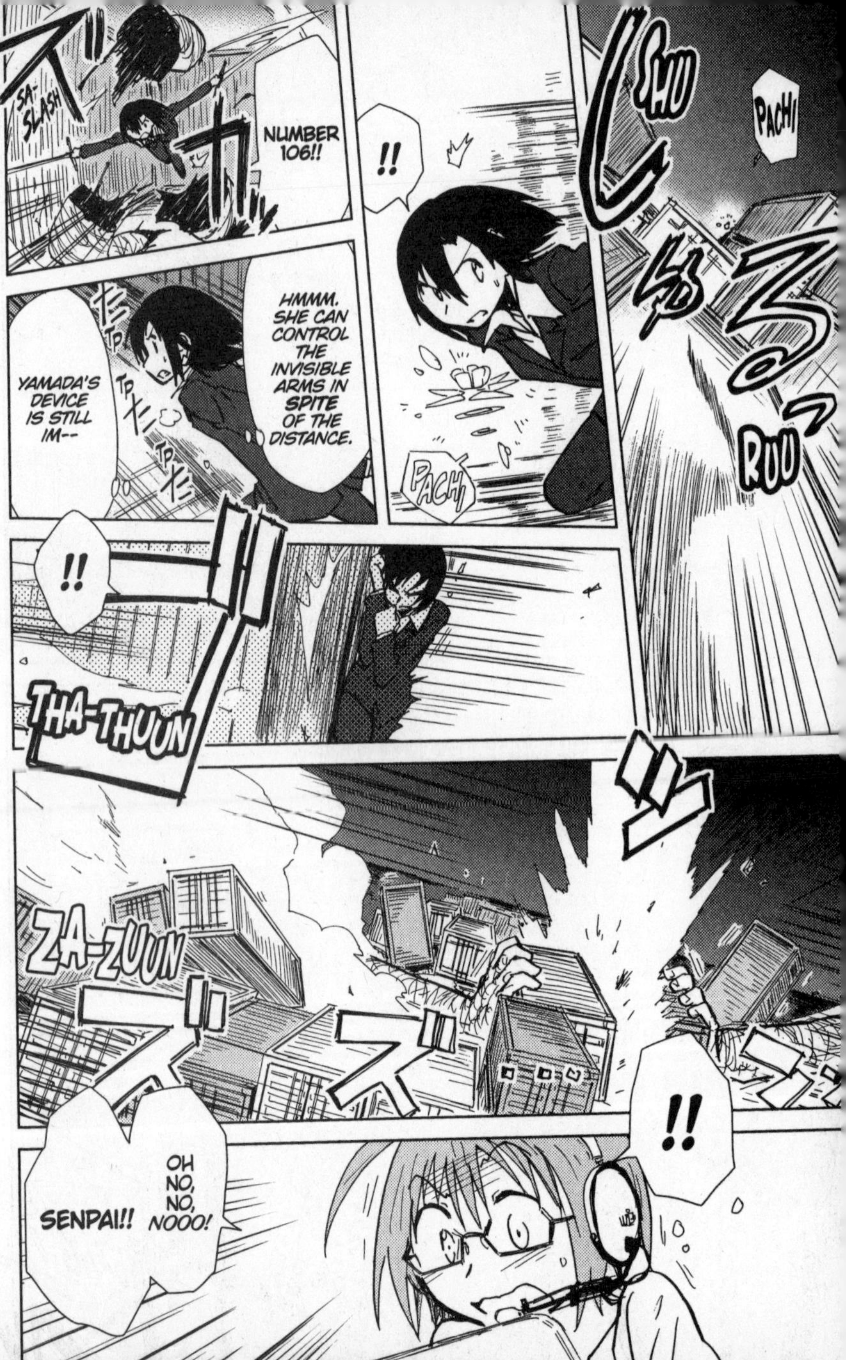
SHU
PACHI
RUU
!!
PACHI
SA-SLASH
NUMBER 106!!
HMMM. SHE CAN CONTROL THE INVISIBLE ARMS IN SPITE OF THE DISTANCE.
TP
TP
TP
YAMADA'S DEVICE IS STILL IM--
!!
THA-THUUN
ZA-ZUUN
!!
OH NO, NO, NOOO!
SENPAI!!

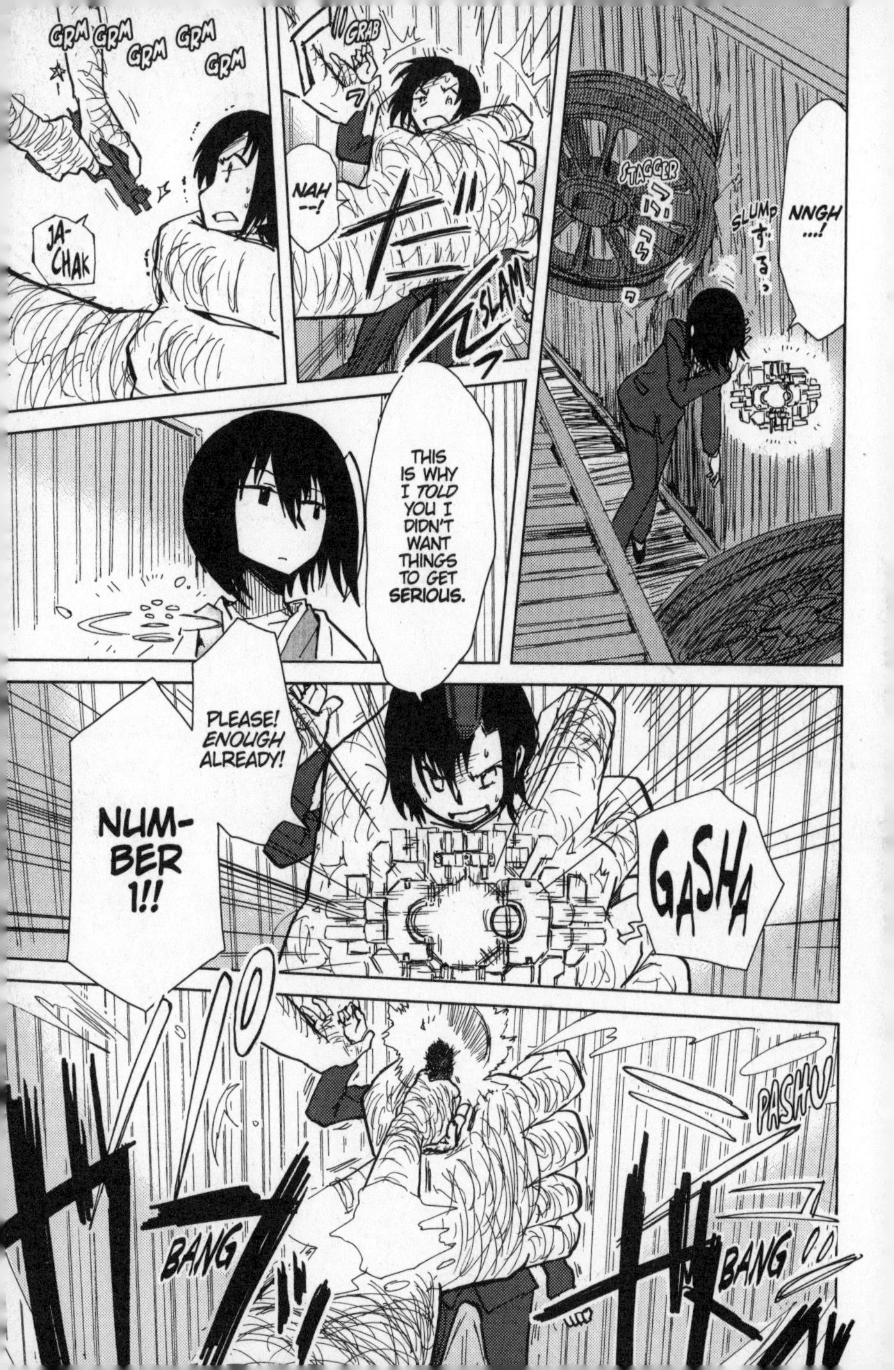
NNGH ...!
STAGGER
SLUMP ずるっ
GRAB
NAH --!
SLAM
GRM GRM GRM GRM GRM
JA-CHAK
THIS IS WHY I *TOLD* YOU I DIDN'T WANT THINGS TO GET SERIOUS.
GASHA
PLEASE! ENOUGH ALREADY!
NUM-BER 1!!
PASHU
BANG
BANG

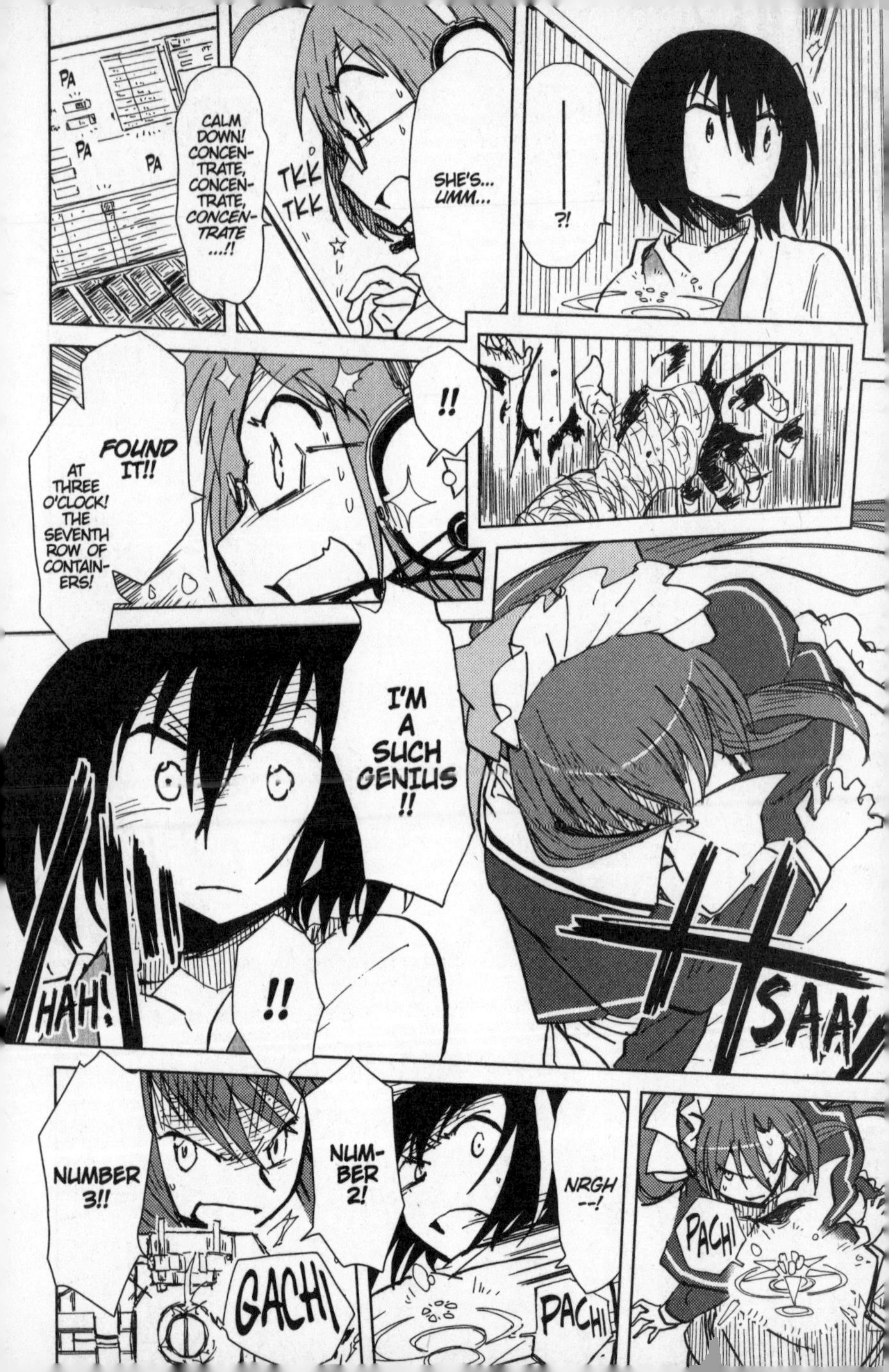
?!
SHE'S... UMM...
TKK TKK
CALM DOWN! CONCENTRATE, CONCENTRATE, CONCENTRATE ...!!
PA
PA
PA
!!
FOUND IT!!
AT THREE O'CLOCK! THE SEVENTH ROW OF CONTAINERS!
SAA!
I'M A SUCH GENIUS !!
!!
HAH!
NRGH --!
PACHI
PACHI
NUMBER 2!
NUMBER 3!!
GACHI

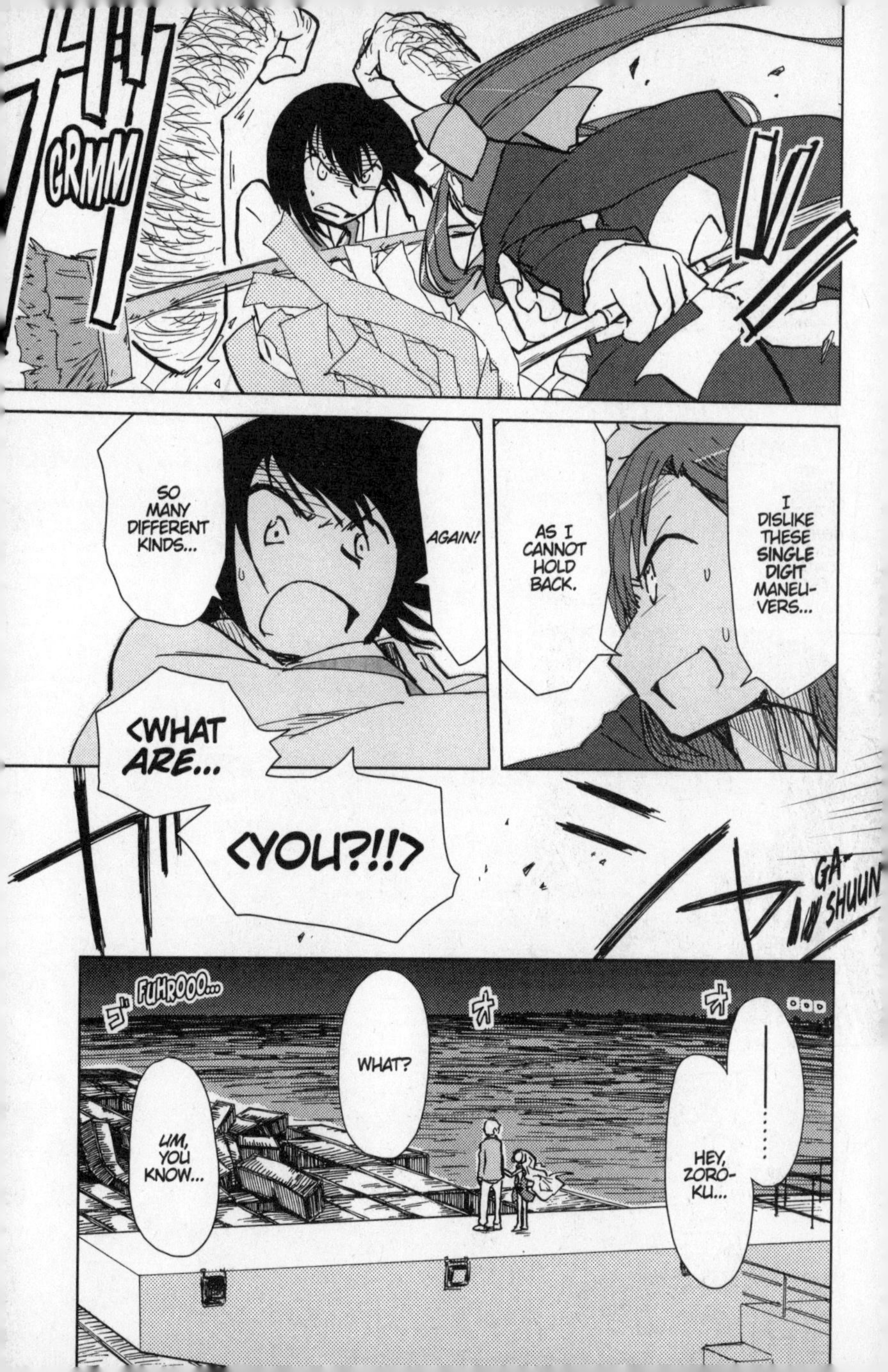
GRMM
I DISLIKE THESE SINGLE DIGIT MANEUVERS...
AS I CANNOT HOLD BACK.
AGAIN!
SO MANY DIFFERENT KINDS...
<WHAT ARE...
<YOU?!!>
GA-SHUUN
...
—......
HEY, ZORO-KU...
WHAT?
UM, YOU KNOW...
FUHROOO...

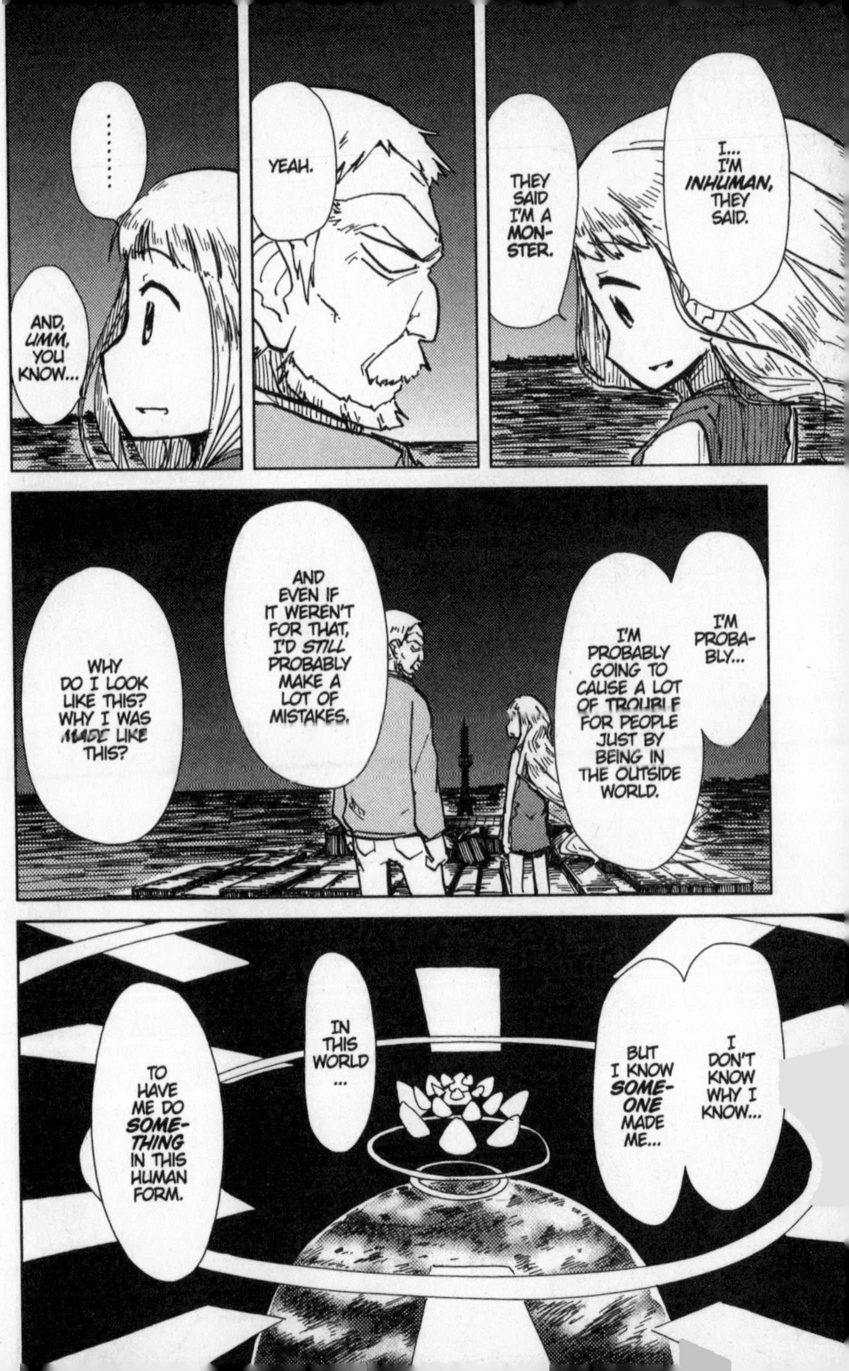
I... I'M *INHUMAN,* THEY SAID.
THEY SAID I'M A MON-STER.
YEAH.
......
AND, *UMM,* YOU KNOW...
I'M PROBA-BLY...
I'M PROBABLY GOING TO CAUSE A LOT OF TROUBLE FOR PEOPLE JUST BY BEING IN THE OUTSIDE WORLD.
AND EVEN IF IT WEREN'T FOR THAT, I'D *STILL* PROBABLY MAKE A LOT OF MISTAKES.
WHY DO I LOOK LIKE THIS? WHY I WAS *MADE* LIKE THIS?
I DON'T KNOW WHY I KNOW...
BUT I KNOW ***SOME-ONE*** MADE ME...
IN THIS WORLD ...
TO HAVE ME DO ***SOME-THING*** IN THIS HUMAN FORM.

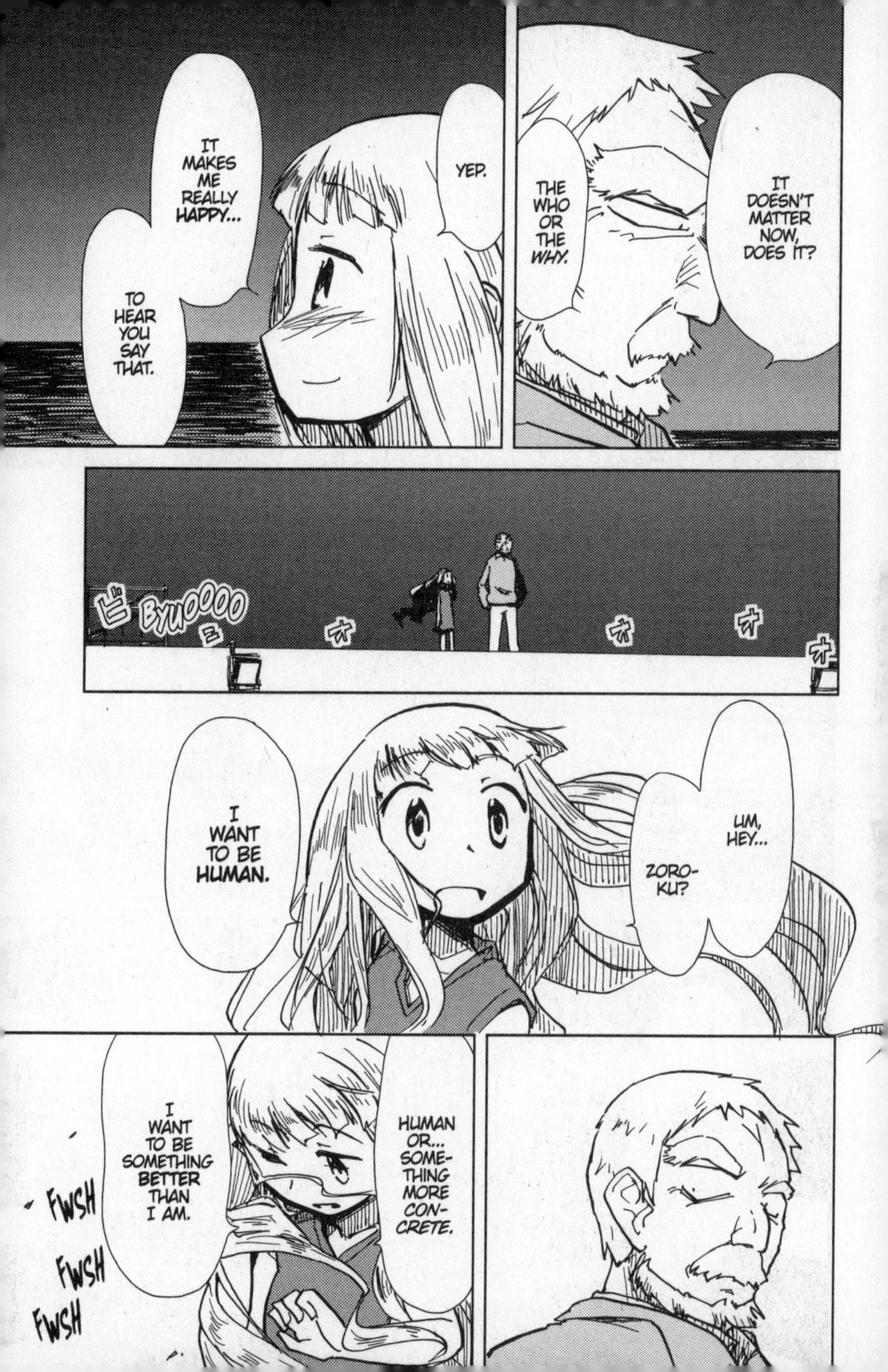
IT DOESN'T MATTER NOW, DOES IT?
THE WHO OR THE *WHY.*
YEP.
IT MAKES ME REALLY HAPPY...
TO HEAR YOU SAY THAT.
ビ BYUOOOO ュ
オ
オ
オ
オー
UM, HEY...
ZORO-KU?
I WANT TO BE HUMAN.
HUMAN OR... SOME-THING MORE CON-CRETE.
I WANT TO BE SOMETHING BETTER THAN I AM.
FWSH
FWSH
FWSH

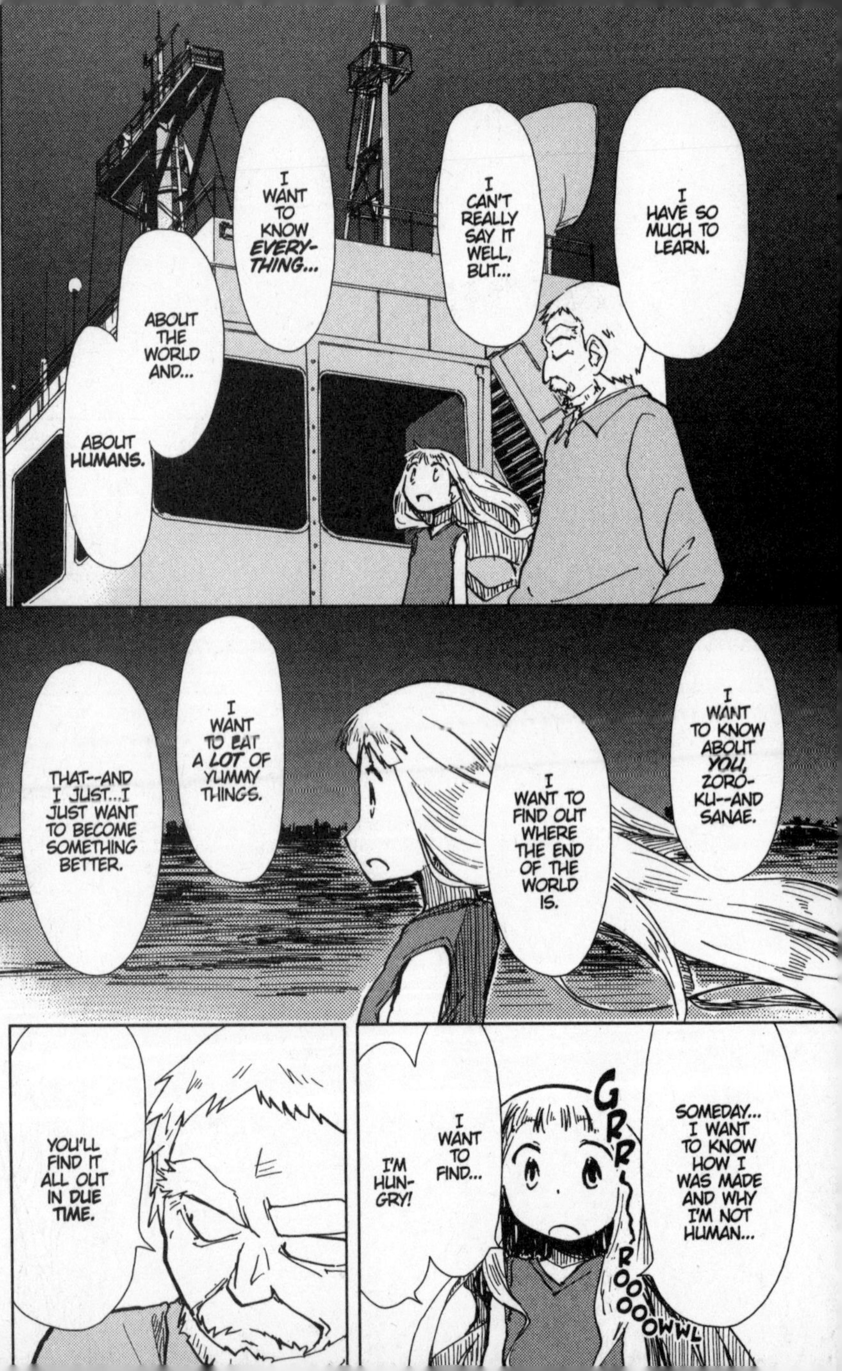
I HAVE SO MUCH TO LEARN.
I CAN'T REALLY SAY IT WELL, BUT...
I WANT TO KNOW EVERYTHING...
ABOUT THE WORLD AND...
ABOUT HUMANS.
I WANT TO KNOW ABOUT YOU, ZORO-KU--AND SANAE.
I WANT TO FIND OUT WHERE THE END OF THE WORLD IS.
I WANT TO EAT A LOT OF YUMMY THINGS.
THAT--AND I JUST...I JUST WANT TO BECOME SOMETHING BETTER.
SOMEDAY... I WANT TO KNOW HOW I WAS MADE AND WHY I'M NOT HUMAN...
GRRR-ROOOOWWL
I WANT TO FIND...
I'M HUN-GRY!
YOU'LL FIND IT ALL OUT IN DUE TIME.

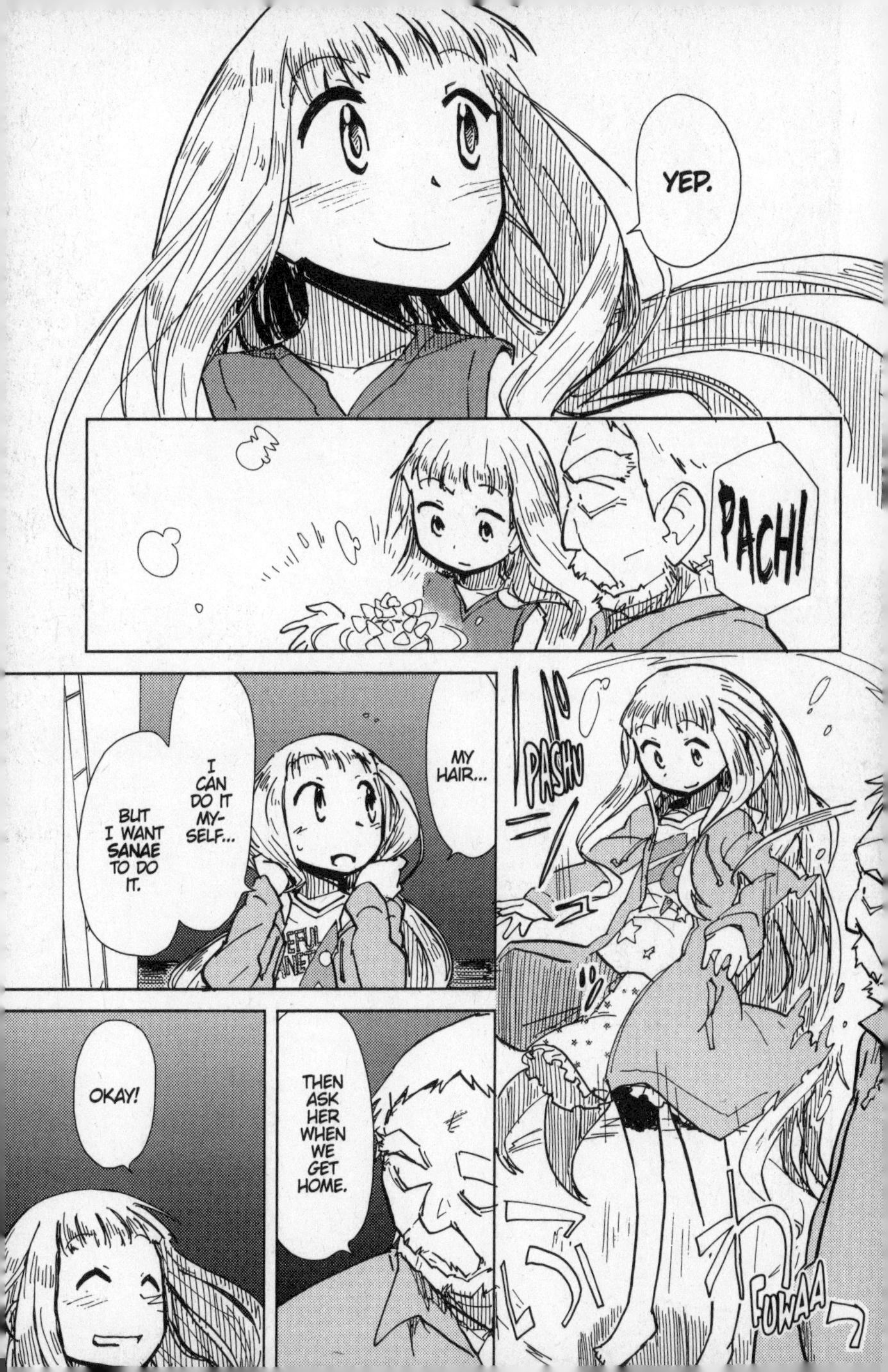
YEP.
PACHI
PASHU
FUWAA
MY HAIR...
I CAN DO IT MY-SELF...
BUT I WANT SANAE TO DO IT.
THEN ASK HER WHEN WE GET HOME.
OKAY!

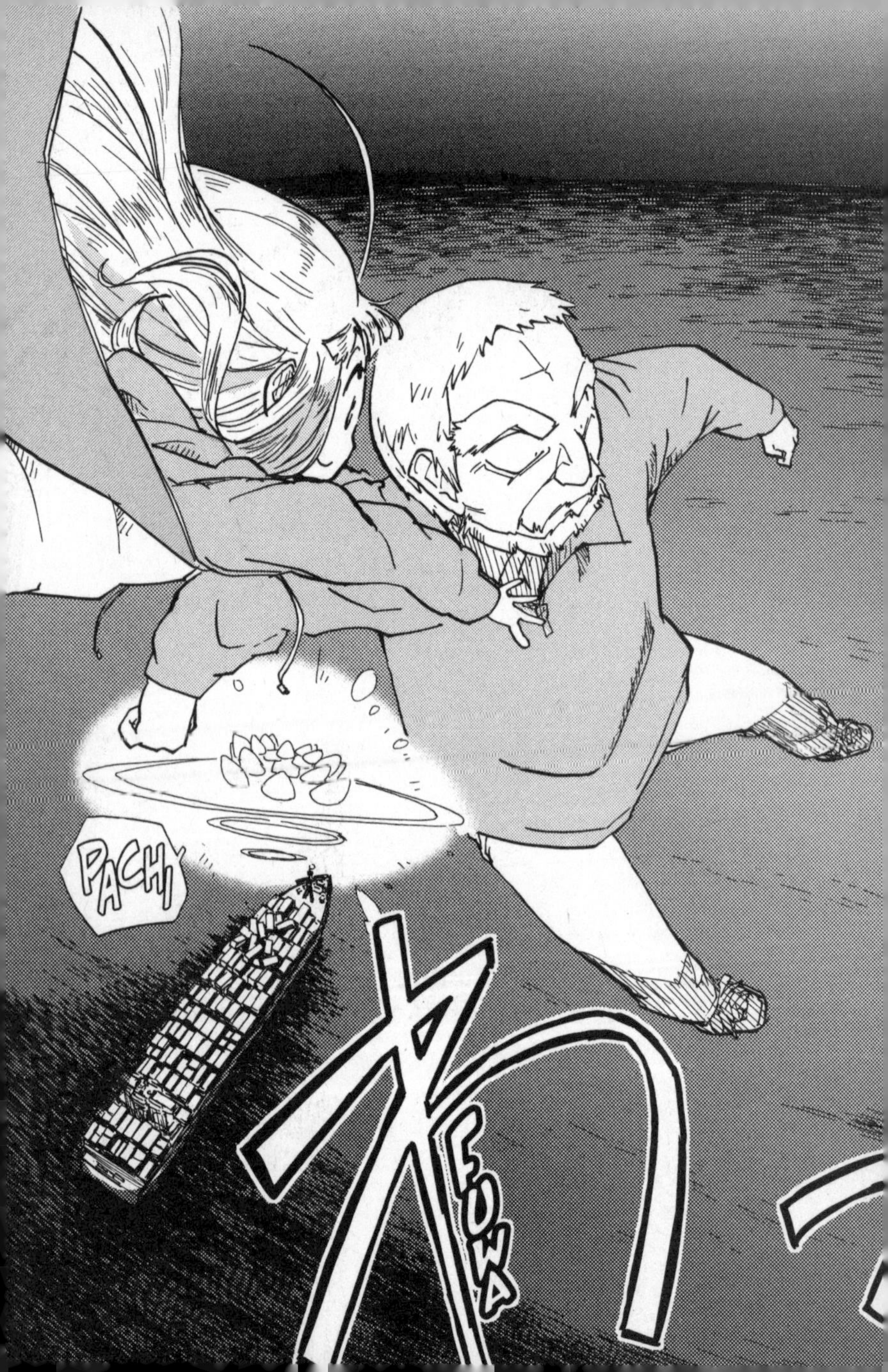
PACHI
FUWA

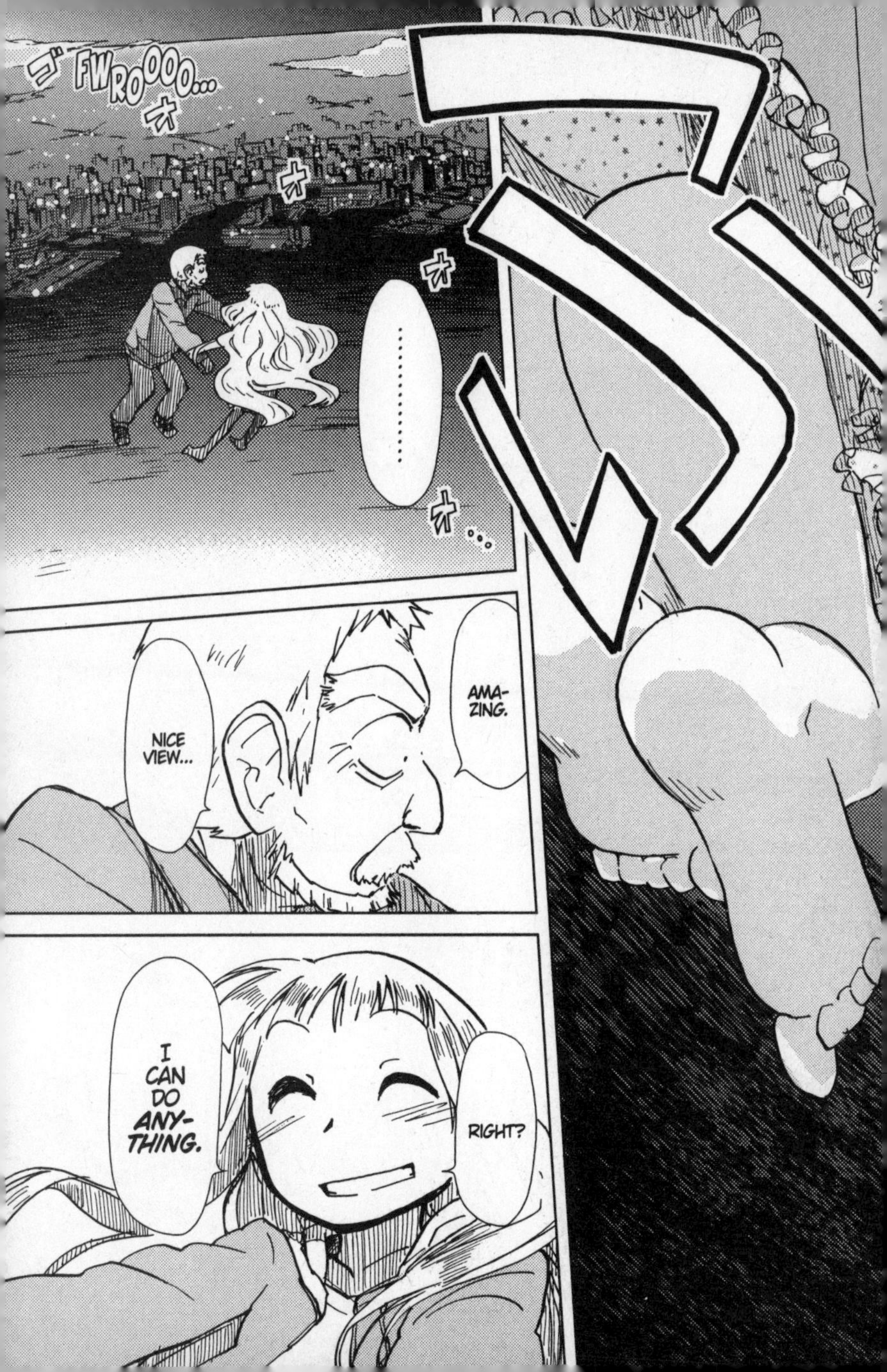
ゴ FWROOOO... オ
オ
オ
オ...
......
AMA-ZING.
NICE VIEW...
RIGHT?
I CAN DO ANYTHING.

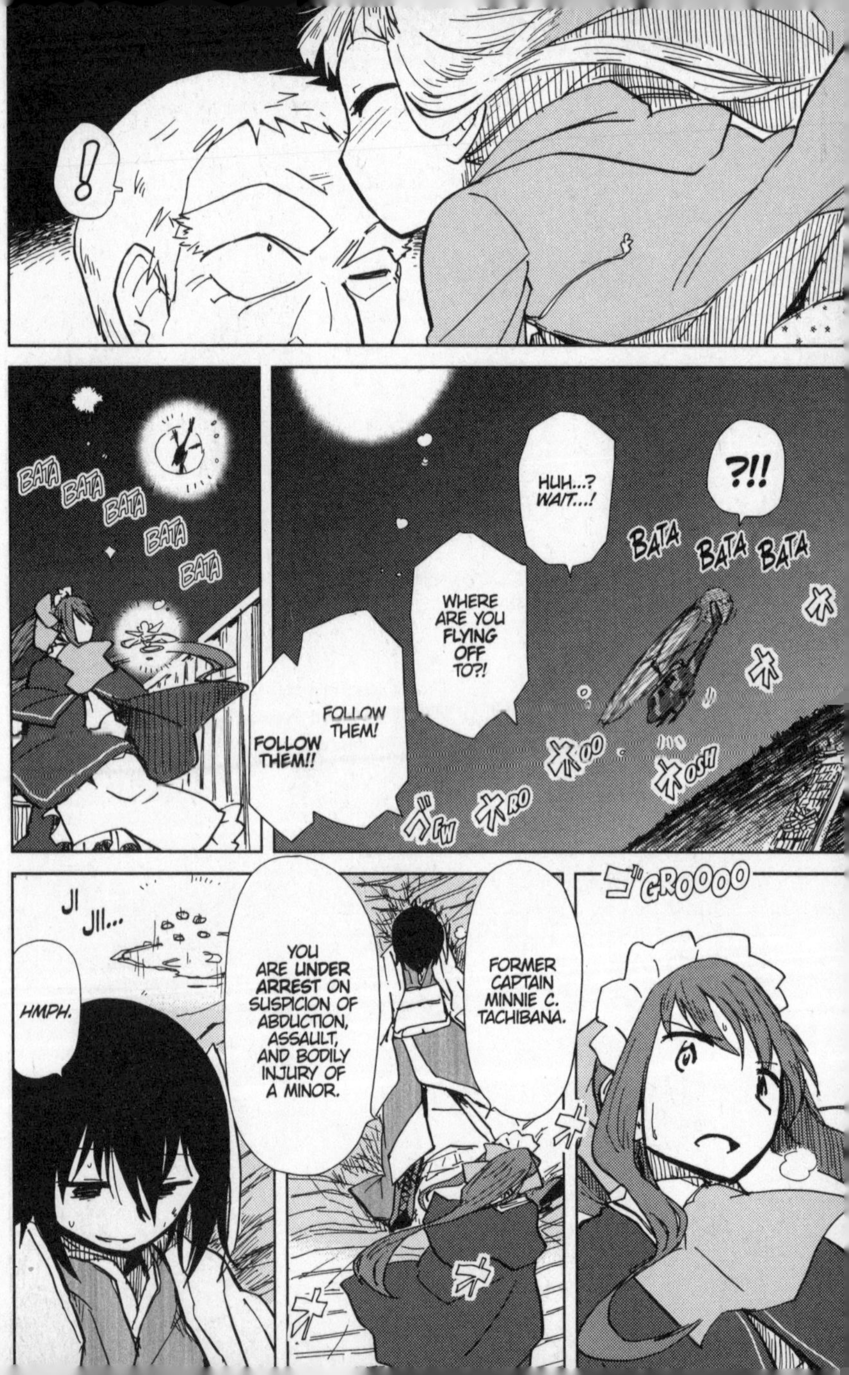
!
?!!
HUH...? WAIT...!
BATA BATA BATA
WHERE ARE YOU FLYING OFF TO?!
FOLLOW THEM!
FOLLOW THEM!!
ホOSH
ホOO
ホRO
ブFW
BATA BATA BATA BATA BATA
ゴGROOOO
FORMER CAPTAIN MINNIE C. TACHIBANA.
YOU ARE UNDER ARREST ON SUSPICION OF ABDUCTION, ASSAULT, AND BODILY INJURY OF A MINOR.
JI JII...
HMPH.

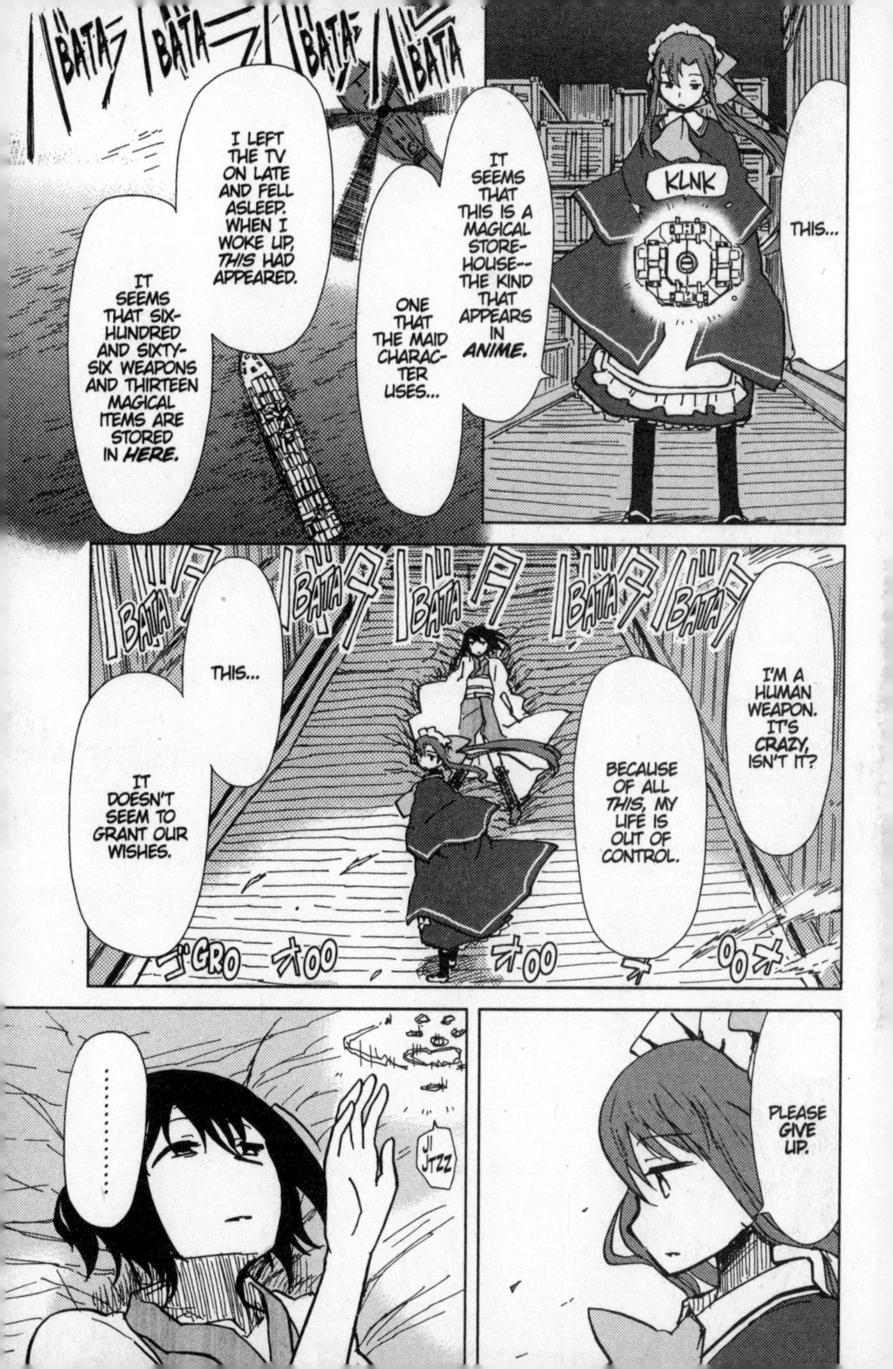
THIS...
KLNK
IT SEEMS THAT THIS IS A MAGICAL STORE-HOUSE-- THE KIND THAT APPEARS IN *ANIME*.
ONE THAT THE MAID CHARACTER USES...
BATA BATA BATA BATA
I LEFT THE TV ON LATE AND FELL ASLEEP. WHEN I WOKE UP, *THIS* HAD APPEARED.
IT SEEMS THAT SIX-HUNDRED AND SIXTY-SIX WEAPONS AND THIRTEEN MAGICAL ITEMS ARE STORED IN *HERE*.
BATA BATA BATA BATA BATA
I'M A HUMAN WEAPON. IT'S CRAZY, ISN'T IT?
BECAUSE OF ALL *THIS*, MY LIFE IS OUT OF CONTROL.
THIS...
IT DOESN'T SEEM TO GRANT OUR WISHES.
OO
OO
OO
GRO
PLEASE GIVE UP.
......
JI JTZZ

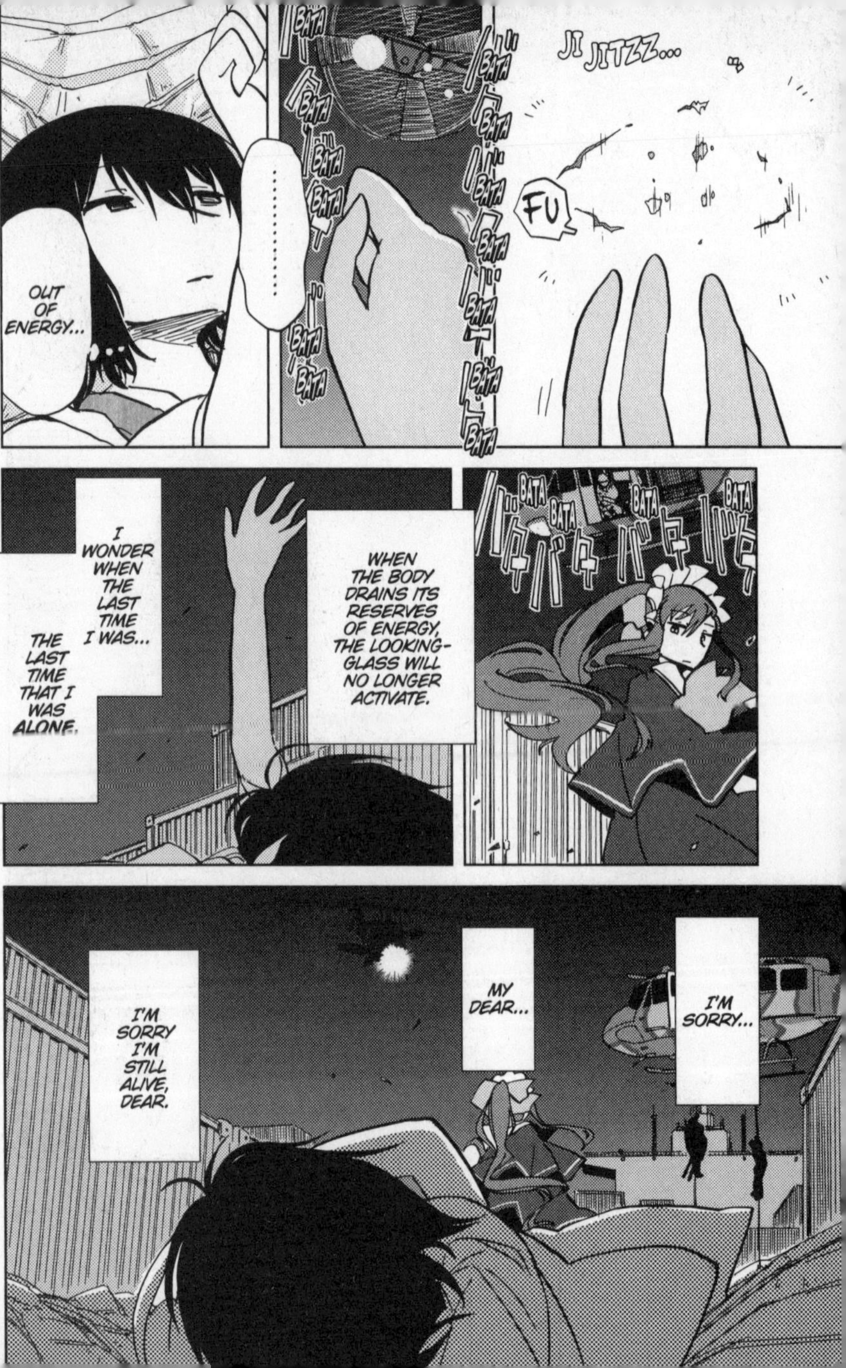

JI JITZZ...
FU
BATA BATA BATA BATA
BATA BATA BATA BATA
...
OUT OF ENERGY...
BATA BATA BATA BATA
WHEN THE BODY DRAINS ITS RESERVES OF ENERGY, THE LOOKING-GLASS WILL NO LONGER ACTIVATE.
I WONDER WHEN THE LAST TIME I WAS...
THE LAST TIME THAT I WAS ALONE.
I'M SORRY...
MY DEAR...
I'M SORRY I'M STILL ALIVE, DEAR.

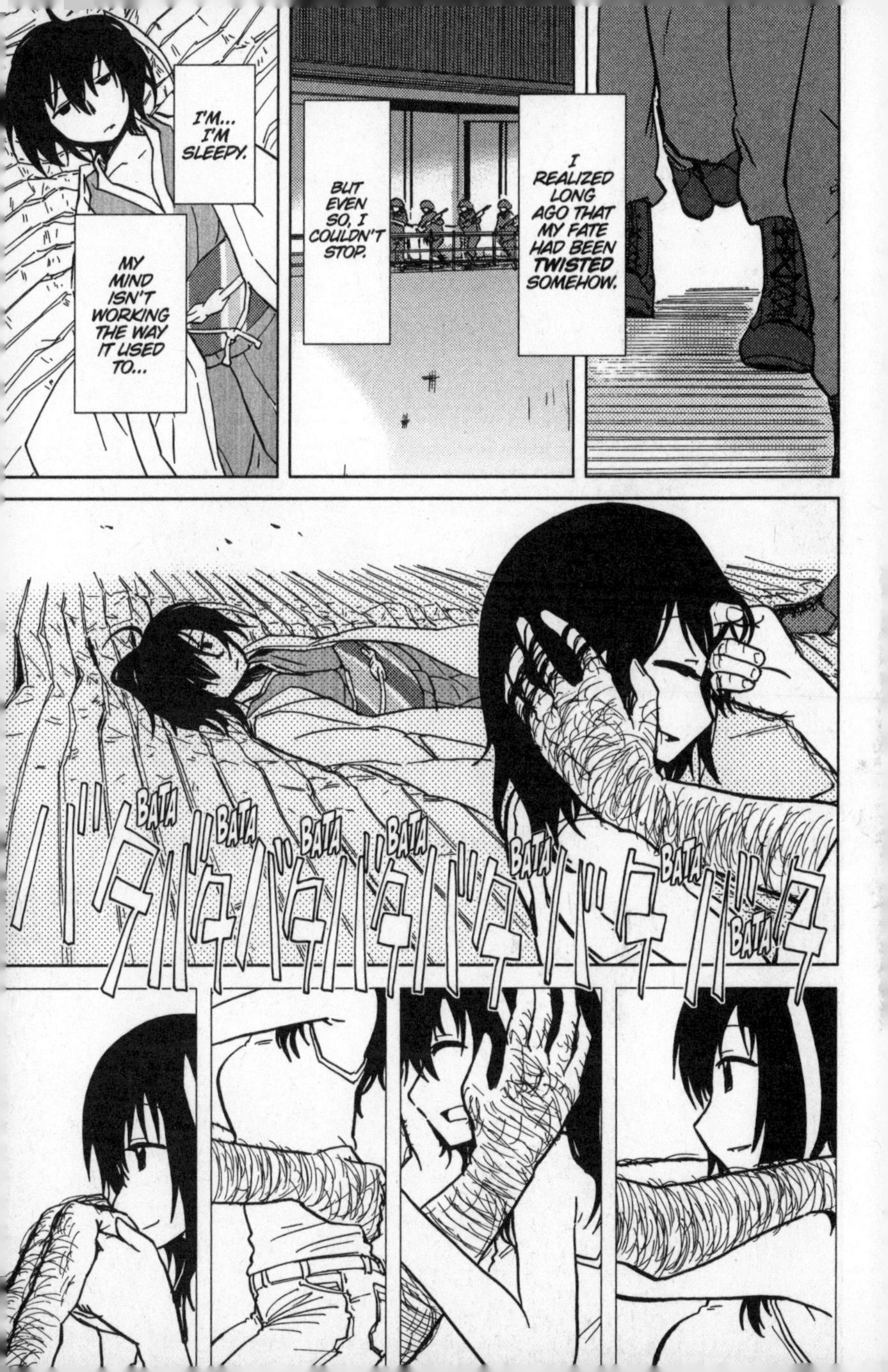
I REALIZED LONG AGO THAT MY FATE HAD BEEN **TWISTED** SOMEHOW.
BUT EVEN SO, I COULDN'T STOP.
I'M... I'M SLEEPY.
MY MIND ISN'T WORKING THE WAY IT USED TO...
BATA
BATA
BATA
BATA
BATA
BATA
BATA

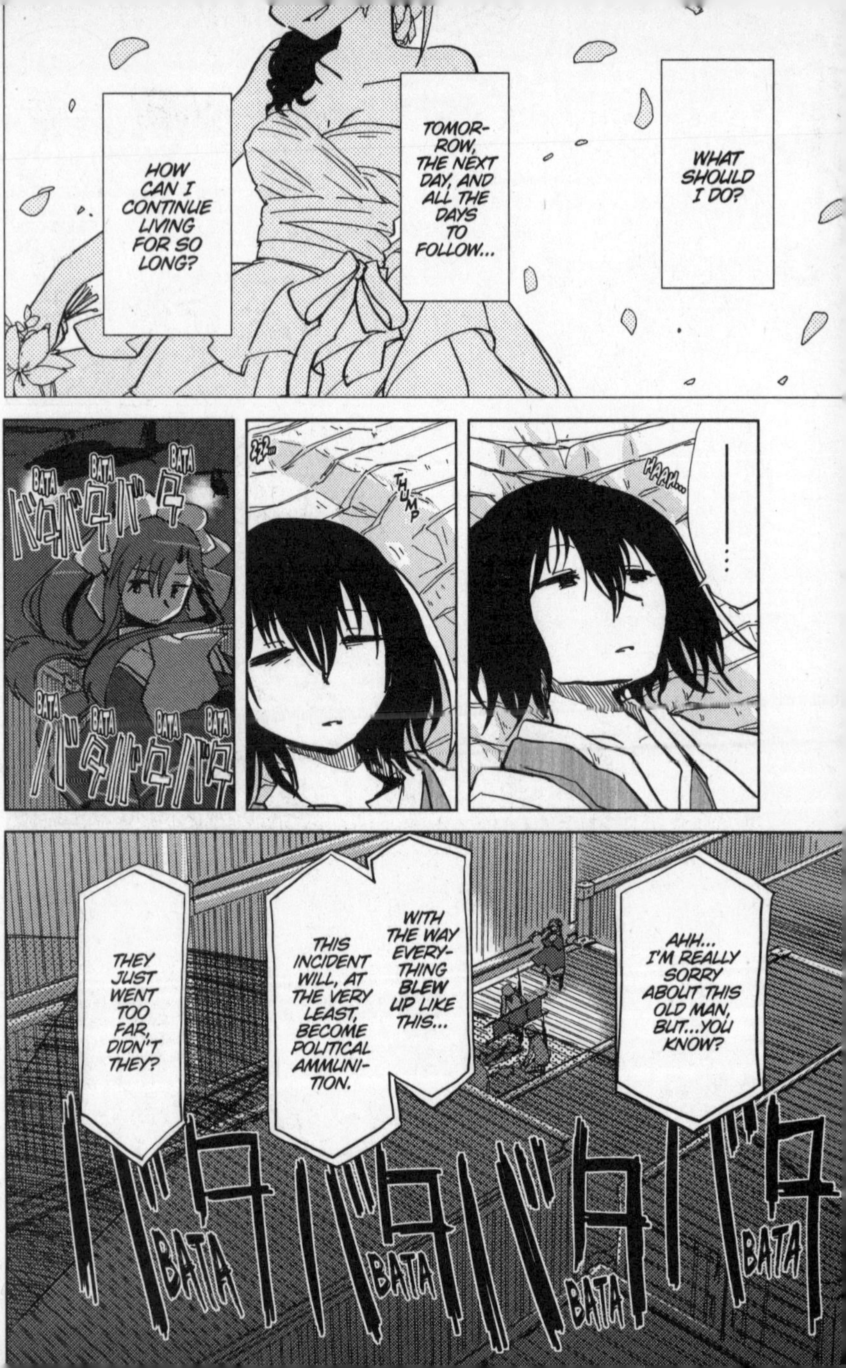
WHAT SHOULD I DO?
TOMORROW, THE NEXT DAY, AND ALL THE DAYS TO FOLLOW...
HOW CAN I CONTINUE LIVING FOR SO LONG?
HAAH...
......
THUMP
BATA BATA BATA BATA
BATA BATA BATA BATA
AHH... I'M REALLY SORRY ABOUT THIS OLD MAN, BUT...YOU KNOW?
WITH THE WAY EVERYTHING BLEW UP LIKE THIS...
THIS INCIDENT WILL, AT THE VERY LEAST, BECOME POLITICAL AMMUNITION.
THEY JUST WENT TOO FAR, DIDN'T THEY?
BATA BATA BATA BATA

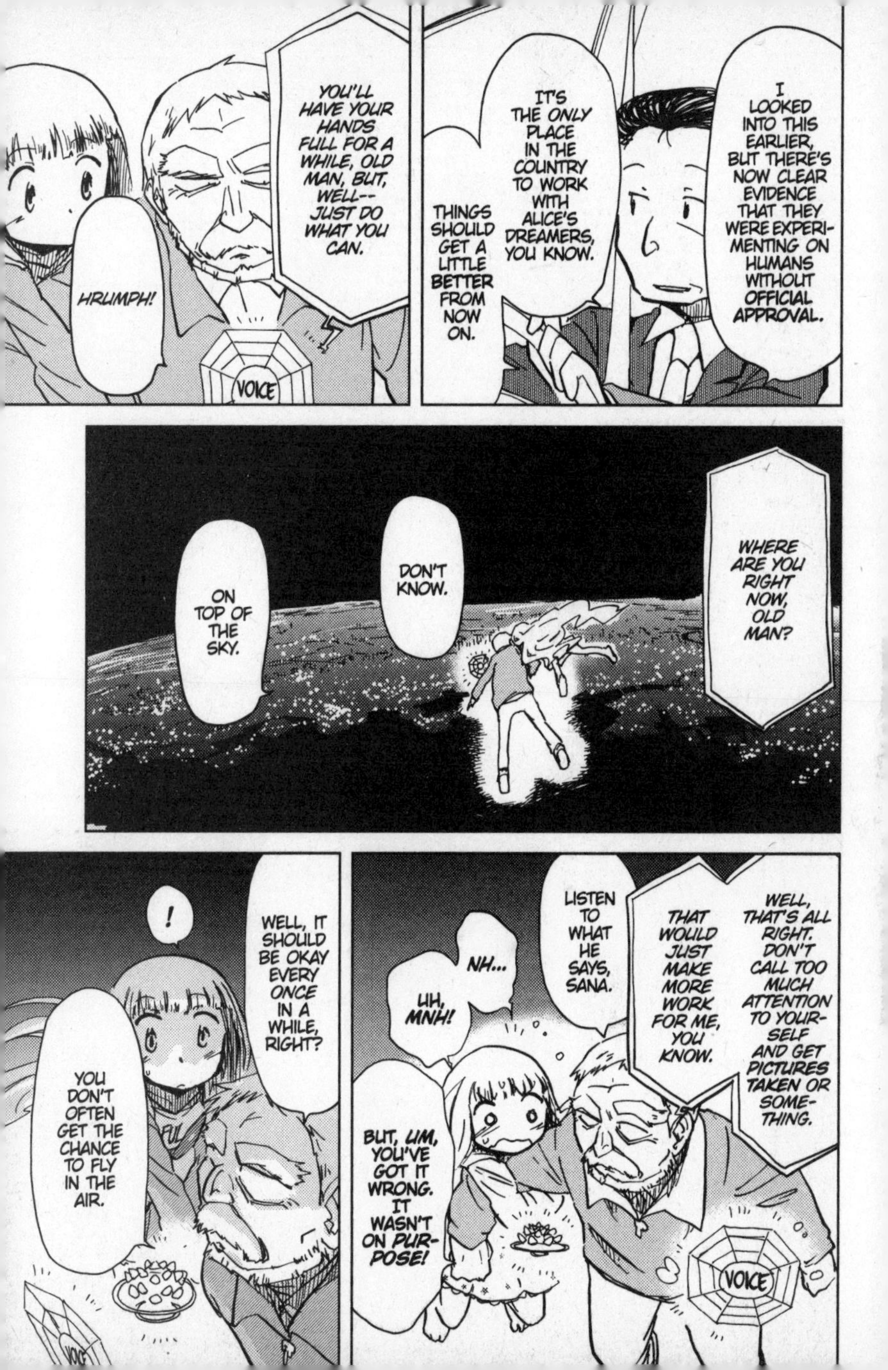
I LOOKED INTO THIS EARLIER, BUT THERE'S NOW CLEAR EVIDENCE THAT THEY WERE EXPERIMENTING ON HUMANS WITHOUT OFFICIAL APPROVAL.
IT'S THE ONLY PLACE IN THE COUNTRY TO WORK WITH ALICE'S DREAMERS, YOU KNOW.
THINGS SHOULD GET A LITTLE BETTER FROM NOW ON.
YOU'LL HAVE YOUR HANDS FULL FOR A WHILE, OLD MAN, BUT, WELL-- JUST DO WHAT YOU CAN.
HRUMPH!
VOICE
WHERE ARE YOU RIGHT NOW, OLD MAN?
DON'T KNOW.
ON TOP OF THE SKY.
WELL, THAT'S ALL RIGHT. DON'T CALL TOO MUCH ATTENTION TO YOURSELF AND GET PICTURES TAKEN OR SOMETHING.
THAT WOULD JUST MAKE MORE WORK FOR ME, YOU KNOW.
LISTEN TO WHAT HE SAYS, SANA.
NH...
UH, MNH!
BUT, UM, YOU'VE GOT IT WRONG. IT WASN'T ON PURPOSE!
VOICE
WELL, IT SHOULD BE OKAY EVERY ONCE IN A WHILE, RIGHT?
!
YOU DON'T OFTEN GET THE CHANCE TO FLY IN THE AIR.

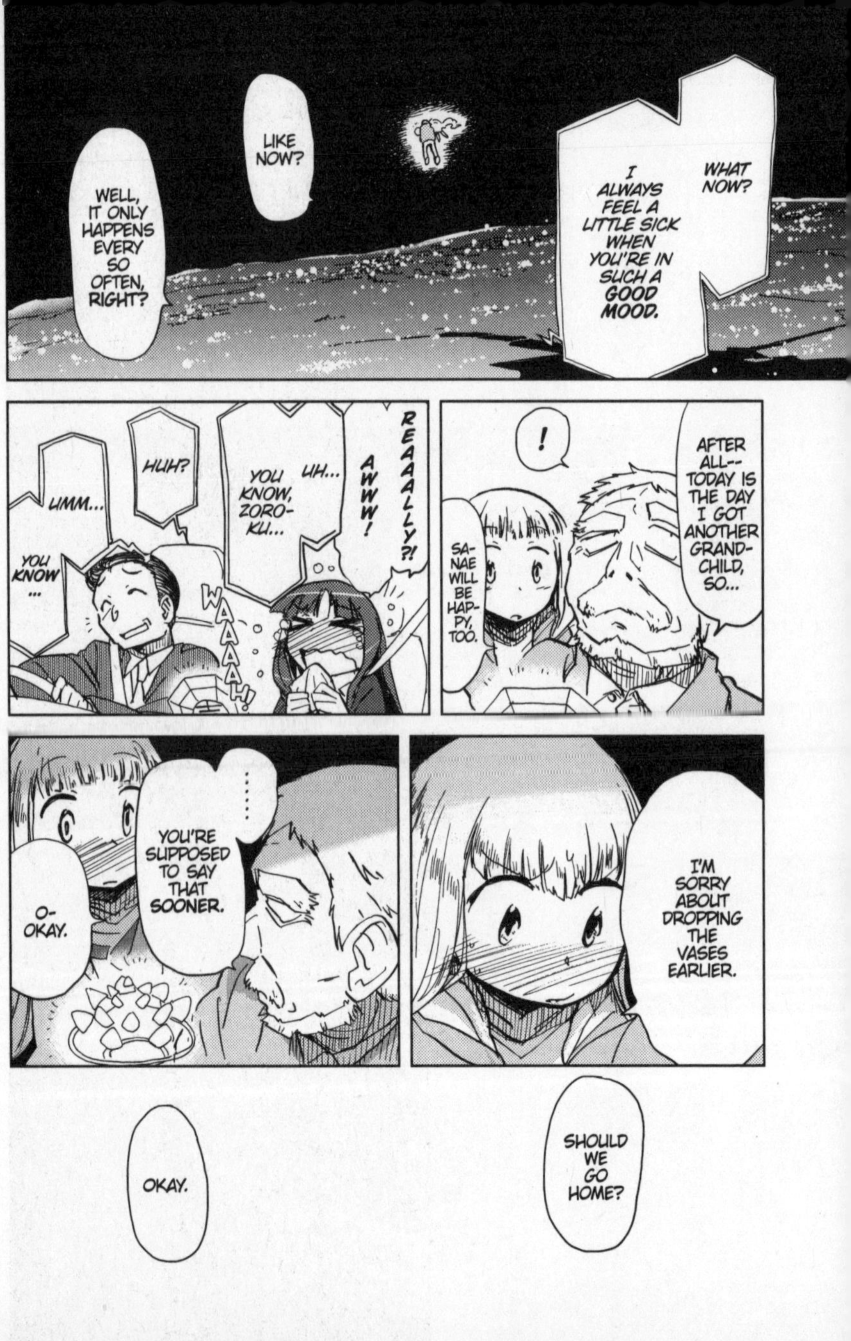
WHAT NOW? I ALWAYS FEEL A LITTLE SICK WHEN YOU'RE IN SUCH A GOOD MOOD.
LIKE NOW?
WELL, IT ONLY HAPPENS EVERY SO OFTEN, RIGHT?
AFTER ALL-- TODAY IS THE DAY I GOT ANOTHER GRAND-CHILD, SO...
!
SA-NAE WILL BE HAP-PY, TOO.
REAAAALLY?!
AWWW!
UH...
YOU KNOW, ZORO-KU...
HUH?
UMM...
YOU KNOW ...
WAAAAAH!
I'M SORRY ABOUT DROPPING THE VASES EARLIER.
......
YOU'RE SUPPOSED TO SAY THAT SOONER.
O-OKAY.
SHOULD WE GO HOME?
OKAY.

To be continued.........

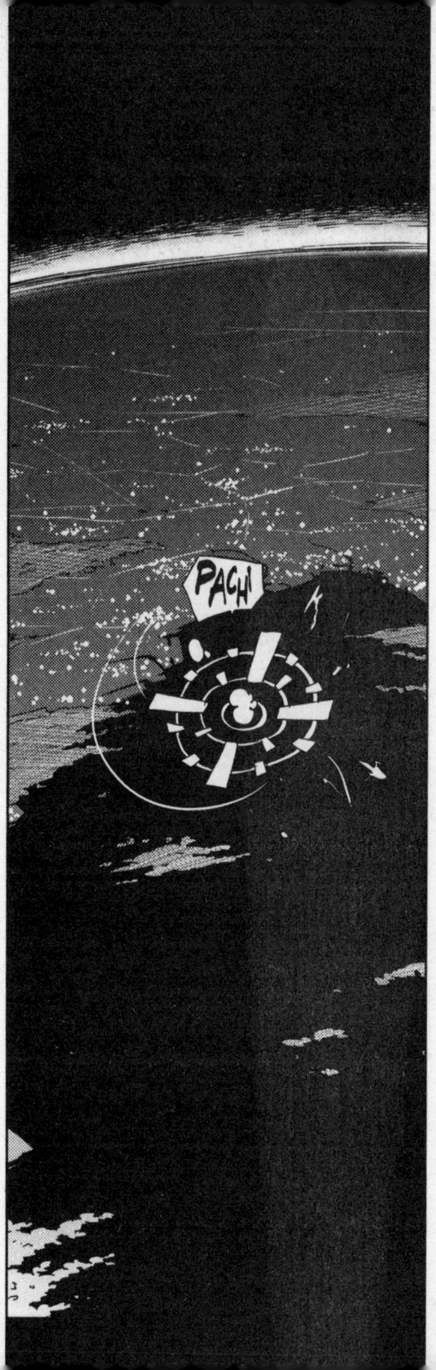
PACHI

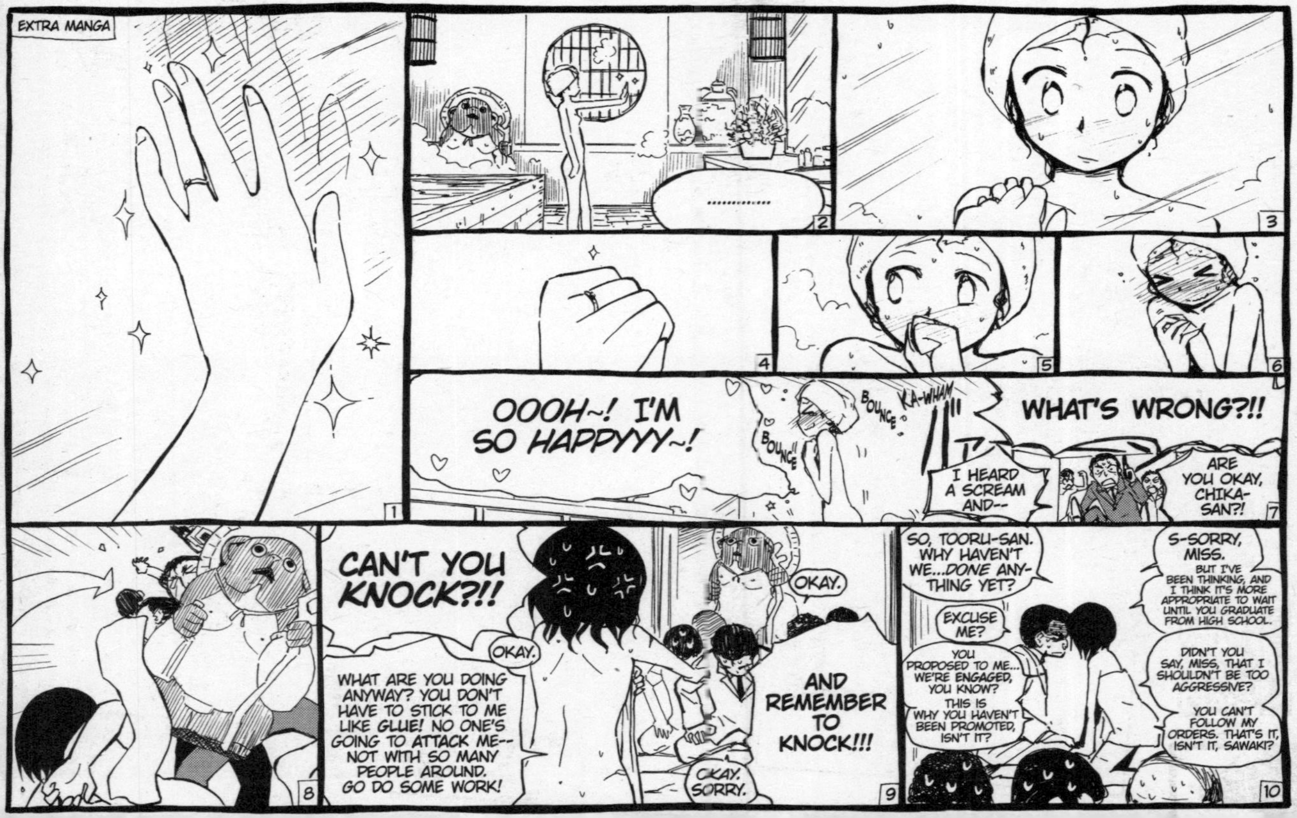
EXTRA MANGA
1
..............
2
3
4
5
6
OOOH~! I'M SO HAPPYYY~!
BOUNCE
BOUNCE
KA-WHAM
WHAT'S WRONG?!!
I HEARD A SCREAM AND--
ARE YOU OKAY, CHIKA-SAN?!
7
8
CAN'T YOU KNOCK?!!
OKAY.
WHAT ARE YOU DOING ANYWAY? YOU DON'T HAVE TO STICK TO ME LIKE GLUE! NO ONE'S GOING TO ATTACK ME--NOT WITH SO MANY PEOPLE AROUND. GO DO SOME WORK!
OKAY.
AND REMEMBER TO KNOCK!!!
OKAY. SORRY.
9
SO, TOORU-SAN. WHY HAVEN'T WE...DONE ANYTHING YET?
S-SORRY, MISS.
BUT I'VE BEEN THINKING, AND I THINK IT'S MORE APPROPRIATE TO WAIT UNTIL YOU GRADUATE FROM HIGH SCHOOL.
EXCUSE ME?
YOU PROPOSED TO ME... WE'RE ENGAGED, YOU KNOW?
THIS IS WHY YOU HAVEN'T BEEN PROMOTED, ISN'T IT?
DIDN'T YOU SAY, MISS, THAT I SHOULDN'T BE TOO AGGRESSIVE?
YOU CAN'T FOLLOW MY ORDERS. THAT'S IT, ISN'T IT, SAWAKI?
10